POWER, POLITICS, AND CULTURE

ALSO BY EDWARD W. SAID

POWER, POLITICS, AND CULTURE

INTERVIEWS WITH

EDWARD W. SAID

Edited and with an Introduction by

GAURI VISWANATHAN

PANTHEON BOOKS • NEW YORK

Pantheon Books and colophon are registered trademarks of Random House, Inc.

Library of Congress Cataloging-in-Publication Data

Said, Edward W.
Power, politics, and culture : interviews with Edward W. Said / edited
and with an introduction by Gauri Viswanathan.
p. cm.
Includes index.
ISBN 0-375-42107-6
1. Said, Edward W.—Interviews.   2. Intellectuals—United States—Interviews.
3. Middle East—Politics and government.   4. Politics and culture.
5. Arab-Israeli conflict—1993—Peace.   6. Orientalism.
I. Viswanathan, Gauri.   II. Title.
CB18.S25 A3 2001b
956—dc21   00-140092

www.pantheonbooks.com

Printed in the United States of America
First Edition
2 4 6 8 9 7 5 3 1

TO MY CHILDREN,

NAJLA AND WADIE,

THE JOY OF MY LIFE

CONTENTS

PREFACE

This collection of interviews covers the years 1976 to 2000, as well as a wide variety of subjects. Except for the first one, which appeared in the Cornell University journal *Diacritics* and was a written exchange between the editors and myself, all of these pieces occurred, so to speak, in a face-to-face situation. Necessarily then, they reflect the immediacy of such encounters, the back-and-forth, the informal question-and-answer language, the circling around, making, and remaking of a point or argument, the challenge and counter-challenge of interviewer(s) and interviewee. They have been edited first of all by the journals, newspapers, and magazines that conducted the interviews in the first place and where they originally appeared, second by Professor Gauri Viswanathan and Shelley Wanger, third by me. As such then, they are a composite of direct discourse and later clarification. No effort at all has been made by anyone involved to make these interviews seem more "writerly." They are therefore principally the records of various occasions, in many different times and places, publications, interviewers (the U.S., Europe, the Middle East, India), and many different situations, moods, and concerns.

Interviews play a role that essays and books do not. Most often in my case, they have arisen as responses to what I have written in my books and articles and, as such, reflect the interests of whoever is conducting the interview. I must say, though, that they have become the steady feature of the life of the publishing teacher and public critic. Wherever I go to lecture or publish a book, I am very grateful that kind and intellectually generous individuals give me the opportunity to answer their questions, on the spot and without preparation. In many ways, interviews are sustained acts of discovery, not only for the person being inter-viewed but for even the well-prepared interviewer. Thus, it is refresh-ingly often the case that someone with a long list of carefully written out questions discards the list and proceeds simultaneously and directly to talk to me—from out of our discussion rather than off a page—and then more discovery often does occur, with results that are usually unpre-dictable. Every situation therefore reflects a specific set of circumstances, and since I have been involved in the public domain as a political activist as well as an intellectual and scholar, all sorts of challenges arise, which I have tried to meet. In any case, it is my hope that despite their infor-mality and relatively wide-ranging nature, these interviews will also an-swer to the reader's interests and concerns—at another time, in another place.

E.W.S.
New York,
March 20, 2001

INTRODUCTION

by Gauri Viswanathan

Few authors today are as prolific as Edward W. Said. The author of almost two dozen books, Said has written on a broad array of topics ranging from literary criticism to Middle East politics to opera, film, and travel. His views, marked by an engaging communicative energy, have reached a wide audience through his publications, articles and books, whether the subject is Joseph Conrad, Richard Wagner, or Palestine and the peace process. He is also the subject of several full-length works and anthologies of critical essays; indeed, there are at least a half dozen publications every year on his work, and books offering critical perspectives on Edward Said have become a growth industry in themselves. So much has been written by and about him that one can be pardoned for asking what new insights a book of interviews can be expected to provide that are not already present in Said's writings or in works about him.

The answer is simple: The interviews Said gave over the past three decades boldly announce that neither his own books and essays nor those written about him have the last word. The first thing to note is not only the number of interviews Said has given, both to print and broadcast media, but also the number of locations in which they took place, spanning Asia and the Middle East as well as Europe and the United States. They confirm his presence on the international stage as one of the most forceful public intellectuals of our time, a man who evokes interest in the general public for his passionate humanism, his cultivation and erudition, his provocative views, and his unswerving commitment to the cause of Palestinian self-determination. Dispersed in numerous publications around the world, these interviews have never before been collected in a single book. Together, they reveal a ceaselessly roving mind returning to earlier ideas in his books and articles and engaging with them anew. One measure of the fluidity and range of Said's thought is his ability to revisit arguments made in his books and essays not merely to defend and elaborate on them but, more important, both to mark their limits and probe their extended possibilities, especially in contexts other than those which first gave rise to them. In other words, Said travels with his ideas as far as they can go, long after they were first articulated, and he applies the same skepticism toward uncritical assimilation of his work as he reserves in general to his now-famous formulation about "traveling theory." In the essay of the same name, published in *The World, the Text, and the Critic* (1983), Said argued that theories developed in local contexts tend to lose their elasticity and become diluted in power and meaning when transported elsewhere. In their attenuated form, theories can be no more than strategic methods, with system and procedure taking the place of genuine thought.

The weakened force of traveling theories challenges the conventional notion that one of the ways influence carries its weight is by claiming a general application, erasing distinctions between places and peoples. Such is the power of empire, too, that the "universal is always achieved at the expense of the native" ("Criticism, Culture, and Performance"). It is only when local knowledge can be brought to bear on texts, which are restored to their situations and locales, that readings can contest the languages of universalism and standardization. An example of the productive uses of bringing in the local context is Said's description of Albert Camus's use of the cultural discourse of the French Lycée to stall the rise of an independent Algeria (p. 111). This is an interpretative method Said uses when he reads his own work in response to interviewers' questions. Extending the critique of universalism to his own work, Said draws attention to the localized conditions of knowledge production affecting one's understanding not only of the works one studies but also of those one writes. Being interviewed in so many parts of the world, he is invariably asked to respond to the concerns most pertinent to those places and to rethink his own work in relation to those different concerns. Take, for example, the question of Said's impact on historians of India. He is asked in an interview at Calcutta ("I've Always Learnt During the Class") whether it is not the case that, as a result of his influence on colonial discourse studies, Indian history writing has been "derailed" from its social history agenda. The interviewer's suggestion is that the writing of Indian postcolonial history might have continued to follow the Marxist trajectory that dominated the school of Indian historiography were it not for Said's interventions in cultural politics, which diverted the scholarly focus from class analysis to a study of the discursive power of colonial texts and their representations. The interviewer's question highlights the fact that, in postcolonial societies, there is no commonly agreed-upon approach to decolonizing the mind, to use N'gugi wa Thiong'o's famous phrase. We learn that what might appear as a revolutionary moment in the Western academy, with the advent of postcolonial studies stimulated largely by Said's work, is received with reserve and caution in some postcolonial societies.

Without minimizing the specificity of different colonial histories, Said's response bemoans the tendency to consider historical study as divorced from considerations of language and form, just as literature is considered to be separate from history and politics. Both literature and history involve the sifting of evidence and interpretation, he points out, and the idea that somehow the writing of history can be hijacked by focusing on discourses of power begs the question of whether facts can be studied independently of the ways in which they have been presented and recorded in language. Nonetheless, the exchange is a reminder that resistances to a writer's influence also signal attempts to restore the local density of different histories. Ironically, both Said and his interviewers agree on this notion, though the point of departure in raising it is the charge that the sense of the local is lost in Saidian-inspired criticism. Once again, Said is provided with an opportunity to expand on his arguments and, through a questioning of this theory's limits, bring himself closer to the particular concerns of the cultures whose journalists and scholars are talking to him.

Said's responses to interviewers' questions enact the way knowledge arises from interactions with others that he describes in *Orientalism, The World, the Text, and the Critic,* and *Culture and Imperialism.* How people know is an important part of his preoccupations, particularly when it is framed as cultural and political exchange, and the interviews go a long way toward illuminating this process. As Said repeatedly points out, his driving interest is in how systems and institutions come into being, how they acquire the force that they do, and what new forms of thought and representation they stabilize through their discursive power. If Said turns such questions inward on his own writings, it is a measure of how insistently he submits to the same standard of accountability to political exigencies and historical circumstances that he applies to the works he studies. The interviews show that the investigation of knowledge production is simultaneously an introspective project for Said, though not necessarily in the sense that its ultimate goal is hermeneutic or psychoanalytical self-analysis. For in more than autobiographical ways, interviews have the virtue of compelling writers to turn their critical gaze on the circumstances that produce their own works, and thus the interviews act as catalysts for self-examination. In Said's case, self-searching reproduces the forms and procedures of critical scrutiny of other texts.

This double movement is amply evident in the interviews collected here. Take, for instance, Said's reflections on the work that catapulted him onto the international stage, *Orientalism*. Obviously, many interviewers come back to this book as a pivotal point of reference for their own queries about the relations between knowledge and power, representation and authority, and about the influence of such thinkers as Foucault, Gramsci, and Vico on Said's articulation of these connections. Many interviewers, riding the wave of poststructuralism, prod Said to think anew about what might be construed as a negative view of agency. In this perception, webs of power constructed by and around discourse rob individuals of the capacity to resist power or rewrite it in terms that restore agency to themselves. In other words, does Said truly believe that individuals are doomed to inhabit the representations that usurp their own lived reality? Is there no way out of the prison of Orientalist representations?

However, far from attributing total coercive power to discourse, Said refers on more than one occasion to Orientalism as a "meaningful" rather than meaningless system of discursive rule. In a move that puts distance between himself and Foucault, Said instead prefers to view Orientalist representations for what they enable through the mechanisms of power. At first glance, "enablement" appears to suggest no more than that Orientalism produces a whole field of study in the form of comparative religion, literary studies, and anthropology, so that its productive value—its establishment of academic disciplines—is really an ironic outcome of negative perceptions of the non-Western world. After all, Foucault had earlier suggested that discourses of power did not constrain individuals so much as they produced civil subjects of the state, so that Said's analysis might appear merely an orthodox extension of Foucault's.

But by placing himself in the narrative as a formerly colonized subject, having gone through an Anglicized education in Cairo that trained him to know more about the Enclosure Act than Arab history, Said makes room for a dynamic concept of critical consciousness. In a major move, he turns Orientalism into a trigger for both critique and self-examination. Let us be clear about one thing: autobiography does not often intrude into Said's works. However, when it does, as in the introductory chapter in *Orientalism*, autobiography is turned to devastating effect. Under a subsection pointedly titled "The personal dimension," Said refers to the "punishing destiny" of being a Palestinian in the West, held hostage by dehumanizing ideologies. This disheartening experience leads him to study Orientalism, as he remarks, in order to "inventory the traces" upon him of the dominating culture. A term borrowed from the Italian political philosopher Antonio Gramsci, "inventory" refers at once to stocktaking and filling out the historical record. The most significant line in all of Said's works, in my view, is the one in *Orientalism* where he writes: "I have tried to maintain a critical consciousness as well as employing those instruments of historical, humanistic, and cultural research of which *my education has made me the fortunate beneficiary.*"

This is a vital key to Said's method and purpose: Orientalism is not finally an annihilating system; rather, in a boomerang effect, it equips its subjects with a critical repertoire that ultimately is used, ironically, to contest Orientalism's power and reach. This conviction pervades much of Said's works and interviews, and it provides the dialectical energy for considering negative representations of "Orientals," not in order to wallow in a rhetoric of victimization but to deflect such representations back toward their perpetrators, using the tools of humanistic research bestowed by them. This partly explains Said's avowed humanism, his repeated insistence on the pleasures of the text. No small part of Said's delight in the works he studies and teaches is that he can read them with keen attentiveness to the imagery, vocabulary, and structure of Orientalist representations, which he insistently shows as being at the aesthetic core of many literary texts. Far from rejecting these works as despicable products of modern Orientalism, Said is clearly fascinated by them, and he believes their aesthetic value is not compromised but rather defined by the political interests that determine their writing in the first place. Thus, to read literature outside its political contexts and origins in the name of aesthetic appreciation produces only false or incomplete readings. Such approaches, he argues, turn a blind eye to the vital conjunction between aesthetics and power.

Said's love of literature is writ large in all the interviews, even in those in which the main topic is Palestine and the peace process. Interestingly, he evokes the pleasure of aesthetics to drive home his point that systematized thinking narrows one's perspective and produces rigidities in place of a creative openness to discovery and knowledge. Even more than his writings, the interviews reveal a man in profound conflict with schematizations of all kinds. At times the conflict is so intense as to make palpable Said's impatience with patterned, predictable reasoning. He does so in ways that self-consciously evoke the dangers and risks of uncharted exploration. For instance, in the *Diacritics* interview "Beginnings," Said points up an opposition between systematized thinking and hedonism, defining the latter as the refusal to ply the well-trodden path. It is the use of the word *hedonism* that compels attention, accounting perhaps for the reason that literary texts embedded in the perversions of Orientalist logic so fascinate him, as if there is an element of alienation in the very thing that attracts him. In fact, at times the literary becomes synonymous with a complex mix of unpredictability, self-indulgence, and unregulated, even unrestrained cognition. Most important, even as literature is believed to evoke cultural tradition and heritage, its resistance to predictable regimens paradoxically breaks it away from the sense of a past, or what Said describes as "freeing oneself of one's past attachments and habits and alliances." The residual hedonism in critical acts is thus for him a strategic form of knowledge.

Said's aesthetic concerns are therefore much larger than what discussions focused primarily on discourse and power in *Orientalism* allow. Such discussions confine his literary criticism to the analysis of representations and stereotypes, and minimize his notion of aesthetic experience as both a response to and an account of multiple cultural influences. On the contrary, his most recent work, *Reflections on Exile and Other Essays,* is the culmination of a critical path which began with the pressures upon him to reveal not a single identity or a single awareness, but rather a composite of cultures, identities, and affiliations. Such complex formations mark the advent of both the modern novel and the modern subject, deracinated and dislocated from one place and one time. In *Culture and Imperialism* Said had already begun to explore imperialism's impact on the novel form by looking for the dissonant textures that firmly located the European novel in the space and time of empire. In evoking the musical concept of counterpoint, he extended the range of analysis of literary texts by listening to the multiple mix of voices playing off against each other. In his interview with Bonnie Marranca, Marc Robinson, and Una Chaudhuri in "Criticism, Culture, and Performance," Said explicitly links his critical method with his experience of exile: "If you're an exile—which I feel myself, in many ways, to have been—you always bear within yourself a recollection of what you've left behind and what you can remember, and you play it against the current experience." This is a marvelous illustration of the productive uses of counterpoint, explaining Said's deep, abiding interest in music for the expressive means it offers him for living, thinking, and reading in modes of simultaneity, connection, and opposition.

Even while Said estranges readings of *Orientalism* that stress only its Foucaultian derivation, there is another kind of estrangement that occurs when he is interviewed in different parts of the globe, especially in the Arab world. One of his most revealing interviews, "*Orientalism,* Arab Intellectuals, Marxism, and Myth in Palestinian History," was published in the Arab periodical *Al Jadid,* in which he responds to the interviewer's queries about the reception of *Orientalism* by Islamic figures. Said is categorical in his rejection of readings that appropriate the book for advancing an Islamic agenda, on the premise that his critique of Western representations of Islam opens the door for claiming him as a spokesperson for Islam. This is a delicate matter, as it might easily be argued that authors who critique distortions in media and literature do so in order to uphold some idea of a "true" representation to which they are sympathetic. To disavow sympathy must surely invite the charge of insincerity at best or betrayal at worst. Said is aware of this, just as he is also conscious of how little control authors have over the ways in which their writings are interpreted or used.

One of the useful functions of the interviews is to engage with this dilemma. If *Orientalism* has become a rallying text around which those frustrated by persistent distortions of their culture and religion have mobilized, Said finds himself challenged to accommodate interpretations that stretch the limits of his own purposes and intents. He realizes he cannot draw a line and claim he has written his work only to correct the historical record in the West and not to facilitate the restitution of those who have been wronged by that history. That dilemma is already raised when Said was asked to respond to the fact that the front cover of one of his books bears an image of a Hamas slogan on a Palestinian wall, announcing that Hamas is the resistance. (The interviewer does not specify which book.) Contrary to his interviewer's probable expectation that he would most certainly be defensive or discomfited, Said calmly states that the image, chosen by his publishers, did not conflict with the theme of his book, which was about protest and anger, and that writing on walls is a legitimate form of protest. By steadfastly refusing to allow the main issue to be diverted to whether he supports Hamas or not, Said keeps injustice and oppression at the center of attention. These should never be lost sight of, we are reminded, and that Said can keep them in view without legitimizing acts of violence is no small part of the challenge he confronted, as well as his achievement, in this interview.

But returning to the subject of *Orientalism*'s reception in the Middle East, in the same interview Said restores a pedagogical dimension to the discussion in reminding his readers that polemics is far easier than careful, serious research and reflection. To that end, he maintains, the purposes of his study were to equip readers with the critical apparatus to empower themselves through rational debate and argument, rather than through a simple reversal of terms—that is, tearing down Orientalism by putting up Occidentalism in its place. To those on the frontlines, this will appear an intellectualist rather than activist argument, and the tone of a number of interviews reflects the tension between these two models of action. The tension is never fully resolved. The call to action that Said makes on numerous occasions can, in some instances, be read in terms of scrupulous research, criticism, and self-understanding. From the point of view of those entering the academy, there is a compelling appeal in such calls, but to those in the places that feed the Western imagination with false images and stereotypes, much more is asked of Said's pedagogy than it can bear. One can hear the demands for programmatic action in the voices of the interviewers, particularly in Asia and the Middle East, and these demands make for a lively dynamic between Said and his interlocutors, which replays, in some respects, Said's articulation of Palestinian self-determination from the groundwork of intellectual responsibility and criticism.

Though for purposes of clarity this book is divided into two sections—"Performance and Criticism" and "Scholarship and Activism"—such distinctions are arbitrary at the same time, since Said rarely talks about literature without also engaging politics, and vice versa. But the division is intended to facilitate the reader's grasp of the parallel and often intersecting strands of development in politics and culture. The interviews are arranged chronologically, progressing in the first section from the thinking that resulted in such works as *Beginnings, Orientalism, Culture and Imperialism,* and writings on opera and performance; and in the second, from the earliest articulations of Palestinian self-determination to the disillusionment of a compromised peace process. The interviews take place in a number of different locations. Indeed, the geographic diversity reveals Edward Said's engagement not only with multiple issues but also with the many different cultural and political circumstances of the places in which he is interviewed. His interviews in the American and European media contrast sharply with those in places like India, Pakistan, Lebanon, the West Bank, and Israel, with interviewers' questions illuminating the particular concerns, crises, and complications of their own societies. As Said himself observes, while a great deal of his work concerns the Middle East, his writings are often received with more enthusiasm in countries outside the Arab world, such as in Latin America, Africa, and Japan, and he turns this observation around to contemplate the relative vitality of intellectual culture in various postcolonial societies.

The original idea for this book came from Anita Roy, a former editor at Oxford University Press, India. She approached me a few years ago to ask whether I would be interested in doing a book of conversations with Edward Said. As someone who studied with Said and learned, in effect, how to think about questions of scholarship, history, knowledge, and power through his encouragement, I did not need to be persuaded about the merits of a book that captured his speaking voice, his interlocutory presence, and his pedagogical engagement. The book may have changed shape somewhat from the time Anita Roy discussed it with me, expanding considerably to include previously published interviews, but the original motivation remains the same. No greater value can be claimed for the interview form than that, unlike books and essays, it preserves the voice of the speaker, teacher, debater, and interlocutor. Said's is a remarkable voice in contemporary criticism. We have seen it amply in print. But those who have had the privilege to hear his lectures know how powerful a speaker and teacher Said is, how much he relishes the occasion for exchange that the format of questions and answers provides. Interviews may not be the same as classroom interaction, but they come uncannily close to capturing the dynamics of a classroom. Unless their lectures are videotaped, few teachers have an opportunity to leave behind a record of the questions that stimulate discussion and the arguments that promote debate. At the end of a class we know we have reached a point hardly anticipated at the start, and we are often fond of mulling over the ways we reached certain conclusions, through stimulus and provocation. Happily, published interviews can capture that spark, that moment of combustion when a well-considered question sets off a chain of exuberant reflection and dialogue. And when the person on the other end is as eloquent, articulate, and thoughtful as Edward Said, reading the interviews is as close as it gets to being in a packed lecture hall.

———

Special thanks go to Shelley Wanger of Pantheon Books for her strong support and attentiveness to detail, to Zaineb Istrabadi for excavating many of the interviews collected here, and to Edward W. Said for his advice and friendship.

PERFORMANCE AND CRITICISM

ONE

BEGINNINGS

I had just published my first book of theoretical criticism, Beginnings: Intention and Method, *and had already written most of* Orientalism *when this interview with* Diacritics *was published. It was the first extended reflection of its kind that I had done.*   E.W.S.

Your scholarly work is commonly associated with what we might term a "critical avant-garde," a constellation of critics, as it were, who are concerned with the philosophical questions encountered in interpretive activity and who are prone to draw on the difficult theoretical reflection which informs a major strain of continental criticism. In this connection, you recently expressed considerable sympathy for the deeply philosophical criticism of Harold Bloom, whose work strikes some readers as being not only recondite and arcane, but also otherworldly, submerged in poetry to the exclusion of the prosaic world, lofted into a prophetic flight toward an ultimate convergence with the literary text. No doubt you would find such an image of Bloom's work quite unfair. Yet one wonders how you respond to the general resistance which the writing of a Bloom or a de Man is prone to encounter from readers who find it to be far removed from the cultural and political arena of our time—unlike your own work, which at the very least has to be read as a direct challenge to the ideological complicities of much academic criticism.

You raise some important points. First of all, let's consider your proposition about a critical avant-garde. No one to my knowledge has analyzed such a proposition seriously, although there seems to be a general feeling about it that literary criticism in the English-speaking world now can be divided into two kinds, French-influenced and non-French-influenced, the former being avant-garde, the latter traditional. This is a sloppy—but by no means passive—feeling, since the evidence commonly (and aggressively) cited for it is either crudely sociological or stylistic, if by style we mean only what kind of vocabulary, authorities, texts a critic employs. The critics you have called avant-garde belong, of course, in the French-influenced group, they are likely to be East Coast critics and middle-aged, they get high salaries at famous universities, they are prolific writers of essays on other critics, they either write about unfashionable authors (Pater, Shelley, Emerson) or about a handful of very fashionable ones (Rousseau, Nietzsche, Freud), they use words like deconstruction and demystification, they are less likely to refer to Empson than to Barthes, their prose does not resemble Edmund Wilson's, and so forth; listing their attributes can be done as a sort of parlor game, and one need only do it as a higher form of gossip—except that by and large the avant-garde critics have two or three serious things in common, so far as their audience, the student of literature, and the reception of their work are concerned. I shall leave aside for now the critical theory—if one can talk about it in so unitary a way—that justifies us in putting them together; now I would like to discuss them as others see them.

In the first place, their work angers a great many people who resent being asked by a critic to read sentences that (a) do not make a "factual" point about the author's biography, the work's textual history, or some such thing; (b) do not tell the reader what to think about a work or author or period; (c) do not spend much time *explicitly* making value-judgments about the work; (d) do not make a fetish of gross chronology; (e) do not badger the reader either with catalogues of other critical opinions or with lists of works testifying to the critic's erudition, sense of tradition, humble place in scholarly life (perhaps "badger" is not the only word one can use here; "fortify" seems relevant too). Take these sorts of things together and you will see immediately that one novel thing about these critics is that their rituals and procedures differ from the ones fathered on academic literary criticism since the end of the nineteenth century. Their notion of what a text is, their addiction to terminological invention, their comparative disregard for biography, their alertness not to "traditions" so much as to "problematics"—all these set them apart. But principally of course, they are *provocative* critics, mainly because they turn the criticism of a text or author into a methodological and self-conscious issue of the first importance; thus the appreciation or valorization of a work or author, which we sometimes assume to be the goal of criticism, turns out here to be its point of departure, in some cases even a hidden point of departure. There is additional provocation in the position they take (and I am using "position" in a very literal way) toward the work; Swift used to say that the bad thing about critics is that because they come after a work, they can always rather nastily crowd out everybody else and ruin a work's reputation. For these critics, however, the work is a contemporary thing, along and within which they place their own; what they do is recreative, in all senses of that word. For all its difficulty their work contains a sense of the pleasure taken in having tried at least to meet the literary text on some other level than the ruthlessly evaluative (which is one of the things Swift feared, since he was thinking—as we all do—of the tyranny of popular reviewers) or the flatteringly appreciative.

The point is that critics are supposed to be commentators from below, as it were, to stand to literature as Howard Cosell stands to Muhammed Ali. If a critic tries to treat a text, whose principal characteristic seems to be its holy fossilization by time, with something resembling co-temporality, even deferential and respectful co-temporality, a lot of people suddenly see red. Intertextuality, which is what the avant-garde critic claims is the *universal* condition of texts (all texts, critical and "creative"), is not supposed to be true of criticism. According to the cant belief of those who think that a critic's main justification is to help the work to be better appreciated, which makes him or her extra-textual at best, the critic has no right to point out, for example, that literature is language, and that criticism is language too, with its own problems and limitations of course, but language nonetheless. I needn't elaborate too much here, since Barthes's *Critique et verité* marshalls all the debating techniques on both sides of the critical fence, and he illustrates too the degree of violence that a certain kind of new criticism produces in the rhetoric of its (usually) self-proclaimed enemies. For avant-garde critics of the kind I'm discussing seem rather mild-mannered when it comes to their opponents; all the ire comes from the other side; this is not a fierce, or combative, or rhetorically aggressive avant-garde; it seems more devoted to its work—rightly so—than to carrying on campaigns against the so-called old guard, which has been very energetic and diligent in going after the critical avant-garde. The latter, to be fair about it, does seem at times infected with a kind of clubby hothouse grandeur, as if all that mattered to it were Derrida and Heidegger and not at all the sweaty workshops in which much intellectual work is transacted.

So anger is a common reaction these critics produce. Another—and this is a more important matter—is that their subject matter is innovative and hence outrageous to an audience that believes a critic ought to confine himself to canonical issues and techniques: explication, commentary, historical background, biography, and so forth. Amongst the Yale critics, for example, you can notice how the titles of some of their books actually deflect criticism onto new subjects: influence (a standard, perhaps *the* standard, concern in school criticism) is associated not with source studies but with anxiety; formalism and insight (two of the code words of the American New Criticism) are tied respectively to transcendence and blindness. Everyone will agree that this avant-garde, like all avant-gardes, is preposterous to a certain degree. Its first order of business is not presence but deferred presence, or absence; for its purposes a text is more an activity than a grounded object—the reversal of expectations is a long and by now well-known list. Yet it is the work of the avant-garde that appeals to students; they seek it out as something that elevates the drudgery of graduate literature work to a higher, and if not to a higher then to a more interesting level. Why this feeling should exist amongst students is a complicated question; to answer it one would have to explain an apparent lack of vitality in historical or traditional scholarship (the extent to which Auerbachs and Spitzers can't be produced any more), the economics of the profession (which with few jobs available is paradoxically more prone to hire a structuralist-type new Ph.D. to teach traditionally conceived, or bread-and-butter, courses than not), and the teachability, marketability, technicability—I'm coining a word for the conversion of avant-garde criticism by opportunists into a technical, pseudo-scientific criticism that pretends to stand for the new and the trendy—of avant-garde criticism itself. But even if we don't go into these matters the fact remains that students flock to the new criticism for the sustained excitement and dignity it communicates, and students feel (wrongly or rightly is not what I want to discuss here) that these qualities are lacking in the established curricular study of literature. The really interesting writing being done by the best people in their late twenties and thirties is directly indebted to the avant-garde. The danger of course is that avant-garde criticism is overesteemed for its comparative neglect of historical, you might say *archival* concern: I'll return to that problem a little later.

Innovation stimulates anger more or less naturally. Besides, other feelings become engaged too: jealousy (why are those characters getting so much attention?), xenophobia (that isn't criticism, it's frogspeak), and a not unjustified hostility to a new coterie (there's *Commentary,* there's the *New York Review,* now there are *Diacritics, NLH,* and *Georgia Review:* are they necessary?). But more fundamentally the avant-garde critics are *literalizers,* that is they take literature at its own word literally, they treat it as language and so outdo (or overdo) the belle-lettrist old guard that believes literature to be Literature, beautiful language, and so forth. One of the commonest refrains now is that people like Bloom, Hartman, and de Man don't write well (I've made the observation myself, and had it made about me: a nice mess which I can't unravel). But what is at issue is not that they are influenced by a foreign tradition (since most of them had their ideas before the French influence, broadly speaking, was felt). Neither is it that they have metaphysical concerns which get in the way of purely (and purified) literary criticism. What is at stake, and makes it possible for "style" to be used as a cosh with which to bang them around, is that their criticism takes language as language, and then proceeds to discuss literature as embroiled in the problems of language. "Style" is the weapon employed to bring literature back to the realm of ideas, humanistic testimonials, and so forth, whereas for the avant-garde the profound question is the embedding of literature in language. That and the way in which language *produces* (rather than is produced by) meaning. In a certain sense, the radicalism of the avant-garde is a conservative one, keeping literature to language and the problems raised by language. And these can be intimate or embarrassing, as when Bloom speaks of an Oedipal struggle enacted between poets whose only spoils of war are lines of poetry. Perhaps one can also say that avant-garde critics of the sort I've been talking about here are *severe* critics in the sense that Vico used the word. To a great degree their severity accounts for the difficulty many people experience in understanding their writing; it is a difficulty that comes directly, I think, from limitation, not from the ambition to do too much.

So much for the reception at present of the embattled avant-garde you mentioned. This is not to say that the avant-garde is the Yale school, since so far as I'm concerned there are many other critics in the U.S.—Girard, Fletcher, Crews, Fish, Riddel, Poirier, the early Sontag, Donato, and others—from whom I learn and who do very different things, but which I would also call avant-garde. Neither can one confine the avant-garde to critics of a certain age; there is Kenneth Burke, there was Blackmur (the greatest genius American criticism has produced) who belong to an earlier generation, yet whose work bristles with invention, brilliance, and independence of the sort I have been talking about.

I can't claim to speak, however, of what people think I do, and in what camp my work belongs, but I do feel that very often—too often in fact—the distinctions between present avant-garde critics and "other" critics are invidious, and don't serve any purpose except to stir up a little excitement. I think that my interest in what is now being written by critics, and what has been written, is very catholic indeed; a lot of the time I am drawn to scholars who do not belong to the avant-garde, since the latter do not seem to be interested as much as I would like in the sheer semantic thickness of a literary text, and that thickness cannot be completely served by psychoanalysis, semiology, and the like. If you read a critic like Harry Levin on Shakespeare or on the novel you are getting a learned and sharp intelligence that can use much of what needs to be used (including Lukács, Bachelard, Barthes, Freud, etc.) because it serves a serious critical aim. You will never need to fear that only some of the problems of Stendhal are being considered, or that a text by Flaubert is studied with no real knowledge of Second Empire France, and so on. So it is probably far too schematic to divide criticism into two hostile camps. In addition I think we should remember that many scholars who themselves write traditional criticism are sensitively alert to and sympathetic with what's being done in the theory of criticism by the avant-garde. We need to acknowledge that criticism is a very complex act: it involves performance, cognition, intuition, style, ritual, and charlatanry of course. All of us can tell a good critic no matter what banner he or she carries; similarly, all of us *know* that it is possible genuinely to *learn* from one critic and not from another. It's not a partisan matter finally.

But you ask about Bloom; let me talk about him a little. I've already expressed my general opinion of his work in some detail, so there's no need to do it again here. I can add two observations of a different sort, however. Bloom is a critic who is not afraid of being theoretical; that is, he is willing to talk in abstract and generalizing language about patterns, forces, processes that inform the production and the reception of literature. Of course he shares this theoretical interest with many of the avant-garde, and it is something I find myself drawn to a great deal. The objections to theory in literary criticism are so boring as to require no repetition now; but one thing that strikes many of Bloom's readers is the extravagance of *his* theory, or to use your expression, its prophetic quality. One's impression is that Bloom seems to have allowed his theory to take over his criticism completely, if by criticism one means the making of discrete judgments, rationalistic analysis, and so on. Moreover the complex variety of literature appears to have been reduced by Bloom to an endless instance of the theory. Perhaps all this is a way of saying that Bloom is a hedgehog, not a fox. But all these objections are mainly, I think, a result of the difficulty that people have both with theory as such, and with the (to them) impertinent pose of a critic who believes he is getting to the very heart of the poetic process. Readers of Georges Poulet, who has many of the same kind of problems with his audience, always say that he is too abstract, or that he hasn't any right to speak for really big authors like Stendhal or Hugo; what such comments reveal, however, is the inability to deal with theory on intellectual grounds. If one doesn't like Bloom's tone, or Poulet's for that matter, and if one feels that the whole idea of trying to penetrate into a poet's consciousness is ridiculous, then one ought to go on to show if and in what way the theory is falsifiable or false (I am using Popperian language purposely), either by proposing a more correct one or by demonstrating seriously—and not simply by pompous exhortation—that the theory is misapplied. There is nothing more indecent in criticism than someone who uses a lot of marginal nonsense (Bloom is too theoretical, or Bloom is reducing everything to his theory) as a substitute for serious refutation; it is total bad faith, on the other hand, to use the kind of third-hand language associated with high humanism to suggest that Bloom has defiled literature and literary criticism.

A second general observation is that Bloom's criticism is semioclastic in a very extreme way. I use Barthes's word for what he was doing in *Mythologies* since the consequence of reading Bloom is that our image of what a poet does, how he works, what his poetry is, becomes shattered. There is nothing so sacred to literature and literary criticism as the mythology of creation. Bloom has made a shambles of that, first by associating creation with contraction and repression, second by turning the poet into a human being who is terribly mired (as Vico was the first to realize) in the difficulties of generation, parenthood, and family life. Latecoming for Bloom is primarily a biological and even sexual term; the affront to polite criticism that the term delivers is unmistakable, and seems unforgivable.

For me Bloom's criticism, when I first encountered it in its mature theoretical form (I had read *Shelley's Mythmaking* when I was a student) as a critic was and still is extraordinarily invigorating. My whole interest in beginnings and origins suddenly acquired a new dimension for me, and many confirmations. I found Bloom's reworking of the old influence topos powerful and elegant in the way that Berg's Violin Concerto reworks that Bach chorale and makes it disturbingly elegant and powerful. Most of all, however, I was impressed with the way Bloom showed that creation was a form of dealing with the past, redoing it in an original or beginning way, so to speak, and since I was a devoted student of Vico the discovery of themes like knowing is making, and the heroism of early poets, in Bloom was quite an experience.

I've always felt, nonetheless, that Bloom implies—without actually saying it—that creation is poetry, and vice versa. He has no discernible interest in the novel or drama, both of which have undismissable connections with history and society. And moreover, Bloom is primarily interested in the struggle between poets without showing necessarily that there are other struggles (as the one, say, between a poet and the language: Mallarmé's case) that play a role as well in poetic creation. But these are objections one might address to emphases in and applications of the theory. My principal theoretical differences with Bloom are of a different sort, which is what I took your question to be getting at.

I don't think it is correct to criticize Bloom for ignoring what you call the prosaic world, at least not from a theoretical point of view. He doesn't say he's not interested in it, or that it doesn't exist, or anything like that. All he says—and I'm not simply trying to defend him, but I'm trying to deal only with the theory—is that poets are primarily concerned with poetry, which is their element and their life as poets; furthermore, he says, creation is an active, anxious, and highly patterned struggle against strong predecessors. For the description of this struggle Bloom has devised not only a complex and brilliantly inventive vocabulary but also a whole series of methodological doctrines. I sometimes feel that the vocabulary is perhaps too schematic or theological, and sometimes that methodologically Bloom refines his work too much in order to take account of figures he has discovered recently (like Derrida for instance). But there is a whole side to Bloom's work which is ignored by his critics, a side which to me is at least as important as the maps, the terms, and the struggles he seems mainly to be describing. And that side is Bloom's ideas about literary history, and the transmission of culture from one generation to the next. Bloom is right to believe that culture doesn't get made ex nihilo, and right also to see the effort expended by poets in getting their poetry into existence. But I think he is wrong to think of poetic and/or cultural history as being either exclusively or preeminently a matter of dramatic struggle between strong and weak poets. A great deal of what matters in cultural history is not what you might call revolutionary but conservative; culture is not made exclusively or even principally by heroes or radicals all the time, but by great anonymous movements whose function it is to keep things going, keep things in being, "elles maintiennent les choses dans l'être" as Foucault says in his book on Roussel. Bloom nowhere takes account of the debt poetry owes to culture or history. The kind of thing that Curtius describes, which is a process of orderly cultural transmission and canon-formation, surely underlies most literary and cultural periods. Not all great or strong writers are rebels; most writers in fact are in fundamental harmony with what they identify as a prevailing culture (perhaps the modernists were an exception). But what attracts Bloom to the idea of poetic struggle and individuality is his notion that for the post-Miltonic writer, influence is almost always felt to be aggressively hostile. Once again I think Bloom ignores the fact that for a great many quite considerable writers, influence can be a benign thing: see, for example, Goethe's relationship with Hafiz (especially in "Unbegrenzt" and "Nachbildung" of the *West-östliche Divan*). The impressive thing about Schwab's *La Renaissance orientale* is that he deals with exactly the periods of most concern to Bloom; only his findings are opposite. The great influx into Europe during the early nineteenth century of Oriental ideas and texts had a very fruitful effect upon such strong poets as Hugo and Goethe; Schwab's main insight is that there is cultural renewal and continuity because poets positively welcome, seek out influence. Of course Bloom suggests the ambivalent feelings of poets toward their predecessors, the paradox of their attraction to and their defense against them, both at the same time. But what Bloom does not spend much time with is the gradation within influence, the various degrees of influence and, congruently, the various kinds of influence, from benign to anxiety-producing. He also neither cares for sports like Hopkins, nor for self-consciously influenceable poets like Eliot.

In any case, let me return to my argument. If you see literary history as quintessentially embodied in the work of heroic, radical figures, whose importance is that their work is epoch-making, you are not misreading cultural history, you aren't reading all of it. I think that is one of the things that Foucault discovered between *Les Mots et les choses* and *l'Archéologie du savior.* The early work had conceived of history as divided into discontinuous periods which follow each other in time the way (these are Foucault's examples) Sade is followed by Nietzsche. Later Foucault had to come to see that the enduring qualities of culture are precisely that it endures, and how it endures, not so much the contribution to culture of great culture heroes like Milton and Goethe. In short, Bloom's theory of poetic transmission conceals, I think, a radically mythologized conception of the individual determinants of culture, and a total disregard for culture's anonymous and institutional supports, which simply go on and on beyond individual efforts or life spans. Instead of seeing culture as finally a more regular, and regularizing business than not, Bloom holds to a notion that delegates tradition (and culture, by implication) to individual figures; I am saying that poetry makes poets, whereas Bloom believes that poets make poetry.

One of the things that I've admired and praised about Bloom's criticism is that he is consistently aware of how much more poetry entails than just the poet's lonely splendors, that in addition to the poet's agonies there are also his antagonists, and these exist in a relatively public domain which Bloom calls "poetry." But he doesn't ever go far enough in acknowledging the material side of this public domain: here I return to what I was saying earlier about the institutional supports of culture, and its roots in prosaic reality. Certainly the romantics were aware of Milton, but they were vitally involved also in the journals, reviews, and competing discourses of their time; how do these bear on the making of poetry, and how does a discourse for poetry common to all the Romantic poets enter the mainstream of their work? My point is that the debate, or the intertextuality that Bloom discusses with such insight and brilliance, scants all the materially productive agencies of the culture that contains, and enables, the romantic poets. These supports are collective, of course: they include social agencies of all sorts (the university, the press, the class system) as well as quasi-invisible agencies which Foucault has quite inventively called the collective system of archive-discourse-statement (*enoncé*).

You will see that far from criticizing Bloom's specific insights into post-Miltonic poetry I am saying that these insights are so powerful as to have ravaged out of all existence the historical scene in which that poetry is set, or in which it takes place. His theory argues that poetry is produced as a result of poets interiorizing their relationship to the world, concentrating it into their psyche by making the predecessor's poetry a symbol of the great world. Poetry is the Poet's struggles with other Poets, and we must look to them for an understanding of all poetic production. Now even if we allow that that is an accurate view of Wallace Stevens or Hardy we must enjoin Bloom (a) to set limits on the theory as an explanation of poetic production universally considered, (b) to cite instances when his view is not an adequate account of poetic production, and (c) to connect his theses about poetry with the historical circumstances of a poet's production. These are some of the theoretical and practical questions his theory raises for me.

I've dodged the main direction of your question long enough. You raise an overtly political question which I couldn't reply to directly without first going into technical, or perhaps professional, critical theory presented by Bloom in particular, and the avant-garde generally. If we move out a little beyond the "field" so to speak, there are certain observations to be made candidly. Elsewhere I've said that I find the New New critics to be quietistic; their concerns and closures are textual ones, the issues that engage them are—from a historical, social, or general point of view—very restricted. They seem uninterested in political questions. The life of society, or the life of society that bears centrally upon texts and literature, does not occupy their attention. I am speaking generally of course; people like Crews and Poirier, for example, do not at all fit what I'm describing. But the Yale critics (whom I talk about as symbolic of a fairly widespread critical community) seem to have willed upon themselves a pronounced *askesis,* a renunciation of everything but the literary work and its problems. This is not to say that what they have to say about literature provides no allusive or implicit comment on the life of society: Bloom's theory of poetry is valuable because he sees the poetic process as a social one, something that takes place between poets, although of course we cannot say that Bloom's poets act as part of a larger group than theirs. You find similar, and similarly limited, refractions of social and communal ideas in the criticism of Hartman and Miller, less so in de Man whose work contains evidence of a submerged, though powerful, sense of metaphysical crisis.

Having said that, I feel I must stop talking about others and speak for what I think I should be doing as a critic; perhaps that is another way of saying that while I share a great many interests with the critical avant-garde I feel myself separated from it on a great many other grounds. Bloom and I have discussed politics only once I think, and we both agreed—not without a good chuckle—that we couldn't be further apart. Until fairly recently I led two quite separate lives, which has always made me acutely appreciative of Conrad's *The Secret Sharer.* On the one hand I'm a literary scholar, critic, and teacher, I lead a pretty uncontroversial life in a big university, and I've done a fair amount of work which has always been plugged into the established channels. That's a function of a certain education, the appearance of a certain social background. Yet I lead another life, which most other literary people say nothing about (and this is a kind of acrobatics which people who know me can manage, with my helping them along: I've been very good at this). It's as if it isn't there, although many of them know that it is. My whole background in the Middle East, my frequent and sometimes protracted visits there, my political involvement: all this exists in a totally different box from the one out of which I pop as a literary critic, professor, etc. Now the second, and older, life is encroaching fairly seriously on the other one, and this is a difficult juncture for me. I am as aware as anyone that the ivory-tower concerns of technical criticism—I use the phrase because it is very useful as a way of setting off what I and the others we've mentioned do from the non-theoretical, non-philosophically based criticism normally found in academic departments of literature—are very far removed from the world of politics, power, domination, and struggle. But there are links between the two worlds which I for one am beginning to exploit in my own work.

Bloom's work is centered around struggle, and very restricted notions of power, domination, and repression. Whatever his political beliefs (Republican or Democrat, Marxist or anti-Marxist) he's hit on something I find absolutely true: that human activity, and the production of work does not, cannot take place without power relationships of the sort he talks about in poetry. One doesn't just write: one writes against, or in opposition to, or in some dialectical relationship with other writers and writing, or other activity, or other objects. Foucault goes a step further, and says that writing cannot materially exist (remember the question that puzzles one of Borges's characters somewhere: what keeps the letters and lines in a book from just sliding off the page?) without a network of agencies that limit, select, arrange, shape, and maintain writing in such a way as to make writing take on a particular form at a particular time. For me Foucault strips out of Bloom much of the dramatic and overly romantic quality I mentioned earlier as a distortion in Bloom's picture of things; Foucault shows how the struggle for domination can be quiet, systematic, hidden, all because discourse (which is always a symbol of victory in language) appears to be inevitable and systematic. Together, and writ very large, these two perspectives fairly describe the contemporary political scene, which itself encapsulates political history pretty much. There is an unceasing and meaningful interaction between forces—classes, nations, power centers, regions, whatever—seeking to dominate and displace each other; now what makes the struggle something more than a random tooth-and-claw battle is that values (moral and intellectual) are involved. One seeks domination over another, in order to dominate and also to exist. You could call these systems ideologies but I think that's too constraining a term: they are systems of belief and universes of effective performance and discourse. It's been said about Marx that he saw this struggle as something exclusively economic; that's a serious falsification of Marx, or at least of the Hegelian residues in Marx. He was perfectly aware that the struggle was materially expressed and economically characterizable, but he was, I think, enormously sensitive to the shaping dialectic, to the intangible but very real figurations, to the internal unisons and dissonances the struggle produced. That is the difference between him and Hobbes, who saw life as nasty, brutish, and short.

I come from a part of the world whose modern history is largely intelligible as the result of colonialism, and whose present travail cannot be detached from the operations of imperialism. Now colonialism and imperialism are not abstractions for me: they are specific experiences and forms of life that have an almost unbearable concreteness. What are imperialism and colonialism but phases of a protracted struggle of the sort Bloom describes as central to the poetic process? What is the ongoing life of a dependent or colonial people but the imposition on that people of a powerful and duplicitous system (discourse) of the sort that Foucault has studied in his work? I am making the transition from poetry and discourse to imperialism and colonialism very abruptly—but I think my gist is clear.

Well then, in my other-than-scholarly life I do certain things which are frequently clarified for me by surprising and unlikely ideas, like Bloom's for example. I will confess to no utopian notions about the end of the struggles I've just talked about, but I guess that what moves me mostly is anger at injustice, an intolerance of oppression, and some fairly unoriginal ideas about freedom and knowledge. The great problem of course is sinking all these things, plus the two lives I mentioned, plus my empirical actuality, plus my profound interest in literature, criticism, and teaching, in some kind of work; and that's where I think I am now, that is I feel I'm able to do that now. And *politically* it distances me rather a lot from the critics and colleagues whose work I've just been talking about, and which I greatly respect and admire. Perhaps we can discuss that.

In your book Beginnings *(1975) you refer to a "radical displacement of traditional thought" requiring a "new fusion between man and his activity," and then affirm that "Marx has cemented his own interpretive activity with man's human activity at a common revolutionary point of departure." The question which arises then is the* placement *of that point of departure, i.e., where in your judgment does it lie for the "committed" critic at the present time?*

The context of those phrases from *Beginnings* is a brief discussion of Lukács, which I'll recapitulate here. Without actually knowing them, Lukács had divined the gist of Marx's views in the 1844 Manuscripts:

that Marx had tried first to recognize, then to overcome the barriers separating man from his work. Out of that analysis, which aside from its perspicacity was a remarkable act of predictive intelligence, Lukács devised his theses on alienation, reification, and class consciousness. More controversially, however, Lukács was attempting to show the extent to which a revolutionary gesture could be made as a metamorphosis from one sort of consciousness to another; he was attacked, and still is attacked, by many Marxists for what is considered to be his idealism on this score. We needn't debate that point here, of course, but we must acknowledge that Lukács was demonstrating the importance, I think, of seeing that if you separate what you do from what you are, you are reifying, giving objectivistic form to things that in reality don't have that form; or if they do, have it in such a way as to require its overcoming. Thus to interpret man's work (as a laborer, literary critic, engineer, or whatever) as radically and organically connected with what man is and a whole entity (despite the fact that his consciousness cannot recognize or accept the connection) is the common and revolutionary point of departure both for the interpreter as interpreter and, Lukács tried also to show, for the proletariat as reinterpreter and upsetter of bourgeois reification.

My interest in these analyses by Lukács is complex, but what immediately concerns us here is what they mean for criticism. I don't think one ought to jump suddenly to prescriptions for committed critics. There is the matter first of what we mean by committed. I can go into that as a *political* issue later, although we need to specify what world we're talking about; indeed the whole notion of worldliness, so far as the literary critic is concerned, is very important and problematic for me. But we can use Lukács's observation to assert that criticism is radically misconceived if it tries to reify (a) the critic, (b) the text, (c) criticism. To treat each of those as if detachable from the others and from society and history is to impose on them a status they have only in their weakest and most rarified form. This is not by any means to say that a text is interchangeable with a lawn mower, or that a critic and criticism are equivalent to what factory workers do. But one of the consequences of the technicalization, systematization, and functionalism of contemporary avant-garde criticism is the assumption that writing and reading can be truly separated from the circumstances that either enable or produce them. It is true that analytically they perhaps ought to be separated, but it is gross *méconnaissance* to believe that the analytic exigency can become, or indeed is, the reality.

On the one hand, you have the scientistic tendency in criticism. One can associate that with the strict semioticians, some stylisticians, theorists of the self-sufficient text, and anyone who believes that criticism, by virtue of its subject matter and its instruments, can acquire the precision of a science. Aside from being completely incorrect about the precision of science—all you need to do is to read historians of science like Bernal, Kuhn, Canguihelm, Holton as well as scientists themselves to realize that the human and social circumstances of scientific work are notoriously imprecise determinants of that work in ways that humanists (and even scientists) haven't adequately dealt with—this view mischievously arrogates to the critic and his or her system powers neither possesses. In fact to turn the text into a message-bearing or purely rhetorical system, and the critic into a scientist of such matters, is to create a fantasy whose main purpose is the aggrandizement of the critic in his or her own eyes.

On the other hand, you have the more subtle tendency amongst avant-garde critics to discuss texts as something to be "deconstructed" from within. Derrida himself is a brilliant philosopher and critic, and he can't be responsible for what people have made of his notions. But to use the deconstructive techniques as a substitute for genetic analysis is, I think, a serious error in perception and judgment. Nothing in a text merely occurs or happens; a text is made—by the author, the critic, the reader—and it is a collective enterprise to a certain extent, as Goldmann used to say indefatigably. To an even greater extent than that, however, a text is a process, not a thing; this is one of the main arguments of *Beginnings,* especially as I was also trying to demonstrate the connection between a text's materiality (as process) and the human effort expended on its behalf.

Now the "committed" critic must be willing to face these things, to deal with them intellectually, and in some ways to incorporate them within his or her work as a critic. To use words like "demystification" and "deconstruction" as if they applied to texts divorced from human reality, or to suggest—as Derrida has done since *l'Ecriture et la différence*—that myths such as "logocentrism" exist at large in Western culture, is to deny the very human ground from which these things spring. I do not think that what I am proposing is a degeneration either into vulgar Marxism or hortatory humanism. I feel that the whole notion of a beginning would be emasculated of its strength if it were taken as advocating a "pure" beginning that stood apart from the dialectical actualities and circumstances which surround us, implicate us, as human beings and as critics. Of course I believe that a critic must analytically be able to separate, demarcate, limit what he or she does, and detach the text from its surroundings. But our great failing as critics today is that we seem never able to reconnect, rejoin our analyses, our *critefacts* as I call them, to the society, agencies, or lives from which they derive. One of the great tonic observations made by Vico is about what he called the vanity (*boria*) of the philologists and philosophers: both classes, he said, saw what they found in texts through a purely textual perspective, as if that perspective was the world.

You appear to view the concept of world *and* worldliness *as a potential mode or lever of articulation which would allow the academic critic to position his work on texts in relation to social and political questions. Can you elaborate on the usefulness and/or polemical thrust of the concept of* worldliness *as you are using it? What is the importance of the ambiguity—worldliness as being-in-this-world, as mundane objectality, materiality, sociality, versus worldliness as the indice of urbane culture, secularity, sophistication—of the term?*

If one has had any direct dealings in or intercourse with the real world of politics, where power is what informs everything, one will realize first of all that the literary academic has no worldly political status to speak of. I would say in fact that a literary professional whose main base of operation is the university must realize that he or she exists in a condition of institutionalized marginality, so far as the system of political power is concerned. Of course we cannot deny that as teachers of literature, as disseminators of high culture, as transmitters of civilization (pick your favorite function) we do introduce and keep alive irrefutable things in the life of society. As Lionel Trilling once said, there is a mind of society, and it is this mind that we address, tutor, doctor, inform, evaluate, criticize, reform. Our role is highly mediated and subtle, insidious even, but as a class of people our impact on the ongoing life of society in its day-to-day and even long-term affairs is very diffuse, hence minimal.

Unlike social scientists, we cannot play—and there is no machinery for us to employ if we wanted to play—the role of consultants to business, industry, or government. No member of our profession has achieved political prominence. To some extent we are technicians doing a very specialized job; to a certain degree also we are keepers of, kept by, and tutors to the middle and upper classes, although a great deal of what we are interested in as students of literature is necessarily subversive of middle-class values. The point is that institutionally, university literary critics/scholars are defused, and held nicely in check.

There are exceptions to what I have been saying. Recent—or post–World War I—history in this country during a few periods shows literary academics enjoying greater political prominence than the low influence I've just described. Certainly during the period of dissent occasioned by the Vietnam War in the sixties some literary academics achieved national importance as part of a national resistance to imperialist war. And the MLA was forced to accept a relationship between worldly affairs and academic ones, but even then we worked by analogy; that is, since there was an announced revulsion from university complicity in such things as counter-insurgency, "scientific" and political warfare, literary academics tended to make an analogy between themselves and their colleagues in the social and hard sciences. The scientists' guilt was also theirs as teachers of literature. Certainly there were no publicly known instances of literary people employed to practice counter-insurgency, and if there was a literary adviser to the electronic battlefield his name (or position) still isn't known: so there was contentment with arguments inculpating (or purifying) us by analogy, and there was much silliness since a *general* guilt could come and go with equal ease. One thing that did not get debated by academic literary people was the responsibility of an intellectual in a time of crisis, particularly his role in making or defining the crisis (I'm thinking of such concrete matters as the connection between the CIA and *Encounter,* the Congress for Cultural Freedom, etc.). We have made the distinction between the profession of literature and intellectual life much too rigid. It's hard to tell now what the lasting results of the Vietnam period are. Some literature was produced: the work of Kampf, Roszak, Ohmann, and a handful of others. But certainly also there was no contribution to a theoretical literature that treated the relationship between literary criticism and worldly politics, at least no contribution that has made a great impact. We seem now to have gone back to a time of quiescence. I very much doubt that anyone now will think of writing a book like Jonah Raskin's *Mythology of Imperialism* which, if you do not allow yourself to be sidetracked by its needlessly obtrusive rhetoric, is a very intelligent work. Not that imperialism has disappeared; it's gone away for the academic intellectual who has returned to writing within a fairly circumscribed political range. The contributions to theory in literary study have left out the role of institutions in literature. Even the semioticians have been extremely remiss about this. As for the rest of the avant-garde, literature for it has been a matter of texts, more texts, and still more texts. Most literary critics, particularly those of the avant-garde, think of themselves as technical critics, as technicians, if you like. It doesn't by any means go without saying that being a technical, advanced critic means that you think of yourself as an *intellectual* in the widest social sense of that word. Far from it. Indeed I think the extent to which—as I said earlier—the critical avant-garde is politically quietistic is a precise dialectical midpoint between, on the one hand, their political marginality and, on the other, their unwillingness to be general intellectuals.

If we have not had a Gramsci or a Lukács to analyze class consciousness or the intellectuals as a class, we have had (and still do have) Marxist groups within MLA and within the profession. (I am confining myself to organized groups.) I have a great deal of sympathy for what they are trying to do, but I think it is a fundamental misjudgment of reality to base one's political work on an unsituated effort to show that Marxism is principally a reading technique. To say that Marxism cognitively and analytically can produce excellent readings of important nineteenth century novels is not in question: how can one deny it? What I am saying is that the doing of Marxist literary analysis alone cannot constitute the basis of a political program in the great world. And to turn a literary or intellectual project immediately into a political one is to try to do something quite undialectical. But to accept the form of action prescribed in advance by one's professional status—which in the system of things is institutionalized marginality—is to restrict oneself politically and in advance.

I'm not trying to be dogmatic about all this, but I do feel that we all have a tendency to closet ourselves amongst each other, and what seems important to us as a class gets promoted into an issue of world-historical importance. One of the arguments I was trying to articulate in *Beginnings* is that each critic needs in some way to fashion for himself a point of departure that allows him to proceed concretely along a given course of work. According to that notion then, such forms as the novel, such objects as "the text," such practices as criticism, are constitutive methods for creating work and "covering" their own beginnings with inevitability and a posteriori logic. I was also interested not only in the transformations of which the idea of beginning is capable, but also in demonstrating (at a very theoretical level) how concrete circumstances and highly abstract appetites (and even fictions) can combine to provide one with an intentional method of formulating projects for oneself. I was examining the way in which one launches oneself from contemplation to a sort of worldly action, although I didn't then (and don't now) pretend for a moment that reading and writing are in themselves otherworldly; of course they're not, but the question is how are they in the world, and how can they be in the world—a terrifyingly complex question. Much of the answer to that is left very implicit in the book, although the last chapter (on Vico) takes it up overtly.

I think it would be extremely presumptuous to try to spell out what critics, committed or otherwise, should be doing, so I won't try. But I can talk a little about these matters, in particular the notion of worldliness, as they appear to me, for me. In the first place, I think we must recognize the marginality of our roles and, more important, that for the first time we are facing some dramatic, explicit impositions on us that make us more marginal as a class. The university, in particular its liberal arts division, is shrinking. Worse yet, our graduate students cannot find jobs; they find themselves standing uselessly before a closed door. We find ourselves torn therefore: what we do as professional scholars/teachers/critics narrows in its focus and its technicality, it is influential amongst students who in turn may not have jobs; what is our response to be?

In the second place, the world itself is shrinking. This is a cheerful McLuhanesque truism only if you think of the world as a problem of communications between its parts. But if you reflect that we face economic shortages of the most catastrophic sort, and that the great line separating the world today is between rich and poor, or North and

South, or developed and developing nations, all competing for such basics as food and resource materials, the shrinking world appears rather a menacing place. In the U.S. we belong to a scandalously wasteful society, which consumes double and even triple its numerical share of resources. In addition, we are the strong man of the world economy (incidentally the idea of a world economy—as Immanuel Wallerstein has studied it—is an extremely important one), and our sense of things (what we call the economic order) is supported by fantastic economic strength, a network of unimaginably powerful institutions (see Barnet and Müller's *Global Reach,* or Pierre Jalée's work, or Harry Magdoff's *The Age of Imperialism*), and a complex system of forces for imposing ourselves on the world, thereby guaranteeing our economic well-being. If you read what Geoffrey Barraclough has been writing recently you will see exactly what I mean.

In the third place, we are—or pretend we are—universalists in our cultural values. In fact, however, we are ethnocentric to a fault. Everything we say or do as teachers of literature applies principally to the Atlantic cultures, which are understandably privileged for us. Our whole sense of literary and cultural history is based on what the Egyptian sociologist Anwar Abdel Malek has called the hegemonism of possessing minorities. Consider, for example, that between 1815 and 1918 European territorial dominion increased from about 40 percent to 85 percent of the world's total surface. Anthropocentrism is "naturally" associated with Europocentrism. Today territorial control has been transmuted into economic and social control.

In the fourth place, what goes on in the developing, or Southern, or Third or Fourth Worlds scarcely occupies attention, or if it does we are unable to make it mesh with what we do as scholars/critics/teachers. I do not believe that the barricades are where we belong. The problem for us is much more dialectical than that, presuming of course that we don't (a) turn our backs on the whole world and (b) declare war on it. Perhaps the lamentable Daniel Moynihan in his grandstanding at the UN does speak for the literary academics: I doubt it, but surely he doesn't speak for all of them. Nevertheless, I think we must somehow take in the realities of the U.S.'s position in the world.

Now it is very hard for a critic to assess the role or the place of his writing in "the world." I've just been speaking of "the world"—very quickly and schematically of course—and it doesn't require a Voltaire to tell us that as authors of books on beginnings, or Hardy's poetry, or Spenser's imagery, the world isn't too much with us at all. What is left to a critic's work if you take away from it in advance any serious impact it might have on the world? To a certain extent the critic will be left with worldliness, in the second sense, worldliness as the index of urbane culture, secularity, sophistication, all of which are signified by critical interchange, critics reviewing other critics, and so forth. In such a world the issues of greatest consequence will be what one critic says about another, the assertion of priorities, values, and imperatives that have the stamp on them of scholastic hermeticism. I haven't any doubt that a certain amount of this sort of worldliness is our lot as critics; the question is how else we can engage with the larger world, and do things there that our peculiar, not to say eccentric, capacities and training suit us for.

If we disabuse ourselves of the idea that "writing" is something that can be reduced unilaterally, terminally, and univocally to an "author" we open a new avenue of approach to the world. This has been Foucault's great discovery. Writing is not free, nor is it performed uniquely by a sovereign writer who writes more or less as he or she pleases. Writing belongs to a system of utterances that has all sorts of affiliative, often constricting relationships with the world of nations, as Vico called it. One can see this most clearly in scholarly writing, or writing that belongs to such disciplines as history, sociology, economics, and philology, disciplines in which the individual writer is born on very heavily by institutions, rituals, exclusions, prohibitions, and a highly particularized, even tyrannical conception of truth and the desire for truth. As I intimated earlier, such disciplines as literary criticism are policed and kept "authentic" by methods that limit what one can say and still be considered as doing literary criticism; it is not a matter of seemliness only, but also a question of the discipline's sense of its own identity, which it must fight—from within and without the field—to preserve. A critic who uses psychoanalysis threatens lit. crit. by stepping beyond boundaries, saying what shouldn't be said, and—if he is like Bloom—doing it with a kind of wounding intimacy.

Let me be a good deal more specific, although I shall have to be confining myself to the limited area I know best. As I mentioned above I have been very concerned about our distance as professionals in this country from the rest of the world. It is too simple to say that most academic critics are lazy esthetes who prefer to contemplate Tennyson than to muck about with the issues raised by Fanon or Barrington Moore. If you have the fortune (or misfortune, depending on your outlook) to know another part of the world—in my case the Near Orient, Arab and Islamic society—you begin to wonder what, except for a mere caricature of that important yet exotic and distant reality, has filtered through into Western society. It's not enough to say that obviously a "foreign" and non-Western part of the world can't be well known; it's much more interesting and valuable to know how and why it is as badly known as it is. In his book on Western knowledge about Islam in the Middle Ages, R. W. Southern makes a superb observation: there was ignorance about Islam, he said, but it was a complex ignorance, and it can be studied actively as a form of *positive* knowledge about Islam.

You can see where that leads—straight to the kind of observation Nietzsche made repeatedly, that knowledge and the will to knowledge are inseparable, and together they are interested, systematic, powerful *interpretations*. In the case of the Orient they did not take place in the abstract. I began to study the "Orient" or what I call the Orientalizations of the Orient. This led me to a study not only of Orientalist philology, but also of history, geography, religion, indeed all those branches of Western knowledge whose principal concern is the Orient. In so doing I was considering such things as the relationship between the rise of modern Orientalism in the early nineteenth century, the growth of Orientalist institutions (societies, exploration and translation funds, academic departments), the increasingly powerful commercial, diplomatic and finally military colonial presence in the Orient, and the work of a number of major artists, including Flaubert, Nerval, Lane, Burton, Disraeli, Hugo, Goethe, and so forth. You could pick up a text by Renan, for example, and see in it the network of predatory interests (interests, by the way, are always created: one should study how they are created, and for what reasons) that connected him with Gobineau, with the French diplomatic service, comparative anatomy, and so forth—all of them encroaching upon, then finally eliminating from the Western Orientalist mind anything but a schematic essentialization which was called "the Orient." A major part of my study has been the way in which Orientalist texts are attempts at textual reconstruction of the Orient, as if the "real" or actual Orient ought not by itself to be admitted into Western consciousness; one sees this in Napoleon's *Description de l'Egypte,* later in Sylvestre de Sacy's chrestomathies, later still in Lane's and Flaubert's tableaux.

The focus of interest in Orientalism for me has been the partnership between a discursive and archival textuality and worldly power, one as an index and refraction of the other. As a systematic discourse Orientalism is written knowledge, but because it is in the world and directly about the world, it is *more* than knowledge: it is *power* since, so far as the Oriental is concerned, Orientalism is the operative and effective knowledge by which he was delivered textually to the West, occupied by the West, milked by the West for his resources, humanly quashed by the West. From such Baconian realizations it is not difficult to see, for example, that most knowledge of something gets into texts according to historical laws, social and economic forces, worldly circumstances which make for important and urgent study. Particularly to a literary critic today, who because of his or her institutionalized marginality seems content with being a commentator from the outside on what transpires in the world. Our interpretive worldly wisdom has been applied, in a sense, to everything except ourselves; we are brilliant at deconstructing the mystifications of a text, at elucidating the blindness of a critical method, but we have seemed unable to apply these techniques to the very life of texts in the world, their materiality, their capacity for the production of misery or liberation, their monumentality as Foucault has spoken of it. As a result we are mesmerized by the text, and convinced that a text is only a text, without realizing how saying that, such a narrow view is not only naive, it is blind.

To reintegrate himself with worldly actuality, the critic of texts ought to be investigating the system of discourse by which the "world" is divided, administered, plundered, by which humanity is thrust into pigeonholes, by which "we" are "human" and "they" are not, and so forth. We will discover that even so innocuous a discipline as philology has played a crucial role in the process. Most important, we should be intent upon revealing the secrecy, the privatizations of texts whose circumstantial thickness and complicity are covered by the otherworldly prestige of art or of "mere" textuality.

In tracing the evolution of the concept of "philology" do you see a

contradiction between the view that all nations are equal as human be-
ings (Herder) and the hierarchical view of nations implied by the "lan-
guage tree"?

On the face of it, yes there is a contradiction. Isaiah Berlin has just
written a study of Vico and Herder that claims for Herder the credit of
being a cultural pluralist who was opposed to cultural nationalism and
the hierarchical divisions between cultures. That is only part of the
truth. The early Herder was typical of the period in conflating the "Orient" with Old Testament history. Between 1769 and 1774 he was converted to a wider view of the Orient, which included Persia, Egypt, and
Phoenicia, and this world he identified with primitivity. Yet by the middle eighties, at a time when texts like Anquetil-Duperron's Zend and
Sanskrit translations were being diffused, Herder became a defender of
Greek art; in the *Ideen* he was saying quite specifically that the Hellenic
aesthetic was preferable to the Asiatic for a European, and one can find
numerous attacks in his later work on the theocratic and despotic practices of Oriental peoples. What I think we must note in Herder is the
tendency always to compare the Oriental unfavorably with the Occidental, and that is almost always the practice of universalizing sciences
like philology and comparative grammar in the early nineteenth century.
Both Schlegels did it, Humboldt did it, Renan did it, Bopp did it.

Yet of course no comparison of that sort is innocent or value-free. My
sense of the comparative tendency which led to the hierarchies of language trees and families is that it is rooted in a desire to valorize three
things: (1) the present (or a particular aspect of the present), (2) Europe,
and (3) the science itself. Consider Schlegel. In his 1808 book on the Indians he shows the affinities between Greek and Sanskrit roots, then the
affinities between both of those and modern European languages. His
idea of the Orient is that it is a classical and immensely distant realm,
yet whose influence lingers now only amongst the modern European
languages, and hence civilizations. The Orient is not at all a place where
modern Orientals live, work, produce; it is a cocoon cloistered away
from the real modern world, but the prestige of its "originality" is transferred onto Europe, which has produced the thinkers whose techniques
—in this case those of comparative philology—allow it to be appreciated
and used. Thus the phrase Indo-European was made of two unequal
parts: the first half is sunk in the past, the second is vital, enterprising,

and resourceful. It is said of Bopp's disciples that they used frequently to quarrel over whether Indo-European ought to be changed to Indo-Germanic: one can see the pernicious nationalism involved, but it was inevitable, I think, once philology made qualitative distinctions between the various language families, and once modernity was associated with the European *état présent*.

For Schlegel, and indeed for all the philologists in that tradition, Indo-European was distinct from Semitic: the latter was agglutinative (the language worked by a system of roots to which were added suffixes and prefixes), it lacked germinative power, it could not perform aesthetic functions. The former was lively, aesthetic, seminal, organic. In that linguistic distinction (if that is what it was) you have the seed of racial theory, since it was not hard to build racial types out of the linguistic discriminations. Every philologist during the nineteenth century made the same distinctions over and over again. In his *The Aryan Myth* Leon Poliakov has studied the symbiosis between racism and such notions as an Aryan type, whose features are those of a hypothetical Indo-European language "set." But Poliakov doesn't make enough of the fact that so far as Europe was concerned "the Semites" were not only the Jews but also the Muslims, and that the whole intellectual program devoted to proving Oriental (i.e., Semitic) degeneracy was practically effective in legitimating the colonial occupation of the entire Orient. But such is the intellectual fashion today that one simply closes one's eyes to that part of reality not in consonance with one's immediate goals. It's ironic too that a book like Poliakov's, which is an attack on racial theory, leaves out that part of history which shows how almost incredibly wide was the net used to gather in Orientals and Semites.

But I'm digressing. If we return to your question then we can see paradoxically that notions of equality based on the idea of "different nations" and all the invidious qualitative judgments made about the inequality of nations and races, these two go together. To a large extent, the reason they go together is a matter of power, whose rhetorical symbol is the word "humanity." Whenever "humanity" or "mankind" was used it seemed immediately to reflect the truth that its user spoke for, could speak for, mankind, at the expense of most of mankind, which couldn't. There's an important study yet to be done by critics on the deployment of generalizations, particularly anthropomorphic generalizations, in nineteenth century European literature. I'm sure one will find that from the romantics on, literary production and political discriminations of the sort I've been discussing, fortify and feed each other.

The figure of the Exotic in Western thought has usually contained the "Caliban" problematic, i.e., the Exotic as a non- or marginally communicative being functioning in the super-imposed, dominant language. This inarticulateness can result in rebellion or submission, but never in the assimilation of the oppressed into the dominant culture. How do you view this question of language in the light of writers (such as yourself) who are forced to accept the language of colonialism as your/their means of expression?

You've touched on a rich and complex question. One thing it reminds me of immediately is how at Joyce's funeral in Zurich the British ambassador there, Lord Derwent, patronized Joyce (perhaps unconsciously) by intimating that for an Irishman Joyce gave the good old English language a glorious shaking-up—I think that's the expression Derwent used. How ironic, since from beginning to end of his career Joyce was troubled by the fact that (as he put it most memorably in *The Portrait*) Ben Jonson's language was not his (Stephen's), and words like "Christ," "ale," "master" did not come naturally or first to him. I remember also the remark made by Aimé Césaire that in praising him once Breton also commented on how amazing it was that Césaire used French like a Frenchman: the barb was no doubt mainly in Césaire's mind, but it was real. Fanon has had much to say about language as a symbol of power for the oppressed, principally in his early works, although it returns as a motif in *Les Damnés de la terre*. I might also mention a series of recent works in French (e.g., Balibar and Laporte, *Le Français national*, Louis-Jean Calvet, *Linguistique et colonialisme: petit traité de glottophagie*, various papers by Gillian Sankoff) that try to deal with the sociocultural pressures involved in language use, particularly as they impinge from the center onto peripheral or colonial groups. The earlier work of Marcel Cohen and Henri Lefebvre is also important in this regard.

The political problem of language has gone through two phases, I think. First you have the period when (as was the case with Algeria) the native writer was compelled to be francophone (or anglophone) without any alternative: of course there was a native Arabic tradition, but that was not supposed to be for the world, but for such arcane subjects as the law, or the *hadith,* and so on. I mentioned above how carefully the colonizer made the colonial native speak his language either as an exhibit or as a sign of tribute to the strong or politically dominant society: I think we have to think in terms of *making someone speak,* in much the same punitive sense that Foucault has studied (in *Surveiller et punir*) the imposition of orthographic or penal disciplines upon European students and convicts respectively during the eighteenth and nineteenth centuries. When the local or native language was studied in the colonies it was always imprisoned within the perspective of a dead or classical language; what the untutored native spoke was a kitchen language, nothing more. Because of the educational system the bourgeoisie adopted English or French, with a good deal of self-conscious pride and also a sense of the distance that separated the class both from the colonial master and from the unfortunate peasant.

The second phase can be subdivided into two parts. First there is a generalized awareness that the colonial language can be used to attack the system of political control—Fanon speaks of this in much detail. Then, the second part, when an abrupt shift to the native language is a symbol of determined resistance to colonial oppression. In Algeria this took place when political agitation against the French included studying and then using Arabic. As a result Algerians today speak a kind of Arabic that is a sort of cross between a spoken dialect and the classical, or written, language. Most other Arabs—with the exception, I think, of the Palestinians whose experience is similar in many ways to the Algerians—move uneasily between the classical and the dialect, which are very widely separated.

English and French today are world-languages. Arabic is either a local demotic or a liturgical language, but one of the great seminal moments in the history of modern Arabic politics was when Abdel Nasser used his speeches as the occasion to attack colonialism in the native Egyptian dialect. Not only was he avoiding the straitjacketing effect of the classical (which Orientalism had legislated into a kind of otherworldly uselessness, so much so that even many Arabs believed the myth) but he was also turning on Britain and France on his own terms, on his own linguistic terrain, so to speak. This is much more impressive a thing than it sounds, particularly when you remember, for example, that the constitutions of at least two Arab countries were originally written not in Arabic but in a European language, and when you consider too that the historical archives of several of the Arab states exist only in London and in English. Add too the fact that there exists in Europe a vast cache of Arabic texts, removed out of the Arab world by the colonial powers during the nineteenth century. Here Foucault's theory of the archive and discourse acquires a very material dimension; the archive of much of modern Arab history resides unmetaphorically, has been deposited in, has been physically imprisoned by, Europe.

Many of the major poets, novelists, and essayists in Arabic have these facts very powerfully in their consciousness. They obviously find it hard to deal with situations in which they are latecomers intellectually to Marxist or other ideas useful in attacking the same culture that produced both Marxism and colonialism. Originality takes on a rather different meaning in such a curious context than it would if one were "first": this is why I find Bloom's charts of influence, and his ideas about strong and weak, first-coming and ephebe poets so suggestive.

There is no doubt that the great cultural and political question facing the Third World generally, and the Arab world in particular, is the articulation of independence—the verbal metaphor here is very central—and the struggle for intelligibility. As a world-language English has a rather menacing side when it is exported; it can (and does) produce a new illiteracy, as Blackmur used to call it, which, when it is allied with the Third World desire for technical expertise and with the electronification of intelligence, makes the language a new form of oppression and enslavement. For if Orientalism was a language whose codes and grids filtered through a schematic Orient for Western consumption, it is also true that the West filters through what schematically ought to be known about itself to the Orient. That Third World and Arab intellectuals can attack these schemata today is a tribute to the transdiscursive power in Freud, Marx, and others.

My own work at present is focused on situating, placing, materializing the discourse of Orientalism: revealing its structures, characterizing it as a language whose institutional and disciplinary presence eliminated, displaced the Oriental as human and put in his place the Orient Orientalized as specimen. I feel myself to be clearing the library of such possessing languages as those of Orientalism, making it possible for myself as an Oriental, and for other Orientals, to speak, using whatever language we feel we need to use. In short, I am writing a work that could be read in either English or Arabic.

As I see it, you seem constantly to emphasize that the basic error (more precisely the ideological distortion) of Western thinking is its belief in a meaningless "Oriental" cultural heritage: inferior language, underdeveloped mentality, no history (or if there is an "Oriental" history, it is always one written by the Westerner for the benefit of the Oriental—who is incapable of writing his own), and finally no "Oriental" literary tradition. Is this last point historically true? Has there been an evolution in the literature produced in Arabic over the years (such as the European novel for instance)? Finally, what role is contemporary literary and artistic production playing in the recent social and political transformations of Arab consciousness among Arab societies? How does it reflect recent changes in the Arab context?

Actually I find the Orientalist turning the Orient into something overly *meaningful,* making the Orient say things, tell things about itself that no region, much less a people or a religion could signify in so schematic and cut-and-dried a way. Renan said that the Semitic mind was "une combinaison inférieure de la nature humaine" he didn't say that it, or the Orient that produced it, was meaningless. One of the dominant motifs in what Edgar Quinet called the Oriental Renaissance of the European nineteenth century was the overestimation of the Orient; Benjamin Constant has some shrewd observations on that phenomenon in his *Journal Intime.* But it is true that the Orientalist, and indeed the European in general, got used to the idea of telling the world, including the Orient itself, what the Orient really meant, and I'm sure you'll find much the same thing happening as "orientals" today tell each other what the "West" is all about. The noteworthy thing about Orientalism was that interpreting the Orient very soon turned into speaking for the Orient (silencing it), as after 1798 the Orient was militarily an occupied territory. Of course all this went on for the benefit of the Oriental, as you put it, who was never consulted, much less involved in such interpretations. I think you must remember that Orientalism thought of itself as doing what it did *in spite of* the Oriental.

Most Arabs would agree, I think, that what has mattered most to Arab culture, aside from Islam itself, is literature. The high point of that literature since the Hegira and until the late nineteenth century was the

Abbasid period, between the eighth and the thirteenth centuries A.D. Between the Abbasids and the modern period there are moments of some literary importance (eighteenth century chroniclers, for example, specialized prose and poetry forms, etc.), but on the whole it isn't a stretch of time with much going on in it that is very memorable, not in my opinion at least, and my opinion is somewhat provincial and not that of a scholar on the subject. I can't possibly go into the Abbasid period here; that would be like trying to talk about the European Renaissance in a paragraph. But yes, it was an extremely rich and stunningly innovative period in Arabic letters. The great difficulty for the Western reader, say a comparatist, is that in order to talk about the literature he would have to be paraphrasing and translating constantly, as so little of it is known. But that's only one problem.

The other problem is that Orientalism for the most part has had very little to do with Arabic literature, or at least with literature as in some way an expression of Arab life. This is one of the most remarkable things about Orientalism as a doctrine, and to a certain extent determined me to write my study of Orientalism. One has the impression that every Orientalist has considered the Arabs as an exemplification of the Koran, or what the Orientalists claim the Koran said: methodologically, this is the equivalent of writing a history of the United States as an illustration of the New Testament. When you consider even the name of the field—Orientalism, or its subdivisions, like Islam or Arabism—you will not be able to find a symmetrical field to it; no one professes Occidentalism for example, and no one will consider a study of Christianity to be a substitute for the study of Shakespeare, or of Saint-Simon, or of American history in the nineteenth century. But these are regular practices in Orientalism. Statistically, I am positive you will find literature to be the least represented of the Orientalist subspecialties, for obvious reasons, since literature muddles the tidy categories invented for Oriental life by Orientalists. The plain fact is that Orientalists do not know how to *read,* and therefore happily ignore literature.

When you come to the modern period, a much more serious distortion arises. As with all national resurgences the various movements of Arab revolution that begin in the post–World War era rely very heavily for their popular diffusion and mass mobilization upon literature; consequently there has been a tremendous development in all branches of

Arabic literature. Read any book written in the West on the modern Arabs and you will never find literature mentioned, much less studied. Most Middle East experts today are social scientists whose expertise is based on a handful of clichés about Arab society, Islam and the like, handed down like tatters, from the nineteenth century Orientalists. A whole new vocabulary of terms is bandied about: modernization, elites, development, stability are talked about as possessing some sort of universal validity, but in fact they form a rhetorical smokescreen hiding ignorance of the area. The new Orientalist jargon is hermetic discourse, whose wisdom cannot prepare one, for example, for what happens today in Lebanon, or in the Israeli-occupied Arab territories, or all through the life of the Middle Eastern people. In short the *presence* of Orientalism means the *absence* of any interest in Oriental literature as an integral part of a society's development. You can get a much better idea of what is going on anywhere in the Arab world by reading five recent poems, novels, or essays than by reading a whole shelf of publications put out by the Middle East Institute, or the Rand Corporation, or by any avowed Orientalist who teaches the Middle East in the various Oriental studies departments across the country. But this should not surprise you if you know anything about either literature or Orientalism.

If you regard Orientalism as a system of *representations* of the Orient, then it should be clear why one of its functions was to avoid literature; such systems *hide* the human being who is the object of study *from* history—Sheila Rowbotham's phrase for what happens to women in bourgeois society is appropriate for the Oriental too. (The parallels between Orientals, blacks, and women are striking of course.) It has seemed to me useful to recall Marx's phrase for Louis Napoleon in the *18th Brumaire;* speaking of Louis's claim to represent the underdeveloped smallholding peasants, Marx says ironically, "They cannot represent themselves; they must be represented." This perfectly expresses the Orientalist's attitude to the Oriental, with the difference only that the Oriental was the victim of total political and cultural usurpation, and of military rule to boot. The banishment of literature is accordingly inevitable.

If it is (somewhat) true that politica manent, *what about the volatility of present schools of criticism? They usually specify strong political concerns and sympathies, but their life span is brief and usually extin-*

guished within critical strife: how is this situation compatible with the
necessary duration of political action?

Doubtless political action and critical schools live according to different calendars, so to speak. Yet a political group or grouping (like a
party) expresses its solidarity with a cause and with itself in very explicit
ways, and this is something literary schools today do not do. There are
much looser affiliations between critics who think of themselves as allied than between members of a party or political action group, so the
difference in time span that you speak about is a function of that principally, and not necessarily of the duration of a political cause. A critic,
even if he feels himself to be a member of a literary school or tendency,
still thinks of what he does not as cooperative, but as something individual, and individualized. Of course this is a dilemma for the critic, this
conflict between the larger ambience of which he is a part and the relatively isolated exercise of his gifts of interpretation, intuition, or whatever: it is difficult to find a way out of it, and I'm not sure one easily can.

A related problem is the extent to which criticism can be systematized; one of the fascinations with semiotics, for instance, is that the
rules of analysis seem not to be dependent on an individual, but rather
upon a community of interpreters. I recall Barthes speaking somewhere
about an ideal of semiotic research as in some way cooperative and
impersonal. Another aspect of systematic criticism is the problem of
whether or not the critic ends up by doing his analysis in a fairly predictable way. You could take Northrop Frye's essay on Dickens as a case
in point, and simply say of it that it is typically Frye-esque. But over and
above such temptations as systematics dangle before us, there is surely a
residual hedonism in every critical act, which may consist in going
against oneself or one's system, or perhaps in quite deliberately freeing
oneself of one's past attachments and habits and alliances. Barthes has
made a whole career of this. I doubt that other critics would want to
strip themselves of this privilege, even though it is very circumscribed.
Schools and systems often exist as a method for warding off such even-
tualities, and that is why I am temperamentally anti-systemic and anti-
school. I think that criticism is fundamentally an activity of discovery
and cognition, not of contemplation or of rigid theoretical imposition.
In the latter there is always the danger of overlooking, or of never finding and experiencing the stray bit of historical evidence; but perhaps this

is another way of saying that I find it especially instructive to ransack the archives, as it were. Aside from the pleasure this gives me, there is the main benefit of allowing theory to feel upon it the impress of material (or at least archival) reality. And this in turn stimulates additional refinement in theoretical activity.

Discussing the nature of the discipline ("Anthropology: its achieve-ments and future"), Lévi-Strauss declared a few years ago that anthro-pology was the daughter of an era of violence: "its capacity to assess more objectively the facts pertaining to the human condition reflects, on the epistemological level, a state of affairs in which one part of mankind treated the others as an object. . . . *It is not an account of its mental en-dowments that only the Western world has given birth to anthropology, but rather as a* consequence *of the fact that exotic cultures, treated by us as mere* things, *could be studied accordingly as* things." *Isn't your forth-coming book on Orientalism (or rather on the* myth *of Orientalism), an effort to denounce the kind of "anthropological imperialism" analyzed by Lévi-Strauss? If so, how do you* characterize *the myth of Orientalism (ideology, mentality, etc.)? How do you go about* demythifying *this myth? and* from where *do you, Edward Said, speak (or rather write)?*

Orientalism isn't a myth, it's a myth-system with a mytho-logic, rhet-oric, and institutions of its own. It is a machine for producing statements about the Orient and it can be studied historically and institutionally as a form of anthropological imperialism. The main point to be made about Orientalism is that it isn't simply a scholarly or imaginative kind of writ-ing (what form is?) with no particular importance for anyone but other Orientalists: it isn't. It pretends to scientific objectivity, and it is today a perfect instance of how knowledge and writing can be brought from the text, so to speak, to the world—with force and genuine political conse-quence. The Orient today is not the equivalent of a disappearing pre-literate tribe of the sort studied by Lévi-Strauss; it is a region of the world with major policy implications for the Western world, the U.S. in partic-ular. So what one studies is the execution and administration of textual knowledge for direct, in some cases, painfully direct political purposes. The limits of my study are, on the one hand, Orientalism as a pre-modern (pre-nineteenth century) system of imaginative geography, and two, Orientalism as a modern discourse whose contemporary relevance is to what Harold Lasswell calls the policy sciences. I am interested in the process by which the first is converted into the second.

My study is divided into three main parts. The first, "the Scope of Orientalism" attempts to characterize Orientalism as a family of ideas that have been in existence in the West since Herodotus, and which culminate in the rhetoric of Cromer, Balfour, Kissinger, and other statesmen. For there is a common element in such ideas as Oriental despotism, Oriental sensuality, Oriental modes of production, and Oriental splendor. My focus is on the dialectic by which the Orient was represented on what I call the Orientalist stage in the West, which until the eighteenth century took Islam to be the main Oriental type. Oriental knowledge during this period is to be found in such works as D'Herbelot's *Bibliothèque orientale,* the *Divine Comedy,* some of the medieval chronicles and in the various sacerdotal attempts (Peter the Venerable, Guibert of Nogent, Luther) to deal with the problem of Islam and Mohammed. These essentially religious works are in striking contrast with the first modern and racialist Orientalist projects, which date from after the linguistic discoveries of Jones and Anquetil; the two projects that I focus on are the Napoleonic expedition (and its learned arms, the Institut d'Egypte and the *Description de l'Egypte*) and de Lesseps' Suez Canal authority. In the second part, "Orientalist structures and re-structures," I study the main philological, historical and imaginative writers on the Near Orient during the nineteenth century; my point of departure is Baron Dacier's *Tableau de l'érudition française,* and I move thereafter to Hugo, Goethe, Renan, Sacy, Chateaubriand, Nerval, Lamartine, Lane, Burton, Flaubert, Doughty, among others. The striking thing about all these writers is the reservoir of knowledge, imagery, and motifs on which they consistently draw, and the way in which each in his own way tried to control the Orient through devices like the tableau, the florilège, the library, the classroom, and so forth. These devices in turn are operated simultaneously by the various religious, educational, and diplomatic institutions in and for the Orient. Thus the structure of the Orientalist imagination is directly projected onto a colonial administration which in turn is converted directly into a system of rules, exclusions, prohibitions placed upon Orientals in the Orient: the three feed each other in a self-confirming process. Finally the third part, "Modern Orientalism," which is an account of how the British and French schools of Orientalism passed their learned legacies and effective techniques onto the American school, and how its dogmas in turn are reflected both in the reward and teaching structure of government and the academy in the U.S. today, as well as in the conduct of U.S. decision making and foreign policy.

Throughout the whole study I am at pains to show the way in which Orientalism was an eclectic system that absorbed, without actually modifying itself, the influences of such "strong" philosophies as positivism, Marxism, Darwinism, psychoanalysis, Spenglerism, and so forth. My polemical intention is to demonstrate how Orientalism is and was a way of being in the world, a way of making statements with authority, and—crucially—a form of disciplined ideological presence. This allows me to deal with the problems of knowledge and imagination, politics and writing, freedom and oppression in the relation between the developed and developing worlds.

These things quite clearly define the process of demystification or de-mythification as you call it. I feel myself to be writing from an interesting position. I am an Oriental writing back at the Orientalists, who for so long have thrived upon our silence. I am also writing *to* them, as it were, by dismantling the structure of their discipline, showing its meta-historical, institutional, anti-empirical, and ideological biases. Finally, I feel myself to be writing for compatriots and colleagues about matters of common concern.

Interview in *Diacritics,*
Cornell University,
Ithaca, New York, 1976

IN THE SHADOW OF THE WEST

During 1981 and 1982 I had been involved in the making of a ten-part documentary film series for Channel 4 in the United Kingdom. I wrote the screenplay for the seventh film in the series, In the Shadow of the West, *which cinematically described the subject matter of* Orientalism *and* The Question of Palestine. *Shot on location in South Lebanon mainly in two Palestinian refugee camps in January 1982, the film eerily presaged the Israeli invasion in June: many of the refugees we spoke to and filmed were made refugees again.* E.W.S.

As a way of raising a number of questions, we wanted initially to go back to the early sixties. Two books were published then by authors whose work has certain affiliations with your own: Fanon's Wretched of the Earth *and Foucault's* Madness and Civilization. *We have, then, the production of two texts, one from within France and the other from one of its colonies, that describe, in very different ways, related mechanisms of exclusion that were embedded in European institutions since the Renaissance. What were some of the forces that might have generated this coincidence of texts?*

I don't really know much about the circumstances that produced Foucault's book, although I could speculate on what they might have been. But obviously Fanon's text—the more significant of the two in my opinion—came out of an ongoing political struggle, the Algerian revolution. It is important that Fanon's book was the result of a *collective* struggle, as opposed to Foucault's work, which evolved out of a different tradition, that of the individual scholar-researcher acquiring a reputation for learning, brilliance, and so on. Apart from their different origins, both were certainly oppositional books. They dealt with not only systems of exclusion, but systems of confinement. Fanon's most powerful image in the book is of the colonial city: the native *casbah* surrounded by the cleanliness, the well-lighted streets of the colonialist town, a European town, violently implanted in a native society. And above all, the common motif in both was that whatever was done in the way of violence to the subject was justified in the name of reason or rationality—civilization. But, I still think that it's important to note that Fanon's book is the more powerful because it is rooted in, you might say, the dialectics of struggle.

Rather than because it comes out of a certain practice of historiography.

Yes, precisely, but more importantly, what is present in Fanon's work and absent in the early Foucault is the sense of active commitment. Ten years after *Madness and Civilization,* in Amsterdam in 1972, Foucault was involved in a television debate with Noam Chomsky. While Chomsky spoke about his own libertarian ideals, notions about justice, and so forth, Foucault backed away and essentially admitted that he believed in no positive truths, ideas, or ideals. And this was not true of Fanon, whose commitments to revolutionary change, solidarity, and liberation were very powerful and appealing to such as myself. Foucault's work was rather a matter of a quite remarkable ingenuity and acuity of philosophical perception. I would also say that the political force of Foucault's work did not become fully apparent until much later, after he had produced more books—*The Order of Things,* for example—and not before the work of several others as well (Jacques Donzelot, for instance). Fanon's work is really the last in a series written by him throughout the fifties, while Foucault's was the beginning of his series.

Let's return for the moment to violence, the subject, and civilization. In Orientalism, *you delineate a broad alliance between Western academic scholarship and the colonialist project, applying concepts of representation in a critique of instrumentalized knowledge. Specifically, how do you define representation and its political economy?*

I'm not sure I could define it economically, or neatly for that matter, but certainly representation, or more particularly the *act* of representing (and hence reducing) others, almost always involves violence of some sort to the *subject* of the representation, as well as a contrast between the violence of the act of representing something and the calm exterior of the representation itself, the *image*—verbal, visual, or otherwise—of the subject. Whether you call it a spectacular image, or an exotic image, or a scholarly representation, there is always this paradoxical contrast between the surface, which seems to be in control, and the process which produces it, which inevitably involves some degree of violence, decontextualization, miniaturization, etc. The action or process of representing implies control, it implies accumulation, it implies confinement, it implies a certain kind of estrangement or disorientation on the part of the one representing. We could take as an example a linguistic treatise, Ernest Renan's work on Semitic languages: what is in Renan's mind as he catalogues his material is the display case in a museum, and when you display something, you wrench it out of the context of living life and put it before an (in this case, European) audience. Because, above all, representation involves consumption: representations are put to use in the domestic economy of an imperial society. In the case of *Orientalism,* I was speaking of an economy whereby the manipulation and control of colonies could be sustained. Now, obviously, there are many other kinds of representations, but these that are produced by and for a dominant imperial culture are the ones that interest me because of the circumstances of my own life, where I was subjected to their authority. I was sent to colonial schools—quite willingly by my parents, there was no force involved—where, by the time I became an adolescent, I knew a great deal about English history, and nothing about my own history, Arab history. What I was being taught was that the only representations that counted were the representations of English history and culture that I was acceding to by virtue of an education. I was also taught to regard myself as somebody whose worth in that economy was considerably less than that of the English, who were, in fact, ruling. And out of that context, I couldn't help but come to understand representation as a discursive system involving political choices and political force, authority in one form or another.

So, as you've demonstrated in your writing, there is a direct and active relationship between domination—political, socioeconomic, cultural— and systems of representation: one produces/sustains the other, and vice versa. In terms of affecting change in structures of domination, is the ultimate goal to transform representations or to eliminate those systems altogether? In either case, what would prevent the establishment of another, equally exclusive, discursive practice?

Representations are a form of human economy, in a way, and necessary to life in society and, in a sense, between societies. So I don't think there is any way of getting away from them—they are as basic as language. What we must eliminate are systems of representation that carry with them the kind of authority which, to my mind, has been repressive because it doesn't permit or make room for interventions on the part of those represented. This is one of the unresolvable problems of anthropology, which is constituted essentially as the discourse of representation of an Other *epistemologically defined as radically inferior* (whether labeled primitive, or backward, or simply Other): the whole science or discourse of anthropology depends upon the silence of this Other. The alternative would be a representational system that was participatory and collaborative, noncoercive, rather than imposed, but as you know, this is not a simple matter. We have no immediate access to the means of producing alternative systems. Perhaps it would be possible through other, less exploitative fields of knowledge. But first we must identify those social-cultural-political formations which would allow for a reduction of authority and increased participation in the production of representations, and proceed from there.

You've dealt with this problem of constructing alternative systems in relation to the exclusionary mechanisms of the Western media in Covering Islam. *Do you think that the implementation of a new kind of instantaneous, global, electronics network that produces and disseminates news could fundamentally change the setup within which people in the West consume representations of what is defined as the non-West? Or is power becoming even more consolidated?*

If anything, the crisis is deepening, for several reasons. First, with the advances in the electronic transfer of images, there is a great deal more concentration of the means of production in so-called metropolitan societies by the great transnational conglomerates. And secondly, so much so, that dependent societies—the peripheral societies in the Third World and those just outside the central metropolitan zones—are to an extraordinary degree reliant upon this system for information about themselves. We're talking now about *self*-knowledge, not only knowledge about other societies.

So that the only categories through which these "dependent" societies arrive at self-knowledge are immanent within that system?

Immanent, precisely. They are insidious because they're presented as natural and real in a way that is virtually unassailable. We have not yet devised the means to deal with a television or film or even a script image, and to criticize the framework in which that image is presented, because it is *given* as reality, mediated so powerfully, and accepted almost subliminally. Finally, and perhaps most important, the response to this growing media dominance, and the solutions offered by the Socialist and Third World countries to combat the situation, are so primitive and crude that they don't stand a chance of dealing with the challenge. For instance, limiting the means of production, government censorship and intervention, and so forth, are more likely to extend the hegemony these measures are intended to combat than to limit it. What the proponents of a New Information Order are saying is essentially that either the West allows them to control their own news production and the entrance of its work into theirs, or they will simply remove themselves from the system and cut the West out. Then what do they offer their citizens as a result? A kind of illiteracy and parochial isolation that simply makes them more, rather than less, vulnerable to the blandishments and consumerist ideology of the prevailing technology and its metropolitan origins.

Then what we are seeing now is an increasing geopolitical stratification, based on access to data networks and to scientific/technological information?

Yes, absolutely, and such complete dependency on these databases as to breed a whole psychological mindset that will carry forward into generations.

Earlier on you explained that you came to understand that the production of representations always involved political choices made in the interest of exerting and maintaining authority. In this case, there is nothing neutral about the way, for instance, sociological information is programmed into a database.

No, of course there never is anything neutral about it: the entire process represents choice and selectivity, exclusions and inclusions, and things of that sort that are highly sophisticated. But what is truly ominous about this monopolization of information production is not so much the problem of access to the information itself, but rather access to the means of *criticizing* the information. In other words, what can we do outside of this system that enables us to treat it as a productive, rather than a natural process? Through what apparatus? The myth of coherence and inevitability about the whole process overrides any consideration of entry at the source, so to speak. There seem to be no options or alternatives and, as a result, resistance is becoming more and more difficult and increasingly the responsibility of metropolitan intellectuals.

Resistance in the form of critical activity.

I think so. It has to be: potentially, you can only do this kind of work in the context of a place like New York where these images and representations are generated, available, and concentrated. I don't see any other way, and I certainly don't think we can rely on rigorous oppositional work from governments—Western, Third World, Socialist, or otherwise.

Interestingly, my experience at a convention of the American-Arab Anti-Discrimination Committee in Washington in a way exemplifies the complexity of the issue, since it demonstrated quite clearly how those who operate within the media system view the problem. The conference was organized specifically to combat the stereotyping of Arabs in the media, the last ethnic or national group that can be represented in caricature form with impunity. Ted Koppel was invited to "dialogue" with me about the problems of representation in the media. Now, Koppel is a very smart man, he runs *Nightline* which has tried to be fair, and so on. But the fact is that Koppel is a creature of the media, and a star to boot. He's a celebrity, which means, in effect, that for him representation as a philosophical issue cannot, indeed must not enter into the discussion. Rather, what is assumed to be the central issue, and the solution as well, is simply getting more time on the media. In other words, he views us as potential guests, stories, issues to be let in on his show; as for us, in this context, we seem to be asking him to let us into the system by giving us air time, exposure, etc. And Koppel's response is that, because he has taken notice of us, *we are in,* the reportage is balanced, and so forth. So the crucial issue—*how* we are represented—is displaced by the essentially technical and commercial problem of who gets on and for how long. On the one hand, Koppel wants to appear independent; on the other hand, he's part of a system, ABC, which is part of a bigger system, the network organization. And on a third, strangely enough, he also represents the interests of the government. All of these journalists, particularly those on a national level—Brokaw, Jennings, Koppel, Rather—do not only give us the *news*, they also (usually unconsciously) represent what's happening from the standpoint of U.S. interests. Journalists internalize governmental norms to a degree that is quite frightening. If the problem were censorship, or even self-censorship, it could be dealt with and pointed at, but what we have here is a process of incorporation and introjection via an efficient ideology of inclusion, so that everything can be and is objectively itemized, framed, formed: the news media can therefore take in *anything*, and incorporate any point of view. For instance, in a radio discussion with some NBC media people, I was asked what I thought of the coverage given to the crisis in Lebanon over the last few months. Naturally, I brought up the fact that they hadn't dealt with the political aspects of the situation at all but, instead, concentrated on the Marine presence near the Beirut airport, which is, after all, a tiny corner of the Lebanese crisis. Well, then, I was told: we did a special on January 4, and identified the Druze, the Shi'ites, every party involved. In other words, they could say with quite literal justification that they had *covered* everything. What in fact occurs is, as Raymond Williams says, a process of setting limits and exerting pressures, so that the focus ultimately becomes: what *our* boys are doing in Lebanon. Everything else simply fades off into nothingness, as the nightly story revolves around the 250 Marines killed, or the 2,000 Marines at the airport, and so forth.

By highlighting the more emotional points of a story, it would seem that journalists are actually making a concerted effort to obscure other aspects.

But the stories are not always emotional, they *become* emotional by virtue of the fact that journalists focus on them. They are not in and of themselves emotional, and could be treated as neutrally as anything else. If you see the Marines at the airport on French or British television, they are only, after all, Marines at the airport.

But newscasters know that Americans will identify with their boys. So it would seem that to concentrate on these aspects of a particular event represents a more programmatic effort to elide the facts.

I don't think it is programmatic, but as I said, a matter of internalized norms. Journalists *assume* that the interests of Americans will of course be the fate of other Americans. There are two points to be made here. First of all, none of these American journalists has, as a citizen, ever been involved in a continuing war-invasion process, unlike an Asian or European, for example. For them, the war is something to be visited—the standpoint of spectacle is very much inscribed in this process. Everything is viewed from the perspective of Washington and New York, as well. Second, the process involves fragmentation: nothing is seen for any length of time, there is no assumed collective memory, and little carry-over from day to day. There is no background, but only a moving foreground. There is no accumulation of history in any of the nightly broadcasts, except when they deal with domestic issues. But in terms of the rest of the world, they give you simply: we were there yesterday, we'll go back tomorrow, so you don't have to worry about what happens between then and now because we'll be giving it to you in a thirty-second slot tomorrow, should the crisis continue. In a strange way, the whole process is antinomian: extremely primitive in terms of its assumptions, but tremendously sophisticated at the same time from a technical standpoint. Bringing you the news requires satellite transmission, the expense of a bureau *out there,* and so on. Not a simple process, but the concept is primitively simple, and self-perpetuating. And, as I said, the most striking feature of the whole operation in my opinion is that every news reporter thinks that he or she is a secretary of state. They immediately ask: what U.S. interests are at stake out there? From a professional point of view, they are not there to report U.S. interests, but a news story in another society, another country, not U.S. interests in that country or society. That is the explicit ideology. Most of the time, however, the interests of those involved are never acknowledged, but always elided, as you say, or assumed in the story. So, as you know, *we* lost Iran, *we* lost Nicaragua, *we* lost Lebanon, and so forth.

A recent article about Israel in the New York Times Magazine *(March 25, 1984) demonstrates that the convention of reportage from the standpoint of our own interests applies as well to media treatment of Israel. The title of the article is revealing: "Israel after Lebanon"—likewise, "the U.S. after Vietnam." In both cases, the emphasis is placed on our/Israel's moral trauma, our/Israel's potential for reconstruction, completely overlooking the fact that Israel and the U.S. were the aggressors, the invaders, and denying the existence of a victim. This kind of cover-*

age implies an affinity between the two countries that goes well beyond the usual (at worst) polite treatment accorded other U.S. client states— El Salvador, for example.

Total, a more or less total identification. Moshe Arens is a perfect example: he's an American engineer. In that same article, the writer reports that Congress voted Arens $200 million more for weapons because, in a private telephone call with Arens at three in the morning, George Shultz *understood* Moshe's emotions about territorial security. The identification with Israel operates on many levels, and it becomes more and more clear that these are two societies that, in a certain sense, have totally obliterated their own history. In the discursive play of current American society, there is very little room for the native American Indian, and in Israel, for Palestinians—they don't belong.

One could point to Israel's military and political links with countries like South Africa and Argentina which, like the United States, have formative nineteenth-century experiences involving the dispossession and extermination of an indigenous population, impelled in part by a notion of societal homogenization.

Homogenization, yes, but also the continued effacement of the native, who becomes a mere cipher in the landscape. Look at the images from Zionist films of the thirties: the land is always displayed as empty. Insofar as Arabs are present, they are acknowledged only as camels and keepers walking across the screen at one moment or another, to supply a kind of exotic local color: This is *not* a field in the Ukraine, this is the exotic East. A camel and a Bedouin pass by—what Barthes calls "the effect of the real": this comes across, that's enough. But the rest of the landscape is empty. And the same idea occurs in America: the pioneering spirit, errand into the wilderness, the obliteration of another society, and the continual sense of enterprise, that enterprise is good for its own sake, especially because a Book says so. It doesn't matter that the enterprise means killing people, bombing apartment houses, emptying villages. But it's enterprise of a particular kind, the kind associated with a new settler society. And with it goes a tremendous hostility to traditional societies, which are posited as backward, primitive, reactionary, and so on: Islam, for example.

So this process of extermination basically becomes a series of technical problems.

Absolutely: on one level, a series of technical problems, and it is carried forth into the media. I think that it is unique in history, this case of a whole society such as Israel delivered, as it were, on the American political and intellectual scene by a massive apparatus for concealing the reality. People would be horrified beyond description if they knew what goes on in Israel and the occupied territories—Chomsky talks about this in his recent book, *The Fateful Triangle*. But it's systematically pushed out, and when Americans do see it, as they did in the summer of 1982, with the invasion of Beirut and the massacres in the Sabra-Shatila camps, after a while it is simply forgotten because it's got no place to go. And always, there are the choruses of praise for Israel's moral superiority, its nobility, the democracy, and civilization, etc.

One of the things that disappointed me in the reviews of *Orientalism* was that a lot of the reviews published by Jewish or Zionist journals missed the point that I was trying to make: that the roots of European anti-Semitism and Orientalism were really the same. Ernest Renan, for example, was a tremendous anti-Semite and anti-Muslim, and his view of both was essentially the same: that the Semites, whether Muslim or Jew, were not Christians and not Europeans, and therefore had to be excoriated and confined. What then occurred is that the Zionists took on the view of the Orientalists vis-à-vis the Palestinians; in other words, the Palestinians became the subject for the Israeli Orientalist, just as the Muslim and others have been the subject for the colonial or imperial Orientalists. Dani Rubenstein, an Israeli journalist, acknowledges this in a recent article where he cites the influence of Orientalism on the administration of the West Bank: there, the colonial administrators have all been Orientalists, Islamic scholars educated at the Islamic Studies Department of Hebrew University. Menachem Milson, former civilian governor of the West Bank, wrote a book on Arabic literature, for example.

You mentioned the core-periphery relationship. Do you see this opposition undergoing a transformation, for example in the fact that the major Western cities encompass increasingly large non-Western populations, what Paul Virilio calls "infra-urbanisms," so that the very heart of what was the imperial core is attracting to it elements of the periphery? Is it at all possible that these population flows, brought about by the ongoing relocation of global production processes, could modify the collective sense of homogeneity, of difference among Western peoples?

Historically, that has not been the case. In fact, I think what occurs, as in England, is an intensification of racial feeling of a very powerful sort, and also movements of revenge—think of the Brixton riots. The phenomenon of the success of a novelist like V. S. Naipaul is intimately related to the problem of the colonials descending upon the core society and threatening to disrupt it with their mindless demands and their native drums. And above all, the real animus of people like Naipaul—and here we come back to the question of representation—is the way in which these "colored people," as they are referred to, are alleged to know how to use the media to attract attention to their plight. That is endlessly the theme, that all native resistance movements, whether urban, black movements in America or London, or in the Third World, have for their root raison d'être never the sense of outraged injustice that they feel, but rather their desire to use the Western media, which is gullible and falls into their trap. Remember how the holders of the hostages in Iran were described as essentially using the American media; the Viet Cong did the same thing. There is always this intense fear that somehow the economy of representation is being abused by the Other, and that, I think, is a very constant motif. At the same time, we hear continual declarations about the openness and freedom of the press.

Naipaul's brother, Shiva, wrote a book about Jonestown in which he infers that any Third World nationalist leader is necessarily a deranged or psychopathic egomaniac. He says, referring to Western liberals and leftists, "Those who ought to know better nourish our crazy dreams of resurrection and redemption, those safely beyond the borders of our madness underwrite our lunacies." How do we account for this identification with the forces of external domination?

In the parts of the Third World that I know, the Naipaul line is symptomatic of the development of a new class of technocrats for whom the center of the world is Silicon Valley. So there is that technocratic identification. Secondly, the first post-colonial generation has now passed. I'm speaking here of the generation from roughly World War II through the early seventies: Sékou Touré, Abdel Nasser, Sukarno.

A generation whose identity was bound up with the vocabulary of national liberation.

Yes, represented in a sense by a kind of nationalist bourgeoisie. Now that period is over, and what these societies are facing is the problematic of the technocrat, which in the end boils down to imperatives like: we have to feed our people, we have to worry about oil, distribution, etc., *plus* we have to face the problem of what is called national security. Those are the issues. In other words, technical services on the one hand, and national security—which really means staying in power—on the other. The nationalist energy is over; something must be found to replace it: so you create outside enemies. Every one of the Arab countries, many of the African and Far Eastern countries as well, depend therefore on a praetorian guard. There's the notion of an outside enemy against which you must defend, imperialism, and so all the old slogans of nationalism are retained. At the same time, there is this great technocratic leap forward—or attempts at such—based on an uncritically internalized modernization model. In such a context, therefore, things tend to break down constantly and, in addition, the insurrectionary stage still has some life in it—you see it in Tunisia, Egypt, Latin America, appearing in one country or another for a time. In El Salvador, you try to have an election and the ballot boxes are stolen. So out of this unstable mix of technocracy and national security you have a nostalgia developing for colonialism or religion—atavistic in my opinion, but some people want them back. Sadat is the great example of that: he threw out the Russians, as well as everything else that represented Abdel Nasser, ascendant nationalism, and so forth—and said, "Let the Americans come." Then you have a new period of what in Arabic is called an *infitah*—in other words, an opening of the country to a new imperialism: technocratic management, not production but services—tourism, hotels, banking, etc. That's where we are right now. And Naipaul derives from that phenomenon.

A significant figure right now, in terms of how his identity has been fabricated by the Western press, is Quaddafi. It seems the main reason that such a wildly distorted image of him has been produced is that he is an independent leader, that is, someone who cannot be bought or integrated into a cold war or trilateralist arrangement for global management.

There isn't much hope that he can be bought off (of course, he's quite wealthy on his own). In all the rhetoric about terrorism, Libyan hit teams, etc., much of it has nothing to do with Quaddafi, but goes back to Dostoyevski and Conrad, who imagined a whole notion of terrorism for its own sake and terrorism as an aesthetic activity, rather than as a political thing. But what is dimly perceived about Quaddafi in all his seeming craziness is that he represents the threshold of a third phase. In other words, first you have nationalism and nativism, then you have technocracy; then the system bifurcates at this point into, on the one hand, nostalgia for colonialism—"come and help us"—and on the other hand, religious revivalism—Khomeini, Quaddafi. In other words, the people who say, "Look, put your faith in the Americans or the Russians, etc.," are now forced to admit that depending on outside powers has been a sordid failure: our people are just as poor as they were, we are still indebted to the IMF or the United States. The only answer, therefore, is Islam. And that is what Quaddafi is, and as such, he is truly formidable. Because if you go through the Arab world and the Islamic world generally, there is a genuine popular sense about "Islam" which threatens every National Security State. The irony of the NSS, at least in the Arab world, is that each of them has failed completely: not one has protected its borders, much less the security of the country. Iran, under the Shah, was an NSS, and was obviously an American client regime. The Arab regimes, nearly every one of them, have been attacked by Israel, invaded, their lands occupied: so, Islam is the answer. What gets lost in all of this is a secular alternative.

The National Security State versus technocracy—this is the conflict for parts of the Third World today. What are the alternatives, what possible models could be constructed?

To go back to Fanon, what you find is insurrection, and the absence of what you might call a utopian dimension, since the ethic of violence really prevents genuine critical reflection. Ideally, what you would like is a connection between Fanon and Adorno, and that is totally missing. In other words, activism, nationalism, revolution, insurrection on the one hand, and on the other, the excessive kind of theoretical reflection and speculation of the sort one associates with the Frankfurt School—which in the end becomes resignation, as you recall. And for the Third World, the former—nationalism, etc.—becomes the National Security State. Somehow, we need another dimension which involves, in fact, thinking about the future in ways that are not simply insurrectionary or reactive.

A critical process which would have to involve the figuration of alternative futures.

Exactly. The point is that I am not talking about inventing utopias or utopianism. Chomsky talks about this in reference to C. S. Pierce's notion of *abduction,* a formulation of hypotheses based upon the known facts. You posit something, take in as much as you can of the present, and out of that, and in fidelity to that—imperfect though our apprehension of the known facts may be—you *abduct* from it a possible future hypothesis. And that process, that dimension, is missing in the present situation. I think it is beginning to develop in certain kinds of critical work done in connection with representation and imperialism in particular.

Orientalism is in some ways a negative book, but at the end I do try to talk about a non-coercive, non-manipulative view of society. You also find this alternative pursued in feminist studies, where the problems are posed really seriously. So, what are the ways of positing a hypothesis based on certain apprehensions, where you do the work of deconstruction and demystification, and yet at the same time posit a direction which is not simply incorporative, but something that deals with the future in some genuinely alternative way? Generally, this is not the kind of critical work people are doing, and in the Third World it is unlikely to develop very much because it cannot be done by one person but has to be a cooperative effort. That's the whole point. So, to go back to Foucault, he is really interested in doing his work on his own, but the collective is where I think the future lies.

Do you see any possible set of circumstances under which there could be any concrete identification between certain sectors in the U.S. and what you and others have described as anti-systemic movements? What would be the common ground of that identification?

I have no doubt that the basis of it would have to be a critique of domination, or of imperialism as domination.

But this critique would obviously take a very different form than it did in the sixties.

Absolutely. The sixties were enthusiastic, utopian. They represent an attempt at recovery and recuperation of certain kinds of, shall we say, primitive or immediate experiences. What I'm talking about is something much more reflective, which would include a critique of imperialism in its cultural forms, not simply as capitalist economy.

Interview with Jonathan Crary and Phil Mariani,
Wedge, New York, 1985

THREE

OVERLAPPING TERRITORIES:

THE WORLD, THE TEXT, AND THE CRITIC

You were asked once to compare Foucault and Fanon, both of whom explore the cultural politics of exclusion, confinement, and domination, which has always concerned you. Discussing Madness and Civilization *and* The Wretched of the Earth, *you conferred a greater power and significance on Fanon's text for the reason that it sprang from the collective struggle of the Algerian revolution, as opposed to Foucault's brilliant and insurrectionary intervention, which was nevertheless individual and remained within the academic tradition. Could you perhaps comment on the dialogue in your work between the concept of critical distance and the cultural politics of commitment and solidarity that you so admire in Fanon?*

I want to begin by saying something more about Foucault and Fanon. One of the things that marks the difference between them is that Foucault's trajectory as a scholar and researcher noted for his interest in sites of political intensity—the asylum, the hospital, the prison, the academy, the army, and so on—moved from what appeared to be insurrectionary scholarship to a kind of scholarship that confronted the problem of power from the position of someone who believed that ultimately very little resistance was possible to the controls of a disciplinary or carceral society. There is a kind of quietism that emerges at various points in Foucault's career: the sense that everything is historically determined, that ideas of justice, of good and evil, and so forth, have no innate significance, because they are constituted by whoever is using them. Whereas the whole of Fanon's work is based upon the notion of genuine historical change by which oppressed classes are capable of liberating themselves from their oppressors. This is an important difference; it's one of the things that I still find especially valuable in Fanon. He not only talked about historical change, but was also capable of diagnosing historically, psychologically, and culturally the nature of the oppression and then addressing ways of removing it.

The second point I want to make is that the solidarity which is implicit in Fanon's work is solidarity with an emergent class, an emergent movement, rather than with an established one. My sense of it is that, had Fanon lived on into the first few years of Algerian statehood, his position would have been a very complicated one, and I don't think that he would necessarily have stayed on; he might have moved on to some other region. Because what happened to many of the militants of the FLN was that they became functionaries in a state system, which has not, for the most part, evolved a class of intellectuals who have retained critical distance. One of the most disturbing things about solidarity is the extent to which you become a prisoner of your own rhetoric of solidarity and the ease with which you can be co-opted into the discourse of power. It's an inevitable thing. Fanon came from a class of militants who later became wielders as well as instruments of state power.

At the same time, there is something very dangerous about critical distance that is literally distance, that allows you to snipe from a position of privilege at abuses of one kind or another. I'm thinking of Eastern bloc dissidents, like Kolakowski for example, who come to this country and denounce communism while garnering every kind of academic and social reward offered to them by grateful anti-communists. That strikes me as being not at all the kind of distance we're talking about. Still other types are the ones that you find throughout the Third World—for example, Iraqi dissidents who are to be found in Syria. The problem in these cases is in allowing yourself to be wielded as a club by a state that has an interest in using you to attack another state. That's the most common phenomenon. But it needn't be a state; it can be a group as well. So for me the real problem is the problem of *where* you do these things—the place—and that raises the problem of constituency and whether you can in fact address several constituencies in ways that are responsive to the problems before them.

Now, as I say, there are cases that don't fall into these categories, and then it's just a matter of choosing the right position. I've never really had to face the problem of solidarity in this way myself, because the causes with which I've been associated—like the Palestinian movement, for example—well, they're losing or at least underdog causes. They're survivors of liberation movements from the fifties and sixties that haven't succeeded and don't really show much immediate hope of succeeding, although I myself haven't lost any of my hope—perhaps stupidly.

So you don't face the same danger of being co-opted.

Some Third World groups and states have tried to co-opt me. They aren't very difficult to resist. And even in the case of the Palestinian movement itself I've made it a point never to accept an official role of any sort; I've always retained my independence. Sometimes I worry whether that's a kind of irresponsibility that I can afford, thanks to the freedom guaranteed by a professorship at Columbia. But I think it's right.

What you say about constituency and the place of the intellectual seems to me significant when thinking about people like Régis Debray, who began by getting deeply involved in political struggles and now is an adviser to Mitterrand.

The model that has always been useful to me is really much more nomadic than Debray, who has always worked out of the French system. What he did with the Bolivians and the Cubans, it appears in perhaps unfair retrospect, was a form of very intense tourism. The model for this kind of activity is George Orwell going to Wigan Pier and writing about it, then going back to London and working for the BBC. I've had nothing to go back to, and I've never thought of what I do in that way. My emotional and political roots are elsewhere, so I've had to be committed to a series of things. It's also temperamental: both my training and my interests are in what could be called *comparative* work. I'm much more interested in traveling across boundaries—in other words, traveling horizontally rather than hierarchically inside one culture. And the things that interest me about comparative literature, for example, are precisely those kinds of crossings-over, as well as anti-specialization and anti-territoriality. All of these things, I suppose, have an origin, in some existential way, in one's background and history; but I think there's also an intellectual predilection for that kind of work, which has always gripped me. I've always been interested in writers and intellectuals who cross cultural and territorial boundaries and make a career in that sort of traffic.

Which is why the image of the exile becomes for you the exemplary image of the intellectual.

Matthew Arnold uses the word *alien* to describe the critic: somebody who isn't anchored in class but is more or less adrift. For me the figure of the exile is terribly important, because you reach a point where you realize that exile is irreversible. If you think of it in this way, then it becomes a really powerful image; but if you think that the exile can be repatriated—find a home—well, that's not what I'm talking about. If you think of exile as a permanent state, however, both in the literal and in the intellectual sense, then it's a much more promising, if difficult, thing. Then you're really talking about movement, about homelessness in the sense in which Lukács talks about it in *The Theory of the Novel*—"transcendental homelessness"—which can acquire a particular intellectual mission that I associate with criticism. And the third term that is very important to me, along with exile and homelessness, is secularism—that is, within the world of the centuries, time, and history, and not in the theological or systematic or "Thomistic" world of high theory to which a lot of Left intellectuals are now attracted.

Hence the importance for you of what you call "worldliness."

Yes, worldliness is another term for secularism, again in opposition to the religious—which has become a much more common attitude, by the way, since I wrote *The World, the Text, and the Critic.* For example, there was an article in *The Nation* recently, which said that the only Left in America is religious now. And last year the summer issue of *Monthly Review* was on the "religious Left," revising Marx's line about religion being the opium of the people. According to *Monthly Review,* Marx really didn't mean what he said about religion to be a criticism; quite the contrary, religion is strength. I could go on and on. There are all kinds of examples of former leftists who now believe that the religious alternative (also known as "liberation theology") is the most important one.

The fourth thing that I want to emphasize is that what I'm talking about is essentially a *Left* alternative: it's deeply tied to a particular vision of social change. This is another reason why most literary criticism, as it's written now, is often uninteresting to me. Obviously I read it—it's my field; it's what I'm committed to in many ways—but most of it says next to nothing to me. To use a Gramscian word, it's the elaboration of elaboration. If you exclude a few people like Jameson (who is inherently

very brilliant, but whose work is also in the elaborate mode and so theoretical as sometimes to engender anti-political and in my opinion quite
religious attitudes), the work that's really interesting is the work of
sports, like Bloom, for example, or Poirier, or Bersani, or Jameson himself, who really can't be assimilated easily to some school or system like
deconstruction or Marxism. I sometimes find more nourishment in historians and sociologists than I do in the work of people who stay within
the territory of literary criticism, which is essentially both religious—the
model is commentary on sacred texts, even when they talk about revising the canon and all that stuff—and so rarified and jargonistic that it's
just not interesting.

The political impulse in Jameson is, in a way, a mirage of politics . . .

I don't think it's so much a mirage in Jameson's case. For him politics
is the condition imposed on us by virtue of the fact that we live in a
world that has lost its transcendence. In other words, his view of the
world is essentially nostalgic. He is a Heideggerian or a Thomist without the transcendental subject, and he knows it and functions in that
mode—somebody who has lost something and is trying to rediscover it
in History with a capital H. But that is really not the historical and secular world of which Gramsci and Vico and others speak. It's a particular kind of late Hegelian vision, a vision that is not essentially political
in my view. It's politics as compensation for the loss of the divine.
There's no direct engagement with historical or political processes, but
at the same time it's a tremendous engagement with the whole tradition
of Frankfurt school critical thought.

How would you contrast your own conception of history to this reli-
gious or teleological vision? Without a philosophy of history such as
that offered by Marxism, how does one think about historical questions
or do historical work?

Obviously I can't offer a quick definition of history, or a long one either for that matter; but what I'm talking about is a particular type of
historical engagement, well inside the Marxist tradition, with, let's say,
an essentially *geographical* bias rather than a temporal one. The attachment to history of most of the theorists in the Hegelian tradition is temporal in the sense that, for them, history originates at some point in the
distant past from which everything becomes possible. It's certainly true
in Hegel's case; it's certainly true for the early Marx; it's certainly true

for Lukács. And it's very powerful. There's an expressed yearning for the recapture of this experience, a grand historical project, whether it's revolutionary or scholarly or whatever. But what I'm talking about is really much closer to the Gramscian conception of history, which is essentially geographical and territorial, a history made up of several overlapping terrains, so that society is viewed as a territory in which a number of movements are occurring. The vision of overlapping and contested terrains is to me a more interesting view of history than the temporal one going back to a *fons et origo*—a miraculous, originating point. Given that, it becomes possible to see engagement in the historical process as in fact a collective struggle—not a struggle to be won by an individual subject trying to grasp the whole of history in all of its complexity, as Dilthey tried to do, but a collective struggle in which various interests interact over particular sites of intensity and contested domains. One of the examples that most interests me is imperialism, where you have an interaction between the metropolitan and the peripheral regions of the world. Another one is, obviously, the class contest between various terrains—emergent, dominant, and so forth—in a given society. Yet another is the whole struggle over authority, which I don't think is historical in the old sense—that is, not an attempt to determine what somebody said back then, but rather an attempt to study the mechanisms of authority of a class or a set of interests. In this respect, the territorial or geographical conception of the historical process is much less likely to be theologized than the one that posits an originary point in the divine.

Yet the individual researcher who wishes to study the past is nevertheless faced with a group of texts which have to be articulated in relation to one another. Now, if you're not using a teleological or totalizing view of history, is there any other perspective around which you can organize your project, or is it simply given according to another set of interests (your political concerns in the present, for example)?

I think there's little doubt that one does organize one's study out of concerns in the present; to deny that is simply bad faith. You're interested in things for all kinds of contemporary reasons. It may be the advancement of your career (to start at the very bottom), but it can also concern your own genealogy, as Foucault would say, your sense of belonging within a particular field. Or, as in the case of so much feminist work, it has to do with the whole problem of the construction of gender distinctions; that's a third case. A fourth case—which I consider to be one of the most interesting—is the uncovering of affiliations that are usually hidden from history. Not only relationships between texts that are normally affiliated to each other (as in, say, the canon of English literature, where the researcher's project becomes a search for an alternative canon). That's not as interesting as what I'm asking, which is: what were these texts connected to that enabled them? It's no use just saying: "Well, what we really need is an alternative canon." We need to find out what gave rise to *this* canon within the social and historical processes that produced a thing called "English Literature." That's just one kind of example. And what I tried to do in *Orientalism* is precisely that.

I guess you could say that a project arises out of two normally unconnected things: convergent political concerns in the contemporary world and a genuine historical curiosity about what produced this situation. And you have to carry it out in a conscious and rational way, with lines of force emerging out of the past for transformation in the present.

Could you perhaps draw a sharper distinction between your concept of affiliation and conventional Marxist theories of ideology, according to which you have a kind of two-tiered structure: a group of texts, on one level, which is indirectly determined by another level that is somehow more "real" or "material"?

I don't like the idea of two tiers. What we're dealing with is historical evidence as it is expressed, or contained, or embodied by texts in many different ways, all of them interacting in a process which, I think, is much more complicated than simply saying that texts are up here and reality is down there. You can't talk about texts as if they had some separate status. There's a difference between a separate status or even a historical particularity, on the one hand, and a totally self-contained element on the other (which is what some of the deconstructionists have tried to assert). I think there's a kind of commerce, if you like, or exchange (I hate the word "dialogic," which is the currently fashionable term). So we're really talking about *many* tiers; and that was precisely the point of the geographical simile I used. What you have is an exchange in which some texts seem to inhabit a level of their own, and some are just considered a kind of trash literature, and so on. It's multi-tiered rather than two-tiered. And once you recognize that, the whole rather invidious distinction between the text and the world is just not interesting anymore. It loses its power to be provocative.

So it's a practical distinction, rather than an epistemological or ontological one?

It's a *provisional* distinction. But a more important question, it seems to me, is: where does the text take place? Again, the emphasis is territorial. And the goal, obviously, is the liberation of as much territory as possible for discussion, analysis, contest. It's a political metaphor as much as it is an intellectual one. It has nothing to do with holding on to territory and keeping people off. Anything that has to do with enclosure, confinement, all of these ideas (which are inherent, I think, in the professional discourse of priests, teachers, etc.) are inimical to the critical enterprise.

This raises a number of issues that come to the fore very powerfully in feminism, which is defined by the fact that it is extra-territorial in a very special way. Women inhabit a world that condemns them, as an "inferior" caste, to exclusion within their dominant cultures; so part of the task of feminism has been the unearthing of women's history—people, texts, and actions that have been banished from sight. At the same time, there has always been the idea that beyond the stage of insurrection there is another, more difficult stage of taking active responsibility for choosing and creating new social forms, which means defending values and choices in a positive sense.

It's certainly the case—in the black movement of the sixties, for example, as in feminism—that in the early stages of a movement there's an attempt to disengage a territory which has been either hidden or discredited in the past, and to give it, through scholarly and critical work, as well as political organizing, a certain visibility and a certain kind of status that it didn't have before. The next step is a double one. On the one hand, you want to assert the value of the hitherto suppressed identity that you've discovered. Once you do that, however, you're faced with phenomena like nativism in the Third World. The same thing happens in a lot of feminist work, where the assertion of value in a feminist canon becomes the order of the day. But to me this is less interesting than the *integration* of that experience into the common experience of the community. Separatism is a first phase, but the next question is: how do you integrate new values into an imaginative community in a world that's full of divisions? This has to do with problems of a more universal sort than those which are reflective of a particular identity that seems to be embattled at the time. A lot of feminist writing is premised on the notion that the feminist perspective gives you a kind of Archimedean point from which to look at history. But there isn't an Archimedean point; you're always involved in a politics. Hence, for example, the inability of a lot of feminism to deal with the problems of race and the question of its intermittent priority over gender. Is race more important or is gender more important in certain situations? These are other matters and priorities than just the assertion of value and preference.

It's true that the former kind of feminism that you mentioned is very powerful and, at the moment, ascendent within the academy; but it isn't the only kind.

No, it isn't the only kind at all. There is a very progressive feminism, which is deeply engaged in politics—Michèle Barrett, for example.

Exactly, Michèle Barrett. And a lot of the British feminists.

Right. But not many American feminists. Or at least not to my knowledge. There are, obviously, some; but I would say that they are a much less active group.

The French-American axis is one that has been given tremendous academic prominence here . . .

Yes. But not only that, the question of gender has become metaphysical in a certain way and psychologized; and so the political dimension and the historical dimension—which in England has produced some really extraordinary works of scholarship—is given less attention in this country. Maybe the influence of the French has something to do with it. I don't know; it's certainly possible.

Perhaps we can move on to another area of interest. In The World, the Text, and the Critic, *you maintain that the critic's chief concern is to draw attention to the realities of power and authority that make texts possible. It seems to me that we have passed irrevocably into a world in which cultural authority—and hence indirectly political power—lies in the hands of the mass media technocracy. If this is true, do you think it should become an important and crucial part of the critic's role to explore the realities of authority and power that give rise to media culture? This is also a question about the politics of the classroom—whether, to some extent at least, we shouldn't be teaching media literacy.*

For the last seven or eight years, I've felt that there is a tremendous problem in the area of what you call the politics of the classroom—in other words, what is to be done in one's actual teaching (as opposed to theorizing about teaching in general). One of the things that is extremely significant for me is that very little of what I write about has anything to do with what I teach, so I find myself teaching, for the most part, the standard courses—the required curricular courses in English and comparative literature, and things like literary theory. When I started teaching theory about seventeen years ago, in the late sixties, nobody was teaching it; but it's become practically half of the curriculum, so that now it's also a kind of standard thing. Whereas, of the two books that I'm working on now, one is on the role of the intellectual, a historical and political study of intellectuals in different traditions from the kind of perspective that I was talking about earlier; and the other is on the relationship between culture and imperialism. Now those are very difficult things to accommodate to the curriculum.

Then the question of popular culture comes up. It's not as if popular culture isn't talked about; there are quite a few courses in popular culture. And I don't disagree with you about the importance of the media and of political representation in the most profound sense, which is what the media is all about. The media represents a kind of discourse of legitimation, which is extremely strong—it's all about consolidation, a certain type of legitimacy, and authority. I think that to try to deal with it head-on on is very bad, because you get involved in jargon and in a kind of instant gratification study, where you look at things that are relatively easy to assimilate and you deconstruct them. My feeling has been that if possible one should try to use the existing structure of the curriculum—say, courses in the English novel or the seventeenth-century lyric—in a way that is geared to addressing, later on, the media environment in which we live. This is why, for example, a book like Raymond Williams's *The Country and the City* is so important. Because he takes the standard curriculum of English literature and puts it in a kind of social context, which is that of a conflict or dialectic between rural and urban classes. That, I think, is a more interesting approach than always dealing with popular culture directly. You're moving your students toward a certain kind of media literacy and criticism—which only a few will really develop, because most students are really interested in accommodating to the system, not in changing it. And I'm very dubious about trying to produce students who are going to go out and change the world. I'm very anti-authoritarian about it. I'm not interested in disciples; I don't want people to be like me. I'm interested in people who are different. I'm not interested in handing people little tool boxes of clichés and methods that they can go out and apply. So, given all of these things, I've really come to a rather conservative view of how one deals with the media problem in the classroom; and I try instead to address it through my writing and, of course, by being on the media, which I also do.

I understand your reluctance before the clichés of popular culture. The problem, it seems to me, is how to talk about clichés in a politically interesting way. Perhaps it's less a question of confronting Dallas *and* Dynasty *head on—that is, analyzing them internally—than of placing them against other literary and historical texts in the culture and exploring the realities of power that make them possible.*

Yes, but what you're not taking into account is that in the case of the canon, you're dealing with a kind of authority, a kind of perception of cultural legitimacy, and a kind of consent that are very different from the easy commodity consumption mode of a TV serial. It's a great danger to mix them up. They're really performing two quite different functions; and until you understand what the functions are, I don't think you should assimilate them to each other. I don't think it's the case that you can "deconstruct," as the word has it, *Dynasty* or *Dallas* in the same way that you would, say, *Bleak House*. So what do you do with them? It seems to me that a much more interesting approach would be to look at the sociology of the form itself, to look at the construction of the media conglomerates, the industry, and the formal tools used, which make up, as you know, an extremely sophisticated apparatus reduced to rather simple ends: pacification, the depoliticization of ordinary life, as well as the encouragement and refinement of consumer appetites. That's the whole point of the media, along with the glamorization implicit in a system of values which says that communism is evil, America is a wonderful place, every woman can become Joan Collins, and so on. I wonder whether that isn't best dealt with allusively, and whether the effort of looking at this kind of stuff shouldn't really come from a quite serious study of the history and sociology of literature in the wider political and social context, which is normally excluded from the classroom.

How you do that is something else. I must say I haven't solved the problem myself.

The thing that I find much more insidious and interesting is the presentation of news on the media and the perception of reality on so-called news or documentary programs. The presentation of sport is no less interesting. Christopher Lasch has written interestingly about the spectacle of sport; but there's a lot more to be done, and I think too much attention has been paid to these serials and soap operas rather than to the representation of other cultures, the representation of reality, the representation of social change, the phenomenon of terrorism—which is tremendously powerful and almost totally ignored from an analytic standpoint. Cooperation between the media and the state is quite unique to our time. I think it's going to define politics in the future.

A current example is the coverage of South Africa, which accentuates the burning and beating up of informers to the relative exclusion of state atrocities, which are going on elsewhere, and which have been going on, systematically, for a very long time.

Yes, that's a very good point.

By way of relating the question of the media to that of the Third World intellectual, one could observe that there has been a linguistic revolution on a global scale; so that by now the Western industrial world enjoys a total monopoly on knowledge . . .

Not a total monopoly. That's really overestimating. And one of the dangers is that you say: "Well, it's there, so we might as well join it." That's simply not true; but it's a common reaction, and the very powerful complicity of political elites in the Third World with this overestimation is quite interesting. A lot of people in the Third World have a stake in imagining that there is a media monopoly, often (but not always) to be able to cooperate with it, because they like it. I can't speak about the entire Third World, but there are parts of it that I know quite well; and if you look, you can always find a fairly significant and impressive group of people who are intensely engaged in the problem of understanding their own condition and their own identity in the world, and at the same time perfectly capable of adopting the critical tools to be found in the metropolitan countries that are dominating them. That's not so rare anymore. Take someone like Salman Rushdie, who is Indian but lives in England. His case has to do with expatriation and exile, but he's really part of something much bigger than just one individual. He can write in a world language and turn that language against its own sources of authority and consolidation. So I think this is really something to be looked at; and one shouldn't assume that the battle is over, and we're all going to sink under Mary Tyler Moore.

I think this is a very important reminder, again, for feminism in the face of the orthodox Lacanian conception of the so-called symbolic, which is seen as all-encompassing and all-embracing. The effect, if not the intention, is that the very tenacious (though assiduously repressed) role that women play in culture becomes invisible and thus denigrated. It ignores the constant eruptions throughout history, in different groups and in different parts of the world, of resistance to the dominant culture on the part of women.

Absolutely. In a sense, the most interesting work that one does on the problem of affiliation is in locating the energy of resistance, which is always breaking out—one finds it everywhere. I've always said that the role of the intellectual is to be oppositional—which doesn't mean that you're simply opposed to everything, but rather that you're involved in the study (and to some degree the enhancement) of resistance to all of these totalizing political movements and institutions and systems of thought (which the Lacanian system, in my opinion, happens to be). And I think that the unevenness and the heterogeneity of the territory that one is looking at has to be the main point of assertion in all of this. If you're going to assume that there is some way of apprehending the whole of reality, then you're simply enhancing this totalizing process. Fish, for example, in going on about "professionalism," is trying to do just that. Everything becomes an aspect of professionalism, just as everything is an aspect of the processes of the carceral society for Foucault. All of these systems that confirm themselves over and over again so that every shred of evidence becomes an instance of the system as a whole— these systems are really the enemies.

They can breed a kind of quietism.

Not only quietism, but also—as in the case of Fish's critics—they can stimulate a lot of fairly trite discussion. Sometimes quietism is the least of the dangers. Adorno's notion of the "totally administered society," for example, breeds an inner kind of quietism, which is itself a form of resistance. It's very carefully formulated *as* quietism and resignation, but quietism and resignation as resistance to the onslaught. In other cases, though, it's really just the question: "How can I make the system work for me?" That's quite different.

Perhaps this is an appropriate place to bring up the politics of the university. What are your feelings about the relation of the critic to his or her role as an academic and existence in the academy? And how do you view the sudden repoliticization of American university campuses in the last year?

The university is a terribly contradictory place. There's no doubt that, within the university, there is an extremely powerful and entrenched hierarchization of functions, authority, and styles of work. And the connection between the university and the corporation in America is rarely looked at with the kind of rigor that it ought to receive; nor is the connection between the university and the state. One of the reasons is, of course, that everybody's too busy to do those kinds of things, and after a while you take for granted the existence of contradictions as part of the environment. I certainly do. I'm engaged in other things that seem to me to be more important. And for me, to be honest with you, the university is a site of privilege.

As for the politicization of the university, the condemnation of apartheid in South Africa, which is a national concern in America now, is to me suspicious to a certain degree. Of course, it strikes me as being important, good, and so forth. How could one oppose it? Even Reagan doesn't oppose it! There has to be something wrong with that. But what also happens—and it's very common in this society—is that the politics of specialization take over. So if the issue is not only South Africa but also the connections between the South African system and other exclusionary systems, the history of exclusions and of racial oppression of the sort that South Africa represents, and a whole set of complicities other than those between the university and the corporations that do business in South Africa—well, none of those issues are taken into account. The perfect example for me (as you could have expected) is the relationship between South Africa and Israel. Nobody ever talks about the fact that the largest and most powerful organic link that exists between South Africa and another society is its link with Israel. That's not an accident. And in the university it's part of a highly professionalized conception of what politics is, of what the role of the intellectual is, and of what the "okay" political issues are. That isn't what I conceive of as politicization. I think politics has much more to do with connecting things that are normally disconnected, with looking at taboos that are usually in the closet and not simply going with okay things just because they're okay.

It's true in a sense that issues like racism and nuclear war are "easy" issues, since relatively few people are actually in favor of discrimination or a nuclear holocaust; but it's also true that the kind of protest that we saw last year on American campuses (and may see again) can open up a lot of other things for scrutiny, at least on the local level: the functioning of the university senate, the power of the trustees. And since you have recently contrasted the utopianism of sixties political movements with the kind of action that you feel is needed now, it seems particularly interesting that the actions of the past year have been distinguished from campus protests in the sixties by their organization, planning, and media-awareness.

There's no question that the differences between sixties protests and the aspects of the recent movements that you referred to are quite striking, and one ought to mark them. But I would still say that one has to look for the imprint of the dominant historical conjunction on political protest, and one of the places that you can see it in the university is in a certain style of what I would call specialization. Looking at the university is one thing, and it's a very important thing to do—to analyze the role of the university in the organization of knowledge, in the promotion of certain kinds of social goals as opposed to others, and to examine the connections between the university and the corporation. I'm not trying to minimize that at all. But I'm talking in a much larger framework about the whole question of political involvement, which has to do with changes in society and the connections between one kind of political system and another; and I don't think those issues can really be raised in the context offered by the university. I said that the university is a highly contradictory place, and I still don't believe that it's the place from which important social movements can be launched. Certain things are possible within the university, certain kinds of reflection and study; but beyond that, since the universities in this society are not part of the state apparatus—they're not part of the political system, as they are in many countries in Europe and in the second and third worlds—a different kind of university style emerges. And to me it's fundamentally attractive. I'm not trying to say that I'd rather be at the University of Damascus. I certainly would not. I'm just saying that certain kinds of things are possible here and certain others are not.

But the main point I want to make is that the protests seem to me to have partaken of the same kind of exclusionism as the larger issue, which is to see apartheid as a single phenomenon having to do with South Africa and not as representative of, or connected to, other relations of the same sort—such as that which obtains between Jew and non-Jew in Israel.

Looking back on the blockade at Columbia, it seems significant that a lot of very young people with little political experience were able to meet activists who are involved in more controversial issues (like the opposition to American policies in Nicaragua, for example) and started to move outside of the university.

Of course. I'm sure that was the case. But I'm speaking in a much more general and perhaps coarse way.

Even in the sixties the student revolts were belated; they came long after the civil rights movement.

The university is a belated place. And maybe it should be—a kind of filter, where things get in very far down the road, rather than right at the beginning.

Interview with Gary Hentzi and Anne McClintock,
Critical Text, New York, 1986

FOUR

LITERARY THEORY AT THE CROSSROADS OF PUBLIC LIFE

"The sense of being between cultures has been very, very strong for me. I would say that's the single strongest strand running through my life: the fact that I'm always in and out of things, and never really *of* anything for very long."   E.W.S.

The work of Edward Said represents "practical criticism" in a new, powerful and, above all, oppositional mode. Said's has been the skeptical voice inside literary theory, constantly reminding it of how impractical its habitual strategies are, since they serve (like the older "practical criticism" associated with I. A. Richards) to split literature and criticism off from wider social practices. By conceiving of "literariness" or "the aesthetic" as isolatable affects open to formal theorizing, critics have marginalized both literature and themselves; and by failing to see the way in which literature—and criticism—are intercalated in a wider field of power and action, they have consciously or unconsciously served the interests of ruling-class power. Said writes against critical modes which, like deconstruction, have a tendency to substitute a pure theoretical consciousness for a critical or oppositional one.   IMRE SALUSINSZKY

The first time I met you, in a class at Yale, I anticipated that you'd speak with a colorful accent, like mine.

I can do that too.

But I was surprised at this New York persona: urbane and rather assimilated. At all events, the story of your life must take the ear strangely. I would like to hear how a Palestinian refugee becomes an English professor at Columbia: I think there must be more than one step involved there.

To describe me as a refugee is probably overstating it a bit. I was born in Jerusalem. Because of my family's business, we lived both in Jerusalem and in Cairo, although after 1948 we were effectively settled in

Egypt. I went to a lot of schools because of these movements—we also spent time in Lebanon, where my family had a summer house. So I went to about nine schools by the time I left Egypt, in disgrace, in the early 1950s to come to America: I had been at a colonial English public school, and was effectively asked not to return because I was a trouble-maker. Then, when I was fifteen, I came to America. I went to boarding school here for a couple of years, and then I went to Princeton. My family remained in the Middle East, so I went back there in the summers; however, I'm the only member of my family who lives here.

Thus, my background is a very anomalous and peculiar one, and I've always been conscious of that. Although Palestinian, we were Anglicans: so we were a minority within the Christian minority in an Islamic majority setting. Then, because of my father's early years in this country (he had come to America in 1911 for a period of about nine years), we always had a kind of outlet to America, and for religious and cultural reasons to England. So England and America were my alternative places, and English was a language I spoke, along with Arabic, ever since I was a boy. There have always been the anomalies and strangenesses of being an outsider, but also of having, as years go on, no place to return to: I couldn't return to Palestine, for various obvious reasons, mostly political; I couldn't return to the Egypt I grew up in; and now I can't return to Lebanon, where my mother lives, and where my wife is from. My background is a series of displacements and expatriations which cannot ever be recuperated. The sense of being between cultures has been very, very strong for me. I would say that's the single strongest strand running through my life: the fact that I'm always in and out of things, and never really *of* anything for very long.

I studied literature because I've always been interested in it, and because it seemed to me that the things around literature, so to speak—philosophy, music, history, political science, and sociology—enabled one to be interested in a number of other human activities. It's been a very good life for me, and I haven't regretted it for a second. The alternative was always to go into business, which was my family background, but that was never a real alternative for me, because of the real social and political background of Middle Eastern business, which was always of a ruling-class type and which I more or less moved away from.

What does your membership in the Palestine National Council involve?

Actually, it involves practically nothing more than the symbolism. I was elected to it in 1977, by the council itself, as an independent member—I have no political affiliation with any official group. In 1977 I went to one meeting in Cairo, and was there for approximately four days. I missed all the other ones until Amman in November 1984—the climactic meeting which sealed the split within the Palestinian movement. I was there for two days, essentially to make up a quorum. I'm a non-active member, to all intents and purposes.

Talking of displacements: if the Palestinian people were ever successful in their national aspirations, for independence and for a homeland, would you remain in the United States or return to Palestine?

I've thought about that a lot. I used to think that I would try to return. Actually, the part of Palestine that I'm from is the western part of Jerusalem: that's always been a part of post-1948 Israel, and it's not a section of the city I feel that I can return to very easily. I really think, now, that the idea and the feeling of exile is so strong in me that I doubt that I'd be able to appease it by a return of that sort.

I'm not sure, in any event, that I believe in what would have to be at the outset a partitioned Palestine. I've stopped thinking that the solution to political problems is to divide up smaller and smaller pieces of territory. I do not believe in partition, not only at a political and demographic level, but on all sorts of other intellectual levels, and spiritual ones. The whole idea of parceling out pieces for communities is just totally wrong. Any notion of purity—that such and such a territory is *essentially* the Palestinian or Israeli homeland—is just an idea that is totally inauthentic, for me. I certainly believe in self-determination, so if people want to do that they should be able to do it: but I myself don't see any need to participate in it.

One of the things which comes across in reading The Question of Palestine *is, for me, a courageous position: you are one of the few commentators within the whole debate who—while you are uncompromising in your description of what Zionism has meant for the Palestinians —continues to insist that the destinies of Palestinians and Jews are interlinked, and cannot be separated out. At the moment, though, what are the realistic outcomes?*

At the moment, there isn't really much to look forward to except exacerbated conflict. I know a great deal about the Arab and Palestinian situation, and there I think the sense of drifting and hopelessness and uncertainty is very strong. I don't think that the ordinary person has given up—there's a great deal of resilience in the people—but what we're really going through is a crisis of leadership, plus a singularly unfortunate and unfair conjunctural crisis: all of the circumstances are against us. The role of the United States, the role of the Soviet Union, the other Arabs, the Israelis: all of these militate against any meaningful resolution in the near future.

But in the middle to far future, it's interesting that a number of Israelis and Palestinians are thinking along parallel lines, precisely in the way that I mentioned earlier: *against* the notion of partition and of trying instead to realize a democratic Jewish/Palestinian state. A lot of this, paradoxically, is due to people like Kahane, who has raised the problem and said that you can't have a democratic Jewish state: it's chilling, and people find it really hard to deal with. I was very interested in a recent piece by Meron Benvenisti, the former deputy mayor of Jerusalem, who has come to the same conclusion as me: we really can't talk about separate peoples, because our lives are interlinked in so many ways, at this moment principally by the dominance of one group over the other. But the whole idea of a separate, differential polity is a travesty of justice and of what was believed to be liberalism and a great social experiment.

That's where the future is: in the evolution, over time, of notions of community that are based on real interdependent experiences, and not on dreams that shut out the other person and half of reality. The principle of military thinking, which is so strong both in the revival of Jewish nationalism and in Arab nationalism, has to take its course over time and, if it doesn't destroy everything, be shown as completely washed up and ineffective. Until it's quite clear that military means are bankrupt—as one would have thought that the Lebanese experience revealed, for the Israelis and the Lebanese and the Palestinians—we're going to have these horrible dips in the lives of people. But I'm a great optimist, let's say for my son's generation.

Your activism as a Palestinian must have in some ways made your work as a literary critic here in the United States more difficult to pursue. Two immediate reasons that come to mind are, first, that as a result, not of Zionist propaganda only, but of Zionist propaganda among other things, a synonymity between "Palestinian" and "terrorist" has been built up in the public mind here. Second, many of the people whom you deal with and are close to—including people like Geoffrey Hartman and Harold Bloom—are Zionists. And any feelings about this issue tend to escalate immediately to being violent and personal and passionate ones. So has it made your life as a literary critic more difficult?

In perspective, one would have to say only slightly. If one sees it in the large perspective of a fairly bloody struggle between two peoples, then what I've had to go through is really quite mild in comparison. Obviously, one misses certain sides of a person if they're withheld because of hostility or fear. In the case of Harold, his ideas, as he told me many years ago, are those of a longtime Jabotinsky/Herut man. He's to the right of the right, but it hasn't inhibited us from talking about it. With Geoffrey, we've never discussed it. I remember being slightly pained during the summer of 1982, when I was with him at the School of Criticism. My entire family, and my wife's family, were in Beirut, being besieged. Not a word of compassion was said. I obviously couldn't say anything, and he didn't say anything. Those kinds of things are what trouble one, on a personal level. It was certainly the case with Trilling, who was a very close friend and a wonderfully generous colleague: a certain aspect of our lives was curtained off and not discussed. So you felt, always, that there was something missing.

On a more public level, the notion of being both a Palestinian and a literary critic is for some people an oxymoron: you can't be. To others, I gather that it's a thrilling and a rather peculiar pleasure to watch somebody who is supposedly a terrorist carrying on in a fairly civilized way. Here's a fairly impressive example. A Jewish psychiatrist, whom I'd met at some political meeting, had come to New York and was all the way down in the Village, but insisted on coming to visit me at my house. She came up—it was an hour by subway—and spent no more than about five minutes. Then she said, "I have to go back, I have another meeting." So I said, "Why did you come?" and she said, "I just wanted to see the way you lived." She wanted to see what it was like for a Palestinian to live in a city like New York, which was a strange proposition to her. She was interested in the fact that I played the piano and things of that sort.

The worst aspect of it is that you know perfectly well that people are attacking you for ideas that seem to abut on their notions of what Zionism is. The most horrendous and cruel irony is that I'm frequently seen as a kind of Nazi type, by people like Cynthia Ozick and the *New Republic* crowd. It is the most outrageous parody.

What happened to Alex Odeh shows how dangerous it can be to speak to this cause here in the United States.[1]

I've gotten death threats, raids on my office, people trying to break into my house, and so on. All of that is there, too. But even in the world we live in—non-political and literary—it's always creeping in. The American Jewish Committee did a review of my book *The World, the Text, and the Critic,* in which the word "secular" was analyzed as really meaning the "secular democratic state" of Yasir Arafat, which really means (they went on to say) death for Jews, so Said is a terrorist, and so on.

I remember that when I showed you the interviews with Frye and Derrida, last year, your response was: "If their problem is going about the world and always finding their own ideas already there to meet them, my problem is going about the world and always finding a distorted picture of my political position there to meet me." Discuss.

It's very disturbing. Usually, when I go to give a lecture somewhere, a huge number of people show up, and there's always a question of security. Even though I'm going to speak on some literary or overtly non-political subject, there's always the danger of violence, of somebody rising in the audience and throwing something or firing a gun at me.

That's a problem. And you can't be private. I've been on the media often, and am fairly well known in that kind of world, so that one's privacy and one's ideas seem totally out of one's control. In other words, it's not just finding them there; it's finding a whole institution which has

---

1. Odeh was the director of the California office of the American Arab Anti-Discrimination Committee. He was killed by a booby-trapped bomb wired to his office door on October 11, 1985. The previous night, Odeh appeared on a local TV talk show to deny the involvement of Yasir Arafat in the *Achille Lauro* affair.

already received and processed what it considers to be your views—whether from a sympathetic or an antipathetic point of view. It's a tremendous effort to control yourself, and not walk away in desperation, because it's very hard to break through into something resembling an exchange of views with people. That's true whether one addresses an Arab audience or an American audience. But, interestingly, if one talks with Israelis, as opposed to with American or even European Jews, then somehow there's a kind of liveliness there. With Israeli Jews, it's interesting, because there's a common experience, though of course it's an antagonistic experience. Still, it's something that you can actually talk about and deal with.

The most interesting thing, from a coldly political point of view—as well as from a philosophical and interpretive point of view—is to watch people talking about things that are not political and to see the question of Palestine interjecting itself. It's certainly the case in this country that, for a certain type of thinker, all questions of self-determination, human rights, and so on are modified—sometimes implicitly—by the shifts in the fortunes of Israel. That's fascinating to watch, and one of the great challenges—not that I've succeeded in escaping from it—is to maintain a consistent position on such matters, on questions of principle, and not to twist them because the audience is friendly and expects you to do something else: nor to make exceptions. So that if you're opposed to religious madness of one sort or another, it would not only have to include Christian fundamentalism or Jewish fundamentalism, but also Islamic fundamentalism. In spite of my openly proclaimed views to the contrary, I'm considered a great defender of Islam, which is, of course, nonsense. I'm really quite atheistic.

A question on your early work on Conrad: did your experience of colonialism have anything to do with bringing you to an author whose work and career are so deeply imbedded in the whole question of colonialism?

Absolutely. I felt, first coming across Conrad when I was a teenager, that in a certain sense I was reading, not so much my own story, but a story written out of bits of my life and put together in a haunting and fantastically obsessive way. I've been hooked on it ever since. I think that he's not just a great writer of stories, but a great writer of parables.

He has a particular kind of vision which increases in intensity every time I read him, so that now it's almost unbearable for me to read him.

Do projects like The Question of Palestine *and* Covering Islam *represent a kind of endeavor which, in your mind, is kept separate from your more strictly literary-critical enterprise?*

Less and less. There was a time when I would do things like *The Question of Palestine* and *Covering Islam* with an eye almost exclusively directed to an audience that had nothing to do with literary matters. But as you know, if you've read them, I draw on certain literary texts, literary techniques, matters of interpretation, which have taught me a lot about the way ideas are transmitted, formed, and institutionalized.

There is no doubt that, until about five years ago, I was leading a very schizophrenic life. I was still confined, or self-confined, to the academic study of English to such a degree that I was routinely teaching courses on the English novel, or the eighteenth century, in a way that had very little to do with my real intellectual concerns. I think that, in the last three or four years, I've devised both courses and ways in which, while I'm not doing overtly political things, my interest in comparative literature has made it possible for me to deal with matters that are closer to my actual concerns: for example, the question of the intellectual; the relationships between culture and imperialism; world literature; and the interrelationships of history, society and literature. In these respects, I feel a lot better and feel that what I'm doing is more integrated.

I want to pick up some of those things in just a moment. But a project like Covering Islam *reveals that side of you which is influenced and affected by Chomsky. Could you describe the relation of your work to Chomsky's?*

I've known Chomsky for almost two decades now. He's a man I admire a great deal. There are a number of differences between us, but I think his kind of intellectual commitment, his relentless erudition, and his capacity for not being put off by professionalism of any sort—whether it's philosophical or mathematical or journalistic—have really encouraged me and a lot of other people not to be defused and put off by disciplinary barriers. And I think he's a very moral man. In many respects, he's a man whose courage and willingness to speak precisely on those issues that affect him most directly—as an American, as a Jew, and so on—have been very important to me.

There are differences between us, but they're not very interesting or important. They have to do, principally, with the need for a certain kind of relationship with a critical mass, in the sense of a people or a cause. Chomsky has always been a solitary worker. He writes out of some sense of solidarity with oppressed people, but his direct involvement in the ongoing political activity of a group of people or a community—partly because of his many interests and the demands on his time—has been different from mine. The second, and perhaps most important, difference is that he's not really interested in theorizing whatever it is that he does—and I really am.

In that sense, Foucault and Chomsky represent the two poles in your mind and practice.

I think so, partly. I suppose, in the final analysis, one has to choose between them, but I've always felt that one in fact could incorporate both of them. In the end, I think that Chomsky's is the more consistently honorable and admirable position, though it may not be the most emulatable position. It's certainly a less cynical position than Foucault's. By the end of his life, I think, Foucault was simply uninterested in any direct political involvement of any sort.

The first book of yours to make any impact was Beginnings. *If one reads that now, and then immediately reads* Orientalism, *it seems that in* Beginnings *you had not found your voice in the way that* Orientalism *has found it: a much stronger, more individual, more theoretically concentrated voice.*

I actually think that *Beginnings* is much more theoretically concentrated. But it may be still ventriloquistic: I felt it important to work through a number of genres, critics, voices. I've always been very taken with choruses, with polyphonic kinds of writing as well as singing. I think there is a kind of consistency through the book, which isn't as relentlessly and ruthlessly concentrated on a particular demystification as *Orientalism. Orientalism* was really a very programmatic book in one sense, but in another it allowed a tremendous amount of latitude. It was a great subject, and I felt it could make a greater effect, but *Beginnings* is a book I still feel very close to. There are a lot of things in it that I haven't completely worked out and that are still, for me, very rich—Vico, obviously, being one of them.

Here's a question which you formulate near the beginning of Beginnings: "*Is there a privileged beginning for a literary study—that is, an especially suitable or important beginning—that is wholly different from a historical, psychological, or cultural one?*" Would it be fair to say that your subsequent work—and most especially Orientalism—has answered that question in the negative?

I think that's probably true. I would say that the shift from *Beginnings* to *Orientalism* isn't so much the literary point of view, but the textual point of view. I was impressed in *Orientalism* by the extent to which, simply by reading something, people could then go out and look for it. That is what I call a "textual attitude," and it's related to the question I framed in *Beginnings*. Now I'm coming around to change my mind a bit. I have felt, for several years now, in a flat-footed and quite naive way, that, given the enormous amount of bad faith and ideological obfuscation that goes on in social science writing of a certain kind, as well as in historical writing, there's something refreshing and immensely appealing about writing—like that Stevens poem you've been quoting—that is purely literary. The literary grace, if you want to call it that, is different. I certainly think it can be *found* in social science writing: certainly, in *Orientalism,* I found that when people like Massignon were not only great scholars but also great writers, it made all the difference, even if their attitudes were completely peculiar. I think I'm coming to a more temperate view of the relationship between literary and other forms of writing.

Something that is there in Beginnings *and then becomes stronger, and is very surprising in you, is the Vichian element. How did Vico, of all people, come to get a grip on you?*

The tremendous impact which *The New Science* had on me when I read it as a graduate student was, first, probably due to the scene that he paints at the beginning: of a feral and Gentile man; the giants; the period right after the flood, with people wandering all over the face of the earth, and gradually disciplining themselves, partly out of fear and partly out of providence. That kind of self-making struck me as being really at the heart of all genuinely powerful and interesting historical visions (you see it in Marx, obviously, and in Ibn Khaldun): the way in which a body forms itself into a mind and a body, and then into a society. That is so compelling, and so powerful; and he uses texts that have been discussed as ornamental or philosophical in a literary way, to inform this extraordinary vision of development and education. That struck me as tremendously powerful and poetic.

Second, he was always doing it by skirting around religious notions, of the creation and so on. That oppositional quality to his work—his being anti-Cartesian, anti-rationalistic and anti-Catholic—was incredibly powerful. I've read him many, many times since then, and always find him enriching and amusing and informative.

Something that is important to Beginnings *is the Vichian opposition between Gentile beginnings and theological origins. This sounds like a question formulated by the American Jewish Committee, but did the resonance of that opposition, for you, have anything to do with the fact that Israel is a society founded, perhaps uniquely, on theological origins?*

I don't think that Israel is unique in that respect. Don't forget that the world I grew up in was a world in which the local product was the manufacture of religions. Certainly it's true of Islam, certainly it's true of Christianity, and certainly it's true of Judaism: they're all related, they're all monotheistic, they all come out of the same "Abrahamanic" (as Massignon calls it) promise or covenant. That distinction I make in *Beginnings,* which Vico makes so strongly, strikes me as absolutely just. If there is to be any kind of history, it has to be led away from these origins. In that respect, Vico is very Lucretian: Lucretius says, in the first book of *De Rerum Natura,* that the worst ills really come out of the suasions of religion. I think that's certainly true, and I was trying as much as possible to register this. But, as I say, I wouldn't confine it to Israel. My own background includes a rather heavy dose, in my mother's family, of Lebanese, right-wing Christians who are as bloody-minded as Kahane. That whole thing is something that I have no use for at all; what I was trying to do was to pull myself out of it.

A big part of the transition from Beginnings *to* Orientalism *is the more powerful influence of Foucault in the second book. Did you know Foucault?*

Not really. I got to know him afterwards, after I wrote *Orientalism.* We corresponded a bit. What I was always impressed with in Foucault was the method. It seemed to me that like Foucault and Chomsky—I don't really want to compare myself with them—I had amassed a great deal of information and knowledge, and that I was also interested in the way in which these are deployed. I think that both of them share a kind of strategic sense of knowledge: a strategic and geographical sense, as opposed to a *temporal* sense, which is what characterizes the Hegelian and, later, the deconstructive modes. Foucault's and Chomsky's is more spatial, and I think Gramsci was terribly important there too, as a mediator for the other two. I was looking for a way to do it effectively, rhetorically, and to organize a large body of information which I had amassed in almost twenty years of reading in the subject.

In *that* respect, Foucault came to the fore. But I was already aware of the problems of Foucault's determinism, his Spinoza quality, where everything is always assimilated and acculturated. You can already see it at the end of *Discipline and Punish*. *Orientalism* is theoretically inconsistent, and I designed it that way: I didn't want Foucault's method, or anybody's method, to override what I was trying to put forward. The notion of a kind of non-coercive knowledge, which I come to at the end of the book, was deliberately anti-Foucault.

In the book, you say that the phenomenon of Orientalism calls into question "the possibility of non-political scholarship." Does that apply as much to scholarship that remains strictly within its own cultural domain or tradition? That is, scholarship which—unlike Orientalism—is not trying to appropriate another culture.

It's the whole question of displacement, which is a Fryean idea: that everything is a displacement from something else. I think it's probably true that all knowledge is a displacement from something, but I think there are degrees. I think that certainly the most malignant is the kind that's doing the most displacing while denying it the most strongly. *That* you find in societies and cultures and moments that are explicitly imperial. You certainly see it in America; you certainly see it in the nineteenth century in England and France. On the other hand, I think it's possible to say that there are relatively benign forms of displacement that occur internally within a culture and within a discipline, of a sort that are variously pleasing and harmless and benign. Somehow, one isn't really concerned about them at this point. I always feel the pressure on me to describe the other kind.

In Orientalism, *you say that fields of learning, and art, are con-*

strained by social and cultural conditions, worldly circumstance, and stabilizing influences like schools, libraries, and governments. You say that learned and imaginative writings are never free, but are "limited in their imagery, assumptions and intentions." Let's come back to what you were saying before about your recent rethinking of whether literature has a specificity within discourse. Is literature necessarily as constrained as, say, fields of learning like Orientalism?

I think that, in fact, one would have to say "yes." The problem with a lot of recent literary criticism, partly under the influence of people like de Man—whom I admired a great deal, and thought was very clever and impressively acute—and Bloom, Frye, and the others, is that a great deal of unnecessary effort goes into defining what is purely literary. I don't understand the need constantly to do that. It's like saying that something is American, and the opposite to it is un-American: that whole field seems to me quite boring. What is interesting about literature, and everything else, is the degree to which it's mixed with other things, not its purity. That's just a temperamental view of mine.

Everything one does is constrained by physical circumstance. One of the things I was always immensely taken with in Vico was the fact that the body is always there. If you read a lot of the critics you've talked with, the body doesn't matter at all. But in fact it *does* matter: we aren't disembodied brains or poetry machines. We're involved in the circumstances of physical existence, and that is very important to me. (I like to play tennis, and squash, and a lot of other physical things.) So those strike me as the more fruitful directions in which to go: outward from the pure, to the mixed and the impure. The constraints are there, but when I say they're "not free" I just mean "free" in an ideological sense. People say "It's a free country": well, of course it's not a free country. That's common sense—I'm not urging some tremendous ideological message. We're in the world, no matter how many times we scream that we're really in the tower.

One aspect in which The World, the Text, and the Critic *differs from, say,* Beginnings, *is the strength of the critique of Derrida. You say that Derrida's criticism "moves us into the text, Foucault's in and out." I wonder if something like the recent deconstructive interest in legal texts could qualify that. In legal judgments, in common law, we seem to be in an area where we can't talk about moving* out *of the text back into society, because the text and social power are identified.*

That is a later development in deconstructive thought. Christopher Norris, in his first book on deconstruction, considers Foucault a deconstructionist. If you're saying that everything that is effectively demystifying or disenchanting—where certain kinds of ideological blinkers are removed, and certain involvements and complicities are revealed—is deconstruction, then I'm for it. But there is another kind of deconstruction, which I would call "dogmatic" or "theoretical" deconstruction, which urges a kind of purity. I don't think that Derrida has been very guilty of it, incidentally—he's too resourceful. But a lot of his disciples seem to argue that way. I remember once giving a lecture in which I talked about Derrida, and one of his disciples came up to me and said: "You made a mistake: you can't use the word 'reality' when you talk about Derrida." Anyway, I think the kinds of distinctions that are made between texts and non-texts are infantile and uninteresting.

Were you attracted to Derrida much, at the beginning?

I met him when he first came to this country in 1966. I've always found him an amiable and extremely genuine person. At times, his work has interested me. But things like *Glas* (although he and I shared a common friendship with Genet) and *La Carte postale* I just found not that interesting. I think he's probably a much better essayist than he is a systematic philosopher, and it's the kind of sporty quality of his work—which you find in some of the essays in *Dissemination*—that I've always thought is quite brilliant. I never really cared for the *Grammatology*. It struck me as a ponderous and ineffective book. I thought that his earliest work, on Husserl's *The Origin of Geometry,* was really quite brilliant.

But finally you think that the general influence of his work has been too much to separate textuality from its surrounding contexts?

He clarified a certain *Zeitgeist,* which is that we ought to be able to talk about texts in a way rather more philosophically than the New Critics did, but fundamentally in the same way, and we needn't feel silly and irrelevant doing it: in fact, we are dealing with logocentrism and apocalypse and phallo-this and phallo-that. You know what I'm trying to say. It gave it a kind of armature that was important for the American academy if it was to think of itself as serious and as dealing with fundamental questions.

But remaining within its own fundamental preconceptions.

That's obviously the case. The attempts to link deconstruction with Marxism and all these other things are interesting, but they're more lab experiments than they are major steps in the evolution of a certain type of thinking.

Another figure within this present series to whom there are many references in your books is Harold Bloom. To my surprise, most of these references are benign. What positive things have you taken from Bloom?

The notion of struggle. That's been the most important thing: the vision he has of everyone quarreling over territory and turf is incredibly persuasive. I don't think there is any doubt about that—that everybody talks both against and with other people, whether it's poetry or not. That's what I found, and how it relates to questions of influence and what is now called "intertextuality." His other stuff, the proliferation of terms like "clinamen," and the gnostic aspects, and the mysterious and prophetic: I find that amusing and charming—because he has great panache—but it's hard for me to take it as doctrine in any way.

The stuff in his interview about criticism being totally personal and without social context . . .

That's obvious nonsense. It sounds clever and brilliant. He's quite rightly taken Oscar Wilde as a model, and if you can pull it off, then you do it. But he's obviously in great need of all kinds of institutional supports, as we all are: he needs an office, he needs workers, he needs grants . . .

Until he won the McArthur Award . . .

But there you are! He didn't turn it down. He didn't say, "Well, I'm just doing it on my own!" He gladly took the money and off he went: he became an institution himself. Obviously, overstatement is very much a part of Harold's arsenal, but there is a difference between overstatement for effect and overstatement as doctrine—such as saying that all criticism is personal. I suppose that on one level it's true: we are ourselves, and we write what we think and not what somebody else tells us to. But that's like saying "Today is Friday": it's a truism.

In The World, the Text, and the Critic, *you begin with a discursus on "secular criticism" and end with one on "religious criticism." You give a list of titles which, you say, illustrate the drift toward a new religiosity in criticism. Most of those titles are by the critics who precede you in this*

series of interviews. However, neither Bloom nor Frye nor Frank Ker-
mode—even though they write books with those sorts of titles—is pro-
posing to make literature the object of some kind of institutionalized
religious worship. Are we really talking about "secular" versus "reli-
gious," or are we talking more about "historicist" versus something that
continues to believe in a supra-historical aesthetic effect?

You can turn it any way you wish, but I think that it's not an accident
that the three critics you just mentioned all write about the Bible.

But one can't take exception to that.

No, I don't agree. I think that it is, precisely, exceptional that the
Bible should emerge in certain types of, shall we say, "theological"
thought, or thought that can be traced back to a God of some sort, to
the divine. I think you're absolutely wrong—I think it's central to their
view. Gnosticism, preciosity of language, obscurity of language—everything that comes out of modernism, which is now crystallized in biblical
work—the privacy of interpretation, privileged or hierophantic language: all of these things are part of a clerical attitude.

Hartman's point was that we cannot get away from the element
of enchantment that literature contains, and that the attempt to purify
that . . .

Who's interested in purifying it? That's the last thing I want to do.
Precisely what they're trying to do is to purify it. I'm interested in illuminating it, or putting it in conjunction with other things. What I'm
interested in is exactly the opposite of purification: not, as in Frye, literature as some kind of separate, total system, but literature as involved
with many other things—in, you might say, an enchanting way.

For instance, one of the things which Frye doesn't develop, but which
I've always wished he had, is the relationship between the scheme of the
Anatomy and tonal music. Music is the great passion of my life. The relationship between literature and certain types of music is a fascinating
one. Those are the sorts of things I'm interested in; not the extent to
which one can isolate literature from everything else. It's a question of
emphasis. Nobody would deny that there is a highly literary quality to,
say, an ode by Keats or a poem by Stevens; but is that interesting in and
of itself, past one's enchantment and one's enjoyment of it? Maybe it's
enough just to enjoy it, but if one wants to talk about it, I think one can

increase one's enjoyment by connecting it to other things. I take that to be what we're all about.

I still don't know exactly what you feel about historicism, as far as literary criticism goes. Do we not sacrifice something as soon as we collapse literature back into any kind of a historicism?

Why is it collapsing? What you're doing all the time is adding words to it that encourage one in thinking of it as a rather impoverishing and reductive method. I would have thought exactly the opposite. Take the example of a critic whom I really respect and enjoy, Raymond Williams, in *The Country and the City*. Now, I suppose that if you were to read one of the country-house poems that he discusses there—one by Jonson, or Marvell—you might say that he is reducing it to its historical circumstances, but I don't think that you could justify saying that. In fact, just as Keats in "Ode on a Grecian Urn" is talking about the way in which a village has to be emptied to appear on the urn, Williams is enlarging the field in which we see a country-house poem. And that seems to me to be anything but reductive. If you're simply saying that a class analysis of "The Wife of Bath's Tale" or "Penshurst"—where all you do is try to show the level of class awareness which comes through in those poems—is reductive, well, it is reductive: but that doesn't seem to me to be a historicist reading in the Vichian sense of the word, or the Auerbachian sense of the word.

As you've become more interested in the Foucauldian type of historicism, isn't it true to say that you've written less about literature, and more about cultural history—things like Orientalism, appropriative structures?

That's sort of tough to answer. I find it very hard, now, to separate out literature from other things, except in the curricular sense. If you say that I write less about literature in the sense of things that appear on English Department lists, then that's probably true. I may have written less about Dickens than about, say, Renan. I've probably written about a wider range of literature, including a lot of Third World writers who are not curricular in the English sense of the word. I suppose that uncanonical works are what I'm writing more about. But I find it rather disturbing to be constantly asked to make distinctions between literature and other things. I mean, I really do believe—Kermode makes this point, too—that some works are greater than others. A Dickens novel is better than a Harold Robbins novel, and it's silly to argue about that. But that doesn't mean that reading a Dickens novel and then writing appreciations of it are actions that are going to satisfy me, in terms of what I'm interested in.

Could you talk for a moment about the connotations of the word "worldliness," as you apply it to literature and criticism?

On one level, it obviously connotes a certain *savoir faire:* I'm interested in the way that great works *make their way,* the way that, in Proust, Charlus can make his way in the world—he's worldly in that sense. That's a rather resonant and deep meaning for me. The second is the extent to which works reach out and hold on to other works, in institutions, in historical moments, in society. Third is a fantastically antimetaphysical quality that I find in the most compelling written works, whether they are what you would call works of literature, or what I would call, say, New Journalism, or essay-writing. In the sense that they really are about some form of engagement, I'm very interested in them. You find that even in Hopkins's poems, for example, where he's really reaching out and trying to get hold of things in an almost tactile way.

You having said that, I wonder if we could choose this moment to look at the Stevens poem. A poem like this, which seems intensely personal: in what sense is it worldly?

I'll tell you immediately: the word "scrawny," the "scrawny cry." Unlike almost all of the people whom you've interviewed, I've never made a great thing out of Stevens. I've always thought of him as a kind of amusing, tinkly poet, who was full of wordplay. He's a failed metaphysical poet, in some way; and very home-made and American.

So what about "scrawny"?

I mean the incongruity of the "scrawny cry" and "Not Ideas about the Thing but the Thing Itself." That kind of Platonic or classically metaphysical statement, and then this poem which slowly unfolds and in the end gives you the "scrawny cry" in a context that is obviously taken straight out of the first chorus in Haydn's *The Creation.* "Let there be light!": and then instead of a great C-major chord you get this little toot. It's a fantastically funny poem, and I think that all of Stevens's poems do this kind of thing. It's a carnival poem; but to see in it some metaphysical parable is impossible, because I *hear* poetry, I don't really read it, and there's always a tinkly, "Asides on the Oboe" quality about Stevens. It's like an orchestra tuning up, but never actually playing a piece.

As Kermode says—and I agree with him—it's not as powerful or moving a poem as "Of Mere Being." Stevens is full of "likes" and "almosts" and "as ifs" and very approximative things of that sort: "It was *like* a new knowledge of reality." It's difficult for me to see it in the kind of grandiose, metaphysical light that I think you feel that it sheds on itself. You know: "a battered panache above snow"; that rather awkward Francophonic quality; the relentless repetition of "scrawny." It's rather Hardyesque, in a way. It doesn't have the stately quality of some of Hardy's late lyrics, but that contrast between the sun and the power of the ending of winter, and the scrawny cry, and the chorister "whose *c* preceded the choir" like an instrument played out of turn, are reminiscent of Hardy.

You haven't talked much about lyric poetry, in your work.

No, I tend to be a plot and narrative person.

Is that anything to do with the fact that lyric is most *resistant to a historicist analysis, and most insistent on its own peculiarity, its mystery, its isolation, its purity?*

I don't think so. It's just that there's a certain privacy to it, which has always meant a great deal to me. For instance, Eliot's "Ariel" poems have always meant a great deal to me, G. M. Hopkins, those kinds of lyrics. There's a certain privacy in them, and in my experience of them, which has made it difficult for me to write about them. A lot of what I write about is not meditative, but quite the opposite: proclamatory. One of the most compelling pieces that I've ever read on lyrics and lyricism is Adorno's piece on lyric and society. It seems to me perfectly possible to read it as a kind of monad, the way he analyzes a late Schoenberg piece, in which all the effort to resist is nevertheless confirming something that is being resisted. I've always found that to be true: it just requires a skillful unlocking.

There are two more critics whom you admire and who seem to me to be antithetical in you, the way Foucault and Chomsky are. I mean Gramsci and Benda, though obviously Gramsci is much more important

*to you than Benda. Gramsci's idea is that there are organic intellectuals,
who emerge from and continue to identify with an oppressed class, and
traditional intellectuals, who try to be Platonic and withdrawn but end
up simply justifying whatever power is in power. To me, you seem in a
sense to be both . . .*

That's a great compliment!

*No, well, I mean that you write, as a Palestinian, about Palestine, and
in that sense are an organic intellectual. The only sense in which I mean
that you are also traditional is that you work in a university. And Benda
is really a defender of the traditional or abstracted intellectual.*

What I admire in Benda isn't his traditional pose, or the affirmations
of the importance of distance. It is his almost clumsy way of saying:
"Look, you've got to tell the truth." It's presented in the most unattractive way possible: the attitudes are essentially conservative; the language
is deliberately a language of orthodoxy and distance. But still, in all,
what one feels is somebody saying: "You've got to tell the truth"—that
paternal admonition that we all heard from our fathers. I find it incredibly tonic and refreshing to read him, precisely because of that. With
Gramsci, it's not so much that organic and traditional intellectual opposition, but the fact that he was interested in everything. Even though he
was very tightly constrained both in his own handicapped body and,
later, in jail, he seemed to be able to experience a fantastic number of
things. The correspondence with his wife and his sister-in-law; all the
immense reading and writing he did, on his own, in prison: that's really
one of the great adventures of human experience. But all of that was
contained within a fairly disciplined commitment to the world in which
he lived.

Everything you've just said has made me think of Nelson Mandela.

There are some people like that. That's what I found in Gramsci. Plus
the fact that he had an incredibly refined mind. You don't get a sense of
being clubbed over the head—partly because of the fact that he was
writing for himself, and under censorship. That one could manage *that*
is something that I've always tried to emulate. To be interested in as
many things as possible: I think that's really what we're best at doing.

*Can the university avoid being simply the institutionalization of what
Gramsci speaks of as the traditional intellectuals?*

Oh yes. I think that the American university is really without precedent. It's difficult to find analogies or predecessors for the strange and incongruous and totally contradictory institution which the American university is. On the one hand, I think it's a very benign institution, as institutions go. Of course, it has its coercive aspects.

But you've shown, again and again, how social scientists, and others within the university, work to legitimize social power.

Yes, but the fact is that people like myself and Chomsky and others *also* exist within the universities.

Without being compromised?

I wouldn't say we've been terribly compromised. I mean, everybody's compromised by affiliation: if a university is taking secret CIA money, as Harvard seems to have done, I suppose everybody is affected in some way. But there's no question that, in some ways, neither Chomsky nor myself would have had the audiences we've had without the university. A lot of the people who listen to us when we speak—it's certainly true in his case—are university students. The university provides one with a forum to do certain kinds of things . . .

But aren't you and Chomsky incredible exceptions, in the way you use that forum?

The exceptions certainly appear from somewhere; they are not out of the blue. And in that respect, I think the university is benign. It can, obviously, co-opt or tame: so what institution doesn't? The most pernicious aspects of the university are not that. The more pernicious aspects of the university—which we're still not quite clear about—are in the way the university is associated with certain social processes. Ethnography, nuclear sciences, etcetera, etcetera: those things are quite clear. But the relationship between the university and the corporation, the relationship between the university and the media: all of these things are complex and troubled matters. Those are much more formidable than mere co-optation. You don't *have* to be co-opted. It happens, but in some cases it could be without consequences that a certain doctrine is co-opted by the university. Like deconstruction: it's entirely a university doctrine, but that it is of the university doesn't make any difference.

What about the pedagogic role? Something that Bloom said struck me very much: all we can hope to do, in the university, is to produce human beings who are capable of sounding like themselves. I interpret that to mean that, within the university, teachers like you have a genuine opportunity to produce human beings who are intellectually strong and independent enough not to be pushed around like pieces on an ideological chessboard—and who are therefore resistant to, for example, Orientalism, or the synonymity of "Palestinian" and "terrorist." Do you feel that function strongly?

Yes, I do: very much so. But again, if one is working with the texts of English literature, then one feels a great constraint. The problem there is that you have a responsibility to the material, which is a real one; but the main goal is to create in your students a critical consciousness. The last thing I'm interested in is disciples. Any kind of overt communication of a message or method is the last thing I want to do. In that respect, it's very difficult to be a teacher, because in a certain sense you ought always to be undercutting yourself. You're teaching, performing, doing the kinds of things that students can learn from, but at the same time cutting them off and saying "Don't try to do this." You're telling them to do it, and not to do it.

Can't a "critical consciousness" very easily become simply an ethic of individualism—that is, as against "class consciousness"?

Yes, you're absolutely right, and I think that in a certain sense the American university is really a breeding ground for that kind of individualism—at its best. It's a great paradox that the best thing you can do is to promote an individualism in a student.

Which is what the system wants.

Which is what the system wants, but in a sense the system doesn't want that: it says that that's what it wants, but really it wants a commodity which is called "individualism." So that's where you are: shortchanging both sides of that equation. You're not allowing individualism to get too far out of hand, as an ideological thing; nor are you allowing the ideology of the commodity to take over everything. As I grow older—I've been teaching for twenty-five years now—I find that teaching is really impossible, in a funny sort of way. At best, you can read with students. It's important, every so often, to bring in a book that you totally admire, and yet completely understand in its limitations. You can just tell your students, "Look, here is something," or "This is a wonderful poem," or just read it and see what happens.

I was reading a comment recently by someone who said that all this stuff about the politicization of English teaching was beside the point, and that what we should do is to be political, to engage in political praxis the same as any other group, and then go on doing our professional work as normal. The reason I mention this is that they said that in this sense Edward Said is exemplary, because he does *engage in praxis instead of just going on endlessly about the politicization of English studies. Anyway, that sounded like quite a good position to me. I'm even thinking of adopting it.*

Why not? The late-1960s notion of the politicization of pedagogical discourse has spent itself, really. For one, you either can do it, or you can't do it. And then, if you want to be political there's nothing to prevent you: there are millions of issues with which you can connect yourself, and there's no reason always just to make a big harangue of it. That's why I like words like "worldly": they are simple, and do the trick, and get you involved, but you don't have to create a whole complicated apparatus to help you make your points. I think that the important things are competence, interest and, above all, a critical sense.

The objection to this, likely to be made by one's Marxist colleagues, is that it's simply naive to think that one can separate one's professional life from one's political views.

But you're not separating it: you're just leading it in different ways. It's like the voices of a fugue. A fugue can contain two, three, four, or five voices: they're all part of the same composition, but they're each distinct. They operate together, and it's a question of how you conceive of the togetherness: if you think that it's got to be this *or* that, then you're paralyzed; then you're either Mallarmé or Bakunin, which is an absurd opposition.

The opposite version of the fallacy of splitting one's professional work from one's political commitment belongs to those Marxists who think that the revolutionary task ends with a radical rereading of Finnegans Wake: *as if Marxism were a literary theory.*

I just came back from England, where I did a day-long conference with Raymond Williams, and we were talking together about the different social contexts in which we did our work. It's very striking that within an English context one *can* talk about Marxism, or at least socialism, as a tradition having a real presence. You cannot talk about that in America, where there is no socialist tradition of any consequence. So the sudden appearance of the most refined and most learned kinds of theoretical Marxism in people like Jameson—whom I tremendously admire—is an extraordinary anomaly. It partakes of the same personal intellectual brilliance—as opposed to its social and political insights—as in Harold Bloom's work. Now, if *that's* Marxism, it's a traveling variety of Marxism which is quite different to what we were talking about.

Reading Lukács and Gramsci, they still talk about the bourgeoisie as being always on the defensive, and as having to elicit an always reluctant submission from the proletariat. Their great blind spot is America. They really could not have foreseen American capitalism. They could not have foreseen that a form of social control would spring up in which, far from being defensive, the bourgeoisie would elicit from the proletariat, not submission, but an entire identification with its own interests. I think that the reasons for that are primarily technological.

But you find similar conjunctions in late-nineteenth-century England, with regard to the empire. There's always a mediating mechanism. In that case it's empire, and empire works here too. And then there's the electronic media that gives everybody, whether a Wall Street financier or a middle-western housewife or a Californian surfer, the sense that they are participants in a gigantic polity, which is all going to the funeral of these poor astronauts who were killed a couple of days ago.[2] It really is an extrapolation from the nineteenth-century idea of nationalism, but it's an imagination that does all the imagining for you, in a strange kind of way. I don't think that Gramsci and Lukács had any idea of that. Plus, in Lukács's case, his idea of the bourgeoisie was that it was the last class in history: it was Austro-Hungarian, it understood aesthetic forms like tragedy and lyric, and it was passing from the scene. That was what the bourgeoisie meant to him, and the proletariat was a great blank. Gramsci, I think, is more eclectic than that. But neither of them could

---

2. A reference to the explosion, two days before the interview was recorded, of the U.S. space shuttle *Challenger*.

have foreseen the enormous and sudden growth of the American empire as a going and quite profitable enterprise. I remember, a couple of years ago, a senior UN civil servant saying, "The Third World leaders speak about Moscow, but in their hearts they all want to go to California." The images are very powerful.

Interview with Imre Salusinszky in
Criticism in Society, London, 1987

FIVE

CRITICISM, CULTURE, AND PERFORMANCE

The following pages take the form of a roundtable discussion with the editorial board of Wedge. E.W.S.

BONNIE MARRANCA: Since you write on music performance, tell us how you feel about this activity in your life, and how it is perceived by others in the literary world.

EDWARD SAID: I think the isolation of musical culture from what is called literary culture is almost total. What used to be assumed to be a kind of passing knowledge or literacy on the part of literary people with regard to music is now nonexistent. I think there are a few desultory efforts to be interested in the rock culture and pop music, that whole mass culture phenomenon, on the part of literary intellectuals. But the world that I'm interested in, the music of classical performance and opera and the so-called high-culture dramas that have persisted largely from the nineteenth century, is almost totally mysterious to literary people. I think they regard what I do as a kind of lark. I've tried to demonstrate my seriousness by giving a series of lectures last spring, the Wellek Lectures at the University of California at Irvine, which are normally very heavy duty literary theory lectures. I gave them on what I call musical elaborations, of which the first lecture of three was on performance. It was called "Performance as an extreme occasion." I was interested in the role of music in the creation of social space. In the third lecture I talked about music and solitude and melody, which are subjects that interest me a great deal. But I don't think one can really worry about music seriously without some active participation in musical life. My own background is that of a pianist. I studied piano quite seriously when I was an undergraduate at Princeton and with teachers at Julliard. So I think what interests me in the whole phenomenon is not so much the reviewing aspect. I prefer trying to deal with the problem of the composer and the problem of performance as separate but interrelated issues.

MARRANCA: Your music criticism seems to be different from your literary criticism. Not only is the subject matter different, but it doesn't seem to be as—let me see if I can choose the right word, because I don't want to mean it in any kind of pejorative sense—it's lighter, it's not as dense and politically engaged. Of course, it doesn't always lend itself to that, depending on the subject matter. On the other hand, the piece that you did on Verdi's *Aida* is a model for a new kind of theater history. But it seems to me that there is something you allow yourself to do in music criticism that is not there in your literary criticism.

SAID: What I'm moved by in music criticism are things that I'm interested in and like. I am really first motivated by pleasure. And it has to be sustained over a long period of time. I don't write reviews; I think that's a debased form, to write a kind of scorecard, morning-after kind of thing about performance. So what I like to do is to go to many more performances than I would ever write about and then over a period of time, certain things crystallize out of my mind as I reflect on them and think about them, and the music I'll play over. In the end, what I really find abides are the things that I care about. I don't know what those are until after a period of time has elapsed. It's a different type of occasional writing from the kind that I do in literary criticism, where I'm involved in much longer sorts of debates. Whereas in this I don't really engage with too much in music criticism, because most of it is to me totally uninteresting. There are a couple of interesting music critics around. Not the journalistic ones. Andrew Porter in the *New Yorker* I think is challenging and quite brilliant at times. And then there are people who write from the extreme right wing, like Samuel Lipman, who writes for *The New Criterion,* and Edward Wasserstein, who writes for the *New Republic,* who are very intelligent music critics. And that's about it. The rest is really a desert—people who write about music in a non-musicological way.

On the other hand, I have had lots of response from young musicologists, who write me about some of the issues that come up. For example, I wrote a piece about feminism in music and the problem of that. And I've written about the problems of political power and representation over years in some of the things I've done for *The Nation.* But my overriding concern is a record of a certain kind of enjoyment, which I think can be given literary form, without drawing attention to itself as a kind of tour de force. "Lighter" is the word you used, I would call it glib and superficial.

Una Chaudhuri: Do you think that performance, as a category, has something to do with the difference?

Said: Tremendously. That's what I'm really interested in. I think the figure who got me started was Glenn Gould. It was really the first extended piece that I wrote which appeared the year he died, or the year after he died—'82 or '83—in *Vanity Fair*. I'd long been fascinated with him. And I also was very interested in the phenomenon of Toscanini. Just because it seemed to me that both of them seemed to be musicians whose work, in a certain sense, was also *about* performance. There was no attempt to pretend they were doing something else, but they had sort of fixated on the notion of performance and carried it to such an extreme degree that it compelled attention on its own, and it attracted attention to the artificiality of performance. And to the conventions of it, and to the strange—in the case of Toscanini—well, Bonnie, you write about it, too, in your essay on performance versus singing—the difference between performers who heighten the occasion and those who turn it into a kind of extension of the drawing room or social occasion. So performance is very interesting because then there's the other problem, that you don't have either in theater, the visual and/or literary arts, in that the performance of music is so momentary—it's over!—I mean, you can't go back to it, anyway, really. And so there's a kind of sporting element that I'm trying to capture. I talked about it once with Arthur Danto who said, for example, if you read his pieces, they're all about going back over to an exhibition, leaving aside what he says and what his attitudes and his ideas are about art. I can't do that. So I have to go back, really, to my recollection. And my attempts, in my own mind, to restate it or experience it in another context.

Marc Robinson: On the whole idea of performance, let me draw you out a bit on opera performance, especially the staging of it. For so many people in the theater, the whole world of opera is a foggy, dead zone that most of us don't go to because the theatricality of it is so conservative. But now many of the experimental directors are going back to opera—Robert Wilson, Peter Sellars, Andre Serban—and trying to revive it from a theater background. Where do you see opera performance going?

SAID: Well, it's a tremendously interesting subject that excites me in many different ways. I think for the most part there is a deadness at the heart of opera performance, largely because of institutions like the Met, which for one reason or another—some of the reasons are perfectly obvious—has been dominated by what I call Italian *verismo* opera—and strengthened in this ridiculous kind of thing by the revival, that began in the sixties, of the *bel canto* tradition. The result of this is that a kind of hegemony has formed between the blue chip opera companies like the Met, and this repertory, and has frozen out a large amount of really extraordinary music. It has hardened performance style into a ridiculous conventionalism which has now become the norm. It infects everybody, even the greatest singers. It is certainly true of Pavarotti, sort of on the right; and on the left, Jessye Norman. You see what I'm trying to say? It's narcotized audiences. The thing I cannot understand is how people can sit through operas at the Met.

ROBINSON: I remember when you reviewed the Schoenberg opera *Erwartung* and were so disappointed. Didn't you say something about how it would be much more rewarding just to stay at home and stage it in your mind?

SAID: Exactly. Or watch it as a concert performance with Jessye Norman. It's the story of a woman who's going mad. And she's looking for her betrothed. The text is written—texts in operas are often very interesting—by a Viennese medical student. The text is not of great literary value, but it's about hysteria and it bears an interesting relation, Adorno says, to Freud's case studies. So it is a minute, seismographic dissolution of a consciousness. Now here is this wonderful singer who hasn't got a clue what it's about, much too large in size to represent neurasthenia and hysteria and all this kind of stuff. As the opera progresses she goes deeper and deeper into the forest losing her mind and looking for her fiancé. And then it's discovered she really might be a patient in a mental institution who's run away. And right in the middle of the set—right in the middle of the stage—is this enormous grand piano. What is a grand piano doing in the middle of a forest? So I opined that the reason she was going mad was that she couldn't figure out what to do with the grand piano. Which produces a kind of—I mean, you could say—it's a kind of perverse version of the opera. It's a glorious misinterpretation of the opera. That's not what's intended; it was supposed to be a deeply serious kind of thing, and it just didn't work. That's what the Met does, and I don't understand how it continues to do that.

ROBINSON: Maybe the consequence of that is there are certain works of music-theater that simply shouldn't be staged. You always hear that with dramatic literature, there are certain "unstageable" texts—an awful lot of Shakespeare . . .

SAID: Yes, that's certainly true, but a lot of those derive from performances where the unstageability of the piece can be made evident, you know, like a late Ibsen play, *When We Dead Awaken*. It has a lot to do with musical performance as well as opera . . . That is to say, how do these—this is a sort of Gramscian phrase—how do these hegemonic canons get formed? I mean, for example, the exclusion of French opera is really quite extraordinary. There is a wonderful tradition of French music and French drama—music-drama—that just doesn't find its way onto the American stages. Think of Rameau; think of Berlioz; think of most of Rossini, aside from *The Barber of Seville*. I mean, Rossini was a French opera writer. Berlioz: you never see him. Bizet is the author of ten operas, of which *Carmen* gets fitful performances—*Carmen* is one of the great masterpieces—but precisely because it's kind of an anti-French and anti-German opera, in a way. Then there's Massenet and Fauré. Why all this *verismo* and then a little smattering of Wagner—Wagner sort of turned into Italian. . . .

MARRANCA: I think the last time we spoke we talked a little bit about the Philip Glass operas, about whether you had seen *Einstein on the Beach, Akhnaten,* or *Satyagraha.* Are you interested in the contemporary repertoire?

SAID: I am. I've heard those and I've seen videos of them—one or two of Glass's things. It's not a musical aesthetic that moves me tremendously. It doesn't seem to me to exploit to the maximum what is available there.

MARRANCA: What about as critical material, in the sense of writing about or looking at the *Akhnaten* opera. . . . Even in terms of political themes I would have thought they'd attract your attention.

SAID: That's true, it's just . . . I don't know. I can't explain it. As I say, I work with fairly strong likes and dislikes, pleasures, and so on . . .

I don't derive the kind of interest from Glass that I would have found, say, in other contemporary composers, like Henze. I think Henze is a more interesting writer of opera.

MARRANCA: I was interested to read in a recent interview—one of the things you mentioned in talking about your writing—how the concepts of polyphonic voice and chorus interest you. Could you elaborate on that in terms of your own critical writing?

SAID: These are things it takes a while to fetch out of one's own interests and predilections. I seem to have always been interested in the phenomenon of polyphony of one sort or another. Musically, I'm very interested in contrapuntal writing, and contrapuntal forms. The kind of complexity that is available, aesthetically, to the whole range from consonant to dissonant, the tying together of multiple voices in a kind of disciplined whole, is something that I find tremendously appealing.

MARRANCA: How do you extend it to your own essays?

SAID: I extend it, for example, in an essay I did on exile, basing it on personal experience. If you're an exile—which I feel myself, in many ways, to have been—you always bear within yourself a recollection of what you've left behind and what you can remember, and you play it against the current experience. So there's necessarily that sense of counterpoint. And by counterpoint I mean things that can't be reduced to homophony. That can't be reduced to a kind of simple reconciliation. My interest in comparative literature is based on the same notion. I think the one thing that I find, I guess, the most—I wouldn't say repellent, but I would say antagonistic—for me is identity. The notion of a *single* identity. And so multiple identity, the polyphony of many voices playing off against each other, without, as I say, the need to reconcile them, just to hold them together, is what my work is all about. More than one culture, more than one awareness, both in its negative and its positive modes. It's basic instinct.

CHAUDHURI: Do you think there are certain cultures and cultural practices that are more encouraging of polyphony?

SAID: Absolutely. For example, in music, one of the things I've been very interested in—and it occupies the last part of the three sections of my book on music, which will appear next year, is a kind of opposition between forms that are based upon development and domination. Like sonata. Sonata form is based on statement, rigorous development, recapitulation. And a lot of things go with that: the symphony, for example, I'm staying within the Western, classical world; certain kinds of opera are based upon this, versus forms that are based upon what I would call developing variations, in which conflict and domination and the overcoming of tension through forced reconciliation is not the issue. There the issue is to prolong, like in a theme and variation, in fugal forms. In polyphony like, in my own tradition, the work of Um Kulthum. She was the most famous classical Arab singer of the twentieth century. Her forms are based upon an inhabiting of time, not trying to dominate it. It's a special relationship with temporality. Or the music of Messiaen, for example, the great French avant-garde composer who I think is divine. You see the dichotomy of that. On the one hand, domination/development; on the other, a kind of proliferation through variation and polyphonic relationship. Those are the culture practices that I think one could use as a typology of *other* culture practices: they're based on the whole idea of community, overlapping vs. coercive domination and enlightenment—the narratives of enlightenment and achievement that are to be found in novels.

CHAUDHURI: I'm very interested in what you say about this idea of inhabiting the time of performance, instead of dominating it.

SAID: Trying to ride it. It's a phrase that comes out of Gerard Manley Hopkins who has a very strange relationship with time in his poetry, especially the last part of his first great poem, *The Wreck of the Deutschland*. There's this whole thing where the question of whether you try to resist the time and erect the structure, or you try to ride time and live inside the time.

CHAUDHURI: I think of theater performance as such, as somehow demanding that the time be inhabited. That is, it makes its own demands, even in the masterful performer, who may try to dominate it, but may not succeed.

SAID: Yes. There really is a difference in musical performance between people who are involved in remaking the music and inhabiting it in that way, as opposed to just dispatching it with efficiency and tremendous technical skill.

ROBINSON: It is also very much in the nature of the exile. I mean, there's a sense that you're either living in the past or living in an ideal future, and the present is such a dangerous equivocal realm where you can't place yourself, and yet you're forced to.

SAID: What's interesting about it is, of course, that you get a sense of its provisionality. That's what I like about it. There's no attempt made to pretend that it's the natural way to do it. It's giving up in a temporal sort of way to that moment.

ROBINSON: Such a balancing act too. Both in terms of time, but also in terms of the exile's relationship to the world. On the one hand, you have the wonderful worldliness or the ability to partake of so many regions. And on the other hand, the enforced isolation. How does one balance between those two?

SAID: I don't know. I don't think there's a formula for it. I think one can call it a kind of traffic between those situations.

ROBINSON: The whole idea of private space connects to that and might be a topic to pursue. I'm often very moved by your idea of the secular intellectual, the secular artist, partaking of the public world in a real, strong way. And yet all the changes that are going on now in Eastern Europe started me thinking about alternatives to that point of view. There was an anecdote of the East German playwright Heiner Müller—he had always been in opposition to the government—who was asked by somebody from Western Europe, "Aren't you excited now that the chains are off, you're able to write your plays that really do take on the political situation, take on the government, what have you . . ." And he said, "No, actually, freedom now means freedom to read Proust, to stay at home in my library." That seems to signal a rediscovery of private space, a retreat from what used to be an enforced secularity.

SAID: Privacy for me is very jealously guarded, because so out of my control is the public dimension of the world I live in, which has to do with a peculiar sensitivity and intransigence of the Palestinian situation. And thinking about it for the last fifteen or twenty years has been very difficult for me to guard. Partly the music has been very much that way, because it's a non-verbal idiom. I've been involved in the thick of these battles over what one says, what one can say, and all that kind of stuff.

The public has been so much with me it's been impossible for me to re-treat into the private. Although, obviously, we all do have a kind of intimate private life. But it's not recoverable for me in any easy way. In the last couple of years—partly because I'm getting older—I've been deeply resentful of how much, quite against my will and intention and any plan that I might have had, public life has usurped so much of my time and effort. By that, I don't mean only politics. I mean teaching, writing, the whole sense of having an audience—sometimes completely unpredictable and against my will. So that inwardness is a very, very rare commodity. I'm not sure that my case is a special case. I think it may be true of more people than we suspect.

CHAUDHURI: Do you think that somehow a certain kind of engaged intellectual is being made to carry more cultural burden than ever before?

SAID: Well, I feel it. I can't speak for others. I find it very hard to speak for others, because I'm in a strange position. I mean, I don't have as much time for reflection. And that's why, for me, the musical experience has been so important. Because it's something that isn't charged and inflected in quite the ways that some of the other things I've been doing have been. I just feel that for the public intellectual it can be extremely debilitating. It's almost paranoid: something you say can be twisted into a thousand different forms or only one different form that can have untold consequences. And in my case, also, I have many quite different and totally impermeable audiences. I write a monthly column in Arabic for one of the largest weeklies in the Arab world. And then the constituencies you have, necessarily, in the world of European languages are also very different. So it's extremely draining, just to try to keep up with it, much less to contribute.

ROBINSON: I wonder if we're going to see some of the models of the intellectual artist change, as is the case already in Eastern Europe, with many who are now retreating from that public role—seeing it as a burden, and now evolving into a secluded hermeticism. A lot of the artists there want to rediscover beauty.

SAID: I understand that perfectly. What we live in, in a way, is what Eliot called a wilderness of mirrors: endless multiplication, without tremendous significance, but just a spinning on. And you just want to say: enough. I don't want too much to do with that. And therefore, one of the things that I find myself thinking about, not only privacy that as we talked about earlier is virtually impossible, but also looking at performance exactly like Gould, who understood this problem, and because of that, therefore, was able to focus and specialize and control what he did to the extent that it wasn't a limitless spinning out. There was this kind of—now this hasn't been written enough about or noted about Gould enough—massive effort on his part from the moment he thought about a work to practicing, preparing, and then performing it, and then recording it. He is one of the unique examples of somebody who was a public performer, whose attempt was to enrich the art of performance by, at the same time, controlling it. There is something, of course, quite cold and deadening about it, at the same time. But on the other hand, it's an interesting model to think about. Not many people do that. Most people tend to be profligate and they want more multiplication. There is a sense in which he wanted that, but he wanted to control it as much as possible. Perhaps because he feared that being on the stage had already showed him what was likely to happen: that he would just become a creature of this public space.

ROBINSON: Genet might be another example, a man who was always preserving the private realm.

SAID: Exactly.

ROBINSON: He was able to understand what went on in the Mideast because of his experience of outsiderhood.

CHAUDHURI: And also in the plays as well.

MARRANCA: Beckett, too.

SAID: But what you feel in Genet and Gould you don't feel in Beckett, that is, that there's a flirting with danger. I've never felt that about Beckett. Who can't admire him—but on the other hand there is a kind of safety in Beckett's work that you don't find in Genet. In Genet you feel the incredible risk involved in all of his drama.

CHAUDHURI: It's also a provocation, isn't it?

MARRANCA: One of the things that strikes me about Beckett is that he's so great a writer and so overpowers theatricality that it's not necessary ever to see him performed. But Genet gains by being in the theater. . . . We've been talking about the private moment and the Eastern European situation, the sense of aloneness and solitude that somehow seems to be demanded after so strong a public life.

The death of Beckett set many people wondering about just what will come after Beckett, of course. And in some ways it seems it's the end of the universal playwright and the international dramatic repertoire. Also, *because* culture has become so public and so much a part of spectacle, and where there's so little emphasis on the private moment, it seems to me that drama, which is such a private, reflective, intimate form anyway, is falling further and further down in the hierarchy of forms experienced by serious people who would ordinarily have gone to theater, those who read serious novels and go to the opera. People like Havel and Fugard became known not necessarily because they are great playwrights. They got into the international repertoire because of their politics and their symbolic value. It seems more and more that drama will be a kind of local knowledge. And in the theater we see the ascendancy of spectacle, of performance, rather than drama. International performers like, say, Laurie Anderson or Wilson, make things that can travel in culture.

SAID: Or Peter Brook. . . . But even Laurie Anderson, and Brook in particular—what underlies them, also, paradoxically is a kind of modesty of means. It's not like a traveling opera. It has, in fact, a kind of easily packed baggage, which you can transport from country to country and do with a small repertory, the same pieces. But I think one thing that you didn't mention about drama—that in the Palestinian situation, for example, which is the only one I can speak about with any assurance—is that the drama has a testimonial value, which is different from symbolic, when you talk about symbolic. That is to say—take Joseph Papp canceling that Palestinian play, *The Story of Kufur Shamma*, last summer. It wasn't because of the content of the play, it was Palestinians talking about *their* experience. *That* was what was threatening. And that's why he had to cancel it. So on that level it is local knowledge, but a local knowledge that is frequently engaged in translocal issues. Things that are of interest to other places. I suppose the burden placed upon the playwright and the performer is somehow to translate this local situation into an idiom that is continguous to and touches other situations.

MARRANCA: In that way, I suppose, drama can travel. But so much of it now, when you compare the theater of the last four, five, or six decades—what used to be considered international and of interest to an international audience—no longer appears on Broadway. For example, when was the last, say, German or Hungarian or French play on Broadway? In this sense the international repertoire is shrinking.

SAID: Although, I'll tell you, Bonnie, I was in Delphi last summer giving a talk at an international conference on Greek tragedy. I talked about Wagner, I believe. Every night there was a performance of a play in the theater at Delphi. And I was there for two performances, the second of which was extraordinary, the performance by Wajda's troupe of a Polish-language *Antigone* . . .

ROBINSON: I saw it in Poland.

SAID: You saw it in Poland. Well, I saw it in Delphi. And the audience was entirely Greek . . . modern Greeks, obviously. It was overwhelming. It seemed to me to have there a peculiar mix of things. It was the "OK cultural festival," it was the antique representation of self that was acceptable to the powers-that-be, because it's sponsored by the Greek government which is in a great crisis at the moment. It was an occasion for the local folk. OK, all that. But in addition, it was for me a very powerful theatrical experience. I don't know which performance you saw, because there were several versions. Where did you see it?

ROBINSON: In Krakow in '85. It was a very bad time, politically, for Poland.

SAID: Were there transformations of the chorus?

ROBINSON: Yes. The chorus changed throughout the play—moving from bureaucrats—maybe Parliament members—to protesting students to, finally, shipyard workers, like those from Gdansk who started Solidarity. In a Polish theater, it becomes extremely powerful. Actually, it's an event that makes me question or at least want to take issue with your idea, Bonnie, about the universality of a play, and mourning the loss of Beckett.

SAID: No, I think what she's talking about—which I'm interested in—the great master theatrical talent that produces, I have to keep using the word over and over again, a masterwork of the sort that created the nineteenth-century repertory theater, that continues into the late symbolic tragedies of Ibsen and Strindberg, and then moves into Brecht and then Beckett. There's a pedigree here that you're alluding to: people who dominate the stage. The model is one of domination. I don't regret its end, to be perfectly honest with you, because of a lot of what goes with it. In the same way that you could say, well what about the great—think of this—what about the great Austro-Germanic symphonic tradition that begins with Haydn, goes through Mozart, Beethoven, Schumann, Brahms, I suppose Wagner's in there a little bit, Mahler, Bruckner, Schoenberg . . . and then what? Nothing. It ends. And you get these local nationalists, you know, Bartók. I mean, it took place, but we can live without it. It can be respected and memorialized in various ways, but I'm not so sure of that, given the damage to other surrounding clumps it overshadows and dominates. It produces a certain canon or canonicity.

ROBINSON: Yeah, and aren't we all trashing the canon!

SAID: Not trashing. It isn't the be-all-and-end-all, is what I'm saying.

MARRANCA: I understand your point of view about attacking universality, of course, but the issue is that in drama there's almost nothing else. There are plenty of musical traditions to follow. There are plenty of great novels that are breaking out of the mode and being enjoyed by wide groups and nationalities.

SAID: Yes, that's true.

MARRANCA: But with drama, the whole thing collapses, because if there's no international repertoire, then it's a gradual decreasing of the form itself. And what's left are just the bestsellers, the topical plays that somehow travel, and then the classics. But maybe two of Ibsen, or a few of Brecht. What I'm saying is the other traditions are so much richer, and the repertories are so wide, but if you begin to have a form which worldwide audiences lose interest in—in terms of the new—then I think it's a problem for the form, and that that's different than, say, the situation in music.

ROBINSON: But isn't that a Romantic idea, that of an international work of art?

MARRANCA: But they still exist in art, if you look at paintings from many, many countries, a lot of it even looks largely the same, and there are good and bad works. I see nothing wrong with large groups of people in different cultures around the world appreciating the same work. That always happens in terms of fiction, for example.

SAID: The way you describe it, it certainly sounds special and peculiar to the drama. But why is it?

MARRANCA: One of the things I hinted at before is that what we are seeing now are international spectacles found in several cultural festivals, works by Brook or Laurie Anderson, whose recent piece can be just as accessible in Japan or Western Europe or Brazil, or someplace else. Often we're seeing a kind of internationalization of performance. When I use the word "performance," I mean something different from the theater. It's not textbound, it doesn't deal with a play. Performance work is often highly technological, it reflects a certain transfer of pop imagery and music.

SAID: Recognizable and commodified styles.

MARRANCA: Exactly. And they are understood by people all over the world now, because of the international youth culture. And that has unseated drama somewhat . . .

SAID: And also because of film and television and all the apparatus of the culture industry.

MARRANCA: So that the great theaters now tend to remain in their own countries and build their repertoires on the classics, redo them, and are rejuvenated by new people. But we don't see this travel in theater that we're seeing in video or visual arts, or fiction, or "performance" as a genre in itself.

SAID: And, of course, in music you find it in the cult of the traveling maestro or the celebrated pianist or the important diva and tenor, and so on and so forth.

ROBINSON: Maybe theater is less suited to this kind of travel because of the holdover of the idea that a play should somehow address the issues of the people in front of it, the audiences. It's the most socially connected of the arts, of course. And I would think people would be reluctant to give up that possibility of engagement that the theater provides, in a much more immediate way than art, music, or TV.

CHAUDHURI: There's another way of looking at this. There has always been this dimension of locality in the theater, this connection to a specific time and place. And it's always been special to the drama. Now, for all its power technology is not going to promote a better means of a direct collaboration with people than the theater event. So that this "local knowledge" characteristic may be what will save the theater, and give it its future.

SAID: But she mourns it. I think you really do have a nostalgia for the great figures. Or the great forms. It's a kind of Lukácian, early Lukács—you know, *The Soul and Its Forms* . . . a kind of Lukácian forlornness and melancholy, which is there. I think you're right. I'm not saying you're wrong.

MARRANCA: To tell you the truth, I'm more interested in the idea of performance than I am in drama, with a very few exceptions. Of course, as a publisher, knowing what it's like to sell books worldwide, on a very practical basis I find a loss of interest in drama.

SAID: What does that mean? You've lost interest in the drama and you watch the performance. In other words, it would matter more to you that Vanessa Redgrave was acting in a play, rather than the play was, say, *Macbeth,* or something like that. Is that what you mean by performance?

MARRANCA: No. I mean something else. I've lost interest in conventionalized stagings of drama. In that case, I would rather sit home with a play and not see it. Though I take a larger interest in performances such as Wilson's work, and some avant-garde performance.

CHAUDHURI: That's really a question of quality, isn't it?

MARRANCA: Yes.

SAID: See, the other part of it is, and I think it's very important for people like us, who are interested in these issues and questions, not simply to celebrate the avant-garde—that is to say, the novel, or the exciting and unusual that come along in the cases of Peter Sellars or Wilson—but also, to stimulate greater dissatisfaction and anger on the part of audiences who now sit sheepishly through unacceptably boring reproductions of masterpieces. That's the part that I find the most puzzling of all. Why is it that the level of critical sensibility has sunk so low? The threshhold for pain is so high, that people can sit through abysmal "conventional" reproductions of classical masterpieces in the theater or in opera or in music rather than experience something quite new in a contemporary work or a dangerous or innovative restaging of a classical work. I don't understand that. Do you understand it?

MARRANCA: Well, certainly part of it, but not all of it, is that the commentary is so bad on the papers of note—that's one major issue.

SAID: Well, there it becomes an important thing to talk about. This is where some of Gramsci's analysis of culture is very important, where you can look at the papers of note and the people who write commentary as sort of organic intellectuals for theater interests. In other words, they are advance guard, in the military sense—advance guard organizers of opinion and manufacturers of consent for important interests in the theater, whose role is to colonize and narcotize and lobotomize audiences into accepting certain kinds of conventions as the norm. I think that's an important part of one's work: to raise dissatisfaction at this time.

MARRANCA: You know, the other thing is that, unlike the art audience, for example, which always wants to see something new, the theater audience and music audience basically want to see the greatest hits in familiar settings. And so the audiences are fundamentally different, even though they might be the same people.

ROBINSON: But sometimes that struggling with those greatest hits can be very fruitful, and writers are doing it all the time. Hofmannsthal will deal with the *Electra* story as handed down and absorb it into a creation of his own. Heiner Müller will write *Hamletmachine* in order to kill *Hamlet*.

SAID: Or, in some cases, to keep adapting to the changing conditions of performance imposed on him by the patrons.

ROBINSON: It seems like there are two ways for contemporary artists to deal with this burden or oppressiveness of the classic tradition, and the canon. One is just to keep pushing it aside and write or compose new work. And then the other one—Hofmannsthal, Heiner Müller—is to try to absorb it and then remake it somehow, to kind of neutralize it, recharge it in a subversive way.

SAID: I'm of the second opinion. In all of the discussions that have been going on in literary studies about the canon, and the whole question of the Western tradition, it seems to me that one of the great fallacies, in my view, has been the one that suggests that you, first of all, show how the canon is the result of a conspiracy—a sort of white male cabal—of people who, for example, turned Hawthorne into one of the great cult figures of American literature and prevented a whole host of, for example, more popular women writers of the time, or regional writers, and so on. . . . Therefore what is enjoined upon holders of this view is you push aside Hawthorne and you start reading these other people. But that is to supplant one canon by another, which, it seems to me, really reinforces the whole idea of canon and, of course, all of the authority that goes with it. That's number one. Number two—half of this is my education and half of this is my age and predilection—I'm interested in the canon. I'm very conservative in the sense that I think that there is something to be said, at least on the level of preference and pleasure, for aspects of work that has persisted and endured and has acquired and accreted to it a huge mass of differing interpretations, ranging from hatred to reverence. It's something that I find enriching as a part of knowledge. So I'm not as willing as a lot of people to scuttle it. My view is to assimilate to canons these other contrapuntal lines.

You could take the extreme view of Benjamin: every document of civilization is also a document of barbarity. You can show—and I've tried to show it in this book that I've been writing on cultural imperialism for ten years—that the great monuments (well, I did it in the *Aida* case) of culture are not any less monuments for their, in the extreme version, complicity with rather sordid aspects of the world. Or, in the less extreme case, for their participation, their engagement in social, historical processes. I find that interesting. I'm less willing to toss them overboard and say, "Let's focus on the new." I mean, I find the idea of novelty in and of itself doesn't supply me with quite enough nourishment.

ROBINSON: The whole canon becomes an incredibly sharp weapon for a non-Western writer, too. Somebody like Soyinka can take *The Balcony,* or *The Bacchae,* or *Threepenny Opera* and rewrite them as parables of colonialism.

SAID: And not only that, but in the best instances—I think more interesting than Soyinka is the work of the Sudanese novelist Tayeb Salih. He's written several novels, but his masterpiece is a novel called *The Season of Migration to the North*—it came out in the late sixties—that is quite consciously a work that is reacting to, writing back to, Conrad's *Heart of Darkness.* This is a story, not of a white man who comes to Africa, but a black man who goes to Europe. And the result is, on one level, of course, a reaction to Conrad. In other words, this is a postcolonial fable of what happens when a black man goes to London and wreaks havoc upon a whole series of English women. There's a kind of sexual fable. But if you look at it more deeply, it not only contains within it the history of decolonization and reaction to Western imperialism, but it also, in my opinion, deepens the tragedy by showing this man's reactive revenge, which to many readers in the Third World, in the Arab and African world, is a just revenge. But Salih does it fresh because it's futile, pathetic, and ultimately tragic. Because it reinforces the cycle of isolation as insufficiency of the politics of identity. It is not enough to just be a black wreaking havoc on a white, there's another world that you have to live in. And in that sense, it's a rich and compelling work because it dramatizes the limitations of Conrad. And I'm second to none in my admiration for Conrad, but this is a quite amazing type of thing which is in the novel, which is quite powerful in its own sense—it's in Arabic not in English—depends on the Conrad novel, but is independent of it at the same time. It's quite fascinating.

ROBINSON: And that may be a solution, as it were, to the whole problem of locality of a work of art. Because what you are describing can be both a very potent work in a local context, but it's also an intercultural work.

SAID: Absolutely. And that's where I finally disagree with Bonnie's idea. In the implied contrast between the local and the universal, I think the local is more interesting than the universal. It depends where you look at it from. If you look at it from the point of view of the colonized world, as Fanon says, the universal is always achieved at the expense of the native. I'll give you a perfect example—look at the case of Camus. Camus is the writer who, practically more than anyone in modern French culture, represents universality. A more careful reading of the work shows that in every instance of his major fiction, and even the collections of stories, most of them are set in Algeria. Yet, they're not *of* Algeria. They're always read as parables of the German occupation of France. You look even more carefully at that and you look for the point of view of Algerian independence, which was achieved after Camus's death in 1962—and of course, Genet answers to this, because Genet was involved in the same issue in *The Screens*. If you look at that and you see what Camus was doing throughout his work, he was using the cultural discourse of the French Lycée—which gives rise to universalism and the human condition and the resistance to Nazism and Fascism and all the rest of it—as a way of blocking the emergence of an independent Algeria. . . . It seems to me, *there* is the importance of local knowledge which you bring to bear upon this text. And put it back in its situation and locale. And there it doesn't become any less interesting, it becomes more interesting, precisely because of this discrepancy between its universal reach and scope on the one hand, and reputation; and on the other, its rather more complicit local circumstances. But maybe we're making too much of it . . .

MARRANCA: I think in some sense we're talking about dissimilar things. Literature and the general secular intellectual life lead a more ongoing life in terms of debate and internal politics than drama does. I simply wanted to point out, if drama was no longer going to add in some sense to an international repertoire, and we were only going to have a local drama, which I value also, then that means something entirely different. For example, in drama we don't really have secular theater intellectuals in the sense that literature does. Almost all discourse and dialogue and debate on theater issues is either in the reviewing mechanisms of the popular papers, which don't have any kind of interesting debate going on internally, or in marginalized journals like our own, or in the academic world. So that theater issues are not brought to bear on general cultural-political issues in the same way that other subjects are treated now, in science or in literature. So I think that this kind of loss is more serious for theater than it would be in the novel.

SAID: I think you're absolutely right, and I think—yes, I see your point. That's a much larger way of putting it.

CHAUDHURI: About the canon—this idea of not just throwing over one canon and putting another one in its place—it really seems that what's missing in that approach is that many people are not looking at how these things are taught and how they're presented. They're really only looking at what is taught.

SAID: Yes, exactly, although "what" is important, also. The exclusion of certain "whats" is very interesting.

CHAUDHURI: But it's almost as if one doesn't want to give up something deeper, which is certain models of evaluating texts . . .

SAID: I call them models of veneration, and that's what they are.

CHAUDHURI: That veneration is transferred to something else, and it leaves you in the same abject position vis-à-vis the text or the art work or whatever.

SAID: Well, it is one of the constitutive problems of academic debate in general, but it's basically unanchored in real engagement with the real world. It's largely theoretical. So the "what," on the one level, is equally important. It's a claim to certain kinds of authority and turf, and so on. But the "how," you know, the "how" becomes relatively weightless, in a certain sense, it becomes one method among others. I'll give you an example of what I'm trying to say. Look at the result of all the massive infusion that American literary, and I suppose, cultural studies in general, have received through "theory" in the last thirty years: structuralism, poststructuralism, deconstruction, semiotics, Marxism, feminism, all of it. Effectively they're all weightless, I mean they all represent academic choices and a lot of them are not related to the circumstances that originally gave rise to them. For example, Third World studies in the university are a very different thing from Soyinka or Salih in their own immediately post-colonial situation trying to write a narrative of the experience. You know how sometimes a critic like N'gugi talking about decolonizing the mind is one thing for somebody who's been in prisons, lived through the whole problems of neo-imperialism, the problems of the native language vs. English, etc. They're very different things than somebody deciding, well, I'm going to specialize in decolonization or the discourse of colonialism. So that's a very great problem.

CHAUDHURI: The academy is actively rendering them weightless . . .

SAID: In a certain sense you can't completely do away with that, because the university is a kind of utopian place. To a certain extent, these things should happen. Perhaps the disparity between the really powerful and urgent originary circumstances of a cultural method, and its later transmutation as a theoretical choice in the university, is too great.

CHAUDHURI: Do you think it should remain utopian? Maybe that's part of the problem, that this is a model that has outgrown its usefulness.

SAID: I think that's where we are right now. We're watching a very interesting transformation. Most students, I think, the good students here, my students—and I know this from direct contact with them—are really no longer interested in theory. They're really interested in these historical, cultural contests that have characterized the history of the late twentieth century. Between racism and imperialism, colonialism, various forms of authority, various types of liberation and independence as they are reflected in culture, in aesthetic forms, in discourses, and so on. So that's where I go. The problem is how you relate that to social change at a time when it seems everything is now moving away from the contests that determined the history of the twentieth century hitherto—the contests between socialism and capitalism, and so on. So it's a very troubling moment. I think the important thing is to be exploratory.

MARRANCA: You know, in fact, in the little piece in *The Guardian* that you wrote, you mention that you felt somehow the history of philosophy and politics, and general drift of intellectual life, was really almost inadequate to deal with the new situations.

SAID: I think it is. I think it certainly is.

MARRANCA: What directions might this view of the arts and sciences coming together somehow in some new understanding take? Where would you like to take it in your world?

SAID: Without getting too specific and detailed, I think that if you take a general thing that you've been interested in, interculturalism, I think that's obviously where it's going. That is to say, various types of integration between formerly disparate or different realms, like politics, history, and aesthetics. But rather than just leaving it at that, it seems to me that new kinds of formations seem to be particularly interesting and important. One would be relationships of interdependence and overlapping. We've had a tendency, you see, to think of experiences in national terms. We say there's the Polish experience, there's the French experience, there's the Haitian experience, there's the Brazilian experience. It seems to me that that's pretty much over, where one could give a certain amount of fidelity and attention to basic national identities. What's interesting is the way the national identities have historically, in fact—and the present moment facilitates that—interacted and depended upon each other. I mean the relationship between Brazil and North America is very, very dramatic now in the situation of the rain forests. The relationship between North Africa and the European metropolis is very dramatic now because of the presence of a large number of Muslim immigrants in France.

What you begin to realize is the universality, therefore, not of stabilities, which have been the prevailing norm in cultural studies, but of migrations: these massive transversals of one realm into another. That seems to me an entirely new subject matter. Refugee studies versus the studies of stable cultural institutions which have characterized the paradigms of the social sciences and the humanities of the past. That would be one major thing. Another would be the study of what I call integrations and interdependence versus the studies dominated by nationalities and national traditions. The conflict between emergent transnational forces like Islam which is a subcontinental presence, it's an Arab presence, it's now a European presence. There's a total reconfiguration of the cultural scene that can only be understood, in my opinion, historically. You could see elements of it already in the conflict between Europe and the Orient, for example, which I talked about twelve or thirteen years ago.

MARRANCA: Do you have any thoughts on interculturalism as it relates to performance or any of the other kinds of things you might want to take to your work, besides the *Aida* model of doing theater history?

SAID: Not at this stage, no, because I'm so mired in *contested* regions between cultures. I'm very much, I'm afraid, marked by that. In other words, I'm really a creature whose current interest is very much controlled by the conflict between the culture in which I was born and the culture in which I live at present. Which is really quite a strange phenomenon. It's not just that they're different, you know, but there's a war going on and I'm involved on both sides of that. So it's very difficult for me to talk about interculturalism, which would suggest a kind of sanity and calm reflectiveness.

MARRANCA: Do you think of interculturalism as a kind of Orientalism?

SAID: Well, it can be. Yes, absolutely. Because I think there's a whole range of what is acceptable and what is not acceptable. We haven't gotten to the stage yet, I don't think, of being able to talk about it in an uninflected way, in a way that doesn't bear the scars of contests between the North and the South, or the East and the West. I mean, the geographical configuration of the world is still very strongly inscribed, at least in my vision of things.

ROBINSON: Drawing out of what's just been said, it seems that there's good interculturalism and bad interculturalism. But after I read *Orientalism* a great paralysis set in.

SAID: Sorry about that.

ROBINSON: Every time I consider or reflect on another culture, I feel the "power" position coming into relief. But is the alternative to that power just a greater distance or isolationism? I don't want that.

SAID: No, no, no. I don't think it's possible. You know, I think one of the great flaws of *Orientalism* is the sense that it may have communicated that there is no alternative to that, which is a sort of hands-off sort of thing. That's not what I would imply. And I think, at the very end I say something like that. That there is a kind of "already given," you know, a sort of messing up and involvement of everyone with everyone else. It's just that I would like to think that the inequalities, as between, say, a native informant and a white ethnographic eye, weren't so great. I don't know how to talk about this without seeming to congratulate myself, but it was interesting, to me at any rate, that *Orientalism*—partly because I think that it was already in the air—seemed to have released a lot of quite interesting work that went way beyond it. It instigated a certain kind of self-consciousness about cultural artifacts that had been considered to be impervious to this kind of analysis. And the irony is it didn't make them less interesting, it made them more interesting. So I think the history of Orientalism—I don't mean the book, I mean the problem—is really the history of human—how shall I put it?—human meddling, without which we can't live.

Look, any time you globalize, let's say East vs. West, you can come up with convincing formulas that always suggest the triumph of the West. That's why Naipaul is successful. I mean, that's the basis for the Naipaul appeal. He says the world is made up of people who invent telephones and those who use them. Where are the people who use telephones? We don't know that. See, you can always fall into that trap; the trap that C. L. James never fell into, because he said if you're a white man you can say you have Beethoven, and the black man's not supposed to listen to Beethoven, he's supposed to listen to Calypso. That's a trap you can't fall into. You've got to be able to make the distinctions and use what you want and think of it as part of the possession of all mankind or humankind. I don't know how to get to that point without waging the struggle on some very local and clearly circumscribed level.

So on one level it seems to me that there's a need for historical understanding of various contests. That's why I don't believe in "literary studies." I don't believe in the study of English literature by itself. It should be looked at with West Indian literature, with American literature, with French literature, with African literature, with Indian—you understand what I'm saying? The deep historicization of the circumstances of production of culture and along with that, an acute understanding of the extent to which every cultural document contains within it a history of a contest of rulers and ruled, of leaders and led. And third, that what we require is a deep understanding of where we would like to go.

Discussion with Bonnie Marranca,
Marc Robinson, and Una Chaudhuri,
Performing Arts Journal, New York, 1991

SIX
_____

CRITICISM AND
THE ART OF POLITICS

*This interview was done by two former students who had gone on to consid-
erable eminence and had remained friends with me. It was one of my first attempts to look reflectively at my life as a young man in the Arab world and to
connect it with my later intellectual and political development.*   E.W.S.

*Edward, could you tell us about Cairo and its strategic importance for
you culturally, politically, both in your childhood development and also
as a kind of pivot of your metropolitan thought?*

Working backwards rather than starting with my early years there,
certainly Cairo has always seemed to be the great alternative city for
someone like myself who spent a lot of time in big Western cities, especially New York, but also London and Paris. But lurking in the background is this figure of a gigantic and, at least from my point of view,
undigested, metropolitan presence in the eastern Mediterranean which I
think I first became conscious of as a kind of antipode to Alexandria.
Both in literature and in my own biography, Alexandria had been the
place where one went for a window to Europe, given the presence there
of foreign communities, great numbers of Greeks, French, Italians, Armenians, and Jews. So powerfully did they impress me as populations
who existed principally in Alexandria, that even today I find it quite
amazing that there are Greeks in Greece, Italians in Italy, and so on. And
of course Alexandria is in literary terms a city with much more resonance in the West than Cairo. Yet I never felt very comfortable with
Alexandria. It just didn't strike me as having the kind of spirit and
sporty, irregular coherence somehow that Cairo did. So there was this
sense of Cairo as an alternative, *my* alternative.

And then Cairo, in my prolonged thinking about it, breaks down into two cities. One the ancient city, the city of the Sphinx and the Pyramids and that whole pharaonic dimension highlighted by modern Western interest in Egypt, especially in the period from Sadat on. Sadat deliberately stressed this aspect by exporting the King Tut exhibition to the U.S., thereby splitting off ancient Egypt in a certain sense, and making Egypt a commodity for mass Western attention in a new way. But then there is the other city which, I note again, was undigested as a whole, nondescript and incoherent for outsiders, except that it was very, very factual in my thought as housing Islamic, Arab, African, anti-colonial experiences, parts of which have never been truly accessible to the West. Yet even within that city, you could separate off the colonial city from its main body, and get a much smaller, more specialized locale made up of sites, for example, like the island on which I grew up, Zamalek, an essentially European enclave where families like my own lived: Levantine, colonial, minority, privileged. And then there are other sections of Cairo, like Garden City, where the embassies were located, where the British embassy was the focus of the central controlling power that was considered to be the counterbalance to the palace during the years of the British occupation from the 1880s until 1952. The British ambassador was the great figure of this site—the high commissioner whose embodiment was Lord Cromer along with all those people who opposed the Egyptian nationalist movement. But of course there was always Arab Islamic Cairo, teeming with all sorts of cultural riches on the everyday level in districts like Gamaliya, Shubra, Bulaq, Ataba, Bab el Louk.

Another thing that I became aware of fairly recently, say within the last fifteen years, was the sense of a very powerful current of thought located in Cairo in which the whole question of Egyptian cultural identity, transmitted historically, was formulated. There is a literature on this topic that I also came to know a relatively short time ago. One of the important figures in this discourse is Hussein Fawzi, a geographer who was later rector (I think) of the University of Alexandria. Anwar Abdel Malek makes very ingenious use of Fawzi in *Egypt Military Society*. I also got a book the other day by an Egyptian parliamentarian called Milad Hanna, in which he too develops the notion of an Egyptian personality and Egyptian culture as a separate thing from the Egypt known to the West, and the work of many coherently discrete centuries. A tremendous emphasis is placed upon the cultural integrity and distinctiveness of Egyptian culture and of Egypt itself as a phenomenon, altogether separate from the Arab environment. Some of the rhetoric is partly a xenophobic reaction to the Arabism of the Nasser period, Nasser being the leader who appeared to have introduced Egypt into the Arab world as its focal point. So there is a retreat from this in the literature I'm referring to, but that isn't all there is to it.

To go back to the early years of my awareness of Cairo: I grew up there, spending a large part of my youth in the place but strangely not as an Egyptian. I certainly never felt myself to be Egyptian, which is one of the perverse things about the city, that it allows you to be there as an alien and yet not feel injuriously discriminated against in any way, nor to feel the hostility of what might have been a culturally xenophobic, deeply enclosed and secret personality. I never felt *that,* but at the same time I also always felt that I wasn't *of* the place. Not because I wasn't in fact, but because in Cairo one felt the presence of a very complex urban and cultural system, which was what you would give the names of Cairo or Egypt to. I never belonged to it, even though I was, and remain, close to it. This is quite special. I've always been interested in how that system is inscribed in the language, in the Cairo version of the Egyptian dialect. It emerges in films and later in television drama, radio, journalistic writing and even the popular literature of the place, with which I became acquainted over the years.

What I am really trying to say is that there is a peculiar paradox in a city at once a great metropolitan center, a great alternative site (1) to the powerful contained interests of the metropolitan West in the Orient and (2) to Alexandria, the Levantine city par excellence; and yet, most impressively, Cairo is a city that doesn't force upon you some sort of already-existing totality. In other words, there's a certain relaxation in the idea of Cairo—at least the way I've gradually grasped it—which makes it possible for all manner of identities to exist unhurriedly within this whole. The idea is an indistinct one but you can actually experience it. All kinds of histories, narratives, and presences intersect, coexist in what I suggest is a "natural" way. For me that defines the pleasurably urban—not Paris, the vigorously planned city as an Imperial Center, nor London, with its carefully displayed monumentality, but rather a city providing a relaxed interchange between various incomplete, partially destroyed histories that still exist and partially do not, competed over, contested, but somehow existing in this rather, in my view, fascinating way. Cairo has come to symbolize for me, therefore, a much more attractive form of the way in which we can look at history, not necessarily to look at it as something neatly manageable by categories or by the inclusiveness of systems and totalizing processes, but rather through the inventory that can be reconstructed. Cairo requires a certain effort of reconstruction. I'll give you a further example here.

When I was in Cairo recently, I was doing a piece on the great belly dancer Tahia Carioca. One of the things I wanted to do was to get documentation for writing the article. I wanted to have pictures. So where would I get pictures? Now the woman herself, Tahia Carioca, was recently divorced. Her last husband, who was thirty years younger than she, left her, and in the process took all her property. She lives in a little apartment by herself, and apparently he took all of her films, all her prints, as well as all her pictures. She has nothing. So I went to the central cinema archives in downtown Cairo with a filmmaker friend of mine, a Lebanese woman who makes documentaries. The experience that I am about to narrate could only happen in Cairo. We went there together, and we walked into this apartment in an office building in downtown Cairo, which is about a block from where my father's office used to be, and I said, well, I'm looking for documentation on the films of Tahia Carioca—I was told by Tahia herself that she made 190 films— a lot of films!—and discover that literally nothing is left of that record in any printed source. I earlier had called the place and asked for what stuff might be available at the archive, and the woman who had put together something for me had gone to visit a friend in the hospital but the file was locked in her drawer, so I couldn't get it. So I said, "Well, surely there must be a bigger file from which all these things came." The man there said I was welcome to look at the library, so we walked down to it. They have a library which is roughly the size of mine here, and my guide said, "Here they are. There are the books." I said, "How can I find out what films she made?" He said, "What do you mean, like a list?" I said, "No, a catalogue with a bibliography of films." He said he wouldn't know and so he asked a lady who seemed to be the librarian. I said to her, "Have you got a list of films?" She said, "Films of what?" I said films, for example, like Tahia's famous *Le'bet il sit*. She said, "No, no we don't do it that way." I said, "Well what way do you do it?" She said, "We have a list of films that are made in Egypt." "Fine," I said, "could we have that?" She said, "We only go up to 1927," and gave me this volume. It's arranged in a completely haphazard way. And then I turned to the man, who seemed to know who I was (the man who had been leading me around), and said, "What do you do?" He said, "I'm a film critic and I work here." "Do you have any pictures?" He replied, "Yes, I think I do have a picture of Tahia." He said he was doing a study on the Mahfouz novels that had been turned into films. So he goes into his office and pulls out a sheaf of pictures, about sixty or so, and we start leafing through them, and we finally find one. She apparently made a film based on one of Mahfouz's middle period novels, so he had her picture in his drawer. I said, "What's the name of the film?" He didn't really know. He turned the picture over and there were some notes on the back—presumably including the film's name—but he couldn't read his own handwriting. And he said he'd find out for me. I said, "When was the film made?" But again he didn't know.

What I felt was a sense of routine muddlement and also of utter nonchalance. How could it be that he didn't know any of the things I was inquiring about? But this is the situation people live in. If you really want to resurrect and reconstruct Cairo's history, you probably could. The proof is that the woman who was with me, the Lebanese lady who was very upset that I didn't get what I wanted, actually went back to the archive and spent a day, quite generously, to help me. She compiled a list of some eighty or ninety of Tahia's films and just gave them to me. It was all done by hand. There were no computers. But much of it is there and even though it isn't, you actually *feel* that it's all there. The question is how to recover it, and that is more or less an individual quest, because the social and the collective enterprise of compiling, let's say, an official history of Egyptian film, which until recently was the central cinematic experience of the whole Arab world, is just not done. It couldn't happen. That infrastructure and organization doesn't exist. What exists instead are these individual enterprises which are allied to each other, undertaken for different reasons but sharing common interests.

There is a kind of entropy but with no sense of loss.

Yes, no sense of loss. I feel the loss because I'm coming from here and I have a deadline and all that sort of thing, but in the economy of the city, that's not the way it works.

What about collectivity, political collectivity, for example?

There are all kinds of interconnecting and interlocking and sometimes, I suppose, competing collectivities. Of course many are the ones that are based on syndicates. Egypt, after all, is modern, and Cairo is a very modern city in many respects, much more highly developed than anywhere else in the Arab world. There is a developed sense of syndical groups and interests—the cinema people, the writer's groups, the lawyers, and then on down through the various vocational and artisanal groups: some of them have a millennium of history behind them. Cutting across them are the new Islamic groups with their own infrastructure, their own economy, their own political and social organizations, education, etc. And then you have the state groups, the official institutes and establishments, say, the people's assembly and the ruling party with its congress. And then I suppose you have at the local level the groups that exist in quarters in Cairo which have attained an identity that is in some instances hundreds of years old. The area of Khan el Khalili, for example. One of the people whom I know quite well in Egypt now is a novelist called Gamal al-Ghitani, who is a younger disciple of Mahfouz. Like Mahfouz, he writes about one district of Cairo called Gamaliya in such works as *Zayni Barakat*. There is a whole literature and consciousness of the area which is itself a collectivity—the coffeehouses and the shoemaker and the brassmaker—a vocational artisanal community. All these exist and they function. How they function all together I have no idea, but they do and you can see they work in the economy of the city. Of course, dominating the whole thing is not only the Azhar and the mosque of Sayidna Hussein, but also such harsher patterns as those provided by the connection between the state and its dependency upon the embassies, the Western powers. You have the imperial dependency relationship, and then you have this vast and complex honeycomb of connections that exist in Cairo on the local and regional level. And then intersecting with them, the Islamic and official parties of opposition as well as the various Sufi brotherhoods. It's an extraordinary thing to contemplate.

The thing that is slightly more difficult for me is the language, Arabic, particularly spoken Arabic. For me—this may be a distortion on my part because I first heard that language before in a sense becoming literate, being able to read it—the language of Cairo, which is a spoken dialect, is quite unique to Cairo. It is extremely eloquent, very concise, clear. It is totally different from any other Arab dialect. And in a certain sense it is a kind of lingua franca, because the radio, to a certain degree the largely colloquial radio of talk shows, the television, film above all, which went through all the Arab world, are all in this dialect. That suggests to me a certain common currency which is then itself connected to the hieratic language of the Koran and the state religion, Islam. The Cairo dialect is also connected to a classical Arabic literary history, and then more particularly to the tradition of Egypt itself, which has its own literary tradition, its own great writers, its own canon, particularly in the modern period. It was very important for me emotionally when Mahfouz won the Nobel Prize. He's one of the summits of this complex urban configuration which is Cairo and which played a tremendous role, not only in the Arab world, but in my own excavations of modern culture.

To stay on the subject of Cairo, could you talk about the autobiographical novel you are writing about your youth?

I've been thinking about it as a memoir, and I've just recently signed a contract to produce it. But what it is exactly is something I really can't talk about now. It's a text that I think exists only in performance and not something I can easily describe. But it would certainly be an attempt to connect, well I'll tell you, the, shall we say, the imaginary and fictional resonances. A lot is based on the following: in much of my childhood there was in a certain sense, an unknowing, a kind of unselfconscious participation without knowing too much, for all kinds of reasons that have to do with my schooling and my family, the restrictions, the sense of belonging and a little series of compartments that led me into the colonial avenues and finally brought me to this country. There was a constant narrowing from the English system into the Western cultural orbit. Part of what I am trying to do now is to go back and to open up the things that I didn't know then, to see if I can do that, since I can only do it through speculation and memory and imagination. The interesting thing about this project is that the discipline that I've imposed on myself as I write the book is that I don't want it to be a book that reads back into those years a political awareness or political program that I have now, if you see what I mean. I don't want to do that. I want to try and do the Cairo-Jerusalem-Beirut axis, which is the one I grew up in, in a pre-political way in which all the political realities of the present nevertheless are somehow there in a figured or implicit form, held in suspension.

Could you talk about your sense of Nasserism in your youth? How acute was that?

Nasserism as such was to me a later development. Nasser came to power after I left Egypt to go to boarding school in the U.S., and therefore I always saw Nasserism through an optic that was at one remove from the society. My family remained in Egypt well after 1952, but, for example, the revolution of 1952 took place while I was here in this country, so that Nasser was always somebody I apprehended through his speeches, through reading about his exploits in the Western media. He was of course universally condemned, deplored here. My experience of Nasserism was one which you might say was already mediated and slightly distanced by a political ideology, which in a certain sense Nasser brought. That is what Nasser in fact introduced, not only into the lives of people in the Middle East but in my own life. Looking back, it's fascinating to me to think through my own relation to the early years of Nasserism, say from 1953 to 1960, which were the last years that I went to Egypt as a sometime resident because I never went there between 1960 and 1975. For that whole period of time, fifteen years, I just never set foot in the country.

During the years from 1955 to 1960, Nasser introduced the nationalization laws—these directly affected my family's business. One of the announced targets of Nasser's "Arab socialism" was the foreign merchant class to which my father belonged and of which he was a great pillar. Nasser introduced a kind of anxiety, a fear, that of course I absorbed simply from being around my father. His worry was that new restrictions were being proposed on trade, commerce, and finance, all of which my father was deeply involved in. And I, in an unnatural and highly emotional way, magnified this into a crisis of the whole society. But one of the interesting things that has happened over the last thirty years, beginning in earnest during the late 1970s and more noticeably now in the last couple of years, when I have gone back to Egypt, is the extent to which I have been able to dissolve that artificial sense of a society in crisis, and see how Nasser and Egypt meshed in other interesting ways.

There's now a whole literature in Egypt about Nasser's secret police, which I saw as threatening exclusively me in a way that made me feel helpless. I felt like a rather passive and isolated victim, the subject of Nasser's repression. But I had not yet begun to discover how many friends of mine had been in jail. One of my closest friends, to whom I dedicated *The Question of Palestine*, was killed in 1960 or 1961. He was a member of the Communist Party, and was beaten to death by Nasser's secret police. So it is a very complex relationship in which there is a great deal of back and forth between myself and Cairo, you might say, as the center of Egypt under Nasser. I was relatively unaware of what was really going on. I then saw Nasser—though one admired him as a great Arab leader—through the prism of my family's interest; now I see that there was a kind of neurosis there which I couldn't deal with. I either worried about the fortunes of my immediate family, or I created this kind of superhuman figure, a figure of Arab nationalism and its defiance of the West and of imperialism, neither of which is absolutely accurate of course. The reality was that Nasser was in constant tension with his own society, and that I never saw until much later.

It was embedded in your own history.

Yes. But not for me to deal with at the time.

To continue with similar concerns, but on a quite different terrain. You just talked now about growing up in the Arab world in a very peculiar position.

Yes, in a cocoon.

And you came to the United States and have spent the majority of your life here. You went to Princeton, Harvard and became as Western as one could imagine, mastering Western culture, in my view in a quite extraordinary way. Western humanism, to give it a convenient label, has been tremendously important to you intellectually. In your work, particularly over the last decade, you've been extremely critical of Orientalism, of ethnography, and yet, not really critical in the same way of, say, Auerbach, Lukács, Blackmur, and Adorno. All of these people, although they were not directly involved in the Orientalist project, nevertheless were part of the discourse of Western humanism, which is part and parcel of that same project.

Every one of the people you mention—with the possible exception of Lukács, about whom I know less, I mean about his views on the non-Western world—in every one of them I could locate for you a place in their texts, in which they are ethnocentric to a fault. In the piece I wrote about Blackmur, I've singled out his rather, I thought, jejune reflections on the Third World. He was, after all, on a mission to the Third World from the Rockefeller Foundation. This was in the days of John Foster Dulles, the cold war, so the influence of the disabling context there is almost total. Similarly with Auerbach. I translated one of his last essays, "Philology and *Weltliteratur*," precisely because it seemed to me to be so interesting a reflection on his own work, but also so pessimistic about the onset of all these "new" languages and cultures, most of them non-European, that he had nothing to say about, except that they seemed to frighten him in some way. He had no concept that they might in fact betoken a new level of cultural activity, let's say in the Third World, that was not previously there.

Even though he spent the Second World War in Istanbul.

There was no discernible connection between Auerbach and Istanbul at all; his entire attitude while there seems to have been one of nostalgia for the West, which gave him the spirit to sit down and write this great saving work of Western humanism, *Mimesis*. So I'm very conscious of that. But, the way I would put it is, that what I have seen myself as trying—perhaps in a rather sentimental way, but it's very conscious, or it has become very conscious in recent years—as in a certain sense, trying to, first of all expose the lapses and the ethnocentric soft spots. But in some way, because I admire the effort nevertheless, somehow to extend their work into areas that interest me. In other words, I'm not exactly answering them, but I'm extending their work into areas they avoid by adopting some of their modes of examination, their attention to texts, their *care*, which I think is the central factor here. It's a kind of scrupulosity, which I suppose you could call humanism. If you pare down that label and relieve it of the unpleasantly triumphalist freight that is carried with it, you are left with something that I think is very much worth saving. The one place where I feel a tremendous lack on my part, through ignorance, is in failing to make as many connections as I'd have liked between the Western humanists and comparable figures in the non-European world.

However, I began to do that in a recent piece that I wrote . . . I may have sent it to you, called "The Voyage In." All the figures considered in that essay were writing in the Western tradition, you know, but the first two, C. L. R. James and George Antonious, are people for whom the West is something that you could in fact have a positive relationship with. But for a later generation, the relationship is inevitably one of hostility. But nevertheless there is a sense in these earlier figures of understanding what the West is all about. In that sense, I'm beginning to draw out patterns from my peculiar background, not so much my ethnic background, but the non-Euoprean background.

One of the reasons that I've been trying to do that has to do with an eagerness to complete work inaugurated by Auerbach, Adorno et al. that I consider to be incomplete by virtue of its ethnocentrism and lack of interest in the part of the world where I grew up. So there is an attempt to claim attention there. But also this moves a little bit into an evolved position about Orientalism, because I've become very aware of how some of the work I've done, especially *Orientalism,* but also *Covering Islam,* has seemed to some not very careful readers to be proposing a kind of indiscriminate conflict between East and West, between Islam and Christianity, between the culture of the West and the culture of the Third World—a set of total oppositions. I've always been taken as in fact proposing that kind of scenario; many of my hostile critics have argued that this is *really* what I'm saying, that I'm really arguing for a resurgence of nativism and that I am to be blamed to a certain degree for the rise of Islamic fundamentalism, and so on and so forth.

This is what you call in the imperialism lectures, "The Politics of Blame." You yourself are being blamed for the politics of blame.

One has to be aware of the way in which certain feelings that you have don't really become clear intellectually until later. They don't provide an intellectual track for you to follow until really much later. For example, Du Bois says that it's very important for a black man in white America to be absolutely scrupulous in discriminating between those aspects of white culture and white civilization that are the enemy, and those that one can align oneself with, draw positive things from, etc. That's really what, in a certain sense, my attitude has been to people such as the ones we've been talking about. Instead of saying that all of them are on one side and all of us are on the other, there may be another mode that can come into play at a level of intellectual and cultural discrimination and elaboration that establishes a different relationship from the purely adversarial or oppositional one.

You call this "The Politics of Secular Interpretation."

Yes, precisely.

Could you say what you intend by this concept?

To go back to the earlier formation which I've given a history of in the third lecture on imperialism. The opposition to imperialism is of course the emergence of nationalism. Nationalism is many, many things. Obviously one aspect of it is a reactive phenomenon. It's an assertion of identity, where the problematics of identity are supposed to carry the whole wave of the culture and of political work, which is the case in the early phases of nationalist struggle against European colonialism. You could see it in the Algerian case, in the Malaysian case, in the Philippine case. You could see it in various aspects of the Arab world, and certainly in the Caribbean. There is an emphasis upon forging a self-identity as a nation or a people that resists but has its own integrity (as in Césaire's *négritude*). But it does seem to me that despite essential virtues there are great limitations to that intellectually as well as politically. The limitations have to do with the fetishization of the national identity. The national identity becomes not only a fetish, but is also turned into a kind of idol, in the Baconian sense—an idol of the cave, and of the tribe. That, it seems to me, then produces, pulls along with it, the rise of what I would call a kind of desperate religious sentiment. This is not everything about the rise of fundamentalism, for example, in the Islamic world, the Christian world, or the Jewish world, but it's an important constituent here.

As opposed to what?

The notion of secularism. This goes back to actual living human beings. Men and women produce their own history, and therefore it must be possible to interpret that history in secular terms, under which religions are seen, you might say as a token of submerged feelings of identity, of tribal solidarity, *'asabiyyah*, in Ibn Khaldun's phrase. But religion has its limits in the secular world. Possibilities are extremely curtailed by the presence of other communities. For example, when you assert an identity, one identity is always going to infringe on others that also exist in the same or contiguous spaces. For me the symbol of that, in the Arab world, is the problem that has been postponed from generation to generation: the problem of the national minorities. Not only the Palestinians, whose denied presence of course proved to be one of the major failures of the Zionist movement, but also the problems with the Jews as a national community to which the Palestinians are only beginning now to try to provide answers in this larger Islamic context. But also there are the many obvious problems with the place of Armenians, Kurds, Christians, Egyptian Copts. The status of all of these groups is extraordinarily inflamed. Therefore, to address such issues, it seems to me that you need a secular and humane vision, one based on the idea of human history not being the result of divine intervention but a much slower process than the politics of identity usually allow. To fight around the slogans provided by nationalist, religious, or cultural identity is a much quicker thing, the formations easier to coalesce around: embattled identities that create traditions for themselves going back to the crusades, or going back to the Phoenician period or going back to the Hellenistic period. I'm actually citing cases of social and religious minorities in the Arab world, where this rhetoric of impossibly early (usually imagined) pedigrees is extremely heated, as opposed to secular interpretation which argues for historical discrimination and for a certain kind of deliberate scholarship. It implies a certain interpretive sophistication. Above all, it argues, and this is the point, for the potential of a community that is political, cultural, intellectual, and is not geographically and homogeneously defined.

At the basis of all this is the extraordinary power and yet the extraordinary failures of the geographical model for human politics. Because what does it produce? The geographical model produces, for example, the kind of thing described in Paul Carter's *The Road to Botany Bay,* which shows how whole entities were fashioned by acts of naming and geographical charting: his example is Captain Cook and Australia. That's really a large part of the history of colonialism. This in turn gives rise to embattled, emergent resistance movements which then in turn, and here's the tragedy of nationalism, fall into homogenized unities, imagined communities. They successfully recapture the geographical identities charted by the imperialists. In the Arab world, for example, the Sykes-Picot agreement of 1916 is the basis for all the national states today—Iraq, Syria, Lebanon, Jordan, Palestine—and for all their "little" nationalisms. These then became reified, stable entities, and on them is built the usually repressive apparatus of the national security, one-party state. Therefore, one has to get beyond geography to these other communities which are transnational which, you might say, are based upon an ideal of secular interpretation and secular work. Obviously I'm not suggesting that everybody has to become a literary critic; that's a silly idea. But one does have to give a certain attention to the rather dense fabric of secular life, which can't be herded under the rubric of national identity or can't be made entirely to respond to this phony idea of a paranoid frontier separating "us" from "them"—which is a repetition of the old sort of Orientalist model where you say that all Orientals are the same. Correlatively, we now have this reactive Occidentalism, some people saying the West is monolithically the same, opposed to us, degraded, materialist, bad, etc. The politics of secular interpretation proposes a way of dealing with that problem, a way of avoiding the pitfalls of nationalism I've just outlined, by discriminating between the different "Easts" and "Wests," how differently they were made, maintained, and so on.

To carry on in the same vein. How do you feel about Gayatri Spivak's negative response to the question, "Can the subaltern speak?"

I have heard her speak a lot about this. She's reacting to the idea that the subaltern can be *made* to speak and thus becomes a kind of new token in the repertoire of dominant discourses.

That certainly happens.

Of course. It's a real possibility. But her position does seem to me to dismiss or not to take seriously enough the various, and in many ways quite unconnected, appearances of groups from Subaltern Studies to various attempts at interpretive political communities in the Middle East, Latin America, Africa, and the Caribbean. For example, certain wings of the Egyptian opposition strike me as very interesting in this respect; they mix Marxism with nativism, with a kind of international sense of Marxist or post-Marxist discourse in the West. Or think of similar efforts in the Caribbean. It seems to me C. L. R. James exactly indicts this notion that the subalterns are always puppets and marionettes who make their speech the same way as the West.

James, while we're on this subject, is really the progenitor of a great amount of quite interesting and quite independent Caribbean literature. The same is true of the African-American opposition movement or the feminist movement in this country. Both have produced, of course, parrots and mimics and all the rest of it, but they have also produced quite important alternative discourses, which perforce overlap with dominant discourses. This by no means invalidates their strength and independence. The same is true in Africa in the work of various intellectuals, poets, and novelists. I don't mean the kind of thing that has gone on about not speaking in a Western language, that to preserve your identity you have to speak in the native language. I'm referring to philosophers, various African ethnologists and ethnographers, and of course the numerous political movements that are not about simply enthroning an idol of the past created largely by the West. They are after some new configurations, some new political process. You can find this in India, you can certainly find it in Japan. It does seem to me that the fear, which is real enough, that the subaltern could be just another form of imperialism does not take enough into account the presence of a genuinely impressive alternative to this outcome, for which in the last two or three years the *intifada* has become a symbol.

What you're really arguing for is a kind of internationalism?

That's too indiscriminate a word. Let's say that these new processes take place in a generally international context. In other words, one can't locate what one is talking about in only one context or in an absolutely new and pure space. The force of the phenomenon that I am talking about is that it takes place in many different places, and I suppose those places taken all together could be considered international. But I think it still has very deep roots in a local and national situation.

So the politics you are recommending is not a cradle of universal values?

No, not at all. I think talk of "universal values" tends to produce a sentimentalism that exactly takes us back to the early days of comparative literature. Woodberry, for instance, the first professor of comparative literature in this country at Columbia in 1892, goes on about congresses of gentlemen scholars, jurists who survey (I think I'm quoting more or less exactly) the scene with a kind of superior detachment, with a general all-encompassing love for all of humanity. Utter nonsense. That's not what I'm talking about.

Let's take the question out of the context of comparative literature and give two examples of internationalism: one, the moment of international socialism, from the end of the nineteenth century and Marx through a certain point in Lenin, let's say up through the mid-twenties; and the second, a genuine international moment and one that surely everything you've said is determined or is made possible by. This is the moment of decolonization, which was genuinely international and remains so up to the present. How would you now situate yourself, the kind of work you do, and the kind of work you think would be valuable to pursue, in relation to that political project, which is after all ongoing?

The point is that decolonization, as I talk about it, is really two moments. The first moment was, you might say, the exhaustion of the classical empires after World War II. Obviously it begins earlier than that, around the period shortly after World War I, and it continues and climaxes in the ceremonies, as I call them, of leave-taking and independence. Of course, the most famous one is midnight August 15, 1947. That is a great moment about which one can feel a certain amount of nostalgia. But the other moment is much more problematic. It's not really over, because the struggle over empire continues in other regions of the world and into the present: Ireland, South Africa, Palestine. That is to say, the drama of decolonization is supposed to culminate in independence, and indeed it did in certain places. But in others it didn't; it continued. Algeria is one of the examples which continues the struggle to be free, now taking alarmingly retrograde forms. In the early sixties so too were Vietnam, Palestine, Cuba, all of the Portuguese colonies of Africa; and then there was the reappearance of a kind of resurgent colonial contest in those parts of the American empire or contiguous to America such as Chile, Nicaragua, etc. There the process seems to continue in surprising ways, not only in actual colonial conflicts but also in the whole drama or spectacle of neocolonialism and dependency, the

IMF, the debt trap, etc. So that's the problem. It's the continuation of the colonization process which has not been contained by the movement of decolonization. That's what interests me, number one.

At the same time, in the decolonized world, and even in the world that is proceeding in its efforts toward liberation, there remains what I call the dialectic of independence and liberation. That is to say the dynamic of nationalism unfulfilled by real liberation, a dynamic whose clear goal is national independence in the form of a conventional or semiconventional state with a whole new pathology of power. The pathology of power in a state like Iran is very different from that in a state like Iraq, from a state like Malaysia, very different from the Philippines, and so on and so forth. Eqbal Ahmed is one of the few people who has tried to talk about this in a systematic way. But as against that, I think the project that continues is that which appears in hints in Fanon, and is figured here and there but not systematically in the works of Cabral, or James. One ought to be able to talk more interestingly about what we were saying earlier, to make more precise the interpretations of various political and intellectual communities where the issue is not independence but liberation, a completely different thing. What Fanon calls the conversion, the transformation, of national consciousness into political and social consciousness, hasn't yet taken place. It's an unfinished project, and that's where I think my work has begun.

For me, the most urgent locus for this problematic is the Palestinian question. During the history of my own direct political involvement, we went from the goal of one secular democratic state, to the immense transformation that in November 1988 took place in Algiers, in which I participated. We turned ourselves from a liberation movement into an independence movement. We talked about two states, an Israeli state and a Palestinian state. Now the principal political struggle concerns the price of having willingly committed ourselves to national independence. It's the tragedy, the irony, the paradox of all anti-imperial or decolonizing struggles that independence is the stage through which you must try to pass: for us independence is the only alternative to the continued horrors of the Israeli occupation, whose goal is the extermination of a Palestinian national identity. Therefore, the question for me is: how much of a price are we going to pay for this independence—if we can get it at all— and how many of the goals of liberation will we abandon? I don't at all mean "liberating" Israel, or the whole of Palestine; I'm talking about ourselves as a movement, as a people. How much of a price are we going to pay in deferred liberation? This involves very concrete problems. What are you going to do about, for example, the three million Palestinians who are not from the West Bank in the diaspora. What formula do we have for that? What is the price we're going to pay in political compromises with our neighbors, Jordan, Israel, Syria, Egypt, etc.? And with the super-partner of them all, the United States? This, after all, is a moment which is dominated by the United States, particularly with the defection of the USSR internationally. Many of us compare Gorbachev with Sadat. By the way, that's not just Alexander Cockburn's notion; it's an idea he got from the Arab context where the exit of the Soviet Union (never a wonderful or even helpful ally) made things worse.

Because you referred to it earlier, can you talk more about the intifada?

Let's begin with the way that the *intifada* has been commodified and presented on American television. Consider the recent statements of Thomas Friedman that it is essentially a series of discrete acts of throwing stones, of firebombing, etc. In fact, it's not a series of discrete acts. It can't be understood that way. It is the creation of a political entity for which the stones are a symbol. The creation of an alternative force which you can't turn off and on. Shamir says, "We will allow elections if the violence is stopped." To suggest that the *intifada,* I mean the model, is the stone thrower who can be prevented from doing that implies either that there's some behind-the-scenes manipulator of the struggle or that it's just a series of blind acts without any basis in any social actuality which is producing these live acts. Therefore, Shamir and others say, you should stop, because we're going to offer you a kind of sop, which is to give you elections so long as of course we retain control through occupation. My interpretation of this is that we should present the *intifada* as an alternative, an emergent formation, by which on the simplest level Palestinians under occupation have decided to declare their independence from the occupation by providing different, not so much models, but different forms for their lives which they themselves administer, develop and have in fact created.

It's an entire cultural movement.

Exactly. It's a cultural movement which says that we are not going to cooperate, we can't any longer live under the occupation, and therefore we must provide for ourselves. Since they have closed the schools, we provide our own schools. They've made health care difficult through the imposition of taxes on the hospitals, so we provide our own health service. One of the aspects of the Israeli system of laws designed to humiliate and punish the Palestinian economy has been to regulate agriculture so that you couldn't plant trees, you couldn't plant fruits, you couldn't dig wells, etc., without the permits, which the Israeli administration either never gave, or made it difficult to obtain. So what has happened is that now with the expropriation of land, with a domination of the network of settlements defended by the Israeli army, there is the possibility for the Palestinians to provide an agricultural alternative to that one. That is to say, the use, for example, of private gardens and houses and the creation of a food delivery service through the collectivization of the bakeries, and the use of children to deliver food in a new pattern that can't easily be dominated by the Israeli military. But it's still very limited.

This new network escapes regulation.

Right. And the same has happened of course in places on the West Bank, which have become in effect liberated zones. The Israeli army has now discovered that it is not possible to enter these places without severe losses. What they have done with the border police is to bring in people who patrol through outbursts of violence. The border police, in a kind of orgy of destruction, kill as many people as they possibly can. But that still, to my way of reading it, proves the existence of these liberated zones, which for a while were free of Israeli occupation. So the upshot is really quite remarkable. We can observe it through telecommunications, through the implements of instant communication which Palestinians have begun to master. There's the whole rural Palestinian world, certainly, but there's also the presence of a complete system of fax machines and telephones controlled by American corporations but not completely dominated by them. One of the great achievements of the Palestinian revolution has been its mastery of this network of communication. It is quite remarkable. It functioned all through the siege of Beirut. All of these situations, which are supposedly dominated by an Israeli siege, have been completely pierced. It's an unprecedented communication network.

So all of this then we can actually watch. In a concrete way we see this new state emerging. What we Palestinians are saying is that we are already practicing our liberation and self-determination. We declared a state; the state is already there. We don't want, we don't need the recognition of others, although we have gotten eighty or ninety recognitions from other states. So the question now, the way we look at it, is not whether the *intifada* is going to stop or not, because it's irreversible. It's a process that has already taken us very far in a direction of self-consciousness, independence, and national liberation. The question is, when are the others going to catch up with us, whether that's going to happen or not. The great problem is that the Gulf crisis set us all back a number of years. There was poor leadership and incredible incompetence. Now the situation is very dark indeed.

There were two things that occurred to me while you were talking. Let me ask the more local one first. You spoke about telecommunication. You've written about this very eloquently, about the control of the media and the way independence struggles in the Third World, particularly the Iranian revolution, but also Palestinians, are represented in the American media, or the "culture industry." But everything that you just said a moment ago shows that to be a half truth. The Adornian notion of a totally dominated and dominating system of mass cultural production is only the apparatus of the media, and that can be mobilized in an entirely different way.

One of the great choruses that you find in the media, indeed produced by the Israeli propaganda apparatus, is that a lot of this is happening *because of* the presence of television. They blame television. That's why Kissinger advised that the one way of stopping the *intifada* was not to let the media in—total nonsense.

Taking up that thread, what would be your attitude now toward the, let's not call it the culture industry, let's just talk about the possibilities of mass communication, etc. Where are the places to intervene? How do you present a counter-narrative, another story, another side of events?

One of the failures of Left writing on the media—it is not only true of Adorno and Horkheimer, but of all the major, shall we say, critiques of domination including the Marxism of Althusser and of Fred Jameson—is that there's a kind of fascination with the techniques of domination.

Foucault ultimately becomes the scribe of domination. In other words, the imagination of Arab people is really an account of the victories of the power dominating them. The site of resistance is eliminated. As opposed to that, I would say people like Gramsci and Raymond Williams take a much less systematic view. I feel much closer to them.

First of all, there's a sense of the fragility of the achievement of the culture industry or the dominating apparatus. After all, just as it was put there, it can also be dismantled or evaded or used to different purposes. There's nothing inevitable or even necessary about it; it's there, it can be taken apart. Second, no matter how dominating an apparatus is, it cannot dominate everything. That, it seems to me, is the central definition of the social process. So what Chomsky says is partly wrong. He sees all information controlled by media that are tied in not only with corporations, but with the military-industrial complex and, indeed, with the government and complicit intellectuals in this country. This analysis is insufficient. There are endless opportunities for intervention (including his own considerable efforts) and transformation that occur within this society. You don't always need to begin at the beginning, that's the point. You could take advantage of the overdevelopment of this dominated apparatus and intervene strategically at certain moments. For example, in the case of the Palestinians where the picture that's presented is incomplete, you can try and complete it, or you can take advantage of the deep contradictions in the society. Such a process would produce somebody like myself, who is a committed Palestinian nationalist on the one hand, and yet through education and certain kinds of intellectual affiliations, a member of the elite. The conjunction of these two makes it possible for me to appear on television to intervene in the ways that I've tried to do. I'm not saying it's the whole story or that it's made tremendously important changes, but at least you get the sense that you are able to combat the domination and to alter the situation and give yourself and others hope.

The most important thing, from my point of view, has been the absence of a master theory for this. It seems to me that's been the great problem with Marxism, or proletarian internationalism. It seems to me that the attempt to invent or devise a discourse that is adequate in its universal contours and detailed power to the new forces of the media or the new social forces outside Europe has not met with great success. It seems to me to have missed a lot of the contradictions, a lot of the untidiness of the moment, etc., many of them due to nationalism, about which Marx had virtually nothing to say. In the conflict between the hedgehog and the fox, the fox in a certain sense is more interesting. The need for a relatively more unbuttoned, unfixed, and mobile mode of proceeding—that's why the Deleuzian idea of the nomadic is so interesting—is to me a much more useful and liberating instrument. Much of what we are talking about is essentially unhoused. You might say the real conflict is between the unhoused and the housed. I don't see the need for a master discourse or a theorization of the whole.

If I could press you on that just a bit. You are absolutely right about the first moment of Marxist theory. It came too soon and too much has changed in the interim. On the other hand, and this is why I stress the notion of internationalism, given the strength of the opposition, of global capitalism—Grenada was one instance, but Cuba, Nicaragua, and Vietnam are others—these individual local struggles simply cannot on their own be sustained, or at least they have failed to do many of the things that they promised. All of these countries are economic wrecks. The reason is that they have not been able to link up in some kind of counter-federation to the Euro-American imperium. Clearly, any Palestinian state will face the same kind of massive opposition, which will try to strangle it in the cradle, so to speak.

Except that the Palestinian issue has already built into it by virtue of the existence of important diaspora communities, both Palestinian and Jewish, an international dimension which connects with South Africa, Nicaragua, etc. Much of the interesting work in the last decade has been the mapping of these networks of connection, of Palestine to Nicaragua for instance. So you already have a kind of blueprint of connections made which could furnish a network for connections to others.

One has of course to reckon (speaking only of the United States) with the presence of localized interests that specialize in single issues and thus, paradoxically, reflect the dominant discourse of division of labor in their counter-strategies. The Nicaraguan or the pro-Sandinista, anti-Contra support is specialized into that, the Salvadorans into another, the South Africans another. We need to find ways that connect these political groups to each other in this society: this cannot be put off. Palestine is very important in this respect, partly because Palestine is always the one that's denied, for various reasons, and also the common factor. You notice that people can talk about Nicaragua and South Africa, but find it very hard to include Palestine. The moment you start pushing, Palestine turns out to be the case that's considered transgressive and slightly messy. And that's why I think an early intellectual effort is very important.

There is a connection in terms of arms trade and counter-insurgency theories, etc., between the Contras, the Saudi Arabians, and the Israelis—that whole connection and the Iran-Contra affair, which wasn't really looked at very carefully. It's not only that there is this massive actuality, but there's also the important theoretical and intellectual perspective which we need to flesh out through what I would call a kind of globalism in the study of texts. This is why, for example, I have very little interest, except residually, in the notion of the national literature, English literature, French literature, and so on. All of these specialties in which professionally we're engaged, whether we like it or not, don't interest me very much any longer, any more than the interest that I have today in things like history and anthropology, etc., is an interest in those fields as fields, but is rather an interest in the connections between them. So that intellectual effort, speaking only for myself, is the direct result of an existential and historical experience in which we Palestinians have been punished by provincialism and the isolation imposed upon us originally by imperialism, but by this very society, which says that you're specialized, you must become "an area expert." All that entire ideology of separation and exclusion and difference, etc.—the task is to fight it. But you can't fight it on one level and be shy or tactful on the others. It's got to be fought on all the fronts. That's where I think we are right now.

What you seem to be saying now, and have also articulated elsewhere, is that because imperialism has constructed and produced so much of the world as we know it, a kind of worldliness is in fact the only viable intellectual, political, or personal rejoinder.

But here's where I think it's been very important to have some live connection with an ongoing political movement. When I talk about worldliness, I don't just mean a kind of cosmopolitanism or intellectual tourism. I'm talking about the kind of omnicompetent interest which a lot of us have that is anchored in a real struggle and a real social movement. We are interested in a lot of different things. We can't be confined by our identities as professional scholars of, say, English literature in the nineteenth century. Nobody's happy with that, but the alternative isn't to just get interested in more things.

Many of our colleagues are perfectly happy with just this narrow professional identity.

I think that's passing. The idea that you can sort of dip in and read *The Nation* and the *New York Review of Books,* and then you listen to a little Mozart, and then you riffle through a volume of Cage's scores. That's not what we are talking about. What has been very important for me, providing a kind of discipline, is the sense of a community and a movement in progress to which I am committed and in which I am implicated. You take all the attacks that brand you, in my case as a terrorist or a kind of delinquent, as a criminal, etc. You pay a price, in other words. But also it imposes upon me some sense of responsibility to a community which is not a specialized group.

For my part, the greatest, most admired worldliness, is that of the great comparatists, the Auerbachs and the Spitzers of an earlier generation, or the Frankfurt critical theorists, people like Horkheimer and Adorno. Especially Adorno, who could really talk about anything, everything. There was this kind of vocabulary of attention to high culture, mass culture, etc. Of course, it was limited by ethnocentrism, as I said earlier, but by and large they broke the disciplinary constraints. Still, they never, it seems to me, confronted seriously the problem of audience, audience viewed as a political and, you might say, human community. Not an ideal or idealized community. In the case of Adorno, some communities he simply took for granted have simply disappeared, can't possibly exist any longer.

Clearly Adorno gave up on the possibility of any kind of political struggle. Once you do that, I think you're saying, then you've given up the real game.

You've given up the real game, which is communication with actual people and communities. Partly this is also true of two intellectuals whose work I've learned from a great deal and been friendly with in all kinds of ways: Jameson and Chomsky. Chomsky's loneliness and his self-imposed marginalization have derived from his unwillingness, for whatever reason, to be involved in the messy political details of a back-

and-forth movement with a community. In the case of Jameson, there has been a sense in which his community is essentially the community of philosophical theorists, or liberated theorists, which gives a very restricted view. Of course both Chomsky and Jameson are very open to solicitations from the political world, and they are very generous people, but their fundamental connection is not to an ongoing political movement. But maybe I'm being too critical of them.

To move on to a related question. You will recall when Beginnings *came out in 1975, there was a whole issue of* Diacritics *devoted to it, including a long interview with you. At that time, you drew a line between your academic intellectual life, which* Beginnings *and the book on Conrad represented, and the political life which you were simultaneously leading. You yourself said something to the effect "It's like I'm two separate people." It seems clear that in the last decade this is increasingly not the case. That is to say, you have begun to integrate these two distinct identities in a much tighter and more immediate way. What is your current understanding, first, of your career in the university in relation to your political life or your political activism, and second, of the way this relationship can or should be negotiated by other university intellectuals who maintain political commitments demanding time, energy, and often certain personal risks?*

I'm not sure that any one can negotiate all the things one does. I wouldn't now talk about a separation as I did in 1976. There I was much more conscious of being a professional scholar of literature in a department which seemed to, not exactly impinge on me, but to demand certain things from me. I don't feel that anymore. And in what I've been writing since *Orientalism,* I've felt that there is a kind of traffic that I've allowed myself between overtly political and cultural, intellectual, and specialized work that makes possible, you might say, a zone which I've existed in without worrying about whether I am really an academic or really a political partisan. Those divisions don't seem to be that interesting anymore. What I've since allowed myself to do, partly because of the pressure of time—I'm growing older, I don't have as much energy as I used to have, and there are more demands on my time—is to be guided by certain things that seem to attract me and let myself go with them. For example, my recent interest in music, on which in the past five or six years I've written quite a lot.

This comes back to your question about mass culture versus elite culture. One of the failures of Adorno, as I read him, is that he thought elite culture was disappearing into mass culture, whereas in fact today one can still witness a very lively concert life based almost entirely on classical music, which as an elite institution has a very powerful social presence in contemporary life. And it's not based upon new music, but on a curatorial interest in the past. That's something to be accounted for. It's a vestige, if you like, but it's still there, and it has a presence, in spite of Adorno's predictions at the end of *The Philosophy of New Music* that this music was going to remain unheard. In fact, we've never had a greater multiplication of classical music, in records but also in concerts and in many interesting types of performance.

All I'm trying to say is that one is provided, largely because of New York, with a panorama of intellectual opportunities for intervention. I've pursued my interventionist bent without trying to theorize or explain or predict it in any way by saying, now that I've written my Conrad book I'll now write my Marx, and from my Marx I should then write the Husserl book, and so on. Instead of following that sequential trajectory, I think I've kept to the idea of trying to do all of these things contrapuntally, given the constant presence in my life of my ongoing Palestinian obligation and political commitment. I've stopped being able to calculate the pros and cons of what I do. I just don't have time to do it anymore. Maybe that's some form of carelessness.

Could you talk more about the importance of music? I know for you personally it's of great moment, as a musician and as somebody who cares about it. But I'm curious about how you would situate the music that you write about and perform yourself, the classical tradition. Does this constitute an autonomous realm of artistic production that doesn't in a sense suffer from the inscription of, let's say, ideology and politics?

It does. I'm right in the middle of these problems and therefore perhaps not well positioned to say something from a large perspective. I'm writing the Wellek lectures that I'm giving at Irvine in a month. In them I try to—they're called *Musical Elaborations*—survey those things that are of particular interest to me. Again and again they converge on the public and the private—the public, in an Adornian sense with all of its processes of power and accreditation and authority and orthodoxy; and the private, which is the position of the listener or the amateur or the subjective consumer of music, like myself. I wouldn't call it an autonomous realm, but I certainly think one can talk about it as having a kind of relatively autonomous identity.

What I've picked for analysis are, first of all, the performance occasion itself, which I talk about as an extreme occasion, but an occasion with a temporality and a locale that are quite marked in the social life of the West, especially the late capitalist West. The second lecture is an attempt to account for that whole dimension within music that goes, you might say, from the technical transgressive of the *diabolus in musica,* forbidden intervals for example, to large questions of morality and aesthetics which culminate in the work of Wagner and Strauss, and perhaps ultimately link up with the question of Paul de Man—that is, of the complicity between music, ideology, and social space. The third lecture is a study of melody as an important aspect of identity in classical music, the contours of the individual melody. My point of departure is the *Contre Sainte-Beuve,* in which Proust says that he can tell the *air de chanson* of each writer. He uses the element of melody to identify the style and the particular signature of every artist: thus each has his own melody. And I then say, well, what about looking at that in terms of composers—the melody of the composer. I was very impressed by the work of the English musicologist Wilfred Mellers, who wrote two books, *Bach and the Dance of God* and *Beethoven and the Song of God*—both attempt to do a kind of musicological analysis of an overpoweringly present theme in the structure, but also in the melody of their work. I'm interested in melody, first of all, on the level of the listener's being imprinted by the composer's identity and then seeing how far that can go into the question of solitude, since composing is a solitary act, into the question of the public profile of the composer. Rather than talk about all of music, I've tried simply to carve out of this long and largely silent experience of musical awareness that I have, to carve out interesting topics that might enable me to talk about music in social and political, but above all in aesthetic, terms.

The main problem I have and don't have any answer to, is that it's strange that, for example, the music of my own Arab and Islamic tradition means relatively little to me as I write this book. I've never been interested in or compelled by it as something to study, although I know it well and have always listened to it. The same is roughly true of popular music. Popular culture means absolutely nothing to me except as it surrounds me. I obviously don't accept all the hideously limited and silly remarks made about it by Adorno, but I must say it doesn't speak to me in quite the same way that it would to you or to my children. I'm very conservative that way.

It's a kind of block, in short. This is somewhat unfair, but one might say that the great Western classical musical tradition is for you an unproblematic refuge of greatness. You could say, of course, that these are great figures, but one might also say, following some of your earlier remarks, that, for example, African popular music is much more global, combining all these strands. It might seem to speak to some, but it falls on deaf ears here.

I don't know about deaf ears.

You yourself don't listen to reggae and rock, but they are the great popular political music of our time, in the West anyway.

I've read a great deal about both, but it's not what I first want to listen to when I listen to music. Perhaps what I'm really writing about is the persistence of this Western classical tradition, and maybe failing in the end to be successful at it. I'm really quite nervous about what I'm doing. It's all very well to write an individual article about a concert that one has heard, or an opera that one has attended, but it's a different thing to put it in this relatively abstract frame that I've called "musical elaboration." But I see it all as part of what Gramsci calls the elaboration of civil society. The social plays a certain role. Nobody would ever deny that rock culture has taken over and in a way is much more interesting intellectually to somebody of my own perspective, but nevertheless it seems to me that there is this kind of strange, maybe neolithic formation that I call classical music in which the great figures are people like Glenn Gould and Toscanini, whose work has really attempted to assert the presence of this tradition, while in other ways, reaching out from it to the questions of mass society, technology, communications, radio programs.

Let's shift our focus somewhat. What do you think now of the scene in not just academic, but general cultural criticism, of literary criticism, to keep it within that realm? Where do you think it's going? What do you think is important that's being done? What do you think are the kinds of things that haven't been done that should be done, etc.? You've asked this question of me enough times, so I'm going to ask it of you.

The reason I ask *you* the question is I really needed to know, because I haven't followed it as systematically as either of you has. I simply lost interest in literary theory about ten years ago. It just doesn't strike me as something that I have needed to be up on, on a day-by-day basis, or as something that is of interest to me in what I'm doing on a given day.

But you do see yourself as intervening in that arena in a very power-ful way. We aren't the only ones who have been affected by this. There are literally hundreds of people who are doing the type of work you have recommended in your own critical practice.

That has to do with a personal relationship perhaps, with accidents. I've been very conscious, for example, of not wanting to impose myself on students in the way in which people like de Man and other members of the (now defunct) Yale school have done, to become part of a school, to formalize what it is that I do in teachable ways or anything like that. I've always thought of my teaching, which I do all the time with great excitement and nervousness, as actually performing acts of analysis or reading or interpretation, rather than providing students with method-ologies that they can go out and apply to situations. In other words, I think of myself as providing opportunities for students and friends, rather than encoding insights in some way that can make them useful tools later on. I just don't seem to be able to do that.

I'm impressed, to get back to the question about criticism, I'm im-pressed by the extent, and I don't understand the reason for it, by the extent to which there seem to be fads and waves. Deconstruction, for example, seems now to be completely exhausted. I don't see anybody doing anything interesting as a deconstructionist. I watched with some interest and eagerness the emergence of something called the New His-toricism, its peak and its now apparent sliding into an orthodoxy of some sort, where people feel they have to repeat the words "New His-toricism." I still don't quite know what it is. I think of the debates that go on in places like *Diacritics* and *MLN,* in *Cultural Critique, the min-nesota review,* etc. My attention is not commanded by them. I don't really know, and I'm finding that I'm in such a scramble most of the time to keep my head above water to answer the deadlines, to meet the commitments, etc., that I've simply lost interest in anything that is meta-critical.

What really compels my attention outside the doctrinal boundaries of "lit. crit.," which I don't read anymore, are interesting, daring, novel attempts to do something from an historical point of view, across discursive lines in often transgressive ways, in ways that try to connect politically and intellectually with other interventions. I've been very interested for the last couple of years, although I haven't written about it, in feminism as one of the sites where those things happen, because there isn't really a unitary feminist discourse as yet. It's still very much going through various phases, independence and separatism, various kinds of metahistorical, metatheoretical ventures. The work of Joan Scott, for example, is very interesting to me. It's a form of contestation which I find invigorating and amazing. But to say that out of it one can derive a particular position strikes me as quite false and quite wrong.

It seems to me that whereas, say, ten years ago I might eagerly look forward to a new book by somebody at Cornell on literary theory and semiotics, now I'm much more likely to be interested in a work emerging out of concern with African history, or, for example, a book that I just read recently by Helen Callaway, *Gender, Culture and Empire,* which deals with the role of European women in Nigeria, and raises the question of imperialism and feminism. Or Jean Franco's new book on Latin American women, *Plotting Women.* That sort of thing is not programmable.

Sort of theorists without portfolio.

Even the word theory suggests something to me that . . .

You would want to abandon that?

Yes, I would. I just feel that's a guild designation now that has produced a jargon I find hopelessly tiresome.

What you were saying just now was that the horizon of literature, and therefore literary criticism, is not the literary text, literary analysis, and formal poetics, etc., but is something wider—culture, history, society. It seems to me you said, "I don't want to have a position." But that is your position, and that has implications.

Well it's not strictly speaking my position. It comes as a strange paradox or, at least for me, an unsolvable riddle. That is to say, I am of the rather strong persuasion that all texts—and the texts that interest me the most are the ones that are most this way—all texts are mixed in some way. This whole notion of a hybrid text, of writers like García Márquez and Salman Rushdie, the issues of exile and immigration, crossing of boundaries—all of that tremendously interests me for obvious existential and political reasons, but also because it strikes me as one of the major contributions of late-twentieth-century culture. There are certain figures who are most important to me, renegade figures, people like Genet, a man who in his own society was an outcast and outlaw, but who transformed this marginality into, I wouldn't say a vocation, because that is something much more deliberate than it was, but a kind of passionate attachment to other peoples, other than friends, whom he lives with and then later quite consciously betrays. There is evidence for this political poetics in his play *Les Paravents*. It's also marvelously the case in his book *Le Captif amoureux*, which has just been translated into English. I tried to focus on this aspect of Genet in a recent issue of *Grand Street*. Those are the phenomena that deeply interest me, the people who were able to go from one side to the other, and then come back.

On the other hand, I'm not one of those who believes that the way to proceed is to find an alternative canon to the great literary masterpieces. I have this strange attachment, again it's a residual or vestigial consciousness, to what I consider in a kind of dumb way "great art." It seems to me that works like *Moby-Dick* or *Mansfield Park* or *Gulliver's Travels* are autonomous literary texts and need to be understood and studied that way. I haven't at all given that idea up. For me these works first of all represent a kind of private experience of pleasure in reading and reflection. That's really what I'm finally discovering. In other words, they represent certain hours of private enjoyment, you might say, that have been companions of my intellectual and aesthetic attention for a long time; they are favorites, in a word.

Let me try to tease something out of that and see where it goes. In your current massive project on culture and imperialism, a lot of your reading and analysis centers on the great nineteenth-century novel and its passage into the high modernist tradition in English . . .

And French. There are parts which you haven't seen which deal with the French novel and then culminate in the early works of Gide and all of Camus. I read them against the colonial background of North Africa and the Levant and that whole group of adventure novels, exotic quests, etc. Then I trace them out further into the literature of resistance in the poetry of Abd el Qadir, the great Algerian warrior of the nineteenth century. I refer to him in passing, but I continue through the work of the early Algerian historians and the attempts to reconstruct the history of the Maghreb. These sections of the book are just notes, but they are part of a picture, as are extended analyses of music. The idea is to present as much as I can of a full portrait of nineteenth-century culture as it bears on empire.

One specifically literary question that one might ask is the following. You use imperialism as a very important new optic through which not merely to read these texts, but to measure their importance, their cultural power, their reach, etc. Does that happen because these are great texts, because of their genius, their linguistic finesse, or any other way you want to term it?

Well, that's an interesting question. That certainly happens in some instances inadvertently. The references to Antigua in *Mansfield Park* are a very important part of the book. I'm sure if you were to look at more focused English writings on the West Indies—there is a great literature in the late eighteenth and early nineteenth centuries that represents the West Indian interests in England—you would find a much more noticeable presence of an articulated imperial attention, one much more noticeable than that in *Mansfield Park*. But to come back to the question of the masterpieces: they're the ones which would be in the common area of examination and investigation of people to whom in the first instance this work is addressed, that is, other students of literature and culture. So in that respect there's the question of availability. Nobody in this group has *not* read Dickens's *Bleak House* or *Mansfield Park*.

Second, the origin or source of their authority. That's the point, too, that they are a part of a canon. I'm very interested in showing the connection between their authoritative presence in the metropolitan culture of Western Europe and America. Making the connection between the authority in the metropolis and their contribution to the persistence of the imperial attitude and the need of imperialism itself is not an attempt to indict them, but to show how, in an almost passive way, because of their magisterial metropolitan achievements, they conferred upon the keeping of territories and subject peoples a dubious privilege of subordination.

Third, they're also symptomatic. They strike me as a symptom that supports the argument I'm making, that there is no dissent, not even in the canon which is supposed to represent, as Lenin and Hobson talk about it, "higher" ideas and higher values, as distinct from the rather base attitudes in the business of imperialism itself. It is a kind of continuity which I'm interested in. In other words, you could trace a line from the actions, from the profits, from the nefarious practices of imperialism in the colonies to the very structure of the novel, to a certain kind of spectacle, or a certain kind of ethnographic, historical, scientific writing. The point then would be that these works do not provide a refuge from the worldliness of the imperial attitude, but in fact confirm it.

And fourth, it seems to me that there's an act here of rebellion against these works which I have read, and which played a very important role in the formation of my consciousness, my aesthetic, intellectual, professional consciousness, as a student of Western literature and culture. I'm reading them now in a way that I never read them before. But more importantly, I'm reading them now in conjunction with the whole process of resistance to them which exists in the Third World, and which I'm also talking about in what was the third of my lectures on imperialism but is now the third section of my book *Culture and Imperialism*. In other words, to read them by themselves is not what I am doing. I'm trying to read them contrapuntally against this movement of dissent and resistance that takes place from the very beginning of imperialism. Of course that's a story we don't really know because, as Barbara Harlow has suggested, not nearly enough work has been done on those connections.

This is a devil's advocate question. Is it possible that such a strategy can become very schematic in the sense that reading Camus with Fanon is going to presuppose that Fanon's rewriting has the legitimacy, the strength of subsequent histories of decolonization, etc.? I'm not saying this to say, "Let's try to salvage these works," but to ask, "Does it exhaust them?"

No, it doesn't exhaust them.

Is Dickens somehow evacuated because we can read his texts as ac-

tive interlocutors in the imperialist project? Then does everything else disappear?

No, no, not at all. That's the point I'm trying to make. Perhaps I'm not making it well. I don't think that at all. Precisely because I give attention to these texts which are "masterpieces," my interest in them is *for themselves.* There is an intrinsic interest in them, a kind of richness in them. These are works by great writers, and because of that fact they are able to comprehend a situation which allows them to be interesting even to the point of view of an oppositional analysis. But it doesn't exhaust the works. The works remain interesting nevertheless. In a certain sense they are interesting and powerful because *they are* interesting and powerful works, not just because they are available to this particular analysis. But the fact is that the analysis has never been done before.

In my imperialism book, I survey the whole, rather peculiar history of important cultural criticism, including that of Raymond Williams himself, who simply never looked at that connection at all, though it is absolutely there. But does it in the end indict the archive as one that is "nothing but" imperialism? Of course this is what people said about *Orientalism,* that I was really attacking all the Orientalists for everything they did. That's a total distortion of my argument. I'm saying that one of the reasons lesser Orientalists were able to do what they did in narrow political terms was partly because they had behind them, not only the resource of a tradition and great social power, but also because the work was interesting in and of itself. For example, Jones or Massignon or Lane, or any of those early scholars, are themselves interesting. They are not simply ideological cartoons lurking beneath the surface of great learning. I'm not saying that their surface and aesthetic achievements constitute a kind of camouflage for a Colonel Blimp or some ridiculous French general lurking underneath. I think it's important to be able to see the two working together in some way; obviously Bernard Lewis can't see it and never will.

But how would you respond to a West Indian friend of mine who said once of Proust, that this novel is simply a kind of decadent, private experience that does not speak to him, to his cultural formation.

That's true of Achebe's response to Conrad. He said, well, people study Conrad, but Conrad is just a racist. No matter how clever a writer he is, however good at depicting local color, in the end his political attitudes are despicable to me as a black man. That's another version of the same argument. But they're not that to me. There's no reason for me to perform acts of amputation on myself, intellectual, spiritual, or aesthetic, simply because in the experience of other people from the Third World, a black novelist from Nigeria like Achebe or your West Indian friend, can make my Proust or Conrad into someone who is only despicable. I can share in feelings of alienation, and extremely severe critique, but I can't fully accept the dismissal of these writers; because they have meant a great deal to me and indeed play a role intellectually and aesthetically in the cultural life of the world in which we live.

But only in certain sectors.

That's true.

Your project suggests not only that one understand the Western tradition in a new way, but that there are all these other cultural traditions, which are in principle equally rich, equally valuable in this slightly peculiar conjuncture we are in. In the New York Times *last Wednesday, there was an article about teaching the sitar and there were all these egregious screeds from neoconservatives . . .*

They called me three or four times to be interviewed for that article and I never responded.

And what was said was that they—you, Achebe, the Left—haven't shown us anything to substitute for the Western canon. I think that's nonsense.

Yes, like Saul Bellow (I think) asking, "Where is the African Tolstoy?" That's the other side of it which is also very egregious. I'm not sure that it's necessary to find another object to study. There are other cultural experiences which may not be as rich—this is where we have to accept the tragic or the ironic other side of what we are talking about. It may in fact be the case that, having happened in Paris in the late nineteenth and early twentieth century, Proust may not have to happen again. And too, it may not be necessary to look again for a gigantic novel of memory and nostalgia. This may lay upon us the obligation to look for other sources of experience which are not codified and not codifiable in that form. That's all I'm saying. That doesn't bother me. When a student says to me, well, you're reading Gide's *Immoralist,* why don't we instead read an Algerian novel of that time? My reply is that there was no Algerian novel at that time, any more than at the time that Mahler wrote his symphonies there was a Trinidadian symphonic tradition. It's the adversarial juxtaposition in this ludicrous way that makes the whole enterprise almost comic; that is what I'm rejecting.

It would be possible and legitimate to say that, for instance, Proust happened, but also that there are other things happening now and they are of equal urgency and therefore we may not want to read Proust or Conrad.

That's something else. Equal urgency is where I might disagree with you. You're posing a theoretical question for which I don't think there's an answer. I am saying that practically, for me, given my particular interest and project, which is very limited I'll grant you, it is urgent for me to read Proust or whoever it is that I'm talking about in this book, who exists within Western culture at a particular moment. That by no means imposes an obligation on anybody else to do the same thing. Somebody who may wish in fact to take up the question, is it necessary to read Proust at all?—it may not be necessary. I'm not saying that it is. It's a private decision on my part to do this, given a certain public and historical reality which is urgent for me, which includes anti-colonialism and anti-imperialism. I don't really know how to extend this into a general program of intellectual attachment. That's my problem. Maybe it's a lack of perspective on my part. Maybe it's a lack of capacity to formulate theoretical models for study and for investigation that I don't feel I have the time for now.

To choose another site in this same problematic. The censoriousness in a certain strand of feminism, American feminism, that would say, "Well, it's just all sexism in the canon and why read it?" To perform this act of excision is ludicrously inadequate. Moreover, to move back to Third World considerations, a figure like García Márquez is not going through this agony about, "Let's substitute all of the canonical figures for Third World writers." It simply doesn't enter into his mode of literary production. It's a peculiar liberal idea of one-to-one substitution and correspondence. It seems to me that involves real political and theoretical consequences.

I'm very interested in Third World literature. In many of the gestures made by writers, but not all certainly, there's a quite conscious effort to redo and reabsorb the canon in some way. Conrad is one of the dominating figures of Africanist discourses that Christopher Miller talks about. That strikes me as really interesting, because it's not just dislodging one and putting in another one, but is really an act of engagement with it and doing something quite different than just substituting for and displacing it. There are various kinds of projects of writing back, revising, reappropriating.

Somebody like N'gugi will say, as he did recently at Yale, "I think my new novel is very interesting because I've tried to make the narrative structure more akin to . . ." Then he listed a host of people he's been reading.

Sometimes the prescriptive and programmatic imperatives of a particular methodological vision strike me again as not exhausting all the possibilities of what one does and what it's possible to do in fact. That's why I'm very uncomfortable with these rather rigorous and I think in the end nativist sentiments. The idea that you shouldn't read Proust because nothing in it answers to you, that could be a false characterization, not so much of Proust but of you. Maybe the three of us are too cosmopolitan.

I think that is in fact part of it. What you've said again and again is that this is the cultural tradition into which . . .

In which I find myself right now.

I can't be other than what I am, you might say. But the point is that there are lots of people in the world who are other than all of us. A lot of them now are students, people from the subcontinent, from Africa, etc., who come to the United States to be educated. They are forced to do very traditional English lit. or comp. lit., but then what they say is, "I want to write on post-colonial fiction." But presumably you would say "yes" to that, or would you?

I don't know: I wonder about that. What I'm interested in having students do, who come with those kinds of concerns and those kinds of backgrounds and imperatives, is to say what it is that the academic situation at Columbia or Stony Brook or Yale, whatever the university happens to be, what it is that is presented to you. And if what is presented to you is in fact a canonical or traditional method, and you are supposed to take all of that in, then the initial process is to understand not so much how that works, but where it comes from. It's perfectly okay to study the curriculum, not by simply reading all the authors in order to fulfill the requirements, but to study it critically and to understand the place of all these things in the procedures of scholarly interpretation and how that has attached itself to various political and ideological formations in the larger society. This dissertation by Gauri Viswanathan, an Indian student of mine, was brilliant precisely because of that. She took as a point of departure the presence of an English curriculum in Indian schools and then tried to discover its archeology. That seems to be the issue that presents itself to a student of the Third World coming here. If you change these sides, if you have done the work here, gotten a Ph.D. and gone through the obstacle course, then you go back to a place like Egypt or the West Indies or India and you're equipped with a professional degree in English from an American or English university. One of the most prevalent and pathetic things of all is to see that precisely the student who was here looking for ways of studying his or her own literature will go back there and be forced by the system there to become the very model of an English professor in America.

The kind of courses that we're talking about, the ones we ourselves want to teach, are unthinkable in most of these countries.

In Egypt I noticed that the curriculum of Cairo University, which is a fascinating agglomerate of Islamic and Arab nationalists, of left-wing and quasi-colonialist attitudes, is all presided over in its content and its procedures by Saintsbury. It's very disheartening, although a lot of the professors I spoke to were aware of it and interested in making changes.

In a conversation I had with Ranajit Guha the other day, one of the first things he asked me was "How old are you?" I said, "I'm thirty-nine." He said, "Aah!" I said I'd written to him because I am a great admirer of his work, and he replied that if I were ten years older I wouldn't be saying that. No one of that generation reads him; he can't speak to the people of his own generation.

Yes, it *is* a generational thing.

But those curricula and the people who perpetuate them are still very much in place.

They have become completely reified, and one can sympathize with the dissatisfaction of students who come here from the Third World looking for ways out. But I'm not sure that the way out is simply by mechanical substitution of post-colonial fiction for nineteenth-century fiction.

And isn't that romanticizing anyway? Then they're taking in what is their own literature somehow. It just defaces the institution.

Totally. It makes a laughing matter out of it, or a shadow figure out of it.

What strikes me strongly, and disagree with this if you think it's not the case, about so much of your literary critical work is the question of narrative and how strongly that impinges on the entire structure of your thought. Not to the exclusion of poetry, but you have concentrated more on narrative. Also, you questioned, and in my view rightly so, the atti-tudes of those like Lyotard who have elevated to a theoretical paradigm the loss of narratives. I just wondered how you would comment on the prominence of this category in your own thinking.

It's really a direct product of the Palestinian experience, and my sense of my own past—I'm sure it's equally true of most Palestinians, even most Arabs and other Third World people who historically were forced to submit to master narratives—that the array of master narratives which are those of the European odyssey have been so extraordinarily dominant. Perhaps in my case it's exaggerated in importance because I was so much a product of the colonial system, but it has played a fantastic cultural role in our lives, so that one of the things I've tried to do is to reconstruct that narrative problem with all of its power and strength and to show its sociopolitical prevalence throughout. And then having done that, beginning to think of alternatives to it. Not just counter-narratives in the case, for example, of the Palestinian recon-struction of identity after 1948, which has always interested me, and the beginnings of the Palestinian political position which has been the ac-quisition of the permission to narrate and that whole business. But also, and I'm at an early stage in this, the interest in anti-narrative strategies of one sort or another.

For example, my interest now in popular culture, so far as I'm inter-ested in it, in the Arab world. This whole excavation of Egyptian cinema that I spoke about earlier is part of that. I haven't gone very far in it be-cause I've been so occupied with the other one, which is really very much a kind of cataloguing and noting of effects. You're absolutely right the way you put it: it's almost crowded out every other kind of interest. I think that Lyotard played a very important role at one point when he first published *The Postmodern Condition,* precisely because everything seemed to be ruled out in favor of what he calls "competence" and "performability." It struck me as simply not the case. I was very interested in the anti-narrative, the anti-linear, in the notion of consecutiveness of efforts, and opposed to that, the whole question of lingering and noting certain areas of experience. At that moment I came to be terribly interested in the work of John Berger, *Another Way of Telling,* in that whole defense against these master narratives and the air of administrative competence that they brought. It may have in a rather artificial way pushed out other interests, but I have not had much time to develop them. Poetry, for example.

I didn't mean to say there was an imbalance, but your interest in narrative is not along the lines of Fred Jameson, who takes Narrative with a capital "N" as the core human experience and looks with enormous nostalgia at what he sees as a diminishment of narrative. It seems to me you look for intersections and renarrativizations.

Right. That sort of thing rather than the grand narrative, in which I simply don't believe. I think it's very hard for First World intellectuals to understand the suspicion with which Third World intellectuals take the question of narrative as in the case, say, of the narrative provided by Western Marxism. Even on the notion of Western Marxism itself, I am critical of Perry Anderson's implicit premise that Western Marxism is the norm by which one judges the progress or failure of Marxism as a whole. I'm not sure that that's the case. There's Marxism in the Third World, for example, which is an interesting story quite removed from the major avenues of the West. Paul Buhle makes the point, actually, in the C. L. R. James book. Western Marxism in Perry's sense excludes Marxism in the Caribbean, which is itself phenomenally interesting and has been politically and theoretically productive. But in Perry's account, Fanon is not to be found and neither is Walter Rodney. The great figures in Africa and Asia, the communist movement of Bengal, for example, are blithely ignored. I'm just not sure that the world historical importance Perry gives to the Western Marxist trajectory is the one I would want to keep with me, although of course I admire it, and Perry Anderson, very much.

I sympathize with that. I was going to ask you a question about Marxism specifically, not just in light of what we said.

Waiting until the end for the most difficult questions.

All of the things we've been talking about, in a way, have focused on the contradictory or at least tensional points in your work. They've all been in and around questions of something called "the Western tradition" as opposed to all kinds of other things that are going on, either at the same time or not, and which may impinge or may not. In the case of Marx, for example, you have drawn attention to the colossal blindness of Marx himself to things outside of Europe, the essays on India, the notion of an Asiatic mode of production, and so on.

Right. Nationalism. He didn't understand that at all.

At the same time, one of the epigraphs to Orientalism *is taken from* The Eighteenth Brumaire. *You have specifically said, not only today, but on other occasions, "I've never said I'm a Marxist." You didn't say, "I'm not a Marxist," but, "I've never said I am a Marxist," which is fair enough. What are the specific political and theoretical reservations that you have about Marxism in particular? One of the things you just said is, "Marxism is clearly not just a Western phenomenon"; it's been tremendously rich and productive in revolutionary movements all over the world. And yet, it seems to me, you've always drawn back from ever making that kind of political and theoretical commitment to Marxism. I'm wondering how you would try to negotiate that problematic.*

First of all, Marxism, insofar as it is an orthodoxy, an ontology, even an epistemology, strikes me as extraordinarily insufficient. The protestations or the affirmations of belonging or not belonging to a Marxist tradition seem to me to be interesting only if they are connected to a practice, which in turn is connected to a political movement. Most of my interaction in the United States with Marxism has been academic. It's hard for me to take it seriously, except as an academic pursuit of one sort or another. But I've never indulged in anti-Marxism either. I may have been critical about certain of Marx's pronouncements, but I've never been an anti-communist; in fact, I've denounced anti-communism as a rhetorical and ideological ploy. But Marxism has nonetheless always struck me as more limiting than enabling in the current intellectual, cultural, political conjuncture.

Do you think that is true within the Palestinian movement?
I think it is especially true in the Palestinian movement.
Can you talk about that?
For example, take the Popular Front, which declares itself a Marxist movement. Insofar as the rhetoric, the analyses, even the organizational practices of the PFLP could be described as anything, they certainly could not be described as a Marxist party. They could be described in other ways, but those of a classical Marxist party they are not. Its analyses are not Marxist. They are essentially insurrectionary and Blanquist, dispiriting to the organization of the PFLP and also "the masses," whom they seem to address. They have no popular base, never did. Not in Oman or in Lebanon nor, to the best of my ability to judge it, now on the West Bank and in Gaza. They have a certain constituency, but the mass party in the Palestinian movement, the mass party in which the majority of the peasantry is to be found, is Fatah, which is not a Marxist party. It is a nationalist party. So, in the Third World revolutionary scene, it is usually the Marxist party which is the party of the minority, and is at some distance from the grass roots of the movement, that is to say, the critical mass which makes the movement into a revolutionary force on the ground.

That's an important discrimination which I would like you to talk about, because clearly what you said is not true of El Salvador, for example. The guerrilla movement there is and has been Marxist from the outset.
In the Arab world there isn't—and I was very very interested in this about fifteen or sixteen years ago when I studied it—in the whole history—again, there are all kinds of personal limitations here which I must admit to at the outset—but in the whole history of Marxist organization, theory, discourse, and even practice in the Middle East, there seems to be no convincing evidence of a Marxism that went beyond Russian Marxism of the twenties and thirties. There has been some presence of those Marxist currents that interest us in the West, the Marxism of early and middle Lukács, the Marxism of Gramsci, later Althusser—although Althusser is a special case, because at a certain moment in the sixties there was a certain Althusserian element in the Arab world, which imported Althusserianism as a superstructural addition, a

fact to be taken account of in the rhetoric of Arab Marxism. But by and large, the development of Western Marxism was not reflected in Arab Marxism. There is, rather, a reaching out to the experiments and the ideas and the gestures of orthodox and unorthodox Russian Marxism of the twenties and thirties, which would include Stalinism and Trotskyism. The Marxist parties were essentially Moscow-oriented. To the best of my ability to judge it, the development of a theoretical Marxism in the Arab world did not seem to meet adequately the challenges of imperialism, the formation of a nationalist elite, the failure of the nationalist revolution, religion, etc.—all the problems that we now face, including Zionism itself. And the interesting and effective, such as they were, efforts were limited to dealing with these other problems that didn't come from within the Marxist tradition. That's played an important role in my own energies.

I've been much more conscious, because of my own particular background, with all of its limitations and drawbacks, of the failures, of the lack of reach, in the Marxist tradition. That leaves, nevertheless, a great deal there to be interested in, for example, the whole notion of class consciousness, the labor theory of value, certain attitudes toward race, and the analysis of domination, etc., which come out of the Marxist tradition. But for me it's much less than it is for you a coherent doctrine. For me it's a series of gestures, sometimes recuperated by parties, sometimes not. Sometimes by experience, sometimes not. Sometimes by theory, sometimes not. It is very difficult for me to identify with Marxism. You say what are you identifying with. I can't identify with a Marxist party here. I can't identify with a Marxist rhetoric here, or a discourse, and the same is true in the Arab world. So in my own experience there is this strange gap. It would therefore be presumptuous for me to say, well, I identify with the Marxism of Lukács, or the Marxism of Adorno. They all strike me as interesting, perhaps historically important texts, but no more than that.

And yet, just to conclude, I've also been very much conscious of Marxism and have tried my best to deal with it in a very vigorous way. I have been conscious of the anti-Marxist gestures of some of the philosophers and theoreticians who interest me, such as Foucault, who is at times hysterically anti-Marxist. I'm aware as well of the anti-

Marxism and anti-communism of most of the American intelligentsia. But in the main, I find myself to a certain degree in sympathy with Chomsky's position, a kind of anarcho-syndicalist position, which has great romantic appeal. Like Chomsky, I am suspicious of Bolshevism and have a general fear of dogmatic and orthodox consensus. Perhaps I'm too interested in alternatives which, it seems to me, Marxism has foreclosed. What I'm really trying to say is that the rhetorical and discursive accounts in Marxism, the accounts that are given by Marxists in this setting we are discussing, strike me often as less interesting than other theoretical and political possibilities that are not comprehended by those statements. I just think intellectually and politically in this country we're capable of a much more active and more effective role without trying ourselves to fetishize ideas about what Marxism is or could be. It seems to me that—given the peculiar structure of an immigrant society such as this, which has nevertheless transformed itself into a society of domination, of class, and of privilege with astonishing kinds of economic and social imbalances and distortions—in this society there's more scope for an intellectual project that isn't so circumscribed.

Would you say that the movement, particularly in the intifada *and I suppose before, has become, even though the PLO is not a Marxist party, nonetheless, would you say that the Palestinian national movement is a class-based movement?*

Yes, to some degree, and I'm distressed now, because of the configurations of the international and regional contacts, of the extent to which, at least outside the occupied territories, the movement is dominated by class interests that are not at all progressive. There is a tremendous confluence of the high Palestinian bourgeoisie in the PLO, and with it an ideological dependency upon the United States viewed as the private fiefdom of whichever administration happens to be in office. There are all kinds of negative things that we can go into in greater detail; they distress me a great deal. On the other hand, you simply can't overlook the fact that Fatah is the most powerful force. Of course, it's probably not as strong intellectually and in leadership—in which the Communist Party, Democratic Front, Popular Front, and the Islamic movements all participate. It seems to me, however, that the idea of a unified leadership is the solution. Some kind of coalition for the purposes of insurrection. But in the final analysis, once you move into action, then there are other considerations, other tactics, that have to come into play.

Gramsci's essay "The Revolution against Capital," a reading of the October Revolution, suggests that the revolution didn't follow what Marx had predicted, but was in some respects a creative departure from, a reaction against, following through all of those things Marx said about the class struggle. I think that kind of superceding is always true, which of course is one of the reasons why Gramsci is such a problem, not only in Western Marxism, but in Italian Marxism too.

It surprised me in your recent writing how favorable you were to Deleuze and Guattari's notion of a politics of dissent that comes out of things like urban movements, student squatters, etc. Taking that together with what one might call your voluntarism of attention—which is a word that you privilege in literary critical terms and I think translate into the political sphere—how would you position yourself now?

Yes, I'm not happy with that formulation. I was just anxious to get to some kind of conclusion quickly, but in fact I would prefer to have a much more open conclusion. It's really a statement of where one could find possibilities for alliances. It derives from a certain despair, really for the most part of finding allies for what I'm interested in doing in the traditional places. My stress upon the informal, the unconventional, the unplaced, is a shorthand for saying one must look elsewhere than in the rituals and performances of conventional metropolitan intellectuals.

This isn't a recommendation for a kind of micro-politics?

Not at all. The more I've looked at that sort of thing, the more it strikes me as a spinning of wheels. To end on a kind of self-critical note, I seem to be in a position of saying about various critical or political projects, well, they're doing this right, but they aren't doing that part right. I don't want to seem to go through ticking off what's good and what's bad. I'm simply registering reactions to things that you're asking about. I'm really much less than perhaps I give the impression, much less certain about what I'm doing and my whole enterprise as I see it now, with this work on culture and imperialism and on music. I'm often concerned that I'm simply dipping into certain formations, certain moments of culture and political experience, and I really do view what I am doing as a suggestion for others to help in, or provide me with ways in which I might go. The one thing I want to resist is the idea of a finished project, or one that can be put coherently into a new language or a new theoretical mode. I feel very strongly about that; it's not what I'm interested in; that's what I want to get away from.

If I ever get around to it, what I may be doing in a few years from now is a book on intellectuals. It would be an attempt to talk about this different style, rather than the one which has characterized the intellectual specialist, the policymaker, or the formulator of new disciplines. What is the word that Peirce uses? Some notion of *abduction,* generalizing from the known facts. A hypothesis of the new situation, projecting forward. I suppose it also is an admission of the fact that I still feel, even with regard to the Palestinian movement, and certainly in the context in America in which I find myself—I still feel, finally, somehow misplaced. I don't feel that I really have found or can ever find a solid, unchanging mode in which to work.

Interview with Jennifer Wicke and Michael Sprinker in
Edward Said: A Critical Reader, Oxford, 1992

SEVEN

WILD ORCHIDS AND TROTSKY

Can we begin with Beginnings?

Yes. The book, I suppose, has an autobiographical root, which has to do with the '67 war. Nineteen sixty-seven was a watershed in my life because up until then I had been two people: on the one hand teaching at Columbia doing English and comparative literary studies with some theory, and so on, and on the other going back and forth to the Middle East, where my family lived.

The war happened while I was here in America. And it was a shattering experience for me, partly because of the distance and partly because of the tremendous upheavals, the consequences of which we are still living with today. I mean, the rest of Palestine was gone; the Arab armies were destroyed; Abdel Nasser resigned on June 9, then returned to power a few days later by popular acclaim. I found myself trying to come to terms with those events, and that is where I hit upon the importance of beginnings, which, as opposed to origins, are something you fashion for yourself.

I had recently reviewed Frank Kermode's *Sense of an Ending*. I wrote about it in the old *Herald Tribune* when it came out and I liked it. I've liked a lot of his stuff. But I noted there that it seemed to me more important in human life to be concerned about beginnings than about ends. And I said it was a situational thing. He tried to universalize matters and argued that the ending was always the most important thing.

I said, no, beginnings sometimes are more important, and I tried to give examples: revolutionary periods, for instance, certain moments in the life of the mind and of general consciousness. The main point was that certain periods, and this was clearly one of them, required a redefinition of one's own situation. And that in order to project where one was to go, one needed a sense of beginnings as starting points.

A major theme of the book was the act of will required: You had to say, "That is my beginning and I am going to go in this direction." And there, the great influence was Vico.

The book went on to try to bring this to bear upon literature and criticism. By that time I had absorbed a great deal of recent Continental theory, and in it I noticed an interest in the same kind of redefinitions, in the importance of refashioning in order to do something new. In other words, the whole idea was associated with novelty, revolution, the inauguration of a new stage, and so on.

So all these things came together, and I found that this new thinking opened up a lot in the study of literature—the novel, for example, which is really about inaugurations. It is a thought that has never left me since then because I keep coming back to it—you know, Daniel Defoe, the whole Robinson Crusoe project, which is central to the history of the novel.

And then the notion of what a text is and how one thinks about texts and how texts very often are associated with particular kinds of conventions and particular kinds of forces, some of which have to be associated with beginnings and breakings off and starting points.

I also took up the criticism that was coming out at the time, especially Derrida and Foucault.

You are generally much more optimistic about the possibilities for beginnings than they are, aren't you?

Yes, absolutely, absolutely. All of us, including them, were very much under the influence of 1968—that is, the startling events of 1968. The irony for me of course is that I was like Fabrizio at the Battle of Waterloo. I was a member of the Columbia faculty, and at the greatest moment of upheaval in its life I was not here. I was on leave. I was at the University of Illinois, in 1967–68, where I had gotten a fellowship at the newly established Center for Advanced Studies.

In the middle of the spring of '68, when the revolution broke out here, I got a telegram signed, I think, by Grayson Kirk, telling me that there was to be an important faculty meeting and "Would you come?"

So I flew to New York. The meeting was being held at the Law School, and I got to 116th Street and Amsterdam, where the entrance to the Law School is, and I noticed that there was a police barrier. I could not get through because I didn't have a valid I.D. So I had come all the way to New York, could not attend the meeting, and of course went back rather forlorn to Urbana.

But the point was that it was part of the period of upheaval. It was also a moment of upheaval on my Arab side, which was deeply depressing. And then there was the student upheaval which was very optimistic. Theoretically anyway, it was like a new dawn.

And above all, intellectually, it was very important because it allowed me to break out of this rigid double structure that I had found myself in and to think in terms of new, and above all *intellectual,* paths—but intellectual in a wide sense. I do not mean professional. I have never been interested in the professional at all. But I saw the intellectual potential to fashion a different kind of life and production for myself, given the sort of capsizing of one life—my Arab life—and the turbulence of the other—my American one. And that is what set me off.

Now, this is where I found problems in some of the French theorists: First of all, it struck me—and this is absolutely central to what I did in *Beginnings* and to what I have done ever since—that even those theorists like Derrida, who appear to be breaking away from all the structures and the orthodoxies, the logocentrism, phallocentrism, etc., etc., in time became prisoners of their own—I would not call it "system," but I would certainly call it their own "manner."

And I became even more disillusioned with Foucault because at least in parts of Derrida there is wit; sometimes there is almost an aspect of triviality because there is so much of it. There is a lot of circling around, a lot of meandering, a lot of, finally, dismissal of stuff, with some interesting insights, particularly in his earlier work.

I felt that Foucault had this initial idea based upon the notion of confinement—confinement and the challenge to the confinement, the breaking loose—which we now know has a lot to do with his own biographical trajectory. A man named James Miller is doing a kind of revisionist biography of Foucault, and Miller's point is that Foucault was always dealing with sadomasochistic impulses, including an early attempt at suicide. So this idea of confinement was very important to sort of getting it down and then breaking it open, hence the early importance to him of figures like de Sade.

But in time, what I think happened—and it was certainly true of Lacan and Althusser—to Derrida, Foucault, and some of the others is that they became prisoners of their own language, that what they were really doing was producing more work in fidelity to what they'd done before. They were maintaining the integrity of their work and, above all, maintaining a kind of loyalty to their readers, who expected more of the same.

In other words, I think Derrida has been very interested in having disciples and followers.

He's founded a school.

The most elite of schools. And I have never been interested in that because it seemed to me to be somehow imprisoning, and finally uninteresting. For me, it has always been a matter of exploration, of self-criticism and constant change in trying to surprise myself as well as my readers.

So I found that to be deeply problematic in their work. And above all, I found—the last point—I found, especially in the early seventies and thereafter, that they were fantastically Eurocentric. They were interested only in Europe—not even Europe, really. They were franco-centric.

And I have always been opposed to any kind of centricity—as opposed to eccentricity—whether it is Afrocentric or Eurocentric or American-centric or whatever. It strikes me as very much the opposite, for temperamental and even ideological reasons, of what I want to do.

And it was at this point in the late sixties and early seventies that for me the notion of beginning also meant, really, the beginning of a fairly deep political and moral affiliation with the resurgence, after 1967, of the Palestinian movement. It happened altogether, you know, between '67 and, say, '71 and '72, and led to the publication, in 1975, of *Beginnings*.

For the first time I felt that it was possible to integrate these two aspects of my life, so that my returns to the Middle East in the summer and during the year and so on were no longer just visits with my family but part of an active political life. Members of my family, schoolmates of mine, acquaintances, friends were all beginning to be part of the movement. And I got into that.

And for the first time in my life, in 1972–73, I found myself restudying Arabic, which I had learned as a kid. It was my first language. But I had never studied in Arabic except when I was in school. But it was an English school, and whatever courses we had in Arabic were marginal. The main thing was to study English history, English literature, and that sort of thing.

In 1972–73 I was on a sabbatical leave in Beirut, and I took daily tutorials in Arabic from an eminent philologist at the American University of Beirut. I began to be aware of, in a serious way, Arabic and Islamic culture.

It was that experience, you see, that began to make me very critical of these theoretical pronouncements because they did not seem to respond to what a large part of the world was experiencing in the aftermath of imperialism, the problems of neocolonialism and, for me above all, the problems of Palestine.

One way to think about Orientalism, *the book you published in 1978 and for which you are probably best known, is that it both is, and in dramatic ways is not, in line with Foucault and his sense that intellectual discourses merge with power to create modes of human oppression that are virtually impossible to challenge. In Foucault, there isn't much that can't be done. Your sense is that more awareness of the confining structures can lead to relative freedom. If I understand you correctly, Orientalism is pervasive, imposing, confining, but finally can be thrown off?*

Yes. It was about that time, while I was working on the final sections of *Orientalism* (which I really began to write, I would say, probably in the aftermath of the '73 war), that it seemed to me that, although it was certainly short-lived, there was some real hope. I'm thinking of the attempt by the Syrians and the Egyptians and, to a lesser extent, the Palestinians to break down the Israeli hold on the occupied territories.

Do not forget that the Egyptians had gone through the holding of the Suez Canal. The Syrians had broken through the Israeli lines on the Golan Heights when it was apparent that they could not do anything, just as almost twenty years later the *intifada* broke out when everybody said the Palestinians were finished.

That has always interested me the most. I mean how—given the domination of one or another powerful system, whether economic, social, or political—one can break through. That is the most interesting thing, I think, about human behavior—that and the way people try to build on it, that oppositional quality.

So that is what I found about Orientalism—that you could study it and oppose it.

At the beginning of the book, you offer a characterization of Orientalism:

> Taking the late eighteenth century as a very roughly defined starting point Orientalism can be discussed and analyzed as the corporate institution for dealing with the Orient—dealing with it by making statements about it, authorizing views of it, describing it, by teaching it, settling it, ruling over it: in short, Orientalism as a Western-style for dominating, restructuring and having authority over the Orient. I have found it useful here to employ Michel Foucault's notion, as described by him in *The Archaeology of Knowledge* and in *Discipline and Punish*, to identify Orientalism. My contention is that without examining Orientalism as a discourse, one cannot possibly understand the enormously systematic discipline by which European culture was able to manage—and even produce—the Orient politically, sociologically, militarily, ideologically, scientifically, and imaginatively during the post-Enlightenment period.

Right. Yes. I would only add that in the modern version that most interested me in the book, Orientalism is associated with imperialism. In other words, it is a style of knowledge that goes hand in hand with, or is manufactured or produced out of, the actual control or domination of real geographical territory and people.

So Orientalism is not just a vicarious experience of marvels of the East; it is not just some vague imagining about what the Orient is, although there is some of that there. But it really has to do with how you control actual populations; it is associated with the actual domination of the Orient, beginning with Napoleon.

Yes. But in a passage like this there is the Foucaultian sense that discourse can initiate domination.

Yes. And I find that it is, in a certain sense, much more mysterious than simply a kind of causal phenomenon. You know, there is domination. Then there is this or there is that. There is discourse, and then there is, you know, invasion.

But the difference is that Foucault always seems to align himself with Power. He is like a scribe of a kind of irresistible, ineluctable power. And I was writing in order to oppose that power, so it was written out of a political position. At the end, although it got to be rather helter-skelter, I tried to show the lineaments of a kind of counter-Orientalism.

How do you come out with a more optimistic view than Foucault does? Is it a temperamental difference between the two of you?

No, I think the real difference is . . . I think it is temperamental, but if you wanted to put your finger on one particular thing and one particular style of thought, I think it's the Gramsci factor.

I read the English translation of Gramsci's *Notebooks* shortly after it appeared in the early 1970s and found it intriguing but unsatisfying. There were too many ellipses; there were too many difficulties in understanding, literally, what Gramsci was about. It took reading the Italian to see what he was actually getting at. There is a very important passage in *Orientalism* where I cite Gramsci's observation that "the starting point of critical elaboration is the consciousness of what one really is, and is 'knowing thyself' as a product of the historical process to date, which has deposited in you an infinity of traces, without leaving an inventory."

Now, that is all the English translation says. But actually, in the original, which I then looked up, Gramsci said, "Therefore, it is imperative at the outset to compile such an inventory." You see? That was the difference. It is saying not just, "There it is," but then, "By *you* making an inventory"—and this is where the influence of Vico was very important—"you give it a kind of structure that allows you then to confront it, dismantle it." And that is what was terribly important for me in *Orientalism.*

But I could not possibly foresee, in writing *Orientalism*—in fact, it has never ceased to amaze me—the incredible transformations of the book thereafter, because it has now been translated into seventeen or eighteen languages. It has been in print for thirteen years and it's selling in all the languages into which it has been translated. I was informed over the weekend that there is a Chinese translation that has not been published yet, but it has been completed. It is also in Japanese.

Is there a relationship between the Orientalism book and your next work, The Question of Palestine?

Orientalism was published in '78, and I had become more directly involved in politics. But expatriate politics have a downside to them. That is to say, you are always at a distance. And even in the days when I was much younger, I could travel a lot, but I was still teaching.

Nevertheless, in 1977 I became a member of the Palestine National Council, and it then occurred to me that it would be very important to continue *Orientalism,* which is a general book, and to look at particular cases—you might say, the other side, since *Orientalism* did not say anything about what "the Orient" genuinely was all about.

I wanted to write a political essay that was fully engaged—I mean, I never pretended that it was anything but that. If you remember, in the beginning I take up many of the same points that I did in *Orientalism,* though this time with specific reference to Palestine. I wanted to show Palestine from the point of view of the victims.

And I think I coined this idea of an alternative history, an instance of which I gave in *The Question of Palestine.* So it is directly related to *Orientalism.*

In fact, I wrote the three books—*Orientalism, The Question of Palestine,* and *Covering Islam*—more or less right after each other. And they appeared within a year of each other. Two of them, I think, appeared within the same year.

The objective of *The Question of Palestine* was to put the Palestinian case before an American audience. It was not meant to be written for an Arab audience, but a Western readership, given that the West had played a very important role in the formation of Palestine. That is to say, the Zionist movement came largely out of the West. It was supported by the West.

I wanted to give Americans a sense of what the dispossession and the alienation of Palestine meant from the Palestinian point of view. It was the first time I was able to write about this from my own experience, and I tried to reach a larger audience with it. In fact, I had a lot of trouble getting the book published.

What happened?

I had been approached by several publishers, actually, in the middle to late seventies, to write a book about Palestine. And the first one shied away after they approached me. Then the second one, or the third one, or the fourth one, gave me a contract.

And when I turned the book in to Beacon Press in the summer of 1978—I remember this very well; I had pneumonia that summer—I got a very long letter back from them, signed by the woman who had commissioned me to do it. She wanted me to write another book, in effect. And, of course, I was tremendously angry.

And so I said, "In that case, you are canceling the contract!"

She said, "No."

And I realized that it was a way of getting me either to write another book or to give her back the advance. So I gave her back the advance.

Then I looked around some more. I went to the publisher of *Orientalism*, Pantheon, and showed it to André Schiffrin, and he refused to publish the book. He said it was not historical enough.

And I said, "What does that mean?"

And he said, "Well, you don't talk about oil."

And I said, "Oil is hardly at the center of the controversy, of the struggle over Palestine between Israelis or Jews and Arabs."

And I realized it was an ideological argument he was making.

So I went to two or three other publishers. And finally, by a chain of circumstances, in the fall of 1978, New York Times Books accepted it and it was published.

And then Schiffrin bought the book in paperback. That was ironic. They would not publish it originally, but they wanted it when it was successful.

Presumably the resistance to publishing it bears out the thesis of Orientalism?

Exactly—that was the whole point. They did not want the *other* person to speak. They did not want me to say these things. And what I was saying had never been said before in English in a mainstream publication. In the late seventies there was hardly anything. Palestinians were already quite clearly terrorists, and they wanted to keep it that way.

That was the point of *The Question of Palestine*. And, if I may say so, it was the first time in English, the first time in a clear way, that a Palestinian had said, "We must live together with the Israeli Jews." I made the point of coexistence, that there was no military option, in the final pages of the book. And these are things that are now echoed—many of them have been echoed not only in Palestinian writing but also in Israeli writing. But I think I was one of the first to actually say that in a clear way, from the Palestinian point of view.

Are there tensions between being a literary scholar and being involved in political issues? Or do they work reciprocally?

I think, on the whole for me, they work reciprocally. The tension lies in the fact that I have tended to resist the exigencies of politics—which have to do with authority, with power, with confrontation, with rapid responses—simply because I have always wanted to maintain privacy for my own reflections, and so on. I have tried to remain outside of direct political office of one sort or another—God knows a good many have been offered me, or suggested for me—in order to be able to reflect in this literary way, which takes more time, requires more solitude.

Politics is the art of the gregarious, in a way. It is the art of being with a lot of other people. And I am not made that way, although I can be very personable and I can deal with people.

Do you feel that the things you say in your political writing have ever compromised you?

Well, I have had to deal with that problem a great deal since the late seventies because one has many constituencies. On the one hand, I am writing for an immediate audience, you know, which is not academic, which is engaged politically. So in America I have a constituency made up of people who count for me—let us say liberals—people interested in the Middle East, who are neither Arab nor Jew.

Then there are policymakers, and it is very important for me to be able to address them. And I take them into account, officials, and so on. Then there are the ethnic and political constituencies. For example, when I wrote *The Question of Palestine,* I was dealing with a largely monolithic but not entirely monolithic so-called Jewish community in this country, and it was my interest to engage their attention and to draw things into focus—which the book did, in part. Of course, it is not just the book. You follow it up. You talk. I did an enormous amount of speaking.

Always, I try to strike a balance between my literary and cultural stuff on the one hand and my political work on the other. And then there was a community of Palestinians. I mean, I was very much writing to Arabs and Palestinians. But then, of course, we are so fractionalized that I got many attacks. For example, the Popular Front published a tremendous broadside against me when *The Question of Palestine* came out, attacking me for compromise, for—what is the word?—capitulationism, all kinds of things. And other people praised it, you know. So I am very much aware of the constituencies with which I'm working.

What is coming through to me is that, in certain ways, your method comes out of the humanistic tradition of Arnold and Trilling, and what you are asking people to do is to apply humanistic values in ways that are much broader than Arnold or Trilling ever maintained.

Or more consistently. More consistently. You see, because there is nothing I disagree with in the broad, humanistic tradition. One of the things I have spent the last seven or eight years of my life doing is writing a kind of sequel to *Orientalism*. There is a big book I have been working on called *Culture and Imperialism* that studies the way in which the broad humanistic principles, the Western principles in which I was educated and feel very much at home, have always stopped short of national boundaries.

I will give you an example: De Tocqueville, right? His reflections on the United States in *Democracy in America* are, I would say, very critical of the American treatment of the Indian and of the black, of slavery in the South.

At the same time, or shortly after that, De Tocqueville—because he was a member of the French Assembly—was very involved in French colonial policy in North Africa. He justified the worst abuses by the French in Algeria, massacres of people, and so on and so forth. And then you realize that what prevented him from being consistent was a kind of nationalism that says it is all right to criticize them, but when it comes to *us,* we are always right.

I have always hated that. That, I would say, is the number one idol of the tribe that intellectually and morally and politically I have always been against. I mean, the idea that there should be three or four sets of principles for the behavior of people toward each other strikes me as one of the most difficult concepts to dislodge.

You see it in John Stuart Mill, the great apostle of liberty and freedom and democracy from whom we have all learned. But he never advocated anything but continued dependence and subjection for the Indians when he was in the India Office. And I attempt, in my new book, to bring these things forward and show how they really work.

And then I go on to talk about decolonization, which I did not do in *Orientalism*. There I discuss it only from the European side. A whole portion of my book concerns what I call opposition and resistance, how from the first moment the white man sets foot in whatever part of the world it is—the New World, Latin America, Africa, Asia, wherever— there is resistance. And that gradually builds. It builds until it climaxes, of course, in the great decolonization that occurs during the period after World War II, to create a particular culture of resistance and liberation, and I talk about that. You see, that is something I did not do in *Orientalism*. Now I will try and show the other side.

And in the new book I advance a critique of nationalism—its short-comings as well as its necessity, because I grew up in that very same world of postwar Third World nationalism. You see, these are my two worlds: the world of the West and the world of the Third World. Nationalism, which is necessary to combat imperialism, then turns into a kind of fetishization of the native essence and identity. You see it in countries like Egypt. You see it in countries like Syria. You see it in Zaire, in Iran, in the Philippines. And the climax of this is, of course, reached in the war between the United States and Iraq last spring—a battle of a kind of, in my opinion, decayed nationalism. Along with that go notions of identity, of essence, Englishness, Americanness, African-ness, Arabness, etc. Every culture that you could think of does more or less the same thing.

Yes. It seems that hand in hand with your critique of nationalism or racialism is a lot of suspicion of religion, of transcendent philosophies.

For me, religion is two things. I grew up in a land completely impregnated with religion. The only natural business of Palestine is the manufacture of religion. I mean, that is what we did, if you think about it for a minute, right? I grew up in the Arabic church, to which my great-grandfather was a major contributor. He translated the Bible into Arabic, and he was the first native Protestant. I come from Protestant stock, an offshoot of Greek orthodoxy. You see, the missionaries in our part of the world hardly converted any Jews and Muslims. The only people they converted were other Christians.

So my family on one side is converted from Greek orthodoxy to Episcopalianism, or Anglican Protestantism. And on my mother's side they are converts to Baptism and evangelicalism. My grandfather was a Baptist minister. So I grew up in that sort of religious environment, as well as bilingually, English and Arabic. I know both rites, and they mean a lot to me, the Book of Common Prayer, the Arabic Bible, hymns, and so on and so forth.

I have no misgivings about religion as a private autobiographical experience. And there is a sense of community among the small number of Christians in that part of the world. We are a small minority.

What I dislike is the hijacking of religion for political purposes, the second phenomenon. Fundamentalism—a term invidiously fastened only upon Islamics—certainly exists in Judaism and Christianity in our part of the world. And in America right now.

Worldliness is central for you.

Worldliness, secularity, etc., are key terms for me. And it is also part of my critique of and discomfort with religion that I am very, I have recently become very—how shall I put it?—ill at ease with jargons and obfuscations. I mean, special private languages of criticism and professionalism, and so on: I have no time for that. It is much more important for me that people write in order to be understood rather than write in order to be misunderstood.

So the critique, such as it is, is not a systematic critique of religion. It really deals with religious fanaticism—that is to say, going back to some book and trying to bring it back to bear upon the present. That phenomenon is comparable to nativism, you know, the idea that there is some horribly troubling present-day situation from which you must escape and find solace in a pure essence back there in time. Then there's the organizational aspect, which has to do with any kind of guild, association, private fiefdom—which automatically, in my opinion, means tyranny and suffering for the designated and excluded others.

Political criticism has now become very common in the academy, and recently, I know, you were involved in an exchange that probably sheds light on some of the new developments.

Well, it was a funny kind of thing and the sort of experience, I suppose, that many of us have had. It was at Princeton, at the Davis Center, and I had sent about thirty or forty pages of the introduction to my new book on imperialism. You send on the piece in advance, and then there is a discussion. There were a lot of people there. I was impressed at how many turned up, mostly graduate students and faculty.

A summary of the paper was given by the director, and then I made a few comments, and the floor was opened to discussion. The first comment pointed out that in the first thirteen or fourteen pages of my manuscript I did not mention any living Afro-American women, etc. Most of the people I was quoting from, it was alleged, were dead white European males.

And since I was talking about the origins of a certain kind of global thought in strangely disparate fields like geography and comparative literature in Europe and America in the late nineteenth century, I said it was inappropriate for me to talk about living nonwhite females.

And then this woman said, "Yes, but then you talk about C. L. R. James."

And I said, "Yes. I mean, there you are. He is not European."

The only answer I got in response to that was a kind of dismissal of C. L. R. James, who is very important to me. I have written a lot about him. The problem, I was informed, was that he is dead. And that was all part of a kind of hostility toward me.

It was a hostile question?

Yes, very hostile. I mean, it was announced as hostile, even before it began. And later, at lunch, she gave me an even harsher treatment, accusing me of one thing and another.

Then I said, "Listen, I don't think you know who I am. I don't think you've read anything I've written, because the last thing I could be accused of is that sort of thing."

And then I was told by her that it was "time to be sent back." She said, "I am going to send you back to your white people now." And she got up from the table and sort of waved me off like that. I thought that was really outrageous.

Another interlocutor during the seminar was this retired professor, whom I have known most of my life (he is also an Arab), defending Orientalism and saying that Orientalism was a very good thing for us. Well,

I don't think he spoke about us, he spoke about those people out there because, without the imperialism that produced Orientalism, *they* would not have been able to do anything, and so on and so forth, and the Europeans taught us how to read cuneiform and hieroglyphics and understand our own traditions, which we could not have done on our own.

It struck me as an absurd thing that academic discourse about the relations between cultures—which was really what I was talking about—and between different groups should always be either conflictual in a clearly marked way—you must be for one and against the other—or completely reductive in an equally caricatural way. You know, one says, "Well, it is all imperialism," and another says, "Without imperialism, we would have been nothing." And that I found very depressing.

One of the great problems is that the polemics on both sides in this stupid debate, about the canon, about culture, and about the university and all that, are so basically ill-informed. First, they do not seek to know much about the historical experience of the West, nor of the non-West.

Second, they are such poor readers that they think whole traditions can be reduced to caricatures, such as, "It is all racist," or "It is this, that, or the other thing." That, it seems to me, goes completely against the grain of the dissenting traditions offered up, say, by anti-imperialism or by feminism. It becomes silly and reductive. And it seems to me to reflect very poorly, not on the American academy—about which I have very positive feelings, because I would not want to exchange my life there for anything else—but on these manipulators of the academy who have become, in a certain sense, floor traders, who are deriving careers from it, like D'Souza and his opponents.

Why do you think the controversies about the academy have risen up now?

I don't really know. It's hard to tell. Probably . . . well, I could speculate. One reason is that, it does seem to me, there is a complete divorce between the academy and the world. The American academic in particular has a unique kind of arrogance, a presumption that he or she can talk about these general issues without any form of commitment to any social or political institution except the academy and the furthering of a career. I think that is one thing.

I think it is also the position of America in the world, where most of us are allowed to act that way because we are singularly untouched. I mean, look at the war in Iraq. It was one of the most horrible experiences of my life, and I did a huge number of interviews and speeches and I wrote a lot of stuff on it. Yet for most of us Americans it was little more than a remote television war. It was forgotten by those in the academy. There was no opposition to it.

So in that respect, I think it is the supreme luxury of the great imperial power to be untouched by things; that is, to talk about them the way in an Oscar Wilde play Ernest and Algernon can just babble on about whether they want to call themselves Ernest or not. It is that kind of thing.

And I think third is this idea of academic specialization. Academics have lost touch with the, shall we say, existential density of real human life, and they talk in these jargons.

I don't know. Those are just speculations. I don't know why it's happening now.

Let me make a more challenging speculation that touches on your own work.

Yes.

If you look through academic literary history, what really tends to happen is that there are people who are extremely innovative in their field—like, say, Cleanth Brooks and W. K. Wimsatt among the New Critics—and what happens over the next couple of decades is that their students and their students' students, for all purposes, routinize the achievement.

Yes.

And that there arose in the American academy strong and innovative work, by you and a very few others, that was politically oriented. But that when any criticism occurs in the academy, it is inevitably going to be literalized.

Yes.

And reduced. And even turned against its initiators.

And slenderized.

Yes, and by dissertation writers who must have terms to get their theses written.

No, I think that is true.

Is that an argument against it? Here comes the hard part. Is that an argument against a politicized form of the criticism? Do you see what I am saying? If it is going to go through the dissertation mill and it is going to become—

No, because it happens anyway. It is not the . . . Look, I think, rather than answering it directly, I first would like to draw your attention to the fact, for instance, that there is now a Conradian industry. There is a Joycean industry. There is a Yeatsian industry, a Dickensian industry. That has nothing to do with politics. There is, perhaps you might call it, a subdiscourse.

Absolutely.

But there are people who are doing routinized work on Dickens, Conrad, etc., all of these people we talked about. Now, that applies to all of the disciplines. It is, you might say, the professionalization of the discourse that we are talking about.

But it seems to me to do no great harm that Joyce becomes an industry and is, for some critics, routinized. When the plight of African-Americans becomes an industry and is routinized and people stand up and denounce you for being a racist based on not having named X, Y, and Z, that does seem harmful.

Yes. Okay. I see what you mean. But is the argument then to remove from academic scrutiny issues like race, like war, like the problematic of other cultures, relationships between cultures? I would say that that is not the solution.

I think what we need is a sense of what the university is about, you see? Here I think we have lost the spirit of the image that I keep referring to from C. L. R. James, who borrows it from Aimé Césaire: "No race possesses the monopoly of beauty, of intelligence, of force, and there is a place for all at the rendez-vous of victory."

In other words, I think the ethic implicit in a lot of current political criticism is that the academic world is a site of contest where you try to put yourself on top by bashing everybody around who does not agree with you. And that seems to me to be a mutilation of the academic quest, which is essentially not to try to resolve all of these contests in favor of one putting down all the others, but rather to try to accommodate by what I call "intellectual work," the intellectual process of research, discussion, etc., and to guard against the slenderizations, routinizations—efforts to push everybody else off the raft once you're on it.

Which I think can be done intellectually. I'm not talking about social or police work. I'm talking about intellectual work that suggests that the academy is not—this is the point I am trying to make—that the academy is *not* a place to resolve sociopolitical tensions. Perhaps it is a cliché to say the following, but it is a place to *understand* them, to understand them in their origin, to understand them in the way in which they are going, in which what is brought to bear is intellectual process. So, in that sense, I do not think the answer is to eliminate the politicized discussion, but to engage it in a rather more generous and open spirit.

When people routinized the New Criticism, there were New Critics who said, "This is a good use of this particular method." And, "This is not such a good one." And it mattered, the subtlety, performance, the acumen of the individual critic. And that is possible to do, I think, with political criticism.

But I don't think most of us, in the literary, humanistic field, have a very good sense of, let us say, the limits and the possible kinds of synchronizations that can occur between reading a literary text and politics in the national or international sense. These are very different things. And most people make the jump from a literary or intellectual argument to a political statement that cannot really be made. I mean, how do you modulate from literary interpretation to international politics? That is very difficult to do.

And most of the people who try it are so ignorant, as was manifest in the argument of the academic who told me, "But he is dead," in regard to C. L. R. James. That is not an argument! That is just silly, and needs to be exposed and dismissed.

But I think that some of the people whom you are correctly characterizing would say that one of their major influences was Edward Said.

Yes, I understand what you mean. Well, then I would say that they are stupidly misreading my books. For example, a review of *The World, the Text, and the Critic,* which I have somewhere, published by a kind of occasional journal of one of the major Jewish organizations, contends that when I talk about "secular criticism" I am using an esoteric method to advance the PLO goal of a secular democratic state to be achieved by killing all the Jews. That was actually said.

That was a creative misreading.

Exactly! A maliciously creative misreading. So one cannot always be blamed for one's misreaders, if you see what I mean, although one should, I think, probably be blamed to a certain degree. So you have to write more, explain more. Unlike Noam Chomsky, whom I admire a great deal, I am not a relentless answerer of letters or of misstatements, but I try, to a certain degree, to do it. But there is never enough time. I am always involved in something else that I want to do.

Interview with Mark Edmundson,
*Wild Orchids and Trotsky: Messages from
American Universities*, New York, 1993

CULTURE AND IMPERIALISM

We'd like to ask you to talk about the general relation between this new book, Culture and Imperialism, *and your previous work, especially the major texts, such as* Beginnings, Orientalism, *and* The World, the Text, and the Critic. *Could you take as a point of departure the way in which, in* Beginnings, *you characterize the task of the critical intellectual as "anti-dynastic"?*

Well, the closest parallel, I think, is with *Orientalism,* because I had actually thought of this book as a sequel to *Orientalism.* I started writing it almost immediately after *Orientalism* was published and after the initial responses in the form of reviews, and so on, came in. At the time, I thought that what I wanted to do was to write something that would deal with some of the problems in *Orientalism.* In fact, I did write an essay called "Orientalism Reconsidered," which I had originally thought of publishing as a kind of appendix to this book and which was in the nature of a response to critics and an attempt to explain further and develop some of the ideas in *Orientalism* that weren't well explained.

In addition, there were two important things that I felt I needed to do: In time, these gave *Culture and Imperialism* a non-dynastic relationship with my earlier books. One of them was to talk about other parts of the world where relationships exist between what I described in *Orientalism* and the more general imperial experience—I mean in places like India, since a number of people who read *Orientalism* were Indologists, or were interested in Indian studies, and so on. *Orientalism* didn't really cover Asia at all. So, I wanted to extend the analysis to include further and different places than the Arab and Islamic Near East. The second thing I wanted to do was to deal more extensively with the response to imperialism, that is to say, the resistances, as well as the oppositional work, of European and American intellectuals and scholars who couldn't be considered a part of the structure of things like Orientalism. Those are two things I obviously tried to do in this book. I also felt that what was most often misconstrued, misrepresented, and distorted in reviews or accounts of *Orientalism* (incidentally, I think there were numerous misreadings of *Orientalism,* mischievous ones in my opinion) was my account of the West; a number of people said that I seemed to be claiming that there was a monolithic object called the West and that I was being very reductive. That was the charge. Of course, I took great exception to that, because if that had been the case, then why would I have written as big a book and had as many different analyses and dealt with as many different people as I did in *Orientalism*? My whole point about the West wasn't that it was monolithic, but extremely varied. So, I thought it was important to stress the changing, and the constantly modified, structure of this material both in this book and retrospectively in *Orientalism*. I think that's one of the important things that I was trying to do.

Also, in the intervening years between *Orientalism* and this book, I had begun to write more about music, and most of my writing about music is really focused on contrapuntal work. I mean, that's what interests me the most; even forms like opera interest me, I think, for that reason: forms in which many things go on simultaneously. And my favorite works in this genre are works that are not what you would call developmental or sonata-form works but, rather, works that are variation-structure works, like the Goldberg Variations, for example, or Bach's Canonic Variations, and it's that structure that I found tremendously useful in writing *Culture and Imperialism*. This has been a long-standing predilection of mine; it's the kind of music I'm most interested in and one of the reasons why I was so compelled by Glenn Gould, which I think had a direct bearing on this book. I wanted, therefore, to try to organize it in a way that was modeled on an art, rather than a powerful scholarly form—the idea of a kind of exfoliating structure of variation which, I think, is the way this book was, in fact, organized. The whole idea of interdependent histories, of overlapping characters, and all of that is very important to the enterprise.

A third aspect of the book that is connected to some of my earlier things is the whole idea of contest; *contestation* is the actual word I use. In *Orientalism*, I think, this is perhaps one of the negative effects of Foucault: You get the impression that Orientalism is just continuing to grow and have more power. This is misleading. I was much more interested in locating the axis of this book, *Culture and Imperialism*, in the contest over territory, which is at bottom what I am really writing about. A fourth issue is, of course, the role of the intellectual. The intellectual is not really a neutral figure; he or she is not really somebody who is standing above it all and just pontificating, but somebody who is really somehow involved in it. One of the people I quote here is Thomas Hodgkin as he talks about the word *collaboration,* and the difference between theories of imperialism that try to "describe it" and theories of imperialism that try to "end it"—so I am really talking about that. In other words, this book was intended to deal with those things that might have an effect on hastening the demise of imperial structure, although I realize it's a kind of impossible goal. So those are some of the things I was trying to do.

There's one major motif that runs throughout your work, even starting with Beginnings, *and that's "the worldly."*

Oh, worldly, yes.

It is prominent in Orientalism, *already in the introduction, and then in* The World, the Text, and the Critic, *and also in* Musical Elaborations, *where the whole discussion links the appreciation of the aesthetic with the worldly, whether we call it history, or whatever. Now, in* Culture and Imperialism, *this motif seems to be omnipresent either in terms of worldliness, or in your use of the term* secular, *or in your insistence on historical particularity, and so on.*

That's very important for me, because one of the things I want to suggest is that the things I discuss are all taking place in a kind of public realm. In the last chapter of the book, when I talk about America, when I talk about the public sphere, that's really what I had in mind. But the whole idea of worldliness is to show that even writers like Jane Austen who are known to be—well, if not otherworldly, then, sort of very fastidious—basically unpolitical, if you like, in the gross sense of the word— were very much the opposite. If you want to look for the public realm in their work, you can find it. So, I talk about, in a sense, exposing a kind of public side, a worldly side of these canonical texts that is usually ig-nored—ignored, by the way, not because it's easy to miss but because in some way to pay attention to it could be like an inconvenience. I mean, why do we need to talk about India when we talk about Thackeray, you could say. Or, others say, why do we need to talk about the West Indies or about the Mediterranean or even about India when we talk about Jane Austen? Or, why do we need to talk about India, or Egypt, or Aus-tralia if we want to talk about Dickens; they seem like extraneous things. My argument is that these, first of all, are the works of very pub-lic authors; nobody could be more public than Dickens. In the second place, obviously, all these authors—Jane Austen is the same—want au-diences and, therefore, solicit their attention by these references. So that's what I have in mind.

There is one point I want to go back to, which I forgot to mention; the idea of the anti-dynastic intellectual is very important to me. To tell you the honest truth, that's a specially important point for me, because ever since I was a student, I was aware of the whole question of disci-pleship, which is fascinating because being a student of somebody and then being a teacher of somebody—that kind of relationship—is repli-cated not only in our lives at the university but even before that when we're students. I have always had a very complicated feeling about this, because I don't like to be thought of as somebody else's person, in the first instance. And, in the second instance, I don't want anybody to be my person. In other words, I stake a great deal on the question of doing something for oneself. It's a form of independence, I suppose, which (a) I cherish, and (b) I don't think the kinds of works I write—like this book, or *Orientalism,* or any of the other things that I've written—I don't think they derive from formulas or concepts that can be handed on. They really derive from personal experience, and that's something terribly important to me.

I talked about this in a series of lectures I gave this last spring at Stan-ford, the Camp Lectures, which are going to be published later this com-ing year. The title of the lecture series I gave is "The Historical Study of Literature and the Intellectual Vocation." In the first lecture, entitled "Historical Experience," I argue that one of the things that happened to contemporary criticism (with, obviously, some exceptions) has been a transformation of the concept of experience into concepts of form and mediation and attenuation. I gave many examples. The one that most easily comes to mind is Hayden White's *Metahistory*, where there's a shift away from the contents of history, which are the historical experience of the historians that he talks about, to their form, their language, and their rhetoric, and so forth. That's been very characteristic throughout; you see it in the work of Jameson, for example, and the New Historicists, in general. I wanted to get back to historical experience. This book is based upon a series of historical experiences that have a great deal of importance for me. They can't, however, be thought of as readymade; in other words, you have to try to reconstitute these experiences yourself, in your work. Hence, the anti-dynastic sense of it. On the other hand, they're not such special and such rare experiences that other people can't understand them; I think they can because they're the experiences of many, many people.

One of the questions we were wondering about has to do with the category of will. Perhaps in light of what you've just said you'd like to talk about that. I can remember from many years ago a review of Beginnings, *by Hayden White, in fact, which specified the will as precisely the central category of your critical practice. In* Culture and Imperialism, *will is still the central object of analysis and, as you've just said, this book is very much concerned with the problem of contestation. Yet, as I read this book, the category of will is now in tension with what I think I will call, for want of a better term, the book's grander humanistic vision, which is motivated by a horror at the activity of the will—which now appears as not only reductive in scholarship and criticism and in such things as identity politics but also horrendous in the world where it produces war—competition and contestation that pits nations, communities, and groups against each other in the striving for identity rather than, as you say at the end of the book, for understanding of the other.*

At the end of *Orientalism*, I talk about a hope for a kind of noncoercive model for the human sciences, because Orientalism, I thought, really had all the elements of a coercive and rather badly intentioned (although concealed) type of will over the other. Of course, *Culture and Imperialism* is very much based on what I think is irreducible, namely, the will to domination over others, but with the added twist, in the case of the empires that I'm interested in, that they have to be others at a fair geographical distance. I find myself baffled by this; I don't really attempt to understand it, because it seems to be there and it doesn't correspond to any experience I myself have had, or any wish I might have had—in other words, to have territory at a great distance. I think it's a very special kind of historical experience and, as I've tried to argue in this book, quite unique to Britain and France at a certain moment and by imitation and in competition with other empires such as the Dutch, the Portuguese, the Spanish, and so forth.

But the thing about the will that interests me in this context is that it's an organized presence that a lot of people participate in, and it's just not a matter of the conquistadors as it was in the case of the Spanish empires of the sixteenth and seventeenth centuries. But here, what could develop was a kind of consensus around a will to dominate, in which the will to dominate really, in a certain sense, disappeared from sight but was there nonetheless. So when the scholar I quote, D. C. Platt, talks about the "departmental view"—that's what I am fascinated with, that there could come to exist a departmental view that India "is ours," and it affected people on the Left, or the Right, or the Center. I mean, John Stuart Mill felt it as much as John Seeley—all the way from the explicit apologists for empire to the ones who were what we would call liberals and, in many ways, our heroes. So, in that respect, the category of will is usually used by me in this book as a kind of negative, let us say, an unsalubrious, devastating thing. I'm very influenced by the figure of Kurtz in *Heart of Darkness,* because that is what he is: he's a creature of will. He seems to me still the most powerful example of that extraordinary and concentrated kind that we can find in literature, even though there are also the images of what I call the great colonial personalities, such as Lugard, Rhodes, Lyautey, and people of that sort. But, somehow, Kurtz, because of Conrad's immense skill, has it in a concentrated form; his plans, his projects, and so on are really what that story is about. And the failure even of somebody like Marlow afterwards (it's always retrospective) to understand what it's all about is what fascinated me.

On the other hand, there is something that is new in this book with regard to my earlier work, and that is, of course, the counter-will; that is to say, the will of other people to resist imperialism's will. I discovered this in my own experience, amongst people in my own community (like the Palestinian community) and elsewhere in the Third World, in Ireland, and so on. *Culture and Imperialism* is punctuated by a number of travels and experiences that suggested to me, in a very immediate way, the existence of a counter-will that was in play all along; what I needed was a vehicle, or method, for representing both of them, namely, domination and resistance, will and counter-will. The tragic part of it is that the contest, in general, did not really provide for a resolution of the problem of the will. In other words, it seemed to go into the next phase, particularly in the world of nationalism. Will is transformed into the will to *have* an identity and an identity politics. So, then, the question is, short of absolute passivity—which is the Schopenhaurian dilemma, in other words, either you become a kind of Buddhistic figure of withdrawal, or you become an artist, or you try to commit suicide—what is the way to resolve this problem of nationalist consciousness, which, I think you're right in saying, derives from counter-will. I think the way to see it is by an effort of a third kind of will that is an intellectual, or scholarly, or historical will to see will and counter-will at work, and to think of an alternative to them which is reflective, non-coercive, meditative to a certain degree—all of which I was trying to do here.

A non-contestatory will?

No, I wouldn't say that; that becomes sort of passive, and there's a kind of celebratory elegiac quality to it.

I put it badly. How is the meditative and the reflective also will?

Yes, I see. I think of it as really having to do with life in the university. I thought about that a great deal, and when I went to South Africa last year, I gave this lecture called the Academic Freedom Lecture on the whole question of what is a university in a very provocative and highly charged atmosphere like that of South Africa. What is the university? In that context, you can say that the university should not be, and cannot be, a place where a victorious party uses the university as a place to expand its program. After all, I was in South Africa at a time when apartheid was beginning to abate. There was a political process of some significance there, although God knows it stalled and has taken many bad turns; but it started with the release of Mandela and de Klerk's speech in February of 1990, and what followed from all that. That struck me as very hopeful. I was speaking, in a sense, in a new situation, in which the anti-apartheid forces were coming back and were beginning to claim their place in, among other places, the university. The dilemma there seemed to me that if, for all of these years, we had been excluded and then we enter, what is it that we want to do? Do we want then to drive out the others, and so on? That was, it seemed to me, what I was addressing there. I argued for a different attitude toward knowledge in the university, in which instead of the potentate ruling territory, I prefer the figure of the traveler traversing it. In other words, there's a suspension of these political devices, of these political contests, if you like, in the interests of a generously integrative, rather than a separatist, enterprise. This, too, is really the message of *Culture and Imperialism*: its opposition to separatism of one sort or another. In my own experience, and it's your experience as well, obviously, we see separatism all around. Wherever one looks, there is this tendency to specialization, fracturing, partitions, separate states, etcetera, etcetera. It seemed to me, therefore, that the university (perhaps I'm attaching too much importance to the university) is a kind of utopian state, but that's what I think it is that enables this kind of study. It's a rather grandiose idea, because most of us tend to think of the university as a place where one has a career, which is certainly true, and there's nothing wrong with that; but, if you wanted to, you could have a somehow more extended idea of what the university is. You know, rather the way, for example, Newman talks about it in *The Idea of a University*. In the late twentieth century, given the expanse of imperialism (which is global, after all), something of this sort is at least useful to get discussion started. And it can be done by individuals. It isn't something that one has to wait for a committee to do. It has to do with the will to overcome these fiefdoms and these specializations and, above all, these fractured experiences in the interests of a larger and more unified whole.

Also, it is interesting that the end of this book, the completion of this book, took place in a rather special way, after all, because about a year, or a year and a half, ago, I discovered that I had a chronic blood disease, and I became very worried about not living to finish it. So, it was very important for me to finish, because, for some months, I thought (irrationally) I was going to die very soon. There was no objective evidence that I would die quickly, but I thought that my days were numbered, and they obviously are. So, it then occurred to me that I was being pushed to finish it and conclude it with an aim not, as I did in *Orientalism,* to open things out at the end of it but, rather, to finish it by making a clear choice between integration and separation. I prefer integration, number one; and the second thing is, there was a moment in the last year, or year and a half, when I became quite fed up with politics, in a way. That is to say, I had been very involved in and thought that I belonged to a phase that had now ended. My political involvement with the Palestinian question, which began, I suppose, by virtue of my birth and my early years, and started again in earnest in 1967, really came to end, as far as I was concerned, with the Madrid peace talks, which, in a certain sense, I thought of as a renunciation of our past, although I supported the negotiations. To my mind, we were asked to declare ourselves and the struggle of our people as effectively irrelevant. All the thousands of Palestinians who had given their lives suddenly appeared now to be in a position that was marginal to what was taking place, namely, an agreement between Israel and the inhabitants of the West Bank and Gaza—which is fine, but it excludes people like me, since we're not from the West Bank and Gaza. I felt that there was a change in the political climate, because we were left high and dry. We were a national movement, the only national movement in the twentieth century in the colonial context or the imperial context, that didn't have an outside patron. The ANC [African National Congress] had the Soviet Union, the Vietnamese had the Soviet Union. There was always an alternative to America. The world had changed, and America had become the only superpower. Actually, it happened as I was writing this book; it was very dramatic. You can see it in the very last chapter. It seemed to me, therefore, that one ought to try to sum up this experience in some way. I wouldn't say I was rather prescient, but, in some way, I felt that the arrangements for the coming phase were going to be highly provisional and that these arrangements likely for the Middle Eastern peace talks were really going to give way to what, in fact, we see now in Yugoslavia, what we saw in the Gulf War, and so on, and so forth. It's not "after imperialism"; there's a late-twentieth-century renewal of it. And I thought it would be better to try to contain it in one work and get it done. That's what I tried to do, maybe too summarily, at the end.

To return to the ideas you expressed a moment ago about the university: In this book, you extend these ideas and analyses to culture in general, or what I would call civil society. Is this why Fanon is so important to you? You seem to use Fanon as a warning. You worry about what happens when a party line occupies the university. But you are also pre-

occupied with the larger question of what happens when, or if, a party line occupies the whole of civil society. So you are extending . . .

Yes, because I had the experience, the quite important experience, myself of the Arab world, where civil society disappeared in the last twenty or twenty-five years. In places like Iraq and Syria, there is no civil society; everything, including the university, has been politicized, has become part of political society. That's a very important example for me.

About Fanon: I was very impressed when I started to read Fanon again in the writing of this book, six or seven years ago, to see how, for example, the very late work, particularly *The Wretched of the Earth,* had a visionary quality to it that had been neglected and ignored by many readers. Also, while I was writing this book (especially in 1988, or 1988 to 1989, or thereabouts), there was a tremendous flurry of stuff, including Sidney Hook's attack, on him; a lot of material on rereading Fanon but trashing him at the same time. I felt that it was really a misreading, or a betrayal, of Fanon to read him in that partial manner, and he became important to me just as a figure who had been misread; I thought that there was something I could do about it. And I talked about it in that context, and, in the process, Fanon became a symbol of a lot of other things than just himself, where the rather limited and foreshortened nature of his ideas about civil society after liberation or after independence were really not that evident in *The Wretched of the Earth,* which is the last thing he wrote.

Let's go back, if we can, to historical experience. I think, clearly, that is a concrete and important advance over some of the dimensions of Orientalism. *I want to ask you to talk a bit about how, as a book of literary historical analysis,* Culture and Imperialism *grasps the complexities of historical experience; I ask this question because it is one of the themes of your book that most critical writing is reductive, as well as confrontational and fragmented. Perhaps you could, in that context, also tell us what the value of literary historical analysis is, and can be, in this kind of late imperial structure. We can take up this question again later, if time allows, when I'd like to ask you to talk a bit about what you imagine could be done to produce more critical secular discourse inside the United States.*

Well, we'll talk about that later. Here's the way I think of it. All the literary analyses, explications, and commentary that I have in this book

I see as under—"under" in the sense of commanded by, or patronized by, or under the influence of, some fairly gross historical realities, which for me are basically two: on the one hand, the reality of the colonized and, on the other, the reality of a colonizer. What I try to do is not lose sight of those experiences that, in their purest form, are never really experienced directly, because there's always something to distract from or complicate them. For example, the plight of a peasant in Egypt during the period after 1882, when Egypt was occupied by the British, would not have changed significantly after the occupation. But there would have appeared, let's say, a new, or relatively new, class of people who mediate between the British and that person, a class who derive from the bourgeoisie, the land-holding class, the cities, and even the countryside. So, I'm not trying to say that everybody is directly "under" in all cases, under the white or colonial master in the imperial world. It's obviously more true in places like Algeria, for example. There are all these degrees. But I would argue that those experiences of domination and being dominated are horizons or limits. They're the setting, and that's what I mean when I talk about geography—that's the geography of that experience, that's the landscape.

Therefore, for me, the job of literary analysis is, first of all, to find the signs of that geography, the references to it in the literary work. I was astonished, because it's very easily found. Nearly everywhere you look—let's say in the novel, although it's also true in poetry, but let's just look at the novel—geography, landscape, and setting are paramount. You can't have a novel without a setting, and the setting is there; it's immediately evident. The analysis of the literary work, then, in the second sense, is to elucidate the setting, which puts the work in touch with this larger historical experience of domination and being dominated, which I was talking about. Then it becomes a rather interesting and intricate thing to try (I won't say to synchronize the two with each other, but), somehow, to make them work together contrapuntally. The discipline of literary analysis isn't, as in the case of the New Critics, just to turn up wonderful figures for their own sake, like metaphors and ironies, and so on, and so forth (although, certainly, one should be aware of those aspects of a literary text), but always to observe these things functioning in a setting and a locale that, so to speak, is commanded at the top. So, I think that's the value of that particular kind of literary analysis.

Now a second point. The literary analysis about which you asked: What I find interesting and invigorating in Kipling is that there are particular kinds of pleasure available, even if one takes into account the rather unpleasant or, let's say, relatively less pleasant, reality of the colonial relationship. This is one of the reasons, I think, that, to this day, many colonials would prefer to read Kipling than they would Forster. In my opinion, there's a much more immediate political agenda in *Passage to India* than there is in *Kim*, which is like an extended daydream. But the range of pleasures offered by the imperial setting is considerable, and I was interested in that for its own sake.

This question of geography is most intriguing if one looks at the way in which the colonized are educated. That is to say, in reading your book, I thought to myself, "If this is as obvious as it's appearing while I read your discussion of Dickens, let's say, then how come, as a student in a colony, I never noticed it?" Perhaps this is the case because when I am in a classroom in a colony learning English literature (and here, I should mention that your discussion of how English gets taught in Arab countries and elsewhere is truly fascinating), I am being taught as if I already knew.

Exactly . . .

And, so, then the goal in the colonial classroom would be to master the techniques of reading that would allow you to get to be one of the chosen few to get the scholarship to go to England and be as good as the English. It is as if geography is, sort of, collapsed—and you could be in Cairo, or Malta, or wherever, but in fact you might as well be in a classroom in England. You could be in England and you'd be doing exactly the same thing.

Well, I don't think it's as collapsed as that. I think one becomes aware of it only when (a) one begins to move, and when (b) the British finally leave—or the French, for that matter, in the case of Algeria. I mean, at the time of colonialism, that setting, that geographical locale that we're talking about, is naturalized; you accept it. I try to say this over and over again: that you really believe because they want you to believe, that it is the destiny of these inferior people to be held by the British, for example, or by the French. That's part of the education of a particular class to which, for example, I belong. You know, Hodgkin calls them collaborators; they're the people who interpose themselves for reasons of class between themselves and the rest of the population. They're the closest to the British. Imperialism always did that, in the French colonies as well. Look at the life of Senghor: He was educated as a Frenchman, then he was sent to Paris, and it was only when he got to Paris that he realized his skin was black, right, and so he was a Frenchman with a black face. But he didn't think of himself as a Senegalese until later. Now, it's always different in the various colonies, but I would say that we accept it as natural because it is "natural" geography under those circumstances. By *natural,* I mean because they're there. In our generation, we didn't see them coming; they were already there. They were there when we were born. So, they're part of the landscape. And you think the world is ordered by the British, or the white man, or the West; you think that, and it isn't until you move and travel, until there is decolonization, until there's nationalism (all of which somebody of my generation actually lived through), that you begin to see it.

Then, of course, I think the main influence on me in all of this is Gramsci. I mean, I was fantastically struck—I say this is the single most important thing that I took from Gramsci—not by the idea of hegemony and the idea of organic intellectuals and all that but by the idea that everything, including civil society to begin with, but really the whole world, is organized according to geography. He thought in geographical terms, and the *Prison Notebooks* are a kind of map of modernity. They're not a history of modernity, but his notes really try to *place* everything, like a military map; I mean that there was always some struggle going on over territory. I think that is his single, most powerful idea. Of course, we all have these ideas, but, in some strange way, all these things I've been thinking about coalesce in Gramsci, and he gave them a quite startling formulation, especially if you compare him with his contemporaries in Europe at the time, such as Lukács and others, who are in the Hegelian tradition, which is organized around a temporal scheme. The geographical, or spatial, scheme is quite a different one; the spatial is much more material. And Gramsci, you know better than anyone, Joe, is really not interested in mediating, transmuting, overcoming, and all those other Hegelian processes by which antinomies are somehow resolved, but he's really interested in actually working them out as discrepant realities physically, on the ground, where territory is the place that you do it. That, for me, was tremendously important.

In a sense you have answered one of the questions we wanted to ask, about the priority of space over time in your book. But if you would allow, then, could we go back just a minute to the problem or the question of the status of literary analysis? I wanted to ask if you could say something more about that in terms of a very important theme of this book—which, I guess, is also, in a sense, Gramscian—that is, say something more about the slow and long-term movements in culture as these transform societies by virtue of the occupation of space. You talk about this often, in terms of the problem of borders; for example, you make reference to Basil Davidson's work on Africa. . . . Given that this is very much, as literary criticism, within the large horizon of empire that you have described, could you say something about the notion of culture's transformations as slow and long-term? And so, could you say something about what you imagine is this book's place, or the place of any such book, in the long history of empires? I'm thinking particularly of some of your language: you speak, for example, at one point of having a hope that this book will have a deterrent and illustrative purpose.

Well, I think first of all, responding to that last point, of the fact that the experience of empire is essentially repetitive but is never perceived as that. You know, there's this wonderful line I quote from Coetzee's *Waiting for the Barbarians,* where the new men of empire come and they just do the same thing that the old men did. This seems to me of extraordinary interest for people who live in this country, where we have this idea that we are going to do things differently or, to paraphrase Laurence Sterne, that they "order this matter better" in Washington. The fact is, the imperial impulse is exactly the same. So, in that respect, if one could put it in all of its drama and detail before the reader, then perhaps it might be a way of stimulating some kind of awareness on the part of people who are the general readers that I address—to realize that our culture as Americans is in many ways similar to the culture of nineteenth-century Britain and nineteenth-century France. In that sense, deterrent; I mean, preventing you from feeling that our imperialism is different. There's no use going down that path, because it's already been traveled, and if you're going to do it, at least then try perhaps for some cynicism so that you're doing it with a full understanding that you *are* doing it. I prefer that to the naive approach most Americans adopt.

But, now, the second point about this is that I think of this book also as highlighting the distinction between independence, nationalism, autonomy, etcetera, on the one hand, and liberation, on the other. That's the motif, obviously, of the final part of the third chapter. That is to say, just to become free of the imperial experience, one usually ends up by repeating it in one way or another. In other words, this is the politics of replication—I mean, the mimic gestures, as Naipaul very cleverly talks about it. It seems to me that that's always there, but what strikes me as very much missing in most of these accounts (partly because of the domination of the discourse or language of politics by the disenchanted political scientists, the politicians, and so forth) is vision—the absence of vision. Liberation, in the end, is neither a state nor is it a bureaucracy. It's an energy of the sort that, for example, you find when C. L. R. James takes Césaire and T. S. Eliot and somehow makes them work together. That is what I am really talking about, although you have to wade through a lot to get to it, because it is, after all, a historical thing. It's not a utopian gesture, but it comes out of an immersion in a particular historical experience of a very powerful kind. So, I think, liberation is really what I am trying to talk about, and freeing oneself from the need to repeat the past. We're back to the *Eighteenth Brumaire*. You know, we're not always necessarily condemned to repeat the past. I'm trying, here, something I explored in a lecture I gave at Oxford in February; I'm trying, here, to move toward some notion of a universalism, that is to say, that it has to be universally accepted that certain democratic freedoms, certain freedoms from domination of one kind or another, freedom from various kinds of exploitations, and so on, are the rights of every human being—which is not the framework of the imperial world in which we live. I'm trying to move toward that in this book and in the works I've done since I finished this.

Now, literary analysis is interesting to me because, unlike some people in my field, I actually like the books, poems, and writers that I read. I think there's something to be said for that. But also because I'm convinced (and this is where I disagree, I think, with both of you on one point) that a lot of people do, too. In other words, I think the idea of the slow building up, you see, itself is a deterrent. Why? Because it's a slow building up of the experience of reading that many of us had; I mean, we're of a generation where whether at school or in one's family, or even later than school and university, one had the experience of reading and enjoying literature. And that is a counter-model to the will of empire; namely, the investment people make over a lifetime in reading, analyzing, and thinking about, and meditating and discussing works of literature or culture, if you like, including music, painting, and so on, about which one feels strongly, in which one feels investment, in which one feels one has invested. It seems to me that this is a very powerful thing to keep in mind. You see it obviously in *Mimesis*—that's what that book is all about, really. You know, my experiences are very different from Auerbach's, and I'm a different person, and I wouldn't want to be even considered in the same category (he is worlds above me). But the general point about an accumulated literacy seems to be something worth thinking about.

I must say that, generally speaking, in the discussions of our profession, of our field, in the last two decades, I've completely lost track of that. There's no way you can find it. Too much energy has gone into technological fixations. It's like car repairing—and I just find it totally uninteresting, and I wonder why that has happened. I think it's probably the American academy, to a certain degree, and the British academy, which doesn't seem to be any better. But, it seems to be possible that if this book is read in a certain way, it might revive interest in that, showing that it's possible to read Jane Austen with a sensitivity toward it as a work of art and yet also to locate it in this other world that I've been talking about at the same time. That's not a contradiction, because I think that's what she was doing. The works I discuss in *Culture and Imperialism* were works that I grew up with, but they weren't *my* works. I read them because I was in English schools, and I don't want to shed or forget them now that I'm politically free of the English. When I talk about this in the first chapter, I say that these realities are part of our experience. No use throwing them out. This is why I have very little time—I'll tell you this in all candor—I have very little time for people who say, "Well, you know, this is all the world of empire, but now we're into a new thing, and so on, and so forth." I'll give you an example.

I was on the West Bank this summer, and I had never before in my life given a speech or a talk in a Palestinian university, but I was able to do just that. It was the only talk I gave while there. Basically, it was a discussion, and it was done in Arabic. First, I summarized this book, because they said, "Say something about what you've recently been working on"; so, I summarized *Culture and Imperialism* in ten or fifteen minutes in English, and then I said, "Let's have a discussion." And we switched to Arabic. The place was full, you know, and it was mostly political questions. They wanted to know about the peace process, and what I thought about the war in Iraq, and about America, and so on, and so forth. This going back and forth was passionately interesting to me. The only moment I felt I lost my cool and my temper was when some man got up and started talking about the West and "the rest of us." In other words, "that's all Western . . . and Islam and us, we're different," and all that. And I said, "Look, I don't want to hear that. I didn't come here to listen to speeches of that kind. I don't believe that anybody can cut himself off from his own past and one's own experience, because one's own experience is necessarily heterogeneous. There's no such thing as a monolithic experience. And to think that you're going to try to recover some primitive, unalloyed pure essence of something that has been corrupted and polluted, as it were, by the West, or by empire, or by Zionism—then you're wasting your time. So, it's much better to accept it and work with that mixture than to try to start to separate it." I feel very strongly about that.

I think there are several things that I would like to say about that, but I'll just mention a couple, and you can ignore whichever ones seem to you not worth following up. I think one thing people would say in response to your question about why the academy has become auto-tinkering is that this happened because, at least in the United States part of the English-speaking world, literature simply does not have a place or anything like the cultural value . . .

You know, I'm not sure that that's true . . .

Well, I say people would say this . . .

Oh, you say people would say so, but also you say it . . .

I don't say it always, I say it sometimes . . .

But, I mean, there are still people out there who read books, don't you think?

I think it's probably truer that inside the academy people don't read.

Exactly. I think you're absolutely right. I have a friend with whom I've been friendly for at least thirty-five years; we were in college together, and graduate school together, and he's a very distinguished editor of Renaissance texts. He's a very literate person; I mean, he went to a very good high school, he studied Latin, and all the rest of it. On several occasions, I've asked him, "Have you read such and such a novel?" I mean a recent novel, say a novel by Robert Stone or one by García Márquez. And he'd say, "You know, after I get done with my editing, I don't have time to read, so I don't read." It's that kind of experience, that somehow what you're doing in your life, in the university, as a professional scholar of literature, somehow crowds out the possibility of literature. Toscanini used to say, "Musicologists know everything but music," which is a parody or caricature, but I mean something of that sort. It's a desolating notion, but I suppose it's true. But that doesn't mean that people don't read at all.

So, nevertheless, there are cases in the profession where the exclusion of literature is almost programmatic. The perverse logic of the so-called canon debate has reached the point now that if, for example, I were to go to a graduate course with your book (which I probably will next year), one of the first questions I expect a student will put to me is, "Why do you think of this book as an oppositional text? It starts with T. S. Eliot." I have problems persuading some of my fellow faculty members that it is important to continue teaching criticism courses with Plato, Aristotle, Dryden, and Kant, which for them seems a waste of time. They would say, "Why don't we start with something more urgent, like Derrida?" It's not that I disagree with you about the importance of literature, far from it. But I see a rather bizarre situation: your book demonstrates the very rich potentialities of literary reading, but, at the same time, it is going to be read by oppositional critics, who might be generally sympathetic with your position politically but who are caught in a web of logic that does not allow them to confer upon certain texts the value that you do. At the risk of exaggeration, I would say that there are people in the profession who are not even trained to read the texts you read in the way you read them.

I would take a more generous view than that, or at least not as jaundiced as yours. But maybe you're right; I don't know. It seems to me that, given a chance, you can pull people away (a) from the canon debate and the fallout from that, which I think on the whole is really very stupid and negative, uninteresting; and (b) from the theoretical urgency or, rather, the urgency of theory, which a lot of graduate students feel—that they really have to be up on Derrida, Foucault, and all the rest of them. You can pull them away from that, or at least suspend their interest in that for a bit, and then expose them to writers like T. S. Eliot, who are opposed to nearly everything that both they and we share in experience, history, predilection, and taste, etcetera. Then, I think, you'll find that there's very often a quite surprising response to contradictions. They will, in other words, take all of these things about T. S. Eliot and accept them—he's a royalist, he's a conservative, etcetera—and say, "Okay, given all of that, let's read him." I think it's possible then to see—I've done it myself with my students—a quite amazing delight in the contradictions that ensue, and the pleasure in ingenious uses of language, imaginative conceptions, the really quite brilliant formal sense in some of Eliot's poetry, and so on. I think that's worth trying, because otherwise we're at an impasse. How much beyond the theory that's being taught and practiced today can one go? Very little. In effect, one has the impression (perhaps you agree with me?) that we're essentially recycling the same material. I mean, some new theoretical book comes out and we rush out to read it, but it's basically the same thing, on the one hand; on the other hand, there's just this going on and on about the distinction between so-called conservatives and those people who want only to read contemporary literature by the people with the right color of skin and the right political ideas. So, the lines have been drawn and— then what? There's nothing. I prefer the other way myself, a way of suspending. It seems to me that you could only do that in the university.

I thought of your book as also having a pedagogical purpose. There is a sense in which it can be seen as offering a possibility of a program of study, of a project, of a mode of thinking.

Maybe. I haven't thought of it in quite that way. It's a thinking through of a lot of issues, in my own way, in a homemade way. It's not meant to be a theory or anything complete like that.

Just one other thing about the literature question. I am thinking of the point that you made a minute ago and I would like to try to bring these three things together—literature, vision, and the universal—because I think the long meditation on study and interiorization of literature provides you with the occasion for vision.

Absolutely.

And therefore this is linked . . .

Or music, or any of the arts that one is interested in.

So, this is linked not only to the desire for a national liberation but also to the possibility of the production of the universal.

Right.

All of that said, I want to come back to what struck me overwhelmingly in reading the book from the very beginning, which is the fact that in many ways this is a book that will strike any reader as both visionary and as having a vision. The vision it has is inseparable from a word that you used a moment ago in speaking about the profession—that's when you said the word generosity. *In my notes, I've written over and over again this term* generosity *to try to name one particular aspect of your book. I've also paid a lot of attention to another word you've used quite often, the word* beseech. *As I listen to what you said about literature, as I also remember what you said about this as a general cultural practice having to do with history and historical experience, I want to bring you back to the question of the intellectual and ask if the issue here isn't for the intellectual somehow to be the person who can respond by memory, by study, to the beseeching of historical experience.*

Yes, well, I think that's certainly one function of the intellectual. In those lectures I gave at Stanford (and next year when I'm giving the Reith Lectures on the BBC, in which the topic is the intellectual and the public world), I discuss particular functions of the intellectual, one of which is what I call a mnemonic function. In other words, part of the role of intellectuals is to recall those things that are there, so to speak, yet forgotten in the heat of battle—you know, usually about one's opponents and about one's own history. So, certainly that, but more: a word I don't use, but it occurred to me as you were talking about it, the word *reconciliation.*

It's like the word integration *or . . .*

Integration, rather—*generosity* is probably too complimentary; but, I mean *reconciliation.* I felt myself for many, many years, and certainly in *Orientalism,* and certainly in *The Question of Palestine,* and to a certain degree in *The World, the Text, and the Critic,* as really being in the thick of a tremendous battle. I don't mean just a literary or historical battle, but a battle on more than one front; I was surrounded by combatants of one sort or another. That partly had to do with my immersion in and commitment to Palestinian politics, especially in America. I don't feel it so much in England, or Europe, generally. This sense of being in an endless struggle was sort of everywhere. I couldn't get away from it. It was relentless. And I realized a number of things. I realized (partly from the example of Chomsky, who has always been very interesting to me, both as a friend and as a person I read) that there's no end to it. In other words, if you're going to go on fighting the battle of truth in a polemical and purely intellectual way, it's an endless war. There's no definitive military solution, is what I'm really trying to say. Obviously, you can try to wipe out the other person; you can try just to sweep the field. But in intellectual issues, it never happens, number one. Number two, in the political arena, given my own experience of politics in the long battle with Israel, in my lifetime or in several lifetimes to come, there's no hope that we can win an essentially military or military-based kind of battle with the Israelis, because it's not in the cards, any more than their winning is. They're not going to go away; we're not going to go away. It has been very important for me to understand that. Therefore, as I told you, I was trying to end this political involvement that I had for various reasons—personal, political, etcetera—but one of the things that occurred to me is that it might be possible to end the conflict with the Israelis not by defeating them but by trying to provide a model of reconciliation for them and their history, and for us and our history, together. It seemed to me that reconciliation was really the model for all of this, the struggle over land and all that that entailed. It's really the question of what you do once you get the land: you can use your independence to push people off, the way they did, because they were the supreme victims of all kinds of colonial and imperial schemes, but the net result was that they started another imperial battle or colonial battle right in their midst. Now, if we were headed in the same direction that we were going, under the aegis of Syria and Iraq, etcetera, arming and fighting and then winning a big battle, what would we do if we lost? We would risk genocide. We would risk further loss to ourselves, because that's the pattern since the beginning; we keep losing.

This is where Gramsci becomes very interesting. Gramsci talks about a mutual siege. You can do it in other ways, where you don't open another front. I wasn't trying to do that. But, rather, you provide models of reconciliation by which you can situate yourself and the other in a territory or in a space that isn't all about fighting, that isn't all about polemics and oppositional politics in the crude and reductive sense of the word.

That's what I was interested in. There are overarching problems; I talk about them in the last chapter of the book. I mean, there's the whole problem of north and south now. There's the whole problem of the environment. There's the whole question of the fractious quality of identity politics. All of these things require new ways of thinking that can't be served and can't be advanced by the polemical and oppositional models of the past. That's what I was interested in very much. So, reconciliation. In other words, modes of reconciliation where you can reconcile (without reducing) histories. That's why, for example, the contrapuntal approach is very interesting: You can reconcile the history of the colonized and the history of the colonizer without an attempt to "be impartial," because there's always the question of justice. It's simply unjust—I certainly don't want to lose the force of that—it's simply unjust for the colonizers to have done what they did. But, on the other hand, that doesn't mean, then, that that entitles the colonized to wreak a whole system of injustices on a new set of victims. I think about it, for example, in the case of the Arab world. I didn't know it at the time, but now I know that nothing could have been more stupid and less farsighted than that, after the foundation of Israel in 1948, many Arab countries, like Iraq and Yemen—partly at the instigation of the Israelis; we know this now for a fact, but leaving even their provocations aside—and after '56, Egypt, threw out their Jews. Of course, the Israelis talk about it as an exchange of population: "We drove the Palestinians out, and they drove the Jews out." But it wasn't the wise thing to do. It wasn't at all a wise or humane thing to do. Of course, the Israelis went and agitated in Iraq, and they provided or threw bombs in synagogues in order to give a sense that the Jews were threatened, and so on, and so forth, and then, of course, anti-Jewish feeling began to prevail. It's an unpleasant mix, let's put it this way. But the point I'm trying to make is that the politics of retaliation—the rhetoric of blame, I call it—is not attractive. There just is a limit to it.

Could we ask a general question?

Of course.

What have we not asked you nor given you a chance to say something about, which at this point you might want to address?

Well, the only thing I would want to say is that there's a certain kind of intellectual energy in this book that one would like to be able to communicate to readers, that it is interesting in itself to discover. I think that's what I find the biggest challenge now, for example, in my teaching. It isn't really just what you tell students about Eliot or Conrad or Hopkins or whomever in a class; but if you could communicate to them the sense not to accept the packaged *idée reçue* that most of us have, to stimulate new lines of investigation that everybody can do for themselves—now that's really what I want to do.

You seem, at the very end of the book, when you discuss the world media and the poverty and paucity of secular critical discourse, to beseech your reader to work toward increasing the possibility of such secular critical . . .

But it can't happen without some personal and intellectual investment. Intellectuals have to be moved, I think, by what Benda said, by a sense of justice; and that's what I find missing, I suppose. In other words, unless people feel that if X and Y are happening because A and B did it in an organized sense . . . I don't mean just individuals. I'm not talking about criminal justice and injustice, I'm talking about social responsibility . . . You know, Conrad says he was moved by a few very simple ideas. I feel the same thing. For intellectual discourse and for intellectual activity, one has to be stimulated not by highfalutin ideas in the appallingly solemn Habermasian sense—you know, the public sphere and the discourse of modernity, which is all just hot air, as far as I am concerned—because there is no moral center to what Habermas does. I think there has to be a kind of moral view, as you find it in Chomsky, or Bertrand Russell, and people like that. I feel that's the only hope in this country.

The problem of this country, ironically—and we're back where we began—the problem in this country, is geography. The dispersion. There's no center. You know, for people in Pittsburgh or Indiana or Illinois or New York or California, there's a certain sense of locality, but there isn't a sense of commonality, and one doesn't have a sense of a national project of one sort or another (especially on the Left). Also, the usurpation of the public space, of the common space, by the media and the corporations, is really very, very, very disheartening. It's a deeply discouraging fact. Those are some of the questions that need to be talked about. Not further refinements of the fifth seminar of Lacan or that sort of thing; I find that to be extremely distracting and pulling the wool over people's eyes.

On the one hand, you refer to dispersal and the absence of center, but then on the other hand, you talk about the mechanisms of what you and others—you and Chomsky, in particular, have written about this—call the manufacturing of consent, which is extraordinarily centralized. We, thus, find ourselves in a very strange situation. We live in a country with many cultures and subcultures that is apparently very disaggregated, but that, at the same time, has a homogenous or quasi-homogenous mechanism for manufacturing consent. The country doesn't have a metropolis binding it together; rather, its metropolis is the airwaves, or the mass media, generally.

I think that's true. The way I put it is this: the homogenization of a certain level of consciousness by the media and by, I would say, also, the system of primary and secondary education. I think that's where a lot of it takes place, where one is taught to be patriotic, to understand certain, carefully selected aspects of the history of this country, and so on. It's very powerful. I wouldn't call it the system of indoctrination; I wouldn't go as far as Chomsky in calling it that. But it has some of those elements. It's also characteristically, I think, a kind of anesthetization of the critical sense. In other words, you take it for granted that, "Well there's nothing that can be done about it," and "They're doing it," and "After all, they're always right," and "We are the defenders of freedom," and so on, and so forth. That was the mechanism of the Gulf War, basically. And then there comes this fantastic local attention to things that are like collecting or tinkering with cars, or collecting beer cans, and so on. Actually, Chomsky makes the point somewhere that if you turn on the radio when you're driving around, you notice that most of what's on the airwaves is either canned news or pop music of one sort or the other, and then when there's discussion—much of the most interesting and complicated discussion on a level of quite amazing sophistication—it is about sports. The American consciousness of sports, with its scores and history and technique and all the rest of it, is at the level of sophistication that is almost terrifying, especially if you compare it with the lack of awareness of what's going on in the world. That's where you get the sense that the investment is being made in those things that distract you from realities that are too complicated—and then you get the need for a savior or some big figure, whether it's Perot or Bush or any of those people, to take over the country.

You probably remember this. There are many, many times when you use a word that strikes me as very interesting. That is the word untutored. *Earlier in the day, we were discussing the precise force of this word* untutored. *I could find you an example if you like; but I wonder, if you remember at all the use of this term, if you could give us some sense of it because . . .*

Well, I mean *immediacy*, basically.

Interview with Joseph A. Buttigieg and Paul A. Bové in
*boundary 2: An International Journal
of Literature and Culture*,
Durham, North Carolina, 1993

NINE

ORIENTALISM AND AFTER

Perhaps we could begin by asking you to say something about your intellectual and political background in the late 1950s and '60s. How did you identify yourself politically in relation to the civil rights and student movements in the U.S. during the period when you were a young member of faculty at Columbia? What from that period of your life was a formative influence on your later work?

Well, in the 1950s I was a student and by 1957 I had finished my undergraduate education. I then went back to the Middle East for a year, basically to play the piano. And then in '58 I came back to graduate school, at Harvard, and I just plunged into that. I did really nothing else but study for five years. One member of my family, in particular, whom I saw in Cairo in those years, was very active in Arab politics, as a Palestinian. This is the period of Nasserism. He was there because Nasser was bringing into Egypt a lot of these revolutionary types from the Arab world. His name was Kamal Nasir, and although he was formally a Baath party member at the time he was also a Nasserite. Later he became a spokesman for the Palestinian movement in Amman in the late sixties. Then he moved to Beirut, after Black September, and in 1973 he was one of the three leaders assassinated by the Israelis in April of that year—I had seen him that very night actually. So that was going on. But I was largely oblivious of it, in the sense that I was focused on my studies. I got my Ph.D. in 1963 and moved to New York, where I took up a position at Columbia in English. Then, too, I was pretty focused on that and writing my first book, on Conrad.

With the emergence of the civil rights movement in the middle six-ties—and particularly in '66–'67—I was very soon turned off by Martin Luther King, who revealed himself to be a tremendous Zionist, and who always used to speak very warmly in support of Israel, particularly in '67, after the war. In 1968 the Columbia revolution occurred, but I was away for that academic year! It was the revolution I missed.

When I returned to Columbia in the fall of '68, I got quite involved in the anti-Vietnam campus activities. Many of the students who had been part of the revolution were students of mine. But it was the period when the emergence of the Palestinian movement was also occurring. And for the first time in my life I got involved in Palestinian politics, as did some of my family and school friends. A contemporary of mine from Harvard, for example, gave up his position at the University of Washington and went to Amman to become a full-time cadre. He was killed in 1976, dur-ing the Lebanese war, in rather obscure circumstances. He was a very im-portant figure in the movement, and there is still a question mark over who killed him and why. He was the one who introduced me in 1972 to Jean Genet, who was in Beirut. He was the man who took Genet around. He's referred to in Genet's last work, *Prisoner of Love* as Abu Omar.

Anyway, I went to Amman in 1969 and got involved in the move-ment—not to stay there, but as an expatriate. I began to write about politics for the first time in my life, to be published in America, and to appear on television and radio. This was all in the aftermath of the '67 war, which was the great event of my political life. I was in Amman dur-ing the summer of 1970 right up until the fighting broke out. I simply had to go back to my teaching. I was there for the National Council meeting. (I wasn't a member then. I became a member in 1977.) That was the first time I ever saw Arafat, in 1970, in Amman. Then, after Black September, the movement drifted into Beirut. My mother lived in Beirut, so I would go there a great deal. That year I married a Lebanese woman, and for the next twelve years, 1970 to 1982, I was very in-volved in Palestinian politics in Beirut, as an expatriate. I always tried to steer clear of the inter-party fighting. I was not interested. For a time people thought I was—as indeed I was, in the early days—sympathetic to the Democratic Front. But I was never a member, and I never got in-volved in the disputes between them. Arafat made use of me, in a way, because I was in America. They came to the United Nations in '74, and I helped with the speech: I put it into English.

Then, of course, during the Carter presidency, I was useful to the movement because some of my classmates were members of the administration. They were people I'd gone to school with. One has to remember that I grew up as an Establishment figure in America. I went to boarding school, I went to Princeton, I went to Harvard. They were things I could draw on, although they were frequently misinterpreted by some of the Palestinians, who thought I "represented" America. When my book *The Question of Palestine* appeared, for example, the Popular Front weekly magazine ran a tremendous attack on me because I was supposed to be a representative of everything bourgeois. In any event, I was plunged totally into politics, simultaneously with my academic work. They were joined, in a certain sense, in the middle 1970s when I wrote *Orientalism*. The book married the two things I was most interested in: literature and culture, on the one hand, and studies and analyses of power, on the other. From then, it continued pretty much unbroken until the autumn of 1991, when I resigned from the National Council.

Perhaps we could ask you something about the character of this marriage of concerns in Orientalism. Orientalism *is often read as a kind of counter-history of the European literary tradition, an exorcising of the political ghost of high literary humanism. On the other hand, the literary quality of the texts which are criticized politically is emphasized and affirmed. This has led some people to detect an ambivalence toward literary humanism in the work. After all, this is a tradition which not only affirms literary values, but has often gone so far as to identify them with human values. Is there still an ambivalence in* Orientalism *toward literary humanism?*

Yes. The heroes of the book, insofar as there are heroes (I can't think if there are any heroines, particularly), the heroes are basically the novelists. People like Flaubert, like Nerval, some of whom were poets as well. There is an ambivalence, however. As Orwell said about Salvador Dali, it's possible to be a disgusting human being and a great draftsman, which Salvador Dali was. So you could be an imperialist and an Orientalist, and also a great writer. That's really what I'm interested in, the coexistence of these two things. What does one do in the face of that? My own profession has been pretty consistent. The tradition has been to separate them completely. More and more I'm perceived as having become shrill about talking about them together.

Isn't the mainstream position rather to suppress *the politics in the name of the human side? Not exactly a separation but an overriding.*

Yes. But it is a *form* of separating, in the sense that you won't talk about *this,* because *that*'s much more important. Even Raymond Williams, for example—whom I revere and loved—has this long chapter in *Culture and Society* on Carlyle. How can you read Carlyle the way he did? Even if it was 1950 or whenever. Carlyle wrote *The Nigger Question* in the 1840s, and it was an appalling piece of racist horror. If you look through his work it's everywhere. The same is true of Ruskin. For all that he was a great influence on people like Gandhi and Tolstoy, Ruskin was a profound imperialist. He really thought that England should colonize the world—and actually said so! So it's not a question of looking for it. It's there. You just have to read it. So you're right. The overriding of one discourse by another is what it's all been about. And I'm interested not only in the way the two coexist, but the way in which you can read the works with these concerns in mind and, by a process of what I call contrapuntal reading, transform the works into the enabling conditions of a decolonizing critique.

This is what I try to do more explicitly in my new book, *Culture and Imperialism.* It becomes possible, for instance, to read *Mansfield Park* from the point of view of the Antigua plantation of the Bertrams, instead of reading it exclusively from the point of view of Mansfield Park. And we can see in that reading the origins not only of the slave revolt in Santo Domingo, but the whole tradition of Caribbean writing that comes out of it: the work of C. L. R. James and Lamming and Eric Williams. At this point, in my opinion, *Mansfield Park* becomes an even more interesting novel, even greater for containing within itself this possibility of reaccommodating it to something else, to another kind of reading, to a different interest. It becomes part of another trajectory, which is not that of the English novel. It becomes part of the Caribbean experience.

Yet Mansfield Park *remains the novel to read. In other words, you stick with the canonical works.*

Yes, of course, because I'm often culturally very conservative. There are good books, and there are less good books.

But there could be several reasons for that. One could say that these books are the books in which certain historical experiences are most significantly sedimented, and put forward a purely strategic defense of them: these are the books which constitute the canon in this culture, and so this is the place we're going to start to unravel it. But you want to say something rather stronger than that it's a strategic starting place?

Yes. *Mansfield Park,* while not my favorite Austen novel, is a remarkable piece of work in its own right. That's where the stakes are highest, in the argument from quality. Because Austen was profoundly implicated in her own society, or a segment of it, it enabled her to see—by virtue of that very limited vision—the necessity of an empire. In my opinion, in an uncompromising way. And that is consistent, despite the fact that Jane Austen has been reclaimed by feminists. The feminism of Fanny Price in *Mansfield Park* is totally untroubled by the slavery and by the sugar plantation. I think one has to note that.

But is the quality of the book intrinsically connected to the possibility of its contrapuntal reading?

I think so, but it would obviously require more than just asserting it to prove this sort of thing. One doesn't have time to do everything. Take *Heart of Darkness* as another example. *Heart of Darkness,* whatever you think about it politically, is *the* novel about Africa. Many African novelists, including Chinua Achebe, who attacked it so, felt the need to engage with it. Not because it's a racist text, but because it is the most formidable work of the imagination by a European about Africa. It has that quality. It's strategically central because it has that quality. The same is true of *The Tempest.* And what one should add at this moment is the word "pleasure." It's not just strategy, it's not just quality, but it is a work in which one can take aesthetic pleasure. Perhaps for some of those reasons, but also because it's a wonderful book to read. I don't by any means put down or denigrate or minimize the role of the enjoyment of the work. One of the arguments I make in my new book about such works as *Kim*—why they're so important by the end of the nineteenth century—is that Kim, the character, is an instrument for Kipling being able to enjoy being in India. Nevertheless, you can't remove from that the imperial quality: that he's there in the service of the British Empire. In the end, he becomes a loyal servant in the great game. But up until that point the major quality, I think, of *Kim* for Kipling is enjoyment— a certain kind of imperial pleasure.

The imperial pleasure is to be able to move across boundaries. So isn't it a pleasure that's intrinsically politically implicated?

True, but other people can also move across boundaries. You'd be surprised. What is interesting is that Kipling is enjoying the pleasures of the Empire in such a way that he is completely blind to what is taking place at the time: namely, the emergence of an Indian national movement. He is blind to this other factor, this other element, forming, emerging, and ultimately overcoming the Empire.

One could say that the subtleties of the text are precisely where it's not blind to the emergence of the national movement.

There are two places in the novel where Kipling talks about changes in India; most of the time he represents a changeless India. One of them is the episode with the old soldier about the Great Mutiny. And he represents it as a temporary madness that came over the Indians. So he saw it, he transformed it into something else, and off he went. He saw it, but he didn't take note of it—as what it was. The second place is later on, when one of the women, the widow of Shamlegh, says that we don't want these new English people who are coming. (It's a reference to the educated young colonial hands, like Forster's Ronnie Heaslop, twenty-five years later.) We prefer the old style. There is a sense in which, according to Kipling, the Indians prefer traditional Orientalists, like Colonel Creighton. So he registers a sense of what the Indians may want, but he doesn't linger over it, and he transmutes it into something else, and off he goes. I don't think there are any other subtleties there, of that sort, that openly refer to the political situation.

It sounds like an opposite example to Mansfield Park. *There you were saying there's a place in the text from which you can reread the text, but here there isn't another place.*

No, there is another place. There is a national movement. For example (it's an important detail), this old soldier who was in the English Army, whom Kim and the Llama visit, is described by Kipling as revered in his village. Now, to my way of thinking, given my own background, somebody like that who collaborated is very likely *not* to be revered. He's likely to be an outcast. So one focuses on that.

Orientalism drew upon a Foucauldian perspective, but that was framed by a Gramscian theory of hegemony. Are there not great differences and tensions between these respective theorizations of power?

Very much so.

Have you continued to maintain that dual perspective?

No. I won't say I abandoned Foucault, but I'd say I'd gotten what there was to be gotten out of Foucault by about the time *Discipline and Punish* appeared, in the mid-1970s. The discovery I made about Foucault, about which I wrote in a small essay called "Foucault and the Imagination of Power," was that, despite the fact that he seemed to be a theorist of power, obviously, and kept referring to resistance, he was really the *scribe* of power. He was really writing about the victory of power. I found very little in his work, especially after the second half of *Discipline and Punish,* to help in resisting the kinds of administrative and disciplinary pressures that he described so well in the first part. So I completely lost interest in his work. The later stuff on the subject I just found very weak and, to my way of thinking, uninteresting.

I was one of the first in America to teach Gramsci, but there are problems in teaching and talking about Gramsci. First of all, the English translation of the *Prison Notebooks* was based on a corrupt text, and conveyed a very false impression. Even when I was working on *Orientalism* I discovered mistakes in it. Secondly, and perhaps more importantly, since it's now possible to read a very good text—the Gerratana four-volume critical edition of the *Prison Notebooks* with a huge apparatus—Gramsci was an inveterate note-writer. He never wrote a consistent piece, except the *Southern Question,* which I make great use of in my new book. It's very hard to derive from Gramsci's work a consistent political and philosophical position. There's a bit of this, a bit of that— mostly, I think, in the tradition of Vico and Leopardi, a kind of Italian cosmopolitan pessimism; along with his tremendous involvement in the Italian working-class movement. But beyond that, methodologically it's very difficult to "use" him.

The concept of hegemony is of use, perhaps.

Yes, it has a kind of gross fascination, a gross applicability, which I still make use of. But as to exactly what it means . . . ? Its most interesting quality is the idea of mutual siege. Hegemony and what is required to mount a counter-hegemonic movement. But that can't be done theoretically; it has to be part of a large political movement, what he called an ensemble. That I find tremendously useful. But beyond that it's difficult to make instrumental use of him.

In Left political culture, there have been at least two quite different uses of Gramsci. One based on a cultural reading of him, the other on what one might call the Turin Gramsci, which is about organic intellectuals, working-class organizations, etc. Are you drawing on both of these?

I think one has to. For example, in the *Southern Question,* he draws attention to the role of somebody called Gobetti, who was a kind of northern intellectual who became a southern activist. What that's all about is overcoming political and geographical divisions between states, between geographical actualities. What Gramsci was doing was improvising in a highly particularized local situation (Italian politics in the early 1920s) in order to put together a counter-hegemonic movement of some sort. That's what interests me most about him. In my opinion, the central thing about Gramsci's thought, which hasn't really been focused on enough, is that it's basically geographical. He thinks in terms of territories, in terms of locales, which is tremendously important to me. The materialist tradition, the pessimistic materialist tradition in Italy, is all about place. It's tremendously undogmatic, tremendously unabstract. You can always find applications to the Italian situation. Most of the theoretical stuff that one reads in Left periodicals today—and for the last ten years, maybe more—is so vague, so out of touch with any political movement of any consequence.

The way you're talking about Gramsci here seems to be in tension with the kind of things you were saying earlier in relation to Austen, about the qualities of the humanist literary tradition.

Why? Gramsci was a literary humanist. His training was in philology and he was passionately interested in Italian and other forms of literature. He read omnivorously. I think there's been a mistake of putting in opposition the humanistic and the political, or radical, or whatever. There's a much longer tradition of the two feeding off each other. If you look at Thompson's *The Making of the English Working Class,* for example, running throughout are example after example of people like Blake, of poets and writers, of the radical movements' use of Shakespeare. I don't think there's this necessary opposition, which goes back, in my opinion, to some phony or factitious Althusserian opposition. It's possible to imagine a literary humanism that is not mandarin, disembodied, or scornful of politics. One can see it actually very much involved in politics. There's a whole tradition of Caribbean writing which, as C. L. R. James says, never had any other background. We're not talking about Africa, we're talking about the Caribbean—it's a transported population. This is its background: precisely these Western humanistic—and political—ideas. So it doesn't trouble me, what you call this tension.

Foucault and Gramsci provided you with alternative theoretical approaches to literary objects that go beyond certain methodologically narrow stances toward the text. They make different kinds of theoretical bridges between texts and their contexts, readings and practices, etc. However, when you come to reject the Foucauldian position because of its problematic, all-pervasive view of power, and you say that Gramsci is to be read only tactically—he doesn't give you a theoretical framework —this seems to open up something of a methodological vacuum. Do you worry about this? Or do you think that other people are worrying too much about having the right theoretical framework?

Yes, I think so. Theory has become a substitute. From my perspective, theory is really not interesting as a subject in and of itself—to write endlessly refined accounts of some theory or other. (I make exceptions. Adorno strikes me as interesting for his own sake, for reasons that none of the books on Adorno have ever touched, namely because of his grounding in music. That's what's great about Adorno. Not so much what he has to say about administered society, or the conquest of nature.) But what's happened, in the years since I wrote *Beginnings* in the early seventies, is that theory has become a subject in and of itself. It has become an academic pursuit of its own. And I am totally impatient with it. Why? Because what has been neglected in the process is the historical study of texts, which to me is much more interesting. Firstly, because there are many more opportunities for genuine discovery; and secondly, because political and cultural issues can be made much clearer in terms of comparable issues in our own time. The question of oppression, of racial oppression, the question of war, the question of human rights—all these issues ought to belong together with the study of literary and other forms of texts; as opposed to the massive, intervening, institutionalized presence of theoretical discussion.

Sticking with Orientalism, *one critic, Jane Miller, in* The Seductions of Theory, *has pointed to the way in which you use all those terms with feminine associations in the discussion of Orientalism, and they are critical terms. Feminism does have a very ambiguous presence in the book here.*

Yes, it does. There's no question about it. What I was doing in *Orientalism*, twenty years ago when I was writing it, was pointing out two things: the extraordinary degree to which the Orient had become feminized by male writers in Europe; and the way in which the women's movement in the West was hand in glove with the imperialist movement. It was not a deterrent. It's only very recently—I would say in the last four or five years—that the questions of race and gender have been joined, in a historical and theoretical way—as opposed to just gender. That's an ongoing discussion, which at the time of *Orientalism* I didn't feel to be a part of the subject that I was dealing with. I think Miller is absolutely right, but it's very interesting that those critiques of *Orientalism* which are now being made were not made then! What is the role of feminism in the Orientalism of a field like music or anthropology, for example? It's very complicated, very troubling, and it's only just come up, I would say in the last three or four years, in discussions at the American Anthropological Association, and various other places. The engagement's only just begun.

Recent feminist scholarship directly related to Orientalism *has supported either a cultural nationalist position or a women's rights position. What do you make of these kinds of arguments?*

For me, they've become very interesting recently, in the last year. Just looking at the Middle East, there's been a sudden efflorescence of quite complex and interesting work on, for example, women's role in Islam and Islamic society. A new book by Leila Ahmad, which was published by Yale three or four months ago, has not yet received a single review in the U.S. Nobody wants to touch it, it's too complicated, quite a troubling view of the whole question. A mass of material is now coming out. In the past we had Nawal al-Saadawi and a few others. But very little. Then of course there are the anthologies—*Let Women Speak, Islamic Women Speaking*—and the translation of women's texts from the part of the world I know best—the Islamic and Arab world. However, most important of all for me are not these theoretical questions, but the emergence here and there of a serious, politically effective, women's movement. That's what it's all about in the end. There is a movement and there is a literature now in the Middle East itself as part of the general struggle against the status quo—which is appalling—in places like Saudi Arabia, Algeria, Tunisia, Lebanon, and, from my point of view, especially in Palestine. The role of women in the *intifada* is extraordinarily avant-garde. So the situation is changing. It's very different from what it was ten years ago, certainly twenty years ago. And for me it's mainly interesting because of the oppositional quality of the women's movement, asserting a set of rights for women essentially denied them by authorities who purport to use the arguments of the Sharia, the Quran . . .

Do you feel that you've taken on board these kinds of discussion in your new book?

Well, I was very interested. But the literature is still small. You get into another problem: what is the relationship between the women's movement and nationalism? In the early days of the national movement in places like Indonesia, India, Egypt, where there were pioneering women's movements, these were basically nationalist movements. They were thought of as part of the general struggle against the white man. I had a striking illustration of the difference between that and the present movement when last year I went to South Africa. I was invited by the University of Cape Town to give a lecture called The Academic Freedom Lecture. Because of the boycott, I had to be cleared by the ANC, which I duly was, and I gave a seminar at the ANC headquarters and at various other places. In Johannesburg, the first talk I gave was at an Islamic center in Linasia, which is an Asian township, mostly Muslim. I gave a talk about Palestine, which is what they wanted to hear about. Then I was told, "We've listened to you, now you listen to us." Which I thought was a fabulous notion, since usually visitors give a lecture and leave. So I heard somebody who spoke about schooling, about legal changes, violence, prison conditions, etc. There was a woman who stood up, whose name I'll never forget, Rohanna Adams: a Muslim name and a Christian last name—fantastic. She was the only one not to use the *Bismilrahim-rahmanulrahim,* which is the statement of faith which Muslims use, and which in South Africa and throughout the Islamic world is sometimes a revolutionary, sometimes a reactionary, thing to say. In the former case, you're saying, "Islam is my guide against you, the oppressors, apartheid," etc. In places like Saudi Arabia it means loyalty to the existing social order. In Algeria it was used against the French: Islam as a political force. She was the only one not to do that. It was her way of not getting sucked into the struggle against apartheid again. She said, "All right, we're struggling against apartheid, but there's still the problem of women. You haven't addressed it, any of you." (Pointing to them all, accusingly.) "You try to put us to one side," and indeed they did. They had the hall arranged so that the women were on one side and the men on the other— talking against apartheid. She said that we have to deal with this.

So, it's a completely different type of women's movement where there's a veering off from nationalism. There's a general discovery—and the women's movement is one of the places where this discovery has occurred—that nationalism has become the catchall for the *oppression* by the new class of minorities: women, religious and ethnic groups, and so on and so forth. The great virtue of the women's movement in the occupied territory in Palestine is not only against the Israelis, but against the so-called Islamic Arab oppression of women. But it's only beginning now to do that. It's changing.

Our final question about Orientalism *concerns your relation to some of the work that it provoked, which goes under the heading of "colonial discourse theory." People often identify* Orientalism *as the founding text of a new theoretical genre. But that genre is then frequently articulated in terms of poststructuralist theory, which is quite different in many ways from the theoretical assumptions and practices of your book.*

Absolutely.

It is also associated, at times, with a political tendency with which, rather surprisingly, you have occasionally been associated by your critics: "Orientalism in reverse," or a simple inversion of the hierarchical relationship between the West and its Other. What these two things have in common is a fixation on the binary opposition between the West and its "Other," and a tendency to homogenize both categories, thereby losing any kind of historical or geopolitical specificity: in the first case, by refusing to go beyond the pure negativity of the deconstructive stance; in the latter, by politically lumping together all kinds of very different colonial relations. What is your view of these developments?

Where I think *Orientalism* was useful was in those works that looked at the cultural component of forms of domination as giving rise to Africanist, Indianist, Japanesist, etc., types of discourses; as having, in a very narrow sense, played an important constitutive role in talking about those places. You could no longer look at, say, descriptions by nineteenth-century explorers of Africa as if they were just seeing what they saw. There was the notion of a collaborative enterprise having to do with the domination of a region. *Orientalism* gave rise to studies of that sort, which I think were salutary. However, it also gave rise to a bad thing, which I didn't intend, and which I thought I had dealt with, but obviously didn't: the problem of homogenization. For example, in the Arab world I'm read by many people as a champion of Islam, which is complete nonsense. I wasn't trying to defend Islam. I was simply talking about a very specific form of activity: representation. The problem then becomes (as some have suggested): you didn't say what the true Orient really was. So what I try to do in my new book (which I didn't do in the other one) is to talk not only about imperialism, but also decolonization, and the movements that emerged from the Third World—all kinds of opposition and resistance.

There is a focus on what I view as the opposition within the nationalist movements—nationalism versus liberation. There's nationalism which leads to the national bourgeoisie, separatist, statist, national security: the problem of the pathology of the Third World state. But there's always the opportunity for the alternative, what I call liberation. "There's room for all at the rendez-vous of victory" [C. L. R. James quoting Césaire]—is a very important phrase for me. It's impossible to talk about the sides of the opposition between Oriental and Occidental separately. I talk about what I call overlapping areas of experience. The whole point is that imperialism was not of one side only, but of two sides, and the two are always involved in each other. That's where the contrapuntal method comes in. Instead of looking at it as a melody on top and just a lot of silly accompaniment down here, or silence, it's really like a polyphonic work. In order to understand it, you have to have this concept of overlapping territories—interdependent histories, I call them. That's the only way to talk about them, in order to be able to talk about liberation, decolonization, and the integrative view, rather than the separatist one. I'm totally against separatism.

As for Orientalism in reverse, there's a literature on this throughout the Islamic world—"Occidentosis": all the evils in the world come from the West. It's a well-known genre that I find on the whole extremely tiresome and boring. And I've separated myself from it and from what I call nativism. I'll give you a perfect example of it. In 1962 or '63, Soyinka, an advanced intellectual, publishes a withering critique of the great nativist concept of negritude. He attacks Senghor, saying that Senghor's idea is really a way of giving in to the concept of the inferior black man. It's the other half of the dialectical opposition. Excellent. In 1991, in his own magazine, *Transition,* which has been reestablished in America with Skip Gates, he writes a tremendous attack on the African political scientist Ali Mazrui, who is a Muslim from Kenya. The essence of the attack on Ali Mazrui is that he is not a pure African. He's an Islamicized and Arabized African. So the integrative liberationist African, twenty years later, in Nigeria, has become a nativist, attacking a man for not being black enough!—the man who had attacked negritude. Those reversals are part of the political situation.

The same thing operates in the Salman Rushdie case. In the Islamic world I've been vociferous in attacking the banning of the book. It's the result, firstly, of the absence of any secular theory of any consequence that is capable of mobilizing people, that is understandable by the people who are laying their lives on the line; and secondly, of the absence of organization. There is no effective secular organization, anywhere, in the fields in which we work, except the state. I mean secular political organization. That's part of the failure which I lament so much. So there is this tremendous thing about authenticity and ethnic particularity. The politics of identity is the problem: the failure to take account of, and accept, the migratory quality of experience; that everybody is a migrant or an exile. In England, for example, the people who have been most vociferous against the *Satanic Verses* are migrants who want to assert their authenticity in an environment which has been basically hostile to them. Rather than saying, "Our experience is very much like that of the Palestinians, very much like that of the Bangladeshis"; instead of seeing it as something beyond the binary opposition, "us versus them," and therefore being able to see it in different terms, there's this obsession about returning to yourself: only in the community, and the purer form of the community, is my salvation—which is, I think, a form of perdition. It's the end of the best things about our civilization, and it's something that I completely oppose. The marginalization, the ghettoization, the reification of the Arab, through Orientalism and other processes, cannot be answered by simple assertions of ethnic particularity, or glories of Arabic, or returning to Islam and all the rest of it. The only way to do it is to get engaged, and to plunge right into the heart of the heart, as it were. That's the only answer; not these retreats.

The idea of secularity plays an important role in your work, particularly as a way of defining intellectual practice. Do you think the term "secular intellectual" bears enough critical force in the current situation? It seems an almost nineteenth-century category, insofar as it sets up the oppositional role of the intellectual solely in terms of a division between the theological and the secular. Secularity seems to define a space, an intellectual space which is oppositional to those who won't allow you to occupy it, but inside the secular space many different oppositional positions would seem to be possible. Is there a specific oppositional content here beyond the secularity?

As you said, it goes back to the secular versus the religious. That's clear. And the space is the space of history as opposed to the space of the sacred or the divine. The second point I take from Gramsci. He wrote a letter, I think it was in 1921, where he says that the great achievement of his generation, partly acting under the aegis of Croce, was that they were involved in the conquest of civil society, taking it away from mythological ideas of one sort or another: he called it the secular conquest of civil society. What interested me was that he also makes the point that the conquest is never over. You keep having to reappropriate as much as possible, which is otherwise going to be taken back. It's a constant reexcavation of public space. Beyond this, we have to describe functions of the secular intellectual. (I don't want to get into the whole question of general versus special, which is, I think, a phony set of categories invented by Foucault. I reject that.)

Instead, I prefer various functions, of which one, for example, is bibliographical: where the role of the secular intellectual, in opposition, is in relation to approved sources and documentation. The role of the secular intellectual is to provide alternatives: alternative sources, alternative readings, alternative presentation of evidence. Then there is what I call an epistemological function: the rethinking of, let's say, the whole opposition of "us" versus the Islamic world, or "us" and Japan. What does "us" mean in this context? What does "Islam" mean in this context? I think only intellectuals can fulfill these functions, in opposition, that is to say, in contravention of the approved *idée reçue,* whatever that happens to be. Then I see a moral function, a dramatic function: the performance in particular places of a type of intellectual operation that can dramatize oppositions, present the alternative voice, and so on. So it's by no means an open category. It encompasses a plurality of particular things and activities.

So the secular intellectual is inherently critical and oppositional? Yours is a more Sartrean position . . .

Yes, exactly.

. . . but not so close to Gramsci, where the distinction between "traditional" and "organic" intellectuals is so central?

No, I think it is. Part of the problem is that the categories of organic and traditional intellectuals in Gramsci are fantastically unclear, and difficult to make clear. The categories are simply not stable categories. At one time you could say that Matthew Arnold was an organic intellectual. When he wrote *Culture and Anarchy* in 1869, he had an affiliation with a particular class. But by the end of the century, he had become a traditional intellectual. People read his work as a kind of apology for culture, without any connection to anything except the Church.

But with Gramsci, one has the sense of a particular audience; that he is addressing a specific audience, an ideal audience, even.

Yes, all of this has to do with an audience, when I talk about a dramatic function. The difference is that I feel we all have different audiences in different constituencies. Just performing acts of routine solidarity, or mindless loyalty, strikes me as not interesting, not important. Although there may be a time for it. The great problem in essentially administered societies, the Western democracies, is precisely the drowning out of the critical sense. That has to be opposed by the secular intellectual and the critical sense revised for various audiences, various constituencies.

This question of intellectuals and their constituencies has been raised quite acutely in the American academy in recent years in ways that relate directly to some of the issues we have discussed regarding the reception of Orientalism: *namely, in the debates about political correctness and the canon. These are debates about exclusion, about boundaries, about what is to be excluded and what included. The position you have taken in these debates looks like a fairly traditional liberal humanist one, of opening up the space, including more texts, but defending canonicity. There are two questions here. The first is that if the way the state works culturally is through exclusion (as you suggest), can you really expect the existing state to open itself up to all these things? The pure liberal state is a fiction of political theory. The second question derives from a piece you wrote in the* TLS *where you ask: "Who benefits from leveling attacks on the canon?" and reply: "Certainly not the disadvantaged person or class, whose history, if you bother to read it at all, is full of evidence that popular resistance to injustice has always derived immense benefits from literature and culture* in general, *and very few from invidious distinctions between ruling class and subservient cultures." This is a strong defense of the oppositional political possibilities of "great texts." But are such distinctions* always *invidious?*

I've never felt the canon to be imposing a set of restrictions on me. It never occurred to me that in either reading or teaching the canon I was like a servant at work in the orchard of some great ruling-class figure who employed me to do that. I took it as requiring a certain kind of attention, a certain kind of discipline. Because I didn't feel that restriction I felt the whole question of the canon—whether it was raised by its defenders or its opponents—to be a very limited one. Secondly, everything I said in that article, and thereafter, concerned not the role of the canon in the state, in the context of the state, but in the university. Now, in my view, the university is one of the last quasi-utopian spaces in modern society. And if it becomes a place for displacing one set of categories in order to put in their place another set of categories, if we're going to read aggressively one set of texts that were forbidden in the past and that are now possible, and we're going to forbid the texts that we read in the past in order to read these texts, I'm against the practice. That's not the answer. In America, the vogue might be for Afrocentrism to replace Eurocentrism. In the Islamic world it is to not read Western texts in order to read Islamic texts. I don't have to make that choice. If that's what it's all about, I'm off. I'm ag'in them both. Just as I'm against William Bennett and Bernard Lewis, and all these who keep telling us that we should only read Homer and Sophocles, I'm against the other ones who say, you'll only read texts by black people or by women.

The question is: Are there open categories? That's really your question. I think there are. But they're not out there, they're what you do. That's what it's all about. It's not about somebody saying: "OK, Said, you can do anything you like." That's not interesting. What is, is what you do in your individual practice as a teacher, a writer, an intellectual. What are the choices you make? Now, if your attitude is venerative, then that's stupid. I'm against that. I've spent a lot of time trying to show the limitations of that. If, on the other hand, your attitude is critical, I think that's what education is all about—to instill a critical sense, a kind of nasty, demanding, questioning attitude to everything that's put before you. But that by no means exempts you in the end from making judgments, from deciding what is good versus what is better, what is excellent, what is lousy. Questions of taste are very important. I don't derive the same pleasure reading a novel by a great novelist and a political pamphlet. It's a different kind of thing. So in the end it's not the categories that are open, it's the possibilities of political and intellectual work that are relatively open, if one knows how to take advantage of them.

Can we return to your own position as a Palestinian working and living in the U.S.? In the introduction to a discussion with Salman Rushdie about your book After the Last Sky *you talked about the dangers of being a "cultural outsider." Is that how you see yourself, as a cultural outsider?*

Yes, I do, without necessarily feeling alienated, if you see what I mean. You could be an outsider, and become more of an outsider, and cultivate your own garden, feel paranoia, all the rest of it. I've never felt that. I've felt discriminated against, but I've never felt that my situation was hopeless; that I couldn't do something to lessen my feelings of marginality. I've never lacked for opportunities to speak and write. Sometimes it hasn't been very good. A couple of years ago I was under a death threat, when some group was trying to kill me. I had to change the way I lived. And it's been very hard for me constantly to be on the defensive in a public situation, in the media, or even socially, in a place like New York, where people look at me and say, "Oh yes, PLO terrorist."

Has that got worse since the Gulf War?

No, it's pretty much the same. Just before the Gulf War, there was a horrific attack published in *Commentary* called "The Professor of Terror"—it was completely libellous—which tried to prove that I plotted the murder of Jewish children and all this sort of thing. It was clearly reckless, designed to provoke me into starting a libel suit, which would tie me up for ten years, and prevent me from doing anything else. So I didn't even reply. Those things happen all the time. But you go on, and that's important. In the Arab world, I feel alienated for political reasons. I haven't been to Jordan or Lebanon in over ten years, for reasons that are entirely political. Most of these places have changed beyond recognition. So my own past is irrecoverable, in a funny sort of way. I don't really belong anywhere, but I've resolved that that's the way it is. It's OK. I don't mind so much. You don't have much choice.

Is it this sense of alienation from the Arab world that led you to resign from the National Council?

I began to be dissatisfied with the tendencies of the Palestinian movement, in particular the PLO, to which I've always been loyal as an overall political authority, several years ago. During the summer of 1991, I was very involved in the preparations for the Madrid Conference. I knew a lot of the people on the West Bank, and since America became central, it was thought that my input would be useful. I thought the emphasis in the Arab world, and above all in the Palestinian movement, on the United States, which was the last superpower, was scandalous, a slavish kind of fawning, almost desperate, cap-in-hand. "Help us, we rely on you," etc. When the United States has been the enemy of our people! I thought it was scandalous. It was very confusing to people, this sudden tilt toward America after the Gulf War. Because of the stupidities of what the PLO did during the Gulf War, there was a sudden dropping in the lap of America and accepting everything that they wanted, openly saying "Only America can rescue us!" It confused people a great deal. They suddenly thought, "What are we struggling about?" What happened after Madrid was that the situation on the West Bank and Gaza got *worse,* and it's getting worse every day. I was also unhappy with the mafia-like quality of the PLO, and I thought that Arafat, whom I've always been loyal to—he's a friend—I thought that his tenure had been too long. It's not been good for us. I began my critique in Arabic about three years ago, in 1989. [See page 343.] They don't know where they're going. It's too in-grown.

Inevitably, perhaps?

Perhaps. But it's also important for independents, such as myself, to say openly what the problems are. One last point I want to make is that, talking about negotiations over the West Bank and Gaza really didn't affect me in a way, because I'm not from the West Bank and Gaza. I'm from what used to be called West Jerusalem. And there was no role forecast for those of us who are exiles. Four million Palestinians (many of them stateless) have no place to go. There are many hundred thousands in Lebanon, Syria, etc. They're not included in these negotiations. It's just about residents on the West Bank and Gaza. So it's their problem. Fine, they're doing a great job—let them go on doing it. And the third reason I stopped, which was very important to me, is that since I discovered I have an insidious and chronic blood disease, I decided I would like to visit Palestine. I tried to go once in 1988 and Shamir refused entry, because I was a member of the National Council. So the resignation makes it possible for me to do that. And in fact I'm going the day after tomorrow. I'm on my way, for the first time in almost forty-five years.

When you go to the Arab world, do you see this as some kind of returning home, or is America now your home?

No, I'm at home in both places. But I'm different, in a way. In the American context, I speak as an American and I can also speak as a Palestinian. But in neither case do I feel that I belong in a proprietary sense or, let us say, in an executive sense, to the central power establishment. I'm in the opposition in both places. And of course it means quite different things. If you're in opposition in Palestine, in the Palestinian context, it means that you support and help shape an emerging national consensus. I played, I thought, a relatively important role in 1988 at the National Council meeting in Algeria where I helped to draft some of the statements and involved myself in a lot of the discussions, pushing toward recognition of the Israelis (UN resolution 242) by two states, all of that—I was for that, because it seemed to me logical, because we had no strategic ally, and because I thought it was right. The Soviet representative had absolutely nothing to say. In fact he was very discouraging. He didn't want us to do that. He said "lie low," etc. But I thought it was important to do that. So I did all of that. And as I said, I support the national consensus. On the other hand, I certainly didn't feel it something that I could deny myself. That if I felt something was wrong I should say it, and I said it.

For example, I've felt for almost fifteen, sixteen, seventeen years that Palestinian policy in the United States is badly organized. The U.S. is not like an Arab country. It's not even like a European country. And they've taken no steps to deal with that. The important thing becomes: how you pursue your criticism. The venue becomes central. I would never speak to a Western press person, because, in that context, it is interpreted as an attack on the national movement, which I wouldn't do. But in the Arabic press, in Arabic, I would do it. But rarely without having spoken to Arafat first. In America I'm totally in the opposition. It's true, in effect, I've become some kind of Mister Palestine to a lot of commentators. But I have never been on television, or press, or any sort of forum in America, without always being on the defensive, or in the minority.

I was on a big Sunday morning program once—I think it was the Brinkley show—and it was one of the key moments of the *intifada*. People were getting killed and beaten and all the rest, and they actually showed a tape of it. The first question to me after the tape was: "When are the Palestinians going to stop terrorism?" But when I give lectures now, political ones, since the Gulf War, and even during the Gulf War, I very rarely get hostile questions. It's quite extraordinary. Opinion has changed so much. The standard official Israeli position has simply nothing to recommend it anymore. We've gone all the way, we've recognized them. We've said we want coexistence, we're willing to talk peace. Why then does the occupation continue? Why does the systematic persecution and oppression of Palestinians continue? That's been a tremendous change.

Do you think the Gulf War was the turning point?

No. During the Gulf War, I took a position which was very much against Saddam, but I was also opposed to American troops. I've always been against Saddam. The only time I ever went to Kuwait was in 1985 and I had a huge semi-public fight with a local luminary who was blathering on about what a great man Saddam was. This was in the middle of the Iran-Iraq War. And I said, "Saddam's a murderer and a pig and a tyrant and a fascist, and you're criminals, and fools," and all the rest of it. And they said: "Ah, we're giving them billions"—and they did, they gave him fifteen billion dollars. And I told them that he was going to be the end of them. During the first weeks after the Gulf crisis the same luminary called me up and abused me over the phone, because he said people had told him that I had appeared on English television, and I hadn't been strong enough in defense of Kuwait. And I said, "Of course I've defended Kuwait. I've been opposed to the occupation, I've been opposed to Saddam, but I won't take the position that Saudi Arabia and your morally and politically bankrupt government and the Americans should now send troops in and start a war. There are many moves that can be made before that." Two weeks later, he wrote a column in the leading Arab, Saudi paper, published in London, in which he wrote in Arabic: "Why I invited the prominent Arab intellectuals to commit suicide." And he mentioned me. He said, "Said should commit suicide because he's been a traitor to the Arabs and to Kuwait."

During the Gulf War, my position was very different from the so-called official Palestinian position, such as it was. Basically, I opposed Iraq, I opposed the depredations of the Kuwaiti regime, I opposed Saudi policy, and I opposed the American position. I opposed the war. But I refused to fall into the position taken by people like Fred Halliday and Hans-Magnus Enzensberger–that in the war between imperialism and Fascism you back imperialism. I was against them both. I think that was the honorable and only serious position to take. It could have been taken by more intellectuals in the West, but to their shame—partly because of anti-Arabism and anti-Islam, and the sort of things I talk about in *Orientalism*—they didn't. It's a scandal. It's a great block. What has the war accomplished? Saddam is still there, he's still killing Kurds, Shi'ites, he's killing everybody. And he may even be supported by the Saudis now. At the same time as they're supporting his overthrow, they're trying to buy him off, as they do everywhere throughout the Arab world.

So your position was to maintain sanctions?

Yes, to maintain UN sanctions, but also to maintain uniformity and consistency of positions, everywhere, not just with regard to Palestine.

What about Cyprus? There are any number of UN resolutions on the Turkish invasion and partition of the country. One of the reasons I was very upset about the U.S. position during the so-called peace process, the Madrid phase, was that it said the Palestinians should strip themselves of their right to representation. No liberation movement in history has ever done that. They nominate. They say: We pick the people, and not you, not the enemy. Secondly, I thought it was a classic mistake, typically imperial, that the United States should make this *its* peace process, with the Soviet Union. You notice—if you look at the letter of invitation to the Madrid Conference, the United Nations is specifically cited as excluded. The United States will oppose any initiative from the United Nations. So suddenly the United States, which had used the United Nations in the Gulf War, had banned it from the peace process! All of these things have to be said.

In a television interview with you and Chomsky, during or immediately after the war, you talked about the persistence of Orientalist attitudes. At the time, that explanatory framework seemed to miss the precision of the West's economic and military motives. The reference to Orientalist discourses appeared almost superfluous in the face of that kind of precision.

Maybe I'm overly sensitive to it, but I don't think a war like that could have been fought, paid for by Arabs against other Arabs with contempt toward the whole procedure of negotiating, without Orientalism. This was not a war about aggression or anything like that. It was a war about cheap oil, and only Arabs have cheap oil: that combination has a particular kind of racial tinge to it. Nobody said—certainly not the Americans—that this is Arab oil for the Arabs, not just for the Kuwaiti royal family. These states—Saudi Arabia and Kuwait—are owned by families. There's no state in the world that's designated like Saudi Arabia—it's the House of Saud—they actually own the country. All of these anomalies were only possible, it seems to me, and produced contradictory and lying discourses about justice and aggression and all the rest of it, *because* they're Arab.

The United States has never supported human rights in the Arab world. I made a study of it. Every U.S. position of importance, whether political or economic or military, in the Arab world has always been taken against human rights. They've opposed human rights for Palestinians, they've opposed human rights in the Gulf, they've opposed human rights in places like Egypt, and so on and so forth. So I think you can't not talk about what we might call cultural attitudes. There was a kind of contempt. The other discourse—what you call economic and military—is not precise enough without this component. There was a massive campaign on the media in the United States: an anti-Arab and racist campaign, the demonization of Saddam. In many ways, Iraq is the cultural center of the Arab world. You didn't know that from the television screen, which just showed those smart bombs going in over Baghdad. Saddam is not Baghdad. And to this day, not a word, not even a word about the people killed. This could only have been done with Arabs.

Do you think that the American anti-war movement did enough?

What anti-war movement? Of course not. I don't think it would have been hard to do it. I think there was a lot of popular ambivalence about the war. The Left position was ambiguous. Not enough was made about the human catastrophe visited upon Iraq and the Gulf generally. Not enough was known about it, you see. A leading article in *Foreign Affairs* in December, just as the United States was about to go to war, began: "Saddam is from a brittle country which has no connection to ideas, books, or culture." This is a description of the country they're going to war against . . . "camel jockeys" and "towel heads," whether they're for us or against us. The same kind of scorn was heaped on the Saudis, and they were the "good Arabs" in this war. This was considered to be a war good for Israel, because Iraq was touted as the country most threatening to Israel. So there was really very little in the way of protest. To call it a movement would be wrong. It could have been a movement.

What would it have needed?

It would have needed organization. Don't forget, this is the period after the collapse of socialism, of the Left. There is no Left in America, like there is a European Left, or a British Left.

The British Left was itself very confused.

Well, if you were confused, what about America, where there is no real Left? There are people who are sort of vaguely Left, who are Left by virtue of sentiment and providence—people like Irving Howe, for example, or Michael Walzer—who are great gurus of the Left. Walzer was for the war. He thought it was a just war. The media was completely in ca-

hoots with the government. It was one of the great satanic collabora-
tions between the media and the government. You couldn't get on.
Radio, however, was very important during the war. National Public
Radio and a few of the national networks carried a lot of stuff. But it
doesn't have the power of television. It was a television war.

In Baudrillard's terms?

What did he say? Probably not.

Baudrillard said it was a hyper-real non-event.

Good old Baudrillard! For that I think he should be sent there. With
a toothbrush and a can of Evian, or whatever it is he drinks.

Interview with Anne Beezer and Peter Osborne,
Radical Philosophy, London, 1993

TEN

EDWARD SAID:

BETWEEN TWO CULTURES

You've said that your background is a series of displacements and expatriations which can't ever be recuperated, that the sense of being between cultures is the single strongest strand running through your life. I'd like to trace some of these displacements, starting perhaps most logically with where you were born—in Jerusalem, in what was then Palestine. Did you feel between cultures even as a child?

Yes, I did. My father was *from* Jerusalem, but he was a rather strange, composite creature. He had lived in the United States before he was married, having come to America in 1911 or 1912 to escape the Ottoman draft. They were going to take him to fight in Bulgaria, I think. He was sixteen or seventeen at the time, so he ran away and came here, to the United States. And then, through inadvertence or wrong information, he got into the American army, which he believed was going to send troops to fight against the Ottomans. In fact, he originally joined the Canadian army, and then didn't stay because he realized they weren't going to send him to the Middle East to fight the Ottomans; he joined the American army and he ended up in France, where he fought and was wounded. He then became a U.S. citizen and around 1919, a year or so after the war, he went back to Palestine and shortly thereafter went into business with his cousin. In the late twenties he established a branch of their business, which was books and office equipment, in Egypt. So actually, when I was born in Jerusalem in 1935, my parents were commuting between Palestine and Egypt. I didn't spend a huge amount of time in Palestine or, for that matter, anywhere really; we were always on the move. We would spend part of the year in Egypt, part of the year in Palestine, and the summer in Lebanon. In addition to the fact that my father had American citizenship, and I was by inheritance therefore American and Palestinian at the same time, I was living in Egypt and I wasn't Egyptian. I, too, was this strange composite, and that is my earliest memory.

You've also talked about being a minority within a minority.

Both my parents were Protestants in Palestine. That really meant that they were separated from the overwhelming majority of Christians, who were of course a minority in an essentially Muslim society. Most Christians in the Middle East—or at least in the Levant—are Greek Orthodox, but my parents were the children of converts from Greek Orthodox. My father became, through his father, an Anglican—an Episcopalian—and my mother became, through her father, a Baptist. It's one of the serendipitous things about the missionaries. When they came to Palestine and Lebanon and Jordan and Syria in the 1850s, they were tremendously unsuccessful in converting either Muslims or Jews to Christianity, which was what they came to do, and they ended up converting other Christians from the majority into these new sects.

As a child, what did that awareness of being between cultures mean to you?

I'll tell you the honest truth: it was miserable. My strongest continuous memory as a child was one of being a misfit. I was incredibly shy. I was terribly anxious and nervous about my relations with others, since I was sort of envious of their being Muslim/Egyptian, or Muslim/Palestinian, and I always had this sense of not being quite right. In fact my next book is going to be a memoir called *Not Quite Right* [which later became *Out of Place*]. I felt always that I was being made to pay for it in one way or another.

I forgot to add an important component to all of this, which is that I always went to English or French schools, so in addition to my problematic Arab identity, there was this other fact of my education where, by the time I was thirteen or so, I knew everything there was to know about English history, let's say, or French history, and next to nothing about the place I was living in. That was the style of education. So it was a perpetual discomfort. My family compensated for this by creating a cocoon around us. We were unusually different and each of us—my four sisters and I—had different kinds of gifts. And so the result was that we lived in a make-believe world that had no relationship (a) to reality and (b) to the history and actuality of the places we were living in.

I can see why you might be a little bit daunted by some of the company you were keeping. As I understand, when your family fled to Cairo in 1947, you spent a few months at a posh boys' school known as "the Eton of the Middle East," where the other students were people like the future King Hussein of Jordan and the actor Omar Sharif.

At the time of course I didn't know that he was going to become an actor. He was the head boy of the school; he was about four or five years older than I was, and he was rather flashy and daunting in the sense that he used to take it out on smaller kids like myself. Prefects in those schools were actually allowed the privileges of masters. There was a lot of beating, caning. I got caned the first day I was in school for talking in prayers or something equally horrendous. But it was a really mongrel atmosphere with all kinds of people, most of whom we knew only by their last names. Omar Sharif—that's his stage name—was Michel Shalhoub, so we called him Shalhoub, and I was known as Said. All the masters were English, and they treated us with contempt. It was a continuous war between us and them. So all in all it wasn't very happy, and after I was there a few years I was kicked out.

Why?

The euphemism was "misbehaving," which really meant causing a rumpus in the classroom, endlessly annoying the teachers. My impression, looking back on it now, is that the teachers were shell-shocked veterans of World War II. When they turned their backs on the class, we were incredibly sadistic and they'd dissolve in shakes and fits. They were British and didn't understand what we were saying in Arabic. An important fact here is that when you arrived at the school you were given what was called a handbook, which had a list of rules, and the first rule was that English was the language of the school and if you were caught speaking Arabic or any other language, you were either caned or given lines or detentions. So we used the language, Arabic, as a kind of assault on the teachers, and they of course didn't understand this. After I was thrown out, my father decided that, although they would have taken me back, my future in the English system was not bright. So I was shipped off to the United States to a disastrously unpleasant puritanical boarding school in New England, where I experienced for the first time the beauty of snow. I'd never seen snow before.

But the school was disastrous?

It was terrible. I should note, by the way, that all along I was very clever at school, and got good grades, so they couldn't completely banish me. At the school I went to in New England—I'd rather not mention the name because it's quite a well-known school—you had to get up at an ungodly hour and do things like milk the cows, and there was a lot of evangelical stuff. I had been so fantastically well trained in the English system that when I came to the United States, it was academically a lark. But the rest of it was quite bad. And there, too, I fell afoul of the system. My impression of it was that I was frowned on for my character or absence of it, something of that sort. So, although at the end of two years I graduated as a senior with the highest average in the school, I still wasn't named either salutatorian or valedictorian. When I tried to inquire, I was told that I didn't meet the moral requirements. And I've never forgiven them that particular infringement on my achievement.

You describe your book, Culture and Imperialism, *as an exile's book. So you're really a creature whose current interest is very much controlled by the conflict between the culture in which you were born and the culture in which you now live. Do you think that in a sense we should all be intellectual exiles? You seem to see exile as a salutary thing.*

I don't know any other condition, to tell you the truth. I'm fifty-seven years old. I went back to Palestine last year, after forty-five years. I took my children and my wife came along, and the four of us trudged bravely around and visited the West Bank and Gaza and all the rest of it, and then we went and saw the house where I was born. And you know, it was patently clear to me that I could never go back. It was nice to be able to visit it after all these years; it wasn't so nice to see what's become of it, from my point of view, because it's irrecoverable in some ways. What must it be like to be completely at home? I don't really know. I suppose it's sour grapes that I now think it's maybe not worth the effort to find out.

Initially, I think you tried to keep literature and politics relatively separate. On one side would be academic study of English literature and on the other your political concerns. I think you led what you called a "very schizophrenic life." How did you find a way to bridge these interests?

The fact is that all of us live in the world. I suppose it was just a matter of time and the right event. In my case it was during the 1967 war. I'd been this well-behaved academic; I'd done all the right things—gone to college, gone to graduate school, got a Ph.D., got a job, had fellowships, written books—and then in 1967 the world I knew completely fell apart. More of Palestine, or the rest of Palestine, was taken by the Israelis—the West Bank and Gaza—and I suddenly found myself drawn back to the area. I've never taught the literature of the Middle East— I've taught some Arabic books in translation, but basically all my work has been in Western literature. So I started to accommodate myself to the somewhat repressed or suppressed part of my history which was Arab. I did several things: I started to go back to the Middle East more often; I got married in the Middle East to a Middle Eastern woman; and then in 1972–73 I took a sabbatical year in Beirut, and for the first time in my life undertook a systematic study of Arabic philology and the classics of the Arabic tradition. By that time the Palestinian movement had been involved in a catastrophic clash with the Jordanians. Because a lot of my family lived in Jordan, I had been in Amman visiting relatives in 1970. When I was there I saw some friends of mine from college, Palestinians, who had gone back and joined the movement. It was quite a shock to see them there and realize that they, too, had gotten involved. Gradually, after the movement moved to Beirut—my family lived in Beirut by that time, in the seventies—I got more and more involved in the politics of the Palestinian struggle. That naturally honed my interest in issues of dispossession, exile, the political struggle for human rights, the struggle to express what is inexpressible, and a whole set of things that since that time have molded my work. My book *Orientalism* really came out of that experience.

Orientalism *is one of your most influential books, and what you do there is look at how the Arab or Eastern world is represented in and by the West. And basically it has been misrepresented.*

All representation is misrepresentation of one sort or another, but I argue in *Orientalism* that the interests at work in the representation of the Orient by the West were those of imperial control and were the prerogatives of power. I tried to show that the invasion of the Orient, beginning with Napoleon at the end of the eighteenth century but continuing as Britain and France spread into the Orient, colored and indeed shaped the representation. Far from it being objective or scientific, as a lot of the professors of Oriental studies used to say in the nineteenth century, especially the Germans but also the British and French, it was really a function of power and continued control over populations that they were trying to rule.

But the resulting images—the caricatures of the inscrutable Orient, the mysterious East, the evil and terror of the Arab world—why were they necessarily created?

I think ignorance played a big role. There was an hostility that prevented what I would call the normal exchange between cultures. One of the things that is quite amazing is that there is a rather stubborn continuity between European views of Islam in the twelfth century and European views of Islam in the eighteenth, nineteenth, and twentieth centuries: they simply don't change. First of all, I argue there's no such thing as Islam, pure and simple; there are many Muslims and different kinds of interpretations of Islam—that was the subject of another book, called *Covering Islam*. There's a tendency always to homogenize and to turn the other into something monolithic, partly out of not only ignorance but also fear because the Arab armies came into Europe and were defeated in the fourteenth and fifteenth centuries. So there is that longstanding sense. Then of course they're part of the monotheistic trilogy. Islam is the latest of the two other great monotheistic religions, Judaism and Christianity, and there's a sense in which the closeness to Europe of the Arab and Islamic world is a source of great unease. Nothing is easier for people to deal with something that is different than to portray it as dangerous and threatening and to reduce it ultimately to a few clichés.

That's what's really appalling, that the whole history of this creation of the Orient involves a continuous diminishment, so that now, for example, in the Western press, the things you read about Islam and the Arab world are really horrendously simplified and completely belie the two or three hundred years of close contact between Europeans and to some degree Americans on the one hand and Arabs and Muslims on the other. It's as if they've always been standing on opposite sides of some immense ditch and all they do is throw rotten food at each other.

And that isn't changing?

No, I think it's actually getting worse. At times of crisis, such as during the Gulf War and also on a continual daily basis in the media in

America, the clichés are getting less interesting and less forgiving and less "true." They correspond less to any conceivable human reality. Islam in the West is the last acceptable racial and cultural stereotype that you can fling about without any sense of bad manners or trepidation.

Why do you think that is?

There are many reasons for it but I think the main one is that there's no deterrent. No Western, or let's say North American person, knows very much about the Islamic world. It's out there, it's mainly desert, a lot of sheep, camels, people with knives between their teeth, terrorists, etcetera. The cultural heritage, the novels and other books that appear in English, are never paid attention to. There's nothing to prevent people here from saying what they wish. On the other hand, the Arabs and the Muslims haven't really understood the politics of cultural representation in the West. Most of the regimes in the Arab world are basically dictatorial, very unpopular, minority regimes of one sort or another; they're not interested in saying anything about themselves because it would expose them to justified criticism. The myths about America and the West in the Arab world are equally clichéd: all Americans are oversexed and they have large feet and they eat too much. The result is that where there should be a human presence there's a vacuum, and where there should be exchange and dialogue and communication, there's a debased kind of non-exchange.

One of the apparent contradictions or complexities in your own life is that, although you've been a member of the Palestinian government-in-exile and you're a champion of Palestinian liberation, you're uneasy with nationalism.

Nationalism can quite easily degenerate into chauvinism. There's a tendency when you're attacked on all sides—particularly in movements like the Palestinians', where we really don't have too many friends—to fall back into the fold and end up by fraternizing or sisterizing with your kind, and everybody who isn't of your ilk, who doesn't think like you, is an enemy. This is especially the case for Palestinians living in the Arab world. It's completely understandable. There was a time when to be a Palestinian was a great noble thing. But the Arab world is now a much reduced place, and there is poverty, economic and social disintegration, so the Palestinians now enjoy a problematic status, to say the least. And people are tired of the struggle that's gone on for so long. Of course on the West Bank and Gaza, there's been a lot of talk about collaborators and agents, and the secret manipulation of Palestinians by the Israelis. People are understandably suspicious because we're talking about the dangers of loss of life. But in general, nationalist movements actually work on that model; they tend in time to grow smaller and more particular and more homogenous. Look at what's happening in Yugoslavia, where what used to be a multicultural state, a multilingual state, has degenerated into "ethnic cleansing." The same happened in Lebanon, where a pluralistic society, with Christians and Muslims, in the end became a perpetual daily bloodbath of people killing each other "on the identity card," as they used to say in Lebanon. If you were asked for your identity card and if you had the wrong name or the wrong religion, you were shot on the spot or your throat was cut.

I'm afraid that the unpleasant aspects of nationalism are also surfacing in societies like the United States, and maybe in Canada also. You have all these different ethnic communities who are now beginning to feel that the problem is how to preserve, against the depredations of the others, their own identity. Identity politics becomes separatist politics, and people then retreat into their own enclaves. I have this strange, paranoid feeling that *somebody* enjoys this—usually people at the top, who like to manipulate different communities against each other. It was a classic of imperial rule. In India, for example, you got the Sikhs and the Muslims and the Hindus dependent on you and suspicious of their compatriots. That is all part of the process of nationalism. In that respect I find myself very unhappy with it.

I can see that the complexity of things puts you in an awkward or a very acrobatic position, because you have to walk two sides, not only politically but also in terms of your raising issues of multiculturalism and "the literary canon." On the one hand you're an advocate of inclusivity and opening things up, and at the same time you are a defender of the literary canon.

I'm a defender of what I would call good work. The main criterion for me in judging a novel or a poem or a play isn't the identity of the person who wrote it. That's interesting, but it's not the major issue. If that person happens to be of the "right" color or gender or nationality, that doesn't necessarily mean that it's going to be a very fine work. You've probably heard of this Palestinian woman, Hanan Ashrawi, who was the spokesperson for the PLO delegation in Madrid. She was a student of mine and she wrote a dissertation under me on the literature of the West Bank under occupation. And one of the things that she discovered in writing this was that being Palestinian and writing about the travail of being under occupation doesn't necessarily produce good poetry or a good novel. That's the point, and it's a very important one to make.

I'm not saying it's not subjective. The determination of what constitutes good work is profoundly subjective. It really has to do, for example, with things like pleasure. I've maintained a long battle with people who talk about objectivity, especially in the media, because obviously everything is based on relatively subjective interpretation. We're really talking about discriminations that you yourself make. In a sense, quality is profoundly subjective—it can't be legislated from above; it can't be that somebody tells you, this is a great book and you'd better believe it, or it is a great book because I say it is. It has to be achieved by a process of investigation and analysis. I think the closest we can come to a rule about great as opposed to not-so-great work, aesthetically speaking, is that great work repays much reading and much rereading and continues to deliver a certain kind of agreeable or pleasurable sensation, whether through enlarged consciousness or enhanced taste and sensibility or whatever, and a lesser work doesn't. We have all had that experience. You read a Danielle Steel novel—and I don't, actually—you don't necessarily want to read it again, but if you read a novel by Dickens, you want to return to it.

You quote Walter Benjamin where he said that every document of civilization is also a document of barbarity, and in a way that's what your book Culture and Imperialism *is about.*

Right. A great work doesn't necessarily mean an innocent work, or a work that's completely unaffiliated with anything that we would call sordid. When *Culture and Imperialism* came out in England, there was a tremendous storm of reviews, a lot of them insulted by the notion that somebody as pristine as Jane Austen—whom I talk about at some length in my book—had anything to do with empire and slavery, even though the evidence is not invented by me, it's what she herself talks about. I don't say that Jane Austen is a lesser writer because of that. I just say that almost all works of art, like all human beings, are connected to what is unattractive and barbaric in some instances. It's really particularly noticeable in these canonical works of the nineteenth century in Europe. We're connected to the practices of slavery and empire largely through what they said about them. So I don't think it's a problem to discover that. The question is: once you've discovered it, what do you do? Do you suppress it and say, well, it doesn't really matter, or rather—which is what I'm saying—do you try to hold it in your mind and say, well, that's there too.

You say you don't want to be reductive, but how do you avoid reading literary classics as colonial or imperial propaganda?

I don't at all read them that way. In the book I said it would be wrong to reduce these classics to a long list of instances of imperialism, or to say that they're all imperial. They're not; they were part of an imperial culture and part of a process which, as the theorists of empire have said, involved not only the most sordid practices but also some of the best aspects of a society. A lot of very brilliant people were involved in empire: great artists, like Delacroix; great writers like Flaubert. Of course the nature of the involvement, the degree of the involvement, is different in each case, and their view is quite different. They're not all the same, that's why there are so many analyses in my books, both in this one and in *Orientalism*. I'm not trying to make the point that they're all imperial, but that they give different views of the imperial world in their work. They elaborate it, they refine it, they ascribe certain kinds of sensations and pleasures to it, in the way that Kipling does, for example, in *Kim*.

You make a very far-reaching claim, though, that the novel and empire-building were inextricably linked, that the novel didn't simply reflect what was going on, but that imperialism and the novel somehow fortified each other.

It is a rather far-reaching claim, but I think it's true.

How does that work?

Well, in the following way. The first English novel of note is *Robinson Crusoe*, and *Robinson Crusoe* is incomprehensible without the imperial quest. He leaves England, he's shipwrecked, he finds himself on an island, and within a matter of days, a couple of hundred pages into the novel, he is the master of everything he surveys. And then you realize that what this island has done for him is allow him to create his own world. In other words, imperialism at that level is associated with a certain kind of creativity. Later, at the end of the nineteenth century, John Seeley said that the central fact of England, the central fact of English culture, of English identity, is expansion. This is not true of every society. My argument is that in the nineteenth and twentieth centuries, England was in a class entirely by itself. The idea is a very strange one: you're sitting in London—let's say you have a little apartment in Hampstead—and you get up in the morning and say, "I control the lives of a hundred people," because if you break down the relationship between the population of England and the population of India, which England controlled for over three hundred years, it really meant that every English person was in control of a hundred or a hundred and fifty people. That fact has to be taken into consideration, *plus* the fact that in no other Western society has there been such unbroken continuity in the imperial tradition as in England, and in the writing of novels. There is no Italian novel before 1860 or 1870. There is no German novel until well after 1870. There is no Spanish novel, with a few exceptions, in the nineteenth century. I'm talking about continuous. The English novel begins formally, according to most literary historians, with people like Defoe in the early eighteenth century, and continues in an unbroken way through the eighteenth, the nineteenth, and the twentieth centuries.

But are you seeing causality where there's only synchronicity?

No, I don't say causality, but I say that there's accompaniment and accommodation. All of the great novelists of the nineteenth century make allusion to the facts of colonial control, such as immigration to places like Australia or America or Africa. The same is true, to a lesser degree, of France. My argument is that the facts of imperial control have an imaginative side to them which is part of the structure of identity. Most novels are really about the creation of a fictional identity, who am I? I am Pip, for example, in *Great Expectations,* or Tom Jones, the foundling. He's found in a bed at the beginning of the novel; at the end of the novel we know who he is. The novel is really a form of acculturation and accommodation, the accommodation of a self to society. Part of this process is that the identity is bound up with imperial reaches. In the case of Jane Austen's *Mansfield Park,* for example, the slave plantation that Sir Thomas Bertram owns in Antigua is used to finance the estate in Mansfield Park, in England. That's the kind of thing I'm talking about, that there's a kind of an imaginative projection in the fiction, in the narrative, that suggests that England is tied up with its overseas colonies in different ways. We're not talking about the same thing over and over again; each novel is slightly different, inflected differently.

Is it too innocent to see it as plot?

It's not innocent at all: it *is* plot. But why that plot and not others, you see? All novels involve choices on the part of the writer, and the fact is that this was a subject ready at hand; it was part of the intellectual, imaginative, emotional property of the English. If you read a German novel, it's a completely different thing. There's no talk about our territories, and we can't go to India; it plays a different function: exoticism or something of that sort. In England it's a place you can go to because we're there, like in *A Passage to India* or *Kim,* or some of Conrad's works. It's literally everywhere. The fact is that the British were nearly everywhere, when you think about it for a minute. By 1918 a small group of European powers were in control of 85 percent of the world. What could be more natural than that possession, which is an historical experience, also becoming part of the imaginative experience? I think it does. I'm saying: it's there, what do you make of it?

What do you make of it?

I think you have to see it as part of something bigger than itself. My point is that this experience is part of reading the English novel. I'm not saying it's the most important part but it's an important part. One also has to remember, which most people don't realize, that these places that Jane Austen or Kipling talk about have had a history beyond what is enacted in the novel. In 1814, when *Mansfield Park* was published, Antigua was a plantation colony of England, but most people who read the novel say, oh yes, well, there it is. But the fact is that that experience continues and Antigua is liberated, becomes independent.

There is a whole literature coming out of the Caribbean, written by people such as V. S. Naipaul and George Lamming and a whole school of Caribbean writers who in fact see the imperial experience in its past—as slave colonies—from a completely different perspective than Jane Austen. What I'm saying is that the fullest and most interesting way to read people like Jane Austen or later Kipling, who writes about India, is to see them not only in terms of English novels but also in terms of these other novels which have come out. You can read them contrapuntally, to use the metaphor for music. They're going over the same history but from a different point of view. When you read them that way you get a sense of the interdependence of these normally quarantined literatures. There's nothing more exciting and interesting than that, because it puts you in touch with great writing. It also puts you in touch with the notion of contest, that a lot of culture involves the struggle over territory of one sort, figurative or real. And it puts you in touch with ideas of human liberation, that people don't endure colonialism for a very long time. I'm sure most people who read Jane Austen know very little about what happened to that place that Sir Thomas Bertram went to. She doesn't say very much about it either, because *she* didn't know what happened; it was just a place where you went to pick up the money and come back to England. You go; if there's a slave revolt, as there was in the novel, you fix it and then you come back. To leave it at that is not to have a very accurate sense of what's going on out there. In a certain sense if you just leave it at that, you're perpetuating the bias of that earlier novel. Other great works—such as *The Black Jacobins* of C. L. R. James, for example—could be read against it or with it, if you like.

It seems as if some of the Victorian novelists just took a very utilitarian approach to empire in terms of plot.

Exactly. But the argument that I make at the very opening of *Culture and Imperialism* is that the world has changed now: it's no longer Indians in India, English in England, and traveling around. The fact is that, for example, most of the European countries today are not pure countries made up entirely of white people. There's a very large Indian community in England; there's a very large Muslim and North African community in France, in Germany, Sweden, and in Italy, and so on, and the world has become largely mixed. Why are these people in France from North Africa? Largely because France was the imperial master, and when these people are running away from depredations they come to France—they're francophonic, they speak French. The world is a mixed world. My sense of it is that what used to be utilitarian in the nineteenth century is now no longer the case, and there are critics who write in English who are not English. When Conrad wrote *Heart of Darkness,* for example, he assumed—obviously wrongly, but that was the bias of the time and I can't blame him for that—that no African could read what he wrote; he wrote for English people. But the fact is that there are now Africans who read *Heart of Darkness*, and what they see in *Heart of Darkness* is very different from what Conrad's white contemporaries in the 1900s saw, and *their* reading has become a factor in the novel. So the novel opens up in a way that Conrad and Dickens and Jane Austen and others never even dreamed of. This is to be welcomed because it shows you a new side of the work and enables you to see things that you couldn't have seen before.

Why is Conrad one of your favorite writers?

I've always felt a tremendous affinity with him because he was Polish and left Poland at the age of about sixteen, lived for a time in Switzerland and France, learned French, and at the age of twenty or so, began to write and learn English, and lived in England and became a member of the British Merchant Navy, serving on sailing ships for fifteen or so years, and then he settled in England. When he became a writer he was in his forties, I think. He remained a Pole; he was outside the English center, in a sense, although he wrote a marvelous English. He had this strange sort of exilic consciousness; he was always outside any situation he wrote about, and I feel that affinity with him. His angle on things is completely unlike anyone else's in the period. He was very friendly with people like Henry James and John Galsworthy, and they were wonderful writers too, but they don't provide you with that strange prismatic sense of dislocation and above all, skepticism, especially the skepticism about identity and settled existence that Conrad does. Conrad is one of the few novelists in English to write in a masterful, although in some cases objectionable, way about places like Indonesia, Malaysia, Thailand, Africa, and Latin America. He was really an internationalist of the imperial period.

He's a very complex figure, and I don't pretend to suggest that my interest in him is entirely because he shares a roughly similar background. Not at all. He's a great novelist and there is something astonishingly complex and brooding and rich about him that makes me keep wanting to come back to him. Nobody really sees things quite the way that he does. I suppose another affinity is that he writes English like somebody who is not a native-born English speaker, and I find that endlessly fascinating. The syntax is slightly off in Conrad; the adjectival insistence is rather peculiar. There are a number of things like that which on a gut level are very interesting to me.

Another aspect of your far-reaching claim is to say that imperialism more than any other literary theory, Marxism, deconstruction, or the New Historicism, is the major determining political horizon vis-à-vis literary theory.

The notion of a global setting in literature comes from the imperial experience. People have global empires—the British and the French certainly did—and now, in the twentieth century, the United States has succeeded to the British and French hegemony. Therefore, it would seem to be lacking in seriousness in the study of culture not to take this larger horizon, this framework, into account. All I'm doing is saying there is a connection. I'm not saying that the connection is simple or direct or causal; I'm saying there are lots of interconnections and interlacings—interdependencies, I call them—between the two spheres. Insofar as imperialism had a global reach, has a global reach, then it is the backdrop or the stage setting for the enactment of some of these literary structures, cultural structures and practices.

Interview with Eleanor Wachtel,
More Writers & Company,
Toronto, Canada, 1996

ELEVEN

PEOPLES' RIGHTS
AND LITERATURE

You wrote somewhere that the Palestinian experience is so fragmented that classical concepts don't apply to it. What about the concept of "rights"?

Well, we are in a unique position of being a people whose enemies say that we don't exist. So for us the concept of "rights" means the right to exist as a people, as a collective whole body, rather than as a collection of refugees, stateless people, citizens of other countries. It has, in a certain sense, the most urgent meaning for us, since, from the beginning of our struggle against the Zionist movement, and later against Israel, our principal goal is to get to step one. We are still a long way from "national rights." In the current climate of peace talks, the so-called peace process that the Americans speak about, there is no phrase signaled by the Americans or the Israelis that suggests that we have "self-determination" or "national rights." We are very much at the starting point.

You talk about "national rights" and "self-determination." But is a nation really a "self" that ought to have rights to determination?

It's a tricky question, but I think that in the case of the Palestinians, yes. We have a long history of residence on the land of Palestine. We were a coherent society with a collective memory, a language—Arabic, of course, which is like the language of other Arab people in other Arab countries—even if ours is a distinctive brand of Arabic. We had sent members to represent us to the Ottoman parliament in the 1870s, and part of the battle, the intellectual and cultural battle, that we've had to fight since the beginning of the twentieth century, has been to show that we are a "people." And as a "people," there are two things open to us:

one is subservience and finally suppression and extinction; the other alternative is to exist in a national state with the rights that are now the rights allowed to most peoples in the world today. We have opted for the second.

But isn't the very idea of a "national state," or a "state-nation," or a "nation-state," one which contains all sorts of traps? I mean one view would say that the idea of a nation is a kind of con trick whereby the ruling elites of different jurisdictions make it sound as though any injury to the elite is actually an injury to every person who lives under their jurisdiction, and the idea of "national identity" and the right to "national identity" serves to make for that illusion, so that in international law you get the idea that invading a nation-state is a matter of violating every individual within it. Isn't that an illusion? Or do you think that's too cynical a view? Or what is it?

It is partly cynical and partly incomplete. In our case, it has to be remembered that there are two levels to Palestinian nationalism. On the one hand, it is an urgent necessity for people, the large majority of whom today, I would say, enjoy no rights at all, precisely because of their national origins. For example, there are over four hundred thousand plus Palestinians in Lebanon, all of whom exist as stateless people, and who have pieces of paper saying "you are stateless." So in a certain sense, this is invidious nationalism. On the other hand, that level can be addressed, as you said, by founding a national identity, having a state, all of the traditional, one might say conventional, attributes of nationalism about which one has mixed feelings because this can lead to all sorts of abuses. But the other level for the Palestinians, which is more important as far as I'm concerned, is that the Palestinian struggle in the Middle East, in the Arab world in particular and with regard to Israel, is a vanguard struggle in that it is a secular struggle in a part of the world where religious nationalism is very, very powerful. I mean the nationalism of Islam in places like Iran, Algeria now, Jordan—Jewish nationalism too as the right-wing organism which has dominated Israeli life for the last twenty years is an example of that, as well as Christian fundamentalist nationalism in Lebanon. So we are different. We are not a religious movement. We are a nationalist movement for democratic rights. The second attribute is that the Palestinian struggle is a vanguard struggle because it is a struggle for democracy in a part of the world where there is no democracy. We make it very clear in our national declaration of independence in 1988 that we are a secular struggle with democratic rights for all people, men and women, religions, creeds and sects. In that respect, we are much more than a small or petty nationalism; and in that respect, it is a brilliant and important struggle.

Jews, of course, are likely to feel threatened by the sort of thing you are saying. You wrote somewhere that Zionism is a touchstone of political judgment in our time. Could you explain that?

Yes. Jews, insofar as they are Zionists, are people who believe in a return to Palestine, that is to say, the ancestral homeland of the Jewish people. They are people who believe that they are entitled for the most part to sole rights in Palestine. What that overlooks, of course, is that there was another people there, and there is another people there now, most of them under occupation in the West Bank and Gaza since 1967, and about 800,000 who are the remnant of the Palestinians who have been driven since 1948, as second- or third-class citizens in a state which is described as the state of the Jewish people, not to say of its citizens (a very important distinction). Now, Zionism achieved very important things from the standpoint of Jews. But from the standpoint of its victims—and Zionism has always had victims—it's a catastrophe that the state of Israel was constructed. It is a conflict, if you like, of tragedies. On the one hand, here were the remnant of the Jewish people, who were massacred in Europe by Western anti-Semites, coming to Palestine. They had come before World War II, but the status and the state of the survivors, and the construction of their state, were on the ruins of our society. This is not a metaphor, because I remember. I was a boy, and I partly grew up in Palestine. I remember what it was like to leave. One's whole family left. From that point of view, it is a conflict between a group of people who came as victims and who, in turn, produced another victim: us—we are the victims of the victims—and it is a most difficult choice, but, I think, a required choice on the basis of rights. You can't deal with the rights of one people at the expense of the rights of another.

Your work as a critic links up in quite deep and subtle ways, I think, with your concerns as a spokesperson for the Palestinian cause. But I think in particular of the fact that a theme in a lot of your criticism is space and geography. One could say that for a lot of previous criticism the main theme had been time and history. You have changed that, or perhaps you and Raymond Williams would be mainly responsible for that.

Well, you know, that isn't to say that if you're interested in geography, space, territory, you aren't also interested in history. I am really interested in the interaction between the two. But I do, it's true, give primacy to geography because it seems to me that the history of the last three hundred years is, in fact, world history, and it is a globalized history. What makes it intelligible, or one of the main things that makes it intelligible, is the struggle over territory. By 1918, 85 percent of the world was under the domination of a handful of states in Europe and America. Since that time, one can understand the cultural and historical experience, say the period after World War II, as the struggle to get back territory that had been taken from people of color in the colonized world. So, that's why it's terribly important to me. I see my own history, and the history of my people, as a function of that struggle over territory; and it was always territory. The interesting thing is that it was never territory taken for the sake of territory. You didn't simply go there, and just say, "Well I like this; I'm going to take it."

I am interested in the antecedent justifications. Australia, for example, is perfect for England because it is far away. It is the antipodes; we could put all our unwanted populations, the felons, there. America is the promised land, so they go there and they colonize it because it is a new Eden. Palestine was the country of the reclaimed promised land for the Jews. But what always happened was a conflict of these justifications with, you might say, the bodies, the realities of the people there. Therefore, it is a struggle over geography, but also over justification and philosophy and epistemology, and whose land it is. Is it the right of the people who live there? In the case of Palestine, for example, one of the main arguments in early Zionist writing—and not only early Zionist writing, but early European writing about Palestine in the twentieth century—was that it was uninhabited, and if it was not uninhabited, it was a land full of neglect, which is a similar argument to that used by French settlers in North Africa when they took Algeria: it was simply an empty land with savages on it. In other words, the right to use land, or the right to imagine the best use for the land, is a right given to the European, to the white man. That seems to me to be the foundation, not only of actual political struggle, but also of the construction of cultures.

It is impossible to understand European culture without some sense, for example in England, of the role played by India or Australia or the Caribbean in English domestic life. All of that strikes me as a fantastically interesting field, and bears always the connection, the relationship, to Williams's *The Country and the City*, the overseas territories, and so on.

You talked about epistemology, and certainly in your work on the geography of imperialism the leading theme, I think, is the idea that the East was constructed as a mystery which it took the West to know about. There is a curious way in which your work on that subject has been caught up in the logic which it, itself, designated—I mean that people have criticized you for writing so exclusively about the European view of the East, and for neglecting agents who actually were in the East. What do you think of the way that this has developed?

Well, I think that to a certain extent they are right. That is to say that when I was writing *Orientalism,* I was really talking about European conceptions of the Orient, which are in some instances so far beyond any local conception of what that geography might be, that they constructed a field and a subject all their own. Even now, retrospectively, it seems to me perfectly okay to talk about it, because it constituted itself as an object that had very little to do with what people there thought. What I have done since then, however, is to look at the struggle over competing conceptions of geography. In my latest book, which will appear in a few months, I really spend half the time looking at how nationalist struggles in Africa, in places like Ireland, in the Caribbean, in India, really had to begin, you might say, with the reconquest of that territory, to do it initially epistemologically. In other words, to reimagine it in the way, for instance, that Yeats reimagined the history of Ireland in terms of its fairies and heroes and great fighters, and so on and so forth. The fact produces—as somebody like Neruda does in Latin America—a new geography which is a reclamation of the land. You find really competing conceptions there. I think that I've been trying to do that, but what is very striking is the extent to which the prevailing conceptions in Europe, in the West, are very difficult to dislodge, because so much is invested in them. It is not just a matter of someone having an idea—but scientific institutions are built around these ideas, like the Royal Geographical Society in England. Rodney Murchison, for example, was a man who, as a geologist, as a geographer, as a surveyor, didn't only think that he was exploring Africa. He actually said it was like a military campaign, and what he was trying to discover about the geography and the geology of Africa was, in a certain sense, adding to the realm of England. Along with that went an enormous institution—the Royal Geographical Society. Those are the things that one has to take seriously and not say, well, you know, they are just Western fictions.

What about that situation of people in the English language, but not in Britain or America? I'm thinking of people, say readers, in Africa reading Conrad, in the Caribbean reading the The Tempest, *in India reading Kipling and Forster. What's that experience of reading?*

Well, it's a very different one. I mean, let's say that you wanted to read as a Caribbean native a novel by Jane Austen, who is, perhaps of all English novelists, the most tied to a particular locale which is very, very English and extremely insular in that respect. But if you read with the eye of a Caribbean, or the eye of an Indian, a novel like *Mansfield Park* or *Persuasion* or *Pride and Prejudice,* you'll find very careful notations there of overseas territories that are very much held. In *Mansfield Park,* for instance, the estate of Sir Thomas Bertram is held by Bertram in Antigua, and the importance of Antigua, therefore, to the economy of *Mansfield Park* is absolutely central. But at the same time you have a kind of illusion of it. It ceases to be important once it is mentioned that he had to go there and take care of it. And it was a slave sugar plantation. If you read with those eyes, you can, then, see that the history of the English novel, great form that it is, is constructed with precisely those territories held in the imagination as they are held in England. A totally different experience emerges from the reading of the novel *A Passage to India* for example. Even more so, Conrad's *Heart of Darkness* becomes not just the explorations of Marlow and Kurtz of that bit of Africa, but really becomes the symbol for Africa and the enslavement and partition and the scramble for Africa. That entails, of course, a much different reading than simply reading as you would for a test or for an English course. You read as N'gugi [wa Thiong'o] and people like Chinua Achebe have read it. You have to read it in a decolonizing way. You have to strip from it all the assumptions that are there; and very often you have people like Achebe and N'gugi reading it and in some cases rejecting it and rewriting its history in terms of their own apprehension of the river and the territory, and so on. In my opinion, it is a much more lively and invested process to read and interpret literature of that sort from the point of view of the colonies, and above all of the decolonizing colonies.

You've mentioned N'gugi and Achebe, so that raises the question of being a writer of English outside Britain and America, the situation of Yeats or [Derek] Walcott. [Seamus] Heaney has a phrase somewhere about how those people are in a situation of being on a forked stick of their love of the English language.

It is not inherent to English by the way. It is the case of French writers too. There is a whole group of very interesting and important Algerian novelists, like Kateb Yacine who writes in French, but was very much a part of the Algerian resistance to French colonization, and of Moroccan writers, like Abdel Kebir Khatibi who writes in French. I think it is a very interesting case which, in a certain sense, N'gugi has finessed by proceeding to write in the native language. He rejected English after having written several very distinguished novels, saying that he wanted to write in his native language. But the challenge is there. That is to say that the language is a field which one can work in, and it depends often on the premises. It is not the language itself which is infected. For example, Achebe says that Conrad shouldn't be read at all, that he is such a racist that *Heart of Darkness* is an unreadable text for Africans, and then he goes off and writes his own novel in English. But I think that the struggle within the language for values, for perceptions, for geographies exactly, is a continuing one, and in a certain sense has to be understood in domestic terms. It is not everybody in England who writes from neocolonial or imperial premises using English. One can always find alternatives to it. I think that's the great task of criticism today—to read novels, not to reestablish the orthodoxies and the perceptions of the dogmas, etc., that anchor the work, but rather to read to understand these, to try also to understand them as dislodged to allow for other places. As Aimé Césaire says, "there is room for everyone at the rendezvous of victory." That was a great example for someone like C. L. R. James—that you could write the history of the French Revolution from the point of view of the great slave revolt in Haiti. That seems to me to be the interesting alternative, not what language would you write in.

Yeats is a particularly interesting example here, I think, because a lot of people would be surprised to see him regarded as a poet of anti-imperialism rather than a poet of modernist internationalism.

Absolutely! I think Yeats is a particularly interesting case because he was very reactionary, at the same time somebody who believed in great houses, in eighteenth-century nobility, and he was Anglo-Irish. After all, he belonged to the Ascendancy. But in a certain sense, Yeats was a national poet, and he was one of the people who forwarded precisely this decolonizing imagination that gave rise to the Irish Renaissance, and continues today to do so. I think it is possible to see Yeats in two ways: on the one hand as a man who slid off at the end of his life into a kind of terribly reactionary, even fascist, politics, but whose poetry, particularly up to "The Tower," and even after it, in the twenties, was really the nationalistic poetry that, I think, can be seen. . . . I mean, in the Irish context, he became a reactionary. But if you compare him with nationalist poets of his time, or like Aimé Césaire later, or Neruda, or Tagore in India, you could see him as belonging to the decolonizing culture, which was an international culture. They knew about each other, and worked from similar premises in local situations that differed widely. To see Yeats as simply a modernist internationalist, as he has been taken, is to miss, I would say, a good part of the vigor and arrogance of his verse. For an Irish person to speak the way he did, to talk about Irish history in the way he did, is an act of *lèse-majesté* whose force is undeniable.

Your first book, Joseph Conrad and the Fiction of Autobiography, *was described by you as an attempt at a phenomenological kind of criticism, and you talked of Sartre and Merleau-Ponty as the inspiration of the book. Is that still the inspiration of your work, or has its direction changed?*

I would say probably yes, but I wouldn't, perhaps, use the word phenomenology. What interested me about those people, Sartre and Merleau-Ponty and Husserl, at the time was that they seemed to situate the study of forms, or it was possible through them to understand the study of forms, as taking place in a context, in a whole environment. And when I grew up as a student, and as a graduate, I was living in an era of high formalism where the work itself—the Cleanth Brookses, the New Criticism—was really the dominant thing. I found that in somebody like Conrad—who at the time was scarcely known (this is in the late fifties and early sixties) except as a writer of highly polished formalist kinds of things—something was missing. And what was missing was what I answered to in his work, the tremendous dimension of exile and dislocation, and so on. There was a vocabulary at hand in the works of the phenomenologists and the existentialists that I made use of shamelessly, exploited, to be able to look at Conrad in that way. It was a study of Conrad's life in his work—not as anecdotal events, that he had been to Africa, or that he had been to Borneo, and put that in a story, and so on—but rather that he was always trying to reconstruct his experience in a whole way, in the forms that would yield to insight and investigative analyses, usually unsuccessfully (I mean Conrad's own unsuccessful attempts to get to the bottom). I found that stimulating, and in a sense, since I have gone on to try to do that, seeing works in a "situation," as Sartre says, in a context, remains very important to me. But all the heavy jargonistic and metaphysical language that goes along with it is now for me irrelevant in a way.

One of the themes in the Conrad book is Conrad's total expatriation, his separation, the way that he tried to relate himself only very artificially to the tradition of novel writing in English, because he was a well-traveled Pole and all that. It seems to me that this theme was taken up in your works of the seventies on "beginnings" which, if I understand it correctly, was a sort of definition of what modernism means, defined in terms of having beginnings rather than origins, of situating yourself in relation to tradition by adjacency rather than by continuity. Do you still think that this idea of a break with tradition is adequate as a characterization of modernism?

It is a break with tradition up to a point, and I think that is an accurate definition of it, in that something cataclysmic happened. In the case of modernism, it was probably the First World War, changes in the economic and political topography of Europe, and a number of other things. Later on, in my current work, I have a new theory of modernism that accommodates itself to precisely this, that one of the things that is directly involved in the creation of what we call European modernism (that would include people like Joyce, Eliot, Thomas Mann, Proust, and all the rest of it) is, in fact, the crisis in the imperial world. One has a sense that in the horizon of their works there is some disturbance at the peripheries which is having an effect, like the plague in *Death in Venice* which comes from the East, and becomes a metaphor for the change in Europe such that it can no longer exist on its own. Therefore, what the writer does is to reconstruct.

It is a break with tradition, but an attempt, sometimes a desperate attempt, as in the case of Eliot, to rebuild, and that's why the great metaphorical figure, for me, was provided by Vico in *The New Science,* that book on beginnings, where Vico is the great theorist of self-invention. The figure he uses, you recall, is that there is a big flood, and after the flood men are left lying around like great giants. In order to live as human beings, they make the choice to construct societies. They have to construct marriage, religion, civil institutions; and that becomes the metaphor for the new world in *The New Science.* I saw that as inspiring the onset of European modernism. But underlying that for me, you see, was the 1967 war in the Middle East which was a great crisis in my own life. I had spent most of my time there. My family was in the Middle East. I had gone to America as a student by myself and I had, more or less, lived as much as possible a life as a student and later as a scholar in America without reference, really, professionally or even emotionally, to this world I'd left behind—and which was shattered in 1967. The rest of Palestine was destroyed, or taken over by the Israelis. The Arab world, as I had known it, grown up in it, had completely changed. This then was my autobiographical impetus, to rethink the whole question of what it means to start again, to begin. It involved acts of choice, acts of designation, rather than things coming from heaven. That is why the emphasis on the secular is so great, as far as I'm concerned. It is a congeries of things, a number of things, working at the same time.

Your most recent book is about music and it's about the pleasure that you personally take in music. It is a curious combination in a way because it contains a lot of discussion of a kind that people would have expected in a book by Said. That is to say, it talks about the development of the institutions of Western classical music, the definition of Western classical music versus the East, and the rise of the cult of soloists and celebrities and solitary listening, and the influence of technologies of reproduction and all of that. But in the midst of that, there is an emphasis on pleasure at a time that people wouldn't quite have expected it. Is this a new development in your work?

I shouldn't like to think so. No. It has been there all along. I must confess to feeling at times rather beset by these contests that I find myself in because I am a Palestinian or because I belong to one or another school of literary or philosophical or political criticism. And it seemed to me that what had been happening, at least in the U.S., was that one becomes almost entirely a creature of those things which are completely professional—or professionalized, which is worse. You lose any contact with whatever it is that you're doing. It becomes just a matter of earning your honorarium or, more, your salary. I like to think of myself in many ways, that I'm moved by what I like, what I want to do, rather than what I don't like or what I am forced to do. So it seemed to me that one thing to do would be to write about music, and to focus on those aspects of music that are completely intimate, and provide a very sustaining kind of pleasure, which has been there all through my life, from my earliest consciousness.

Given that you were born in Jerusalem, how did you become inducted into European literature?

I grew up really bi-culturally. I always went to English schools. Both Palestine and Egypt, where my family subsequently lived, were British colonies. I guess I belong to the elite of our country and we were sent to British schools. So I grew up studying English in school and speaking Arabic at home and with my friends. So I have no memory of not looking at European books. It has really been a very serious study all my life. But I always felt I wasn't European at the same time. Perhaps it was the schools I went to that made me feel that, because there were always English teachers and mostly Arab boys (I went to boys' schools). One felt sort of excluded, and that being educated in the language and the literature was a process of trying, unsuccessfully, to acculturate to it. One was always found wanting.

Would it be facile to say that it was an easy assimilation to make because so much modern, modernist, European literature is about exile and displacement, and that you were exiled and displaced, so it was your literature?

I wasn't always exiled and displaced. I always felt slightly divided, because I come from a Christian minority, and within that minority in Palestine—about 10 percent of the Arab population of Palestine which is mostly Muslim—we were a Protestant minority, even smaller, so there was always a sense of being slightly askew, off from the center. The fact that I went to these schools and became good at speaking English and French was added to the peculiarity of the whole thing. So, in a certain sense, I felt peculiar, and this literature seemed to resonate with what I felt. Not all of it seems that way, but certainly modern literature does, yes, and that's what I am interested in. I never really felt completely at home in earlier periods of literature when I was getting my professional degrees as a scholar of literature. I loved the eighteenth century, but it seemed like almost studying a foreign culture, whereas the twentieth century, particularly with its expatriate figures, its wanderers—like Joyce, and so on—was much closer to me.

People with a taste for periodization or even a mania for periodization, tell us that modernism is over, and we are now in the epoch of post-modernism. What do you think of that?

I suppose it's true to people who think exclusively in terms of America and advertising culture and the media, pastiche, and that sort of thing. But if you are aware of other worlds than, say, Madison Avenue and high-tech architecture, you will realize that the battle for the modern, and therefore modern as in "modernity," is, for example, in parts of the world that I am familiar and affiliated with, like the Middle East, a very important one. It is, indeed, *the* battle. Don't forget, we live in an age where the whole question of what the tradition is, and what the Prophet said, and the Holy Book said, and what God said, and what Jesus said, etc., are issues that people go to war over, as in the case of Salman Rushdie, who was condemned to death for what he wrote. That is for us the battle—the battle over what the modern is, and what the interpretation of the past is. It is very important in the Arab and Islamic worlds. There is a school of writers, poets, essayists, and intellectuals, who are fighting a battle for the right to *be* modern, because our history is governed by *turath*, or heritage. But the question is, who designates what the heritage is. That is the problem. For us, the crisis of "modernism" and "modernity" is a crisis over authority, and the right of the individual, and the writer, the thinker, to express himself, or herself, for it is also the battle over women's rights. So the whole question of postmodernism to us is an interesting sort of Candidean question in the West. But for us, modernism, as in modernity, is the issue of the moment.

I've noticed that in several contexts recently you described yourself as being on the conservative side in certain debates. And, I think, you were talking in particular cultural debates in the U.S. about the authority of the canon. One of the ways in which this has been formulated is in terms of the idea of political correctness, "PC," very much an American tele-phenomenon. Is the question about PC, from your point of view, just another "red scare," the idea that there are people on the campuses who are trying to gag anybody whose views they don't agree with?

Yes and no. The idea that there is a small Left cabal in the American universities who are running things and are declaring what can and can't be read, that's total tommyrot, total bullshit. But on the other hand, there is an important and interesting debate, and that is, what do we people, let's say, the subalterns, or the oppressed, or the formerly suppressed, or whatever designation, people of color, what do we do as we confront the canon? The alternatives are generally formulated, in my opinion, in rather impoverishing ways. One way to say it is, if we are people of color we are not going to read anything by whites; if we are women, we are not going to read anything by men; if we are gays, we are not going to read anything by straights; and so on. That is to replace one canon with another. I have no sympathy for that, because it simply condemns us, you, to a new marginality. There is nothing easier for political correctness bashers—who have turned themselves into an industry in America today—the people who write books like *Tenured Radicals* or Dinesh D'Souza's book on "illiberal education." It's all tommyrot . . . let's see what these people want; let's give them departments of African-American studies; let's give them gay studies; let's give them all that; but let's get on with it.

The other alternative is not to substitute one canon for another, not to become Afrocentric where you were first Eurocentric, gynocentric where you were first phallocentric, but rather to say, let us try and understand the construction of the canon and what these objects serve. That's number one. And number two, most important from my point of view, is how are they related to each other. In other words, it seems to me that the history of imperialism and the history of colonization, the history of oppression as experienced by blacks, by Palestinians, by gays, by women, all that is built upon segregation, on separation. The worst thing ethically and politically is to let separatism simply go on, without understanding the opposite of separatism, which is connectedness. In that respect, I am very conservative. I want to see how everything works. I am not just interested in Palestinian themes in American literature, or Palestinian themes in French literature. What I am interested in is how all these things work together. That seems to me to be the great task—to connect them all together—to understand wholes rather than bits of wholes.

Interview with Jonathan Rée,
Alif: Journal of Comparative Poetics,
The American University in Cairo, 1993

LANGUAGE, HISTORY, AND THE PRODUCTION OF KNOWLEDGE

Gauri Viswanathan, a former student of mine, was Visiting Professor of English at Colgate University when she conducted this public interview with me in 1996, as part of the University Colloquium Series. E.W.S.

Edward, you've often written that something like scholarship matters in the real world, that there's a battle which is fought out over imagery, information, and vocabulary. Your work has been influential in making readers aware that knowledge production is never disinterested, that it is deeply rooted in the materiality of history, circumstance, and location. This is a materiality that you've often described as worldliness, with its own stakes in the outcome of cultural production. My first set of questions has to do with developing alternative knowledges. If scholarship, such as Orientalist knowledge, has created blocks of knowledge that support prevailing orthodoxies, your work suggests that scholarship can also undo those structures. So, first of all, in the battle against the grand narratives sanctioned by official knowledge, what, in your view, is the starting point, for those whose history has been denied to tell their own stories? Does the telling of one's own story require access to such public institutions as the media, or government, or universities?

Well, perhaps later on. But I have a very contradictory and perhaps, in some respects, conservative view about scholarship. In the first instance, I don't believe that one can provide a counter-alternative to the prevailing orthodoxy or the grand narrative of the official kind, without some really serious understanding of what that narrative is in the first place. Nor do I think that you can start out by telling your own story. I think one really has to understand and respect the structures of knowledge that over the years have been contributed to by men and women. I learned this very early from Vico, who makes you understand that history is not divine or sacred but is made by men and women. And, in order to understand the world in which one lives and the world of scholarship in which these activities take place, I think one really has to have a very strong sense of what it means to do scholarship. And, to the extent that I was able to do that, it took me a long time to try to master the techniques of traditional scholarship. It's not something you can just blow away and say it's all dead white males or imperialist clap-trap. I'm very interested in the process by which people produce things. So, I think that's the first step, and then, I think, the second step is gradually to acquire a point of view, and not just because you're looking for an angle but because, in some way, you relate to it. In my own case, it was, perhaps, a coincidence, I didn't think it was a *happy* coincidence, that I grew up in a colony as did you—but you grew up in the *post*colonial period, didn't you?

Right.

Right. [Laughter] Well, you see, you didn't have that advantage, right? I grew up in two British colonies, and I really had to learn more about England than Arab history . . . and I *did* learn more about England and English history and King Canute and King Alfred and Shakespeare and the Enclosure Act and all kinds of facts that were completely nonsensical to somebody from my background.

It still continues in the postcolony.

Yes, it still does but not quite this way. That is to say, the school I went to in Egypt before I came to this country was called Victoria College—it was modeled on a British public school. When you enrolled in the school, they gave you a handbook which contained a little statement, "English is the language of the school." If you were caught speaking Arabic, which was the native language, you would be punished. So, it was that powerful. In a sense, I *had* to absorb it. Your book, *Masks of Conquest,* is, to a certain degree, about that: when you have English teachers teaching a lot of natives, one of the things they try to teach you is that you can acquire some of the knowledge of England and its poetry and language, but you can't ever *be* English, which is quite different from the French system of imperialism, where they trained people to assimilate to France. So you grow up learning the language and culture and history of this place that was your master and, at the same time, are forced to concede that, although you were learning it, you could never be a part of it. And so that strange disjunction provided me, many years later—I didn't know it then—with a kind of perspective on it: the realization that you could absorb it and yet remain alienated from it.

But to what extent and at what points do you ever separate yourself from that experience of colonization?

I didn't for a long period of time. These were the last days of British rule in Egypt in the late '40s and early '50s, and the last years of King Farouk, who was the ruler of Egypt just before the revolution. And so there was a tremendous social volatility and tension in the school. There were these English teachers and here we were this other group of Arabs and Armenians and Jews and Italians—all expatriates. There was a struggle going on, and then, in the end, of course, I got involved in it, and I was thrown out. So then I came to the United States and immediately embarked on a traditional education. I had a great appetite for reading and studying, and my head was buried in books. I had no political or social awareness of any movement, and it wasn't until later, in the middle '60s—I had already come to Columbia by then—that I suddenly realized, with the 1967 War, that the world I had grown up in, the ideas that I'd absorbed about the world I came from, second-hand or fifth-hand or whatever, were suddenly all being changed to a tremendous degree. And, for the first time, I began to feel some restiveness at the imposition—at the self-imposition on me—of academic discipline. And then, with the beginnings of Palestinian nationalism, I became involved in a movement, and I think that's the way it happened.

Would the direction of your thought and career have been substantially different, for instance, if you had continued to live in Egypt and to grow up in the region? You raised an intriguing idea that your coming to the United States and going through a different set of academic, intellectual experiences brought you to a boil sometime later. But—and this has been my own observation in India—in schools and universities, sometimes the kind of critical consciousness that's producing rethinking of fields and disciplines comes from outside—for example, Indians who may have gone abroad and then come back. Whereas those who continue to work in India feel a little more enclosed, and perhaps their sense of alienation may not be that strong.

It's difficult to tell, because the world I grew up in—Palestine, Egypt, and Lebanon—has changed so much: Palestine by the establishment of Israel in 1948, Egypt by revolution, Lebanon by twenty years of civil war and continued turbulence. The world I grew up in no longer exists, it was physically changed. So I think if I'd remained in the Middle East, I would have probably had the choice of two things: either I would have gone into politics directly, as many of my generation did, particularly if they were educated and belonged to a certain class, and there were some traditions in my family of that, or—and probably the two are not separate from each other—I would also have had to scramble, to keep going, because when a country is destroyed, or you have to move, or there are cataclysmic changes in one's life, you spend a lot of your time, as people now do in the Middle East, worrying about what's going to happen tomorrow. So, you don't really have that much time for reflection and so on. And I think what happened to me by coming to this country was that, for a long time, I was shielded, not only by the institutions, but also by, I think I always thought this was a tremendous stroke of good fortune, the fact I never really had any good teachers. [Laughter] I mean they were all okay. They were *good* teachers, but they were not *great* teachers. I remember around 1986 I went to visit C. L. R. James, the Trinidadian historian and writer and essayist, who by then was very old. He was living in London, and he was very near the end of his life; he must have been in his late eighties. He was obsessed with cricket, and, of course, I grew up in a cricket-playing culture, and so there was a little bit of that to talk about. Then, all of a sudden, in the middle of the conversation, he turned to me, and he said, "Did you ever have any really great teachers?" And that was the first time I'd ever thought about it really *that way.* "Anybody who," he continued, in his rather enthusiastic way, "*really* stirred you?" And I thought back to *years* of schooling, and, you know, I had a lot of schooling, and I had to say, I didn't. And I thought, what a pity, but then a few years later, it occurred to me that if I'd *had* a great teacher, I would have spent a lot of time trying to get out from underneath the sheer force of it, whereas, this way, I had had good teachers who had presented me with a lot of information, opportunities to read, and so on, but I never took in any systems of ideas. Imagine if you were a student of Fred Jameson, for example, you'd be wrestling with that for a long time, in both a good and a bad sense. I didn't have that, and so what I did was to discover for myself and that enabled me, I think, later on to be open to these other events around me.

A consistent strain in a lot of your writings is the need for independent judgment and a kind of critical consciousness that stays clear of prevailing orthodoxies or ruling dogmas. I'm interested here in what you have to say about how this has something to do with your not-so-exciting teachers. You've said this many times yourself, that you've not cared to turn out students who do what you do, think like you do, because that perpetuates a priestly tradition which is very much against what you consider to be the intellectual's role in society.

Yes, I never was a disciple, and it's not really interesting to me to have them. Some people produce disciples. The world is still full of Paul de Manians, or de Manian disciples, and all the structuralists have their imitators, and I've always thought that that was uninteresting because in the end you never really learn anything. I have a very childish sense that I'd like to learn new things all the time, and I'm driven by that. I think, also, the need to reformulate and rethink is paramount in what I've tried to do.

Your stance on professionalism illuminates your sense of the intellectual's function in society, to speak beyond his or her own discipline.

Yes, but I don't think you can actually do that. As I said earlier, it's a bit contradictory, because I don't think that you can go beyond the realm of professionalism unless, in a certain sense, you've understood what professionalism *is*. And I think that it's very important, for me at any rate, to insist to students or to people who read me or listen to me, that there's a need to understand the investment in those things, not to just dismiss them as silly and uninteresting. I think the whole question of system-building is deeply interesting. As I tried to suggest in one of my essays called "Travelling Theory," even the production of a theory is rooted in historical and social circumstances, sometimes great *crises,* and therefore, to understand the theory, it's not important to see it as a kind of abstract thing but rather to see it as something that emanates from an existential *need*. And then, of course, it gets used again. Once it becomes appropriated by others, of course, it loses that particular charge, but therefore, it's the job of the intellectual and the historian to try to understand it *in terms* of that early beginning.

But do you think this kind of dilution, this weakening of the original motive, is inevitable?

Well, it does seem to be most of the time. In other words, if you look at the distinctions between the Hegelians and Hegel or between the Marxists and Marx, there is a loss of urgency as the system gets elaborated, worked over. Of course, there are moments of tremendous, wrenching transformation, for example, Lukàcs when he talks about Marx and Marx*ism* introduces into the system a very powerful tear, a very powerful transformation. But that's rare. Most people appropriate the ideas of others. I think that's what human life is about, we appropriate from others, and we acclimatize and acculturate, and what happens is that the force of the ideas loses a little. I've recently become interested in ways in which theories are borrowed, and used again and made even *more* radical. One of the examples that struck me very powerfully was the insight that Lukàcs had of the subject and the object. The tension between them, in *History and Class Consciousness,* is used by people like Lucien Goldmann and Raymond Williams and made slightly softer. It becomes an academic, if you like, *purely* intellectual, as opposed to a social and political issue. But in the case of somebody like Fanon, I discovered fortuitously that Fanon had *read* a French translation of Lukàcs and *used* the subject-object dichotomy, which is a very abstract and Hegelian idea, and introduced it into the colonial context, in which the conflict and the contrast, the opposition, is between the settler and the native, and Fanon, then, shows that it has to explode: There's no way of reconciling the two. So there, a theory in which Lukàcs, in the beginning, shows how the subject and the object can be reconciled to each other, is transformed into something much more radical, but *most* of the time that doesn't happen.

Would you say, particularly when you wrote Orientalism, *that you were attempting to do something like that with Foucault, and take Foucault where Foucault dared not go?*

I was much more interested in the material than I was in theories. By that time I had already begun to lose interest in Foucault, actually.

But Orientalism, *for better or for worse, has been taken as theoretical text. Would you like to respond to a certain reading of the work that may have, in fact, gone beyond you at this point? For instance, take the reading of discourse as power. You talk about Foucault in the opening chapter, but you also indicate the* limits *of Foucault, that he's not particularly interested in imperialism or with non-Western cultures.*

Or non-French.

Yes, exactly.

His interests are much more limited even than Europe.

Yet, you know, one of the critical readings of Orientalism *that has persisted over the last two decades or so, is about your rendering of discourse as power, for instance, the notion that you're really interested in how that power is* constituted *rather than how it impacts on the subordinated peoples.*

Right.

How would you like to respond to that reading?

Well, I think that's a fair criticism of *Orientalism*. I think I was very limited in what I was trying to do, that is to say, I was trying to look at the way in which a certain view of the Orient was created and accompanied, or perhaps was used to subordinate the Orient during the period of imperialism beginning with the conquest of Egypt by Napoleon. And that's all I was trying to do. I had *nothing* to say about what the Orient was *really* like. I said *nothing* about the possibility of resistance to it. That's a fair criticism, because one of the things that I think Foucault is very wrong about is that he always writes from the point of view of power. It's strange, most people think of him as a rebel, but he had this side to him which James Miller writes about in his book on Foucault, suggesting that all of Foucault's work is really an exemplification of his peculiar form of homosexuality and his interest in sado-masochism. So you could say that Foucault is always talking about power from the point of view, on the one hand, of the way power always wins; and then, succumbing to that power, he talks about the victims of power with a certain amount of pleasure. And I think that always struck me as wrong, and my attitude to power, in *Orientalism* and elsewhere, has always been deeply suspicious and hostile. It took me another ten years to actually make that more explicit in *Culture and Imperialism*, where I was very interested not only in talking about the *formation* of imperialism, but also of *resistances* to it, and the fact that imperialism *could* be overthrown and *was*—as a result of resistance and decolonization and nationalism. But in *Orientalism*, I never talk about discourse the way

Foucault does in *The Archaeology of Knowledge,* for example, as something that has its own life and can be discussed separately from the realm of the real, or what I would call the historical realm. I think perhaps one of the things of which I am most proud is that I try to make discourse go hand-in-hand with an account of conquest, the creation of instruments of domination, and techniques of surveillance that were rooted not in theory but in actual territory.

Some readers might come away from the book saying, "We don't hear the voice of the colonized."

Well, they're right, they *don't* hear it.

What about the person who's writing the book? Is it not possible to make the argument that you as author *are writing from the position of the colonized?*

Well, it was done with irony. I relied on the techniques of disenchantment and demystification. I was trying to show that this massive and authoritative series of studies by scholars were really flawed in all kinds of ways, and so I was talking about them ironically, sometimes even sarcastically. And I didn't allow the voice of the colonized to appear through them, because I wanted just to focus on them. And my own voice appears, really, only at the end of the book, when I start asking questions. I say, well, who could survive such a thing? I think it's bad for the Orientalist, and as bad for the Oriental, that is to say, both lose in the encounter, and that's the only time that I speak that way. But the rest of the time the tone is fairly even, and not until ten years later did I write what I consider to be the sequel, namely *Culture and Imperialism,* where, in fact, I do talk about the colonized.

Can I move to a related, though somewhat different subject? It picks up on this notion of your writing from a certain set of experiences and history. In After the Last Sky, *you revisited Palestine, primarily through photographs, but in the last couple of years, you've returned to the place where you were born, and you've made several trips to the region, and you've just now come back from the West Bank. Would you like to talk about that trip?*

I began to inform myself about events in Palestine during the two years since the Oslo accords were signed. I began to acquire, for the first time, a fairly large Arab readership—most of my writing is in English.

But then starting in the latter part of 1993, after Oslo, I began to write regularly for the leading Arab newspaper in Arabic. Sitting in New York, going through years, two, three years of chemotherapy, I found that the energy that I got out of anger and political disputation could be invigorating in many ways and had gotten for me this quite large audience.

And then, my son got a Fulbright, '94–'95 and spent the year in Egypt and then, on his own, worked as a volunteer on the West Bank. He took no money from us, working in something called the Democracy and Workers' Rights Center as a volunteer for $100 a month. And then, of course, the pressure mounted: Don't you want to come and visit? And I thought about it, and finally I went. It was very hard, because I felt that the so-called autonomy for Palestinians was terribly unfair, and the Israelis had created a map—one of the things you learn about imperialism is that it is always the natives who don't have the maps, and the white people who do—and this is certainly the case in Israel. I knew that during the entire negotiating period, the Palestinians had no maps; they had to rely on the Israeli maps. And so I arrived in Palestine via Israel— of course I had to go to Tel Aviv to get to Jerusalem, and I felt a very strong sense of discomfort that I had never experienced before, even more than the first time I went in 1992, because here, I had become quite notorious for publicly attacking Yasir Arafat and the Palestinian Authority and criticizing the Israelis and the Americans. So I arrived in this place, and the next morning at 9:30 on the "Voice of Palestine," which is Arafat's private radio station inside Palestine, there's a half-an-hour program which was devoted to nothing but cursing and attacking me. And, of course, the lowest cut of all: I was described as a mere Orientalist for my views, and as an agent of the CIA acting against the Palestinian people, etc. But after a couple of minutes of horrified shock, I took it as a great compliment that they had to take account of my presence there. And I spent the next couple of weeks going around Palestine with my son, and I was really hoping there would be a new Palestine since it had so engaged my son. But my sense of the whole thing is that the Palestinians are now passing through a very, very dark period. Because of the closures, you can't go from one area to another. We spent hours in the territories being stopped at Israeli roadblocks, and they examined our passports, and pulled us aside, that sort of thing.

What, in your view, are the possibilities of dialogue and understand-

ing on the Palestinian question? How has your thinking about the future for Palestinians informed your other work, including literary criticism?

The question of dialogue applies to questions having to do, for example, with multiculturalism and the relations between cultures. It also has to do with the relations between members of different communities in the United States, outside the United States, in Europe and so on. We have before us endless examples of, not the dialogue of culture but the clash of cultures, which can sometimes, as Samuel Huntington, alas, is right about, be very bloody. And a lot of people like Huntington have made a universal out of this, and have said cultures or civilizations today are so different that we have to accept the idea they are going to clash, that they cannot communicate except through opposition, sometimes through even exterminatory relationships. I deeply disagree with that. I think the history of cultures, if you take a long view of them, suggests that cultures really are not impermeable, they are open to every other culture. The newer Conservative movement and the rhetoric of people like William Bennett and Dinesh D'Souza and others suggests that there's such a thing as Western culture which has a kind of independent existence different from all other cultures. That's total nonsense. Historically, it's simply not true. And I'm not so much of a deconstructionist that I don't allow myself to say whether things are true and untrue. In this case, we're talking about falsifications of human experience and human history. And, therefore, it seems to me, that one of the prime motivations of a lot of my own work, whether in *Orientalism* or *The Question of Palestine,* is to try to expose the historical roots of clashes between cultures *in order* to promote the possibility of a dialogue between cultures.

Now I come to the second part of your question: why the whole Palestinian experience has been so important for me in works of scholarship and discussions that have nothing to do with Palestine, and has provided me with a lot of insight. I don't think you can have understanding, any more than you can have understanding *between people,* in an abstract sense. I think understanding always has to be rooted in history, it has to be rooted in an ongoing relationship, and I'm enough of a student of Gramsci to know that relationships are never equal, that there's never anything like an equal dialogue. Edward Thompson was one of the first to point this out in his 1926 book *The Other Side of the*

Medal. Thompson was an Englishman writing for English people at the height of a very inflamed period of Anglo-Indian tension, in which he said, look, what you have to understand is that, as the colonizers of India, we have simply been insensitive not only to the harm that we've done to the Indians, but also the harm that our *representations* of that relationship did to them. That is to say, if we continue to represent them as savages, as violent, as barbarians in need of disciplining and education, we're going to inflame them, because, he says, we've produced a psychological hurt, which, far from being resolved by power, or by understanding in a general sense, is going to be increased. And therefore, he says, we have to accept the fact that we have done wrong, politically, in India, to the Indians.

And I've always felt this about the Palestinian and the Israeli question. That is to say, I believe very strongly that what happened to the Palestinians is a particularly egregious case of this. To this day 55 percent of the Palestinian population does not live on the West Bank and Gaza, they live elsewhere: refugees, stateless, in Lebanon, 400,000, in Syria, 800,000, in Jordan, 1,000,000, and in America, Europe, scattered everywhere. They have a very strong sense of an attachment to Palestine yet confronted with an enemy, Israel, that has (a) done this to them, (b) has entitled the whole Jewish people the right to return to Palestine, or Israel, and become citizens through the law of return, something that is denied to the Palestinians who were born there. Somebody born in Poland or France or New York can become an Israeli citizen if he or she has a Jewish mother and can qualify as a Jew. Whereas Palestinians live as refugees in camps ten miles away, are not allowed to be citizens, have to be second-class in their country of birth and their place of origin. Despite my formative years as somebody who was relatively privileged in all of this, because my family was well off, and I didn't suffer the ravages of living in a refugee camp, we've had to live with the rhetoric that suggests that *we* are causes of Israel's insecurity, that *we* are the terrorists. One of the books I edited and wrote in was called *Blaming the Victims*—that's the psychological wound that Thompson talks about. I don't believe that there can ever be a reconciliation until there's a recognition by Israelis of what they have done and what their society has cost another people. I'm not saying that every Palestinian wants to go back to

Palestine, and I certainly don't want my family's house back, which is now the headquarters of something called the International Christian Embassy, the most fundamentalist, right-wing, Zionist, pro-Israeli, Christian organization in the world. I come from a Christian minority, but when I saw this Christian headquarters of the International Christian Embassy, I couldn't even go into the house. My daughter said, couldn't you show us where you were born, and the rooms, and where you grew up, but I couldn't do it, it was too much for me. I think most Palestinians would say, well, we can't have Palestine back, there's another people there, and so on.

But we do want recognition that something happened here. Most people haven't read the Peace Process documents, for simple reasons: (a) they're not available, and (b), the last document is 450 pages. What kind of a peace agreement is it, that it takes 450 pages to spell out how the Palestinians are going to be confined in these little territories of theirs? It's obviously not a peace agreement. But one of the most insidious features of it, to come back to the Indian example, is that *in* it, Israel, time and time again, clause after clause, absolves itself of any responsibility for what happened before September of 1993. That's not a way to deal with a conflict, and that's why a real dialogue, a real framework of understanding, a real reconciliation, of two cultures, in this instance, Arab and Israeli, can never take place. There has to be some sense of equity, or at least moving toward equity, for the reconciliation to take place.

The last point I want to make is important for America. One of the ideas that was part of foreign policy in the '70s—I'm speaking as an amateur—was that you could do conflict resolution, and I was involved in some of this until I became utterly disgusted with it and quit. I think it's very insidious. But the idea was that you could bring the warring parties together. They used to do it for Northern Ireland and for the parties in Northern Ireland, for the South Africans, for the ex-Yugoslavians, and bring them together, and try to have them talk to each other *as if* the conflict was basically a matter of misunderstanding; you know, you don't understand me, and I don't understand you. A guy who was in graduate school with me worked in the foreign service business, apparently, with psychological conflict-resolution. He wrote an article called "Foreign

Policy According to Freud." So it was just a matter that these people were neurotic, and it was always the weaker person who had to make the most psychological adjustments, and I think that's completely nonsensical, that's not the way you get out of a conflict like that. You really have to deal with the true source of the conflict. It goes back to power. And I don't think it can be done unless the victim is able, in a certain sense, to carry the discussion into the heart of the person who's doing the victimizing, because there are all sorts of things that insulate us from the reality.

This might be a good point for the audience to ask questions.

AUDIENCE MEMBER: Where does the economic factor fit into your question concerning the distribution of resources on a global scale?

Let me start with the Palestinian/Israeli situation. The economic arrangements that have been made, and I generalize here because there isn't time to go into every detail, are such that the Palestinians have become more dependent economically upon the Israelis. Which means that any time that there is a sense, as happened after the bus bombings and so on in February and March, on the part of Israel, that it wants to punish the Palestinians, it can just close the borders; and now there's 70 percent unemployment. Where 80,000 to 100,000 people used to cross the border, say from Gaza, and go into Israel and work as day laborers—slaves, really, but at least they had a job—now maybe 3,000 or 4,000 can go in. You can imagine what that's like. That's built into the agreement. I'll give you another simple example of how the economic agreement works. There is no continuity between the territories, that is to say, if you live in Gaza and you want to export tomatoes to another one of the Palestinian autonomous territories, in this case, Jericho, which was another place that was given autonomy—you have to traverse about 60 or 65 miles of Israeli territory. So what happens is you bring your tomatoes to the border, you have to unload them, and they can be examined for bombs and all the rest of it, and then loaded on another truck, which passes through Israel, and then it comes to Jericho, it's unloaded, and put on another truck, which then goes to Jericho. Now, I'm talking about only one truck, but in, let's say, in normal conditions, if there's a lot of trade from Gaza to Jericho, from Nablus to Ramallah, you with your truck of tomatoes could be stuck at the border, waiting for the Israeli guards to examine it, offload it, put it on another truck, and it sometimes takes three days. Of course, in the meantime, the tomatoes are rotten, especially in the summer, and it's discovered that it's cheaper to import from Jericho, from the west, let's say from Jordan, across the river, even from Spain, than it is to import them from Gaza. So there, the economic plays the role of making certain that reconciliation can't really take place because the separation in levels of power and economic advantage is so great. It's legislated. And I believe similar patterns are to be found through, for example, the work of the World Bank and the International Monetary Fund in countries like Egypt, for example, where the idea is to immediately strip the government of the public sector, institute privatization, and throw open the market, making it possible for a transnational corporation to exploit it. For example, to bring in machinery to manufacture shirts that are going to be made there because it can be done more cheaply, and then shipped to the United States or France, and, if there's another place, let's say Indonesia, that's cheaper, then the factories are closed and the machinery goes to Indonesia. The market is really controlled. But, in fact, what you're producing is a set of certainties, that the market is always going to be advantageous to the person with capital and power, who can be there and move at the expense of the underdeveloped, the native, etc., the working class and the peasants, and so on and so forth, who really have no recourse. And I think that's very much part of the economic discourse of global economics. It seems to me absolutely disastrous as to where it might be leading: the consequences in terms of things like famine, illness and the population growth. In my part of the world, the great problem which is never looked at in this way is the development of fundamentalism. Here we talk about it as if it's just the Iranians and the Syrians and these crazy, mad terrorists, but I would say, for example, on the West Bank, the emergence of Hamas has much more to do with the results of the Peace Process, the results of the *intifada,* the results of the occupation. Ninety percent of what Hamas does is not, in fact, to produce terrorism, but economic opportunity through education, and so forth, through day care centers, through food supply, things that the government either can't or won't supply. That's how they develop. Islamic fundamentalism begins as a protest and then takes on a life of its own. They seem to have produced opportunities where you have economic disadvantages and political stagnation, where as a citizen you have no possibilities.

AUDIENCE MEMBER: How do you see the situation in Algeria? A lot of us already have a kind of interest in the Israeli/Palestinian conflict, but what about Algeria where people feel less engaged or less involved? When you speak of dialogue, what kind of dialogue do you imagine in this kind of situation?

At this point, I think dialogue in Algeria is very improbable, it is almost doomed. There is, of course, a historical dialectic in Algeria which is easily perceived. There is the atrophy of the FLN, the enlargement of the bureaucracy—again, a typical third-world pattern that Europe plays a part in—and the relationship between France and Algeria *after '62,* which is very symbiotic. And Algeria, which of course has oil, and at one point was a net exporter of wheat, fruits, and vegetables, has now become a net importer of it. So there's a skewing of the economy due partly to the pressure of France and the North, but also, partly, to the abuses of the bureaucracy and the one-party state, producing, in classical Marxist or Hegelian fashion, its opposite in what is called Le Fis, *al-jabhat al-inkhaz,* the salvation front, Islamic Salvation Front. They win the elections, the government moves against them, and you have not only a polarized situation but you have, of course, a war going on, in which killing as many people as possible is the order of the day. Then there is the creation of the third force, again, uncertain as to where they belong. On the one hand you have the Islamists, on the other, the government, and then the third force, in the middle, which includes killers who want to prey off both sides in Algeria. It's not much talked about in the press, which has an interest in perpetuating this conflict. The result is that you have a very large exiled community. You also have a terrorized population, extending to the war on journalists, again, not only from the Islamists and the government, but also from some other force in the middle that provokes rogue elements in the army, and the Islamic front, which has an interest in keeping this going. You have a situation which is so polarized and so charged, that I think here, as I've also thought in the Palestinian/Israeli situation, the role of the diaspora could be more important than it's given credit for. That is to say, the role of dialogue inside Algeria is impossible now. But I think a dialogue between factions, in places like France, Germany, and Italy where there are Algerian exiled or diaspora communities, might be possible. And, if such an instrument were likely, going back now to the idea of UN peace-keeping, it might be possible to develop out of this some international presence that would cool things down, making dialogue in Algeria itself work at some other date. But I think under present circumstances, the framework is so flawed and so charged that one can only be very pessimistic about it.

AUDIENCE MEMBER: What about the anti-terrorists bill? Why do you think that both Democrats and Republicans, the majority in each party, are pushing it?

I think there's general hysteria, which is an example of how a concept or a word like "terrorist" acquires a life of its own and begins, almost in an Orwellian fashion to dominate *life*. I think the end of the cold war has something to do with it. It used to be possible to think in terms of us vs. them. Now, it's us vs. the terrorists. Then it used to be us vs. the Communists.

AUDIENCE MEMBER: How is that impacting Palestine and Lebanon?

I don't want to go into all the ramifications which have been talked about a lot in the press about how it impacts locally in the United States on civil liberties and the dangers of all kinds of abuses. But look at the ramifications *internationally,* given the rhetoric, for example, of the Sharm el-Sheikh Conference, which took place after the bombings in Israel. My fear is that there is now a mounting pressure led by the United States and Israel on *Iran*. There have been some very menacing statements made by the Israeli Deputy Minister of Defense recently, which were not reported in this country, suggesting that the Israelis and the Americans might think of a strike against Iran because Iran has been identified as Terrorist Central. It's easier to deal with terrorism, as Peres said in Sharm el-Sheikh, if it has a post office box and an address and a face and a name, and in this case it's Iran. That, to me, is horrifying, because it suggests that you can call anyone a terrorist and go after him on the local level. But, if you *do* this on an international level, then the likelihood of war is much greater, especially if you have the power to start it. And, I noticed just the other day on C-Span, that Secretary Perry was giving a talk to a large Jewish organization, but it was entirely in those terms. He was talking about the need to have a preemptive strike, to punish, and he was talking in the context of weapons of mass destruction, especially as they might be used by "terrorist states." And he was laying forth a horrifying scenario, which, I think, has opened up new modes of thinking about conflict and opportunities for conflict in the manufacture of enemies in the future which, I think, we have to be very vigilant about.

AUDIENCE MEMBER: You suggested that the relationship between cultures is historically oppositional.

Yes, there are oppositions, but it's not *only* oppositional. There's borrowing and sharing.

AUDIENCE MEMBER: How do you understand the nature of the hostilities between Palestinians and the Israelis, if the suggestion was that there's a kind of symbiotic relationship between cultures?

Well, I think when people start to use phrases like: this is a very ancient thing, and it goes back to times immemorial, something to resist and to militate against is the idea that this is genetic, or that it is *rooted* in the traditions of these two cultures—that, just as the French and the British have always had a hostility toward each other, so, too, have Arabs and Jews. I think that that's a construction that has no real validity. One can show, in the instances of *most* conflicts, that there are historical, real reasons for a conflict that didn't exist with that kind of intensity before, and that you can foresee and project a time when they wouldn't apply, *if* the sources of the conflict were addressed. And I think this is the case here. I think it's wrong to talk about it as Arabs and Jews. I've always resisted that formulation, because I think it's Palestinians and Israelis in this sense, or Palestinians and Zionists before the establishment of Israel. And I think there one could talk about one dominant vision which suggests that "this is a Jewish home, and we should go and take it and build there because we've been persecuted" and that has a certain validity to it. The only problem is that there was always somebody else there. And what is interesting—that can be seen in other contexts as well, let's say now between Greece and Macedonia, or between Greece and Turkey, the north and the south in Ireland—is that it really is a conflict rooted in a particular experience of conquest, or, let's call them inequities in power, where one took and the other had to give up.

And that is transformed and made more intractable by the conflict of images in the media. And I think those can be treated by confronting, or at least analyzing, where such images come from, and how they necessarily exclude, downgrade, deprecate, demonize, or dehumanize the "other." Notice that I'm not saying that Israelis do it more than Palestinians or Palestinians do it more. I'm just saying that these are the general features of it. But what I want to resist in some ways is the notion that these are conflicts that are so radical and primal that there is no way of addressing them. I think they have to be looked at, as I've always said, as historical, existential, and rooted in histories that refused at some point to acknowledge each other. And *that's* where the problem is: acknowledgment, not as an abstraction but connected to political action and political forms.

Interview with Gauri Viswanathan,
Colgate University,
Hamilton, New York, 1996

THIRTEEN

I'VE ALWAYS LEARNT
DURING THE CLASS

I was quite ill and weak from the side effects of chemotherapy for leukemia during my first visit to India, 1997. But I was also exhilarated at the nonstop welcome that was everywhere in evidence, particularly among students, teachers, and journalists. Rarely have I experienced such a high level of interaction and keen debate. E.W.S.

You may have always been a teacher, but you are also a prolific writer and an activist. How do you reconcile all these identities? What does being a teacher mean to you? In what role do you feel most comfortable?

I think that of a teacher. I've been teaching now for almost forty years. And I've always learnt during the actual class. There's something that eludes me when I read and think without the presence of students. So I've always thought of my classes as not a routine to go through but rather an experience of investigation and discovery. And I depend very heavily on reactions from my students. In the early days, when I started teaching I used to overprepare, plan every second of a class. Later, because I had such exceptional students at Columbia, I found that students' comments would stimulate lines of thought and discussion that I hadn't expected before. And very often that found its way into my writing.

You have always focused on the problems of the Arab world, especially Palestine. But as an exile in America do you ever feel that you are orating into a void? How interested are, say, your students in the issues which engage you most?

In the beginning, I certainly felt that I was only addressing my students. Later, as I began to write politically, I was conscious of a larger audience. Not my students. I've never used my classes to talk about political activism of the kind that I've done. I've stuck pretty carefully to the notion that the classroom is sacrosanct to a certain degree. But, the more I wrote the more I discovered that by writing one could get an audience, specially on the question of Palestine. Since there was a dearth of voices, I was able to create, in a certain sense, a kind of constituency for what I was saying and it became quite large. The latest phase is that, since the early nineties I've been writing two columns a month for an Arabic newspaper. For the first time I now have a regular Arab readership, which has been very important for me. My work is so often translated into many different languages and I go to countries and places where the terms of debate and understanding of what I've written are so different that I'm constantly surprised. But I've never had the feeling of speaking into the void. I think the audiences I get in universities and academic associations, professional groups and activists are very stimulating and I love the debate.

Your work on Orientalism has profoundly affected the writing of Indian history. But, has your work affected the historians of the Arab world?

In the Arab world, sadly, my work has really not been as deeply understood as I think it has been elsewhere. In the Arab world I'm read as a kind of defender of Islam against the evils of the West. Which is a caricature. The theoretical side, which I share in common with, say, Indian, European, or Japanese intellectuals, is missing there. In the Arab world, there's not much interest in material that isn't directly about them.

A new historical consciousness, however, is very slowly emerging and most of them are affected by the kind of criticism I've done. In Beirut last July, there was a conference—I think the first of its kind in the Arab world—devoted to my work. It was called "Towards a Critical Culture." But that's a tiny sample. Arab intellectual life is in a state of torpor, political asphyxiation and intellectual indifference. So it is really among the younger Arab intellectuals in the diaspora where I think the change will come.

You've been educated in orthodox and elite institutions. How did you develop into an anti-establishment intellectual from such a background?

You see, my background was always conflicted. Before I left for the U.S., I had a colonial education and I felt out of place. There was something that didn't correspond between what I felt to be myself and that kind of education. So I always felt that two educations were going on—

the conventional education at school and the self-education taking place to satisfy the other self that was excluded. That almost always produced rebellion of one sort or the other. I was always known in school as too clever or smart to be thrown out but too unorthodox to be considered one of the prize students. In the end I was thrown out at the age of fifteen for my political involvement. So I was sent to very elite schools in America. Then it began all over again. During my eleven years as a student there I never developed close relationships.

When you write, for whom do you write? For yourself, for other intellectuals, for policymakers, for activists, for whom?

I write most of the time for an occasion rather than for a person. I certainly don't address policymakers. In the U.S. I'm really considered outside the consensus. My readers tend to be people on the left who are themselves outside the consensus and looking for alternatives to the prevailing worldview. For Arab readers, I try to reach out as wide as possible, for there I feel that I'm trying to change opinions. But I also write for myself. For instance, the memoir I'm writing now is really a search for a lost time and those on music satisfy my own long-standing interest in these issues.

Some people allege that because of your influence Indian history writing has been derailed. Too much attention is being paid to literary and aesthetic representations of colonial rule than, say, to social, political, and economic domination. How would you respond to that?

I'll hope not. I'm nothing if not historically based. I've always said that the study of literature is basically a historical discipline. No use in separating one from the other. There's a constant tension between the world of aesthetic and the world of historical action, which I'm interested in explaining. I've always had an aversion to theoretical web spinning. But one can't neglect the theoretical and the aesthetic—they are important components of human experience. My views are more inclusive than exclusive. I don't think of the study of literature or history as separate or competing; they support each other. The whole process of writing, whether about literature or history, involves sifting through evidence, and in the end arriving at interpretations. I would find it very surprising and even perverse if I was understood as derailing the study of history.

Has education ever been a part of your political agenda?

There was a period when I was actively involved in it. Between '77 and '82 there was a project to establish an open university in Palestine. I was asked to prepare the humanities curriculum. I was very interested in producing an imaginative and comprehensive system for university students who have undergone the peculiar experience of being a Palestinian. It was conceived as anti-imperialist and liberationist, trying to instill knowledge by discovery than by rote. I was profoundly shocked when my proposal was tremendously criticized. The general consensus was that education for us had to be a form of national self-affirmation, which I found antithetical to my interests.

I generally try to talk about the questions of education, about the development of a critical consciousness, about education as a form of resistance against the invasion of the mind by wall-to-wall television, prepackaged news and the rest. There I feel I am continuing it.

Lastly, I always spend a part of each year in one or another Arab country, where I spend time in a university interacting with students, trying to stimulate a kind of discussion and debate which they don't normally get. I'm impressed by the fact that everywhere you go in the Arab world, once you sweep away the collective self-identity imposed by the environment—the television, government, political rhetoric—and deal with students on one-to-one basis, there's tremendous curiosity, eagerness and sheer intellectual energy that is bursting to go somewhere. I find these extremely valuable and rewarding.

Interview with Damayanti Datta,
The Telegraph, Calcutta, India, 1997

PART TWO

SCHOLARSHIP
AND ACTIVISM

FOURTEEN

CAN AN ARAB AND
A JEWISH STATE COEXIST?

Your PLO is scattered across the Middle East, the camps in Lebanon are under siege again and Yitzhak Shamir is prime minister of Israel. Have things ever been worse for the Palestinians?

I think they were worse, yes. Before the late 1960s, when the Palestinians were buried under a lot of rubble and forgotten, there was a sense of complete despair.

You're more isolated than ever from the rest of the Arab world.

Yes. The Arab states have never been more openly hostile, and I'm not just talking about the PLO. It's easy to say they don't like the PLO—that's the Syrian position—but in Egypt every Palestinian has to renew residency every six months; in Tunis Palestinians are not allowed in even if they have U.S. passports.

Look, any organization that is without a territorial base is going to come up against one or another Arab government. Palestinian nationalism is troubling to every regime in the area, regimes whose major fear is of being abandoned by the Americans. So Palestinian independence is going to face a quite brutal series of assaults. The gloves are off, no doubt about it. Which isn't to say we're blameless. Or that we've been brilliant. We're trouble. We represent a disturbance.

And you think it's possible for an Arab and a Jewish state to coexist?

Absolutely, yes.

But if the Israelis reject UN Resolution 242 (which also calls for the return of lands Israel occupied in 1967 in exchange for peace with neighboring Arab states), how could they possibly accept a Palestinian state?

It'll be a long time. No Palestinian expects either the United States or Israel to give anything up. They will give it up through the increasing cost of holding a population hostage. . . . We're dealing with a people that has a genuine history of suffering and oppression, so the ideological dimension is important. And for a lot of Israelis the issue is either prolonged, endless conflict, or an attempt to come to some kind of accommodation. If not, we're both doomed.

Why don't you, once and for all, renounce terror?

We're not in a position to renounce anything that confirms our status as essentially terrorists, which is what the Israelis have since the middle 1970s been trying to convince the world of. That all Palestinian acts of resistance are acts of terror. It's blatant hypocrisy, it's a lie, from a state that commands its bombers from a height of 10,000 feet to bomb refugee camps.

Nonetheless . . .

Nonetheless, I'm telling you about the image. Images are formed by the media, and you know as well as I do that you're not interested in covering *Al Fajr* [an Arab newspaper published in Jerusalem], but you do cover random outrages by individuals who attempt to blow up a bus in Israel. Have you ever actually done a body count? Have you? Have you any idea of the disparity between Israelis killed and Palestinians killed? I mean, we're talking hundreds to one. So. When has anybody in the Middle East renounced terrorism?

Why do you think you have such a hard time convincing anybody of all this?

Because we are a non-Western people from a civilization that has *always* been in conflict with the West. The world of Islam has always been a historical competitor, and it has never capitulated. So the one thing people don't understand is, why do you Palestinians whimper? Why don't you go away? Forget it. But we don't.

Maybe time is running out.

They said that five years ago—the midnight hour. The fact is, every Israeli realizes they have no military option against us. What are they going to do? Kill everybody? So some of us say, We fight on. And we keep saying, We're going to live together with you. That no matter what they do, we're a shadow.

And terror is a means of doing that.

I'm against terror—random, horrid. This scheme to put a bomb in an airliner, I'm totally against it. I'm talking about resistance in the occupied territories [the West Bank and Gaza]. Yesterday, Shamir said again: We have no interest in giving them up.

It seems quite clear the Israelis are not going to give them up.

It was very clear in Algeria. And they fought for what? 130 years? Then they gave up.

You want to see two independent states.

Independent or connected; not hermetically sealed, I wouldn't have thought.

. . . So how will you convince them (to share sovereignty)?

I don't have to. Because they are perfectly aware of the alternative—a permanent state of siege, committing themselves and future generations to an endless state of war. The choice is settlement, reconciliation, partition. It's evident to a three-year-old that the alternative is a permanent state of war in which one population is doomed to be hewers of wood and drawers of water.

Many Israelis have an absolute determination not to give their land up.

They don't have to. They can stay. There's what, 50,000 Jews in the West Bank—and 700,000 Arabs inside Israel [proper] who are citizens. So there are cases of populations having bits of each other in neighboring states. That's not the problem; the problem is sovereignty.

And you accept Israeli sovereignty over the rest.

I accept it because I consider it to be a reality. I also consider it to be the result of the particularly tragic history of the Jewish people. But above all, I don't believe in dispossessing people. . . . You'd have to find a mode of sharing. . . .

Tell me. Why, when Palestinians are being discussed or interviewed, why is the format always adversarial?

Because the image that persists is one of a people whose chief tactic is violence.

And you know that's a stereotype, a media cliché. So half our discussion is about terrorism, which is not the question of the hour.

My fourteen-year-old son and I were watching the television news two weeks ago and he said, "Apartheid has become very trendy, hasn't it? When are we going to become trendy?" Then he paused and said, "I guess never." I think all of us know that.

For many Jewish people, the issue is: never again.

And part of our job is to educate them that what we're talking about is not a repetition of World War II.

Meanwhile, the clock is ticking.

It's a very big clock, with many dials. And things can change direction. The Arabic word *sumud* means persistence. Staying fast. In the phase of the Palestinian struggle that ended in 1982, the role of the exile was paramount. Now we've turned our attention inward: to those who are staying there. Okay, the burden is on us. And the history of the Third World is one of strategic states that have been dismantled.

There's nowhere in the world where people are less inclined to dismantle them.

They said that in Algeria, they said that about the British in Kenya. Who could have imagined that after 300 years of colonization in India they would have left? They come and they go.

Interview with Timothy Appleby,
The Globe and Mail, Toronto, 1986

FIFTEEN

SCHOLARS, MEDIA,
AND THE MIDDLE EAST

*The idea for this debate at the twentieth-anniversary meeting of the Middle
East Studies Association of North America—a bit of* mano a mano *between
the senior British Orientalist and myself, aided by two younger men, journalists who took opposite positions on the Middle East—came from Leila
Fawwaz of Tufts University. It grew directly out my book* Orientalism *(1978),
which seemed to have polarized the field of which, ironically enough, I was
not a member. Three thousand people turned up to watch what took place on
November 22, 1986.* E.W.S.

BERNARD LEWIS: During recent weeks, as interest has built up in this
meeting, I have heard it referred to in terms of the Roman circus, the
Spanish bullring, the American boxing ring, and, from one of my more
imaginative colleagues, as the "shoot-out at the MESA corral." I do not
think of my coming here this morning as that of a gladiator, a bull-
fighter, a gunfighter, or any other fighter, nor as a duel. I come as a
scholar through an organization of professional scholars to discuss a serious matter which is of vital concern to all of us.

A case in point. I do not regard the serious matter which we are here
to discuss as one of the many problems and conflicts which at present
beset the Middle East—Iraq-Iran, the Arabs-Israel, fundamentalist-
secularist, or the like. There are ample other fora in which these can be
discussed and, *in sha allah,* solved. Perhaps more important, I think we
all know that nothing which we say or do here this morning is going to
have the slightest effect in the Middle East. We can change nothing. We
can't even change each other's opinions. What we can and should discuss is ourselves, our own role, our own duty as scholars, our duty
toward our discipline, toward our colleagues, toward our students,

toward the media, and beyond the media, toward the general public. And that is something which concerns us directly and where what we discuss, what we decide, can and, indeed, should determine how we conduct ourselves in our profession and our vocation—our duty being to understand and to communicate what we have understood to others.

In principle, of course, this problem, this duty, would be the same whatever the third term might be in the sequence the scholar, the media, and the Middle East. In principle it could be the same whether we substitute the Far East or the Middle East, the Far West or the Middle West, or India, or any other part of the world. In principle. In fact, of course, we all know that it is different. And the Middle East, in particular, is different for two reasons which I may mention here. One is that it is *our* region, the one with which we are concerned, all of us professionally, many of us personally in a variety of ways. And another reason—I think it is in a way more important and also rather difficult—and that is that the Middle East as an area of study for scholars in the Western world presents peculiar problems different from those of most other areas. It is different than a situation in which we study a part of our own society. That I think is self-evident. It is also different from a totally alien society, at least in its earlier history, its former civilization. The Middle East is not like India or China which dawned at a fairly late date on the Western horizon, and concerning which we have no important pre-judgments, no inherited tradition, or attitudes, or stereotypes; nor they of us. The connection between the Western world—which for this purpose extends from California to the Soviet Union, inclusive—and the Islamic world go back to the very beginnings of Islam and have been shaped by a whole series of events, particularly by the see-saw conflict between the two worlds.

This similarity in some respects, difference in others, makes it tempting and dangerously easy to go astray. We are dealing with a society in many ways akin to our own, quite apart from the general humanity we all share; there are historical and cultural affinities, genuine affinities, between the Middle East and the Western world, genuine affinities which can easily give rise to false analogies. A simple example: we may try to explain things to those who are not familiar with Islam by saying the Qur'an is the Muslim Bible, Friday is the Muslim sabbath. You must have heard these statements often enough. Up to a certain level, at a rather superficial level of discourse, these statements are accurate and informative. But as soon as we pursue them a little further they become dangerously misleading. The Muslim approach to scripture is different from the Jewish or Christian approach to scripture, and you can satisfy yourself immediately by simply reversing the proposition: the Torah is the Jewish Qur'an, the Gospel is the Christian Qur'an. It doesn't make sense, does it?

In the same way, to take a more contemporary and more complex example, when we use such words as "revolution," they may have a different resonance in Islamic society against the background of Islamic history and tradition than that which they have in the West. In the Western world, the associations of the term revolution are the major revolutions of modern history—the American, French, or Russian. In the Islamic world there is a quite different revolutionary tradition, nurtured on different structures and classics, alluding to different history. What matters: the evocative symbol is not the storming of the Bastille, but the Battle of Karbala'. In order to understand, in order to seek to understand movements in another civilization, we must try to understand it in its own terms, in relation to its own history, to its own traditions, and its own inspirations.

The result of this situation is often that we resort on both sides to stereotypes, to stereotyped images and explanations. In the course of the centuries-long confrontation, traditional attitudes have evolved on both sides. Among Western visitors to the Middle East, for many, many centuries now, two stereotypes have predominated: one political, that of arbitrary despotism; and the other, shall we say personal, that of unbridled sexual power. The one relating to the sultan's palace, and the other to the women's quarters of that palace. We have a whole series of descriptions presenting Middle Eastern government, Islamic government, Ottoman government—whatever we chose to call it—in terms of arbitrary, limitless, irresponsible autocracy. In the same way, Western travelers loved to dwell in immense detail on what went on inside the harem, about which they certainly knew nothing. One can see them drooling visibly in their largely imaginary descriptions. From this kind of thing—you can call it bilateral—while Western travelers to the East speak of licentious men, Islamic travelers to the West usually speak of lascivious women. One wonders why, if this meeting of East and West is really a meeting of licentious men and loose women, they didn't get on better.

The answer to a stereotype is not, of course, a negative stereotype. And you do not refute the myth of unbridled autocracy by claiming that what existed was perfect democracy. You do not refute the myth of the subjugation of women by insisting that women have rights far beyond those claimed by NOW.

What are we to do? I see that I have one minute left. What I shall offer are general principles of how I feel a scholar ought to behave. You will probably say, "Yes, that's apple pie." To which I would answer, "Maybe." But don't forget, we are living in a time when apple pie is under attack, when we are told that since perfect apple pie is impossible we should eat raw dough and crab apples. I don't share that opinion. I feel that such values as civility, trying to maintain a decent level of debate to cool rather than to heat passions, to persuade rather than to shout down an opponent are values worth preserving and ones which we as professional scholars in particular owe to the society which employs us.

EDWARD SAID: There is, of course, a fairly wide spectrum of scholarly work that is being done on the Middle East: the MESA Convention program is evidence enough of this. Yet scholarly work in this as in all other fields is limited by contemporary social, political, and economic— that is, contextual—actualities. No scholar ever feels that his or her work is well known enough, and nearly every one of us believes that public tastes and what is easily accessible for those tastes miss the importance of a given area of knowledge. There is no abstract knowledge: all of it is situated relative to other scholarship, to the realities of distribution and circulation, to the social institutions, rhetorical traditions, and methodological procedures of the field, as well as to the political interests and the facts of power and dominance in a given society at given periods.

To speak about scholars, media, and the Middle East here and now is to speak first of the contemporary United States. And in the U.S. it is also to distinguish first between the mainstream print and broadcast media, and the fringe left- and right-wing press; second, it is to distinguish between scholarly work on the Middle East that effectively remains secluded within the various specialist publications, and those views and images of the Middle East in wide public circulation, where they are either confirmed, or refined and repudiated by scholarly experts.

Roughly speaking, there are a small handful of essential thematic clusters in today's media coverage of the Middle East.

1. The pervasive presence of generally Middle Eastern, more particularly Arab and/or Islamic, terrorism, Arab or Islamic terrorist states and groups, as well as a "terrorist network" comprising Arab and Islamic groups and states backed by the Soviet Union, Cuba, and Nicaragua. "Terrorism" here is most often characterized as congenital, not as having any foundation in grievances, prior violence, or continuing conflicts.
2. The rise of Islamic and Muslim fundamentalism, usually but not always Shi'i, associated with such names as Khomeini, Quaddafi, Hizballah, as well as, to coin a phrase, "the return of Islam."
3. The Middle East as a place whose violent and incomprehensible events are routinely referred back to a distant past full of "ancient" tribal, religious, or ethnic hatreds.
4. The Middle East as a contested site in which "our" side is represented by the civilized and democratic West, the United States, and Israel. Sometimes Turkey is included here, most often not.
5. The Middle East as the locale for the re-emergence of a virulent quasi-European (i.e., Nazi) type of anti-Semitism.
6. The Middle East as the *fons et origo,* the hatching ground, of the gratuitous evils of the PLO. Yasir Arafat, whose poor media image is probably beyond repair, is the ranking figure in this cluster of motifs whose basic message is that, if they exist at all, the Palestinians are both marginal and entirely to blame for their misfortunes.

As it happens, these motifs coincide almost perfectly with current U.S. policy, and, as the superpower with by far the most interventionary force in the Middle East—in money, arms, and political influence—we can safely characterize the United States therefore as being abetted in its policies by its media. How far this situation contradicts the rhetorical proclamations of a free, nonpropagandistic press I shall leave to your sense of charity. But that the picture of the contemporary—even the historical—Middle East is misrepresented tendentiously I shall not leave to your charity: I shall say it myself. It is a deeply flawed, deeply antagonistic, deeply uninformed and uninforming view that regulates what is covered and what is not covered. But to a considerable degree it has worked—and this is the shameful part—because of the active collaboration of a whole cadre of scholars, experts, and abettors drawn from the ranks of the Orientalists and special-interest lobbies, among whom one, the Zionist lobby, has garnered a vastly disproportionate strength, given that Israel in the Middle East contains only four million inhabitants.

Thus, in every one of the six constellations I have identified there has been a major role played in formulating and affirming the circulation of this reductive material by members of a profession, and its friends, who *do* know better, but who do what they do consciously to maintain American hostility toward the vast majority of the Middle East's people; encourage that hostility in its ideological fantasies; and hasten it toward less, rather than more knowledge, sympathy, and above all understanding. And, it must be added, there has been no significant scholarly deterrent or corrective to these views in the media; those experts and scholars who might have provided less distorted, more interesting views have either not come forward, or have not been chosen by the powers that be.

Some specifics are in order. As against the six clusters I mentioned, no sustained, meaningful, and undeterred exceptions to them are to be found in the pages of the following (and here I speak of news coverage and opinion): the *New York Times,* the *Washington Post,* the *New Yorker,* the *New York Review of Books,* the *New Republic, Commentary, Foreign Affairs,* the *American Scholar, Partisan Review, Policy Review,* the *Atlantic Monthly, Dissent,* the *New Criterion, Midstream, Tikkun, Moment,* and the *American Spectator.* CBS, NBC, ABC, and PBS in essence work within the same paradigm. Most of the provincial papers, journals, and TV outlets depend on the mainstream majors to a large extent. As a test of my overall thesis, ask yourselves whether any of you can think of a media outlet whose guiding principles vis-à-vis Middle East coverage include the notions that Islam is never to be criticized; that the PLO, while prone to a few excesses, is basically democratic and lovable; that one or another Middle East state besides Israel is worthy of unrestricted U.S. aid; and that Christianity and Judaism are basically violent, hypocritical, and depraved religions. No such publication exists, whereas in fact all the ones I've mentioned give unexamined support to precisely the *opposite* views.

And why not, you may well ask. For, after all, the media can call on a substantial roster of experts who regularly represent the Middle East *for* the U.S. media and U.S. policy. Note—and here i's must be dotted— that this roster virtually—but not completely—excludes Muslims and Arabs—although many are available; it includes people whose political sympathies are clearly inscribed in what they write, although—and this is the pity of it—some of the scholars persist in characterizing what they do as impartial, or detached, or expert. This is the point, and it raises to me the profoundly interesting question of how these scholars continue to practice their art while remaining hostile, or at least antithetical to and substantially reserved, about its central object: the religion and culture of Islam. The roster I have in mind is responsible for what is essentially the entire gamut of media representation of the Middle East. It includes: Bernard Lewis, Elie Kedourie, Walter Laqueur, Ernest Gellner, Conor Cruise O'Brien, Martin Peretz, Norman Podhoretz, J. B. Kelley, Daniel Pipes—I could go on.

I could supply you with a list of people who either could do a better or more informed job, or whose efforts to do the job have been systematically rebuffed. The U.S. media is, I would say, much more predisposed to hearing Bernard Lewis explain the TWA hijacking by a long, abstract, general account of Shi'i history until the Middle Ages, than in hearing about the widespread, ongoing debate between nationalists and supporters of Islamic tendencies, or between various factions within the Islamic tendency itself. The media is prone to welcome, I would say it is primed for, Gellner's theses that Muslims are a nuisance and viscerally anti-Semitic, that their culture and politics can be discussed in thousands of words without a single reference to people, periods, or events. The media is far less interested in discovering whether there is a significant correlation between assertions about Islam based exclusively on classical texts on the one hand, and on the other what Muslims in various countries, belonging to various classes, different genders, in differing social systems, actually do. Never are polls conducted by Arabs and

Muslims cited; never are the old clichés that Islam is a political religion and that there is no distinction between Islam and Islamic life, ever violated by history, reality, events, people, or production.

Obfuscation is one thing; active insinuation quite another. Why do learned Orientalists lend their authority to a symposium on terrorism edited by the Israeli UN ambassador if not as Orientalists in order to *connect* Islam directly with terror? And why, out of all the prodigiously complex, even painful, realities in the 150-million-strong Arab Islamic world and its history, do classical Orientalists find only Islam's poor knowledge of Europe and its anti-Semitism to discuss? Why are poetry, plays, novels, novellas, and essays never discussed? What has Islam become but a crudely and indiscriminately represented bogeyman, certified by the Orientalists?

Aside from the fact that expert scholarship of this kind now in full view of readers of the *New York Review of Books,* the *Times,* and *Commentary* has no counterweight to oppose it, it is on its merits a disgrace to the world of intellectual production in the social sciences or humanities generally. Why is it that no prominent Africanist, Sinologist, Indologist, or Japanologist speaks in this patronizing and deflating manner?

The answer, to conclude, is that scholarly expertise on the Middle East has paid a very high price for its entry into the mainstream media and the halls of policy. It has sacrificed information on what goes on in the Middle East—Israel included—almost completely. It has sacrificed understanding and compassion totally.

Leon Wieseltier: For my sins as a scholar, probably, I've been forced to live among journalists for the past four or five years of my life. So it is largely about journalists that I wish to speak. I begin my remarks by saying that it is beyond any doubt that there is a disgraceful and almost systematically distorting image of Islam presented in the American media. More often the distortions are about Islamic culture and religion and society than of Islamic politics, and such distinctions must be made. Sometimes these distortions are anti-Muslim; sometimes they are not. One does not have to be anti-Muslim to be anti-Quaddafi or anti-Khomeini, though I'm sure it helps. Just last week, more evidence of this distortion was given as Washington assumed as its conventional wisdom concerning Mr. McFarlane's mission to Iran that there are no moderates in Iran, that it was almost a definitional matter that anyone who lived within the borders of Khomeini's Iran was crazy. About this I have no argument. There are, however, a number of complicating and, I think, important points or qualifications that I would like to introduce into the discussion for the purpose of arriving at two rather broad and coarsely stated conclusions.

The first is that some of this almost insurmountable ignorance about the Islamic way of life is owed not to any particularly anti-Muslim prejudice, but to the almost insurmountable ignorance of the American media about everything foreign to the United States. The intellectual shallowness of journalists needs no documentation by me. A system of foreign policy reporting according to which a man who has spent five years in Warsaw must land in Beirut on Tuesday and be an expert about it is well known to all of you. The lack of linguistic competence doesn't help, though in the case of a man like Thomas Friedman of the *New York Times* who does know and speak Arabic, it shows quite clearly what difference the language makes. The coverage of India, of China, of Africa in the American media is just as disgracefully ignorant as the coverage of the Middle East.

Second point. The coverage of Israel, of the Jewish point of view, call it what you will, of Judaism certainly, and indeed of the American way of life—the distortions contained within that coverage in the Arab press are no less spectacular than some of the distortions that are contained in the Western press about the Islamic way of life. Are those distortions anti-Semitic? Sometimes they are. But sometimes they are not. Indeed, the interesting thing about them to my mind is not whether or not they are anti-Semitic, but the extent to which they point to the more common difficulty of the interpretation of one culture by another culture across vast cultural differences.

Three. There is a very delicate question of stereotypes about which I have time only to speak crudely. Stereotypes are the sort of lie that succeeds precisely because there is always a grain of truth in them. And I include the anti-Semitic stereotypes of the Jew in that generalization. For example, there has emerged since the revolution, since Khomeini's revolution in Iran, the famous and fabulous stereotype of the Muslim fundamentalist. Now, it seems obvious that Muslim fundamentalism is, of course, exaggeration based on ignorance of a very complicated phenomenon. It is obvious that the full intellectual, theological, cultural, political, and social meanings and machinery of the Iranian revolution have not been understood in this country; and yet, the stereotype of the raving or radical Iranian Shi'i fundamentalist student or the stereotype that we created by a kind of collusion between those students themselves and their leaders and the Western media—many of the events that led to the worst American prejudices were staged for the purpose of reaching American living rooms.

Four. There are biases in the coverage of Israel, too. I will try to deal with them quickly, and no doubt we will discuss them some more. First, the war in Lebanon in my view was a wrong war and, in some ways, a disastrous and disgraceful war. But the vilifications of Israel that appeared in the American press during that war were as egregious a violation of journalistic principle and intellectual honesty as I have seen. Second, on the question of the West Bank, it is the common prejudice of the American media that Israel should vacate all or most of the West Bank as soon as it can. This is a prejudice that I happen to share. It is a prejudice that I am sure most of you happen to share. For that reason, it is a prejudice that we do not find particularly offensive. But it is, nonetheless, a prejudice. Third, the matter of the coverage of the Palestinians. This is a rather complicated question. But one thing seems clear to me on this simply in reading the American media. That is, that the notion that the Palestinian people, by this late date, by November 1986, have been erased or made invisible seems to me perfectly ridiculous. Which intelligent leader of the American media does not know that the Palestinians are a stateless people, that they were occupied in 1967, that they live under occupation, that they have lived for generations in camps and shanty towns, that they are as unwelcome in the Arab world—indeed, probably more unwelcome in the Arab world—than in the Jewish world, that a resolution of the Arab-Israeli conflict probably depends upon a solution of the Palestinian problem, and so on. All this seems to me not only [not] unknown, but to have reached the status of cliché.

My final two coarsely stated conclusions. (I think they're rather exquisite.) First, I think that the time has come to consider the limitations of media criticism and criticism of the press as a primary form of political discourse for the following reasons. One: the criticism of the press, by now, at least has the effect merely of reproducing and intensifying the very problem of bias that it deplores. Each of us has our own favorite sinners. My friends can point to Jonathan Randall; my enemies speak of other correspondents. I'm not sure there's anything to be gained by this except the simplification of the entire field into a cast of monsters versus heroes. Second: the obsessive criticism of the media flatters the very media it denounces by attributing much too much power to it. It seems to me that despite all the biases in the coverage of the Middle East, it is still possible for an intelligent man or woman to see the story within the story. There are events that happen even if reporters fail to cover them. There are events the truth of which can be seen even if reporters mis-cover them. We are not all mindless puppets of the networks, of the large newspapers, of the media conglomerates. It is possible to read newspapers critically, to watch television broadcasts critically, and to evaluate critically what we have as the evidence of our own eyes.

Final point, and this is the question of objectivity. Let me start this way. Objectivity may seem like an antiquated, bourgeois notion serving really to disguise all kinds of political, institutional, and cultural inter-ests. That indeed may be the case. But it seems to me that there is a basic philosophical and methodological decision that one must make. And that decision is whether or not the truth is available, whether or not there is something that may be called the truth about which honest men and women may disagree, about which they may dispute by pointing to evidence and adducing proofs and fighting over texts and over phenom-ena of history that require difficult interpretation. And not even the all-invasive, all-intrusive media, in my view, have succeeded in destroying the notion of the truth of a situation.

Finally, press criticism, media criticism, in the Jewish case, in the Palestinian case, and other cases seems to me sometimes to be not just a contribution to the discussion, to intellectual discourse or political criti-cism, but a crutch that begins even to hobble action. If the Jewish case in the United States is heard, if the Jewish case is understood better here than in the other cases, it is not because the Jews came to a country that was distinguished by any native or essential hospitality to Jews or Ju-daism. The anti-Semitism and the prejudice and the hostility the Jews faced in this country when they arrived was certainly as great as any anti-Muslim feeling that exists now. But what the Jews did was, they organized intellectually and politically. They founded institutions such as the Anti-Defamation League and they proceeded to see to it that their case would be heard. I think it is probably fair to say that it was a milestone in the history of Palestinian representation in this country when an organization such as the Arab Anti-Defamation League [sic] was founded, quite obviously and quite correctly on a Jewish model. The Jews knew that the world would not understand them properly. But when the Jews were in trouble, they did not wait for the world to understand them properly; they acted to save themselves. I think for vulnerable people, for minorities, the people who live in wretchedness, the important point finally—and to me this was Zionism's great lesson—is that what is really important is not that the world understand you: what is really important is that you understand yourself and that you save yourself. Thank you.

CHRISTOPHER HITCHENS: As a transplanted English radical, I come before you today with the queasy sensation of having been outdone in point of English joviality and emollience by Professor Lewis and out-pointed in matter of radical style, irony, and passion by Professor Said. I stand before you, therefore, somewhat naked, and propose to begin with what I hope will be the day's only uncontroversial remark, which is that no thoughtful person, I imagine, in this audience, with any special knowledge of any subject or any area in the Middle East will be satisfied with the way in which that subject is discussed in print, whether in the general press or in learned journals. My own small area of expertise in the matter, which is the island of Cyprus, I find vindicates this self-pitying proposition. Most coverage and discussion of it is at least three of the following things: totally ahistorical, lacking any historical perspective; a very slight but perceptible reverence toward whatever the current official or administration thinking might be; and a wistful, elusive feeling that truth lies somewhere between any two propositions that may recently have been taken on it. Concerning the Middle East, I want to argue, and specifically the conflict over Palestine, a subjectively even-handed treatment, inadequate as it is, is very often abandoned and sometimes suspended completely.

Now, any examples I might select would, *ipso facto*, be selective, even if I had three times ten minutes in which to speak. But the following selections, taken, naturally, *from* context as all quotation selection is, trying to anticipate that criticism, seem to me to be emblematic rather than to be anecdotal. I have chosen them less for journalism per se than from that bloody crossroads where journalism and scholarship and we today are met.

First, the book by Joan Peters called *From Time Immemorial,* an attempt to show that there was no such thing even as a Palestinian problem; that there was no such thing as a Palestinian people. Its reception in this country ranged from the respectful to the moist and the adoring, and came from all corners of the academy and the press. It isn't so much important, and I haven't the time, to stress the massive evidence that has since accumulated that the book was a mere concoction, as it is to underline the extraordinary difficulty that that evidence had in finding its way to print. Only after extensive ridicule of the book in the Israeli and English presses in particular, were any mild reconsiderations published in this country, in which it was interesting to see a number of people fall on both sides at once. But too late.

Second, the book *The Fateful Triangle* by Professor Noam Chomsky. I don't want to pay Professor Chomsky any unintentional compliments, because I think he deserves far better, but it's correct to say that his book on the Lebanon war was, at its time of publication, unrivaled. That is to say it had no competitor. There was no other book about the engagement of the United States and its Israeli ally in the Lebanon war. And the book was published over the uniquely timely intersection of the events of that war at the vote. Long, very densely and highly footnoted, written by one of the few American Jews with an international scholarly reputation. What was its fate? It was unreviewed by the *New York Times;* it was unreviewed by the *Washington Post;* it was unreviewed by the *Los Angeles Times;* by the *New Republic;* by my own magazine, *The Nation;* by *Commentary;* and by all the magazines on the list that even Edward, with his speed and dash of delivery, didn't have time to complete reading. A no less than scandalous, I dare to say, scandalous, state of affairs.

Third. "Flashpoint," a public broadcasting package with three films intended for screening last April on the question of Palestine. The three films broke up, as such packages of three often do, into two pro-Israeli segments and one made by an anti-Zionist Jew. Public broadcasting stations in the cities of New York and Washington, D.C., among others declined to screen the pro-Palestinian third of the capsule. The *New York Times,* the journal of record of the *bien pensant* and the only journal of record for the benighted greater New York City area, reviewed the film that was not screened and said it was—and I'm quoting—"not far from the films produced by the Third Reich."

Now, I work in a cynical profession and I've set my colleagues the following puzzle. This is all you know; you have to say what the topic is. PBS film is banned from the screens of New York. The *New York Times* does not comment on the banning but describes the unseen film as Nazi. My question to my colleagues is, what was the film about and what view did it take? Not even the most conservative of my friends and colleagues has failed to guess the answer without hesitation. I find this cynicism gives me very little pleasure. I find it unattractive. So is the knowledge that is widely disseminated and internalized in my profession that if a critic of Israel dares to make these sort of points he will face either the repellent allegation that he is anti-Semitic if he's a Gentile, or that he is a victim of Jewish self-hatred, if, as so often, he is a Jew. This latter-day version of Morgan's fork with its blackmailing and authoritarian implications is present in the minds of every journalist that I know. And it's agreed with varying degrees of resignation that whereas life is indeed unfair, the three examples I cited above could not occur so flagrantly in a debate on any other question.

Let me suggest two reasons I think this might be so. And I'll give you another quotation. It is the following. You have to guess where it comes from. Put simply it says, "American journalists are interested only in two topics in the Middle East: Israel and the United States. Whatever takes place that is related to these countries is amplified and broadcast to the world. Whatever is not is virtually ignored." That is from "The Media and the Middle East" by Daniel Pipes in *Commentary,* in the bizarre context of an argument that the entire United States press is ranged against the Israeli case—one of the unintended ironies, of other unintended ironies, which all of those readers of Dr. Pipes have long learned to cherish.

Second, more vulgar, but less escapable—simple racism. Where did the following appear? The description of a play at the American Repertory Theater in this town: "The universalist prejudice of our culture prepared us for this play's Arab, a crazed Arab to be sure, but crazed in the distinctive ways of his culture. He is intoxicated by language, cannot discern between fantasy and reality, abhors compromise, always blames others for his predicament and, in the end, lances the painful boil of his frustrations in a pointless, though momentarily gratifying, act of bloodlust." That is a signed comment by the owner and editor of the *New Republic*. I disagree with you, Leon; I'm sorry, I don't believe that could appear about an Indian or an African in any other magazine in this country. As to whether it should be said at all of any ethnic or racial group in a magazine that, once, boasted Walter Lippmann and Edmund Wilson, "is a question for those who toil in that vineyard."

We would be open to the charge of self-pity if we located this problem just in the workings of the media or the academy. The two are caught—and I realize I'm going to have to save some of this for my rebuttal—naturally, between a state policy which favors Israel for opportunistic reasons (a simple administration decision on which is the right course), and a public opinion with a vulgar prejudice against the swarthier type of Middle Easterner. The second can be seen in almost any kind of contemporary cartoon, not exempting those by the liberal *bien pensant,* such as Herblock of the *Washington Post,* where the unpardonable dual stereotype shows Arabs and Iranians as the most malodorous and subversive desperadoes, again exactly mirroring the fork on which European anti-Semites used to attempt to impale the Jews. Exactly mirroring and duplicating that fork.

And the former is evidenced by coverage which naturally annexes Israeli terminology, to be more precise, the terminology of the Israeli right. I will return.

CHAIRMAN: It is time now for the second round or the rebuttal, or the continuation of remarks.

LEWIS: First, a brief word on the remarks made by our two representatives of the media. Yes, of course, it is very easy to find examples of prejudice directed against all parties in the Middle East, and this does not prove that the media as a whole are biased one way or the other, merely that the media's idea of impartiality is to balance opposing prejudices. And this, of course, is understandable, on television in particular. It makes a much better television than presenting a balanced and reasoned point of view. And we have just seen in the elections which have taken place in this country—where the discussion is not of remote places and foreign people, but of immediate domestic issues—how difficult it is (and most would say impossible) to arrive at any serious or balanced discussion in the circumstances of television and to a lesser extent in the other media.

It is a real difficulty, and we will all naturally concentrate on those passages which are offensive to us, in a sort of masochism of the reader, which is universal. I don't think it can be assigned to any particular direction. Ignorance is of universal implication.

When I was cut off by the chairman, I was about to say one or two things about the duties of the scholar as I perceive them. Professor Said very obligingly exemplified some of the points I was going to make, one way or the other. The apple pie I was about to offer you, shall we say truth and objectivity, are much misunderstood words, and perhaps are not appropriate at the present time. Obviously, we all have our allegiances, we all have our prejudices, we all have our opinions and in a free society we are all entitled to advance them.

What then are we to do? If for truth and objectivity we substitute honesty and fairness, I think we are talking in more practical rather than theoretical terms and enunciating something which we can all understand. For example, it is hardly either honest or fair to try to refute someone else's point of view not in terms of what he says, but of motives which you choose to attribute to him in order to make your refutation easier. It is hardly an example of truth or fairness to use the smear tactics that became well known in this country at an earlier stage, by lumping together writers, scholars, and journals of very disparate characters and origins, and thereby conveying rather than asserting that they are all the same, that they constitute one homogeneous, centrally directed, conspiratorial whole.

Much of what was said about the media I would agree with, but how far beyond the media shall we pursue it? I do not recall any scholar arguing that terrorism in the Middle East is congenital. I would be very surprised if any such thing could be said. Nor that terrorism is inherently Islamic. In the colloquium which was quoted, the point which I made—and anyone who is interested can check it quite easily in the printed version—was that, to say that terrorism is Islamic, is an absurdity in the sense that Islam is a religion like other religions with an ethical and moral standard, and is opposed to terrorism as such. The only way in which that expression has meaning is in the rather more political character, of Islam, particularly at the present time. At the present moment almost all political movements tend to acquire a political character, and terrorism is, after all, a political movement.

SAID: I felt that in the first part of the discussion there was broad agreement that there is distortion, that the media does x, y, and z, and so forth, and that as scholars we should be doing other things. Given the constraints of time, I talked about a group or a number of scholars and journalists, intellectuals and journals and newspapers. And I would be perfectly happy to take the point case by case and to show—not that they were all directed by some outside source, far from it—that there is a set of motifs that keeps turning up in the media. The six that I mentioned I'm not going to repeat. But I felt that the scholars who knew more about the Middle East—and I guess I agree with all my colleagues on this panel—that it is the duty of scholars to act in the interest of truth and justice and fairness and honesty. I felt that there wasn't enough of a deterrent to this essentially mischievous misrepresentation of the Middle East, and that, in some cases, far from preventing the distortions from getting greater, they were actively assisting in a sense of participating or collaborating within this framework to make it worse. And the examples I gave seem to me bear it out. For example, Professor Lewis mentions the symposium on terrorism. In the introduction of the book, Ambassador Netanyahu says that the two central sources today in the world of terrorism are the Islamic world, Islam, and the KGB. And then framed by this discussion we have only three representatives from the scholarly discussion of the Middle East who essentially say, Professor Lewis says, if I may quote him here more or less verbatim, "it's foolish to say that Islam is a religion that promotes terrorism. It's a great religion like Judaism," and so forth, but then he goes on to say in the next paragraph that it is correct to use Islam as a designation for terrorism in the modern world.

Now, there's also the context of the book, the context of public discussion in which it is left to no one's imagination that Islam produces terrorism. I think the insinuation there is quite clear. I don't think it's the case that in talking about Islam today we have experts trying to promote understanding, not only of the diversity of Islam, of the Islamic world—and I speak now as a person who is interested in learning more about it rather than less. It's not a question of promoting it, but rather of concentrating on a few simple points: that Islam is essentially political. What in this context does the word political mean? It could mean anything. But it does seem to suggest that, mostly, Muslims are running around making political points and doing nothing else—you know, that they might live, and produce and die and write and think and feel.

It reminds me of a story by Groucho Marx, one of my favorite Groucho Marx stories. He's coming down in the elevator in a hotel in Italy and a group of priests come in the elevator. One of them turns to him and says, "Oh, Mr. Marx, you know my mother is really an admirer of your films." So Groucho turns to him and says, "Hey, I didn't know you guys were allowed to have mothers."

That's number one. And the other point which needs to be made in this context is the suppression of information that might show the Middle East as a rather more complex place than writings of this sort generally allow. So if you're going to talk about Islamic terrorism, what about in the same context talking about Jewish terrorism, or Christian terrorism? For example, if you want to show that there's anti-Semitism in the Arab world—I'm sure there is; there's anti-Semitism everywhere—one has to make distinctions between quotations from a newspaper, trends, public policy, beliefs, and ethnic characterizations. All of these things are lumped together and produced in a series called anti-Semitism in the Arab world, or the Arab and Islamic world. So that's one problem, the question of distortion.

Then the other problem, and this is the last point I want to make, is the constant protestation that what we are doing is scholarly and objective. I'm all in favor of these things. But I would think we have to allow that the public is rather more intelligent than that. Protestations are not enough. One has to demonstrate these things by fairness, by a wide scope, by quoting the whole context, not just part of it, and stop pretending that what we are about is only scholarship. In fact, as I'm sure everyone here knows, we are dealing with extensions of a conflict that occur and the protection of the guild; that is, the ritual protestation of formulae about one thing or the other are not going to dispel the truth. The truth is there as Leon quite correctly said, and one can perceive it. That one point of view is essentially much more represented than another, nobody in this room would deny. That's the point that had to be made.

WIESELTIER: I'll comment on a few of the things that were said here, and my comments may, with any luck, add up to a coherent argument. It seems to me that Edward Said has drawn a caricature; that he has taken extremes of Jewish and Israeli opinion, put them together, and come up with some alleged mainstream position which characterizes the Jewish state, mainstream Jewish institutions, the American Jewish community, the American Jewish press, and the American non-Jewish media. Who, for example, or where in any of those institutions is the equation of Palestinians with Nazis made? The equation is made in many disgusting quarters of the Jewish community. It is made by many Likud front groups. It is made by a group called Americans for a Safe Israel. It is encouraged by Sephardi demagogic politicians and Ashkenazi demagogic politicians in Israel. But where in the mainstream Jewish community, within the Labor Party, within much of the Likud party, within the American Jewish community, is that particular or any of the other repulsive ideas that he cited, where exactly are they to be found?

I will not stick Edward Said with Abu Nidal. I would prefer not to be stuck with Meir Kahane. Each of us have our big problems. But the fact remains that both of us are doing our best to solve these problems, and we are not alone in our communities.

On the question of Jewish terrorism, one of the reasons that Jewish terrorism is written about less frequently than Palestinian terrorism is because until quite recently, that is to say from the period of the 1930s and 1940s until sometime in the late 1970s, Jewish terrorism occurred less frequently than Palestinian terrorism. And that is simply the historical fact.

On the other hand, with the outbreak of Jewish terrorism in Israel and on the West Bank, there have been many people, as Edward Said knows quite well, who have been screaming loudly and hoarsely in condemnation and denunciation and acting politically both to bring those

people to justice and to destroy not only the political and physical infrastructure that made those acts possible, but to destroy the intellectual
foundation of that kind of extremism.

And I refer to people here, not merely to Noam Chomsky, with
whom one may be permitted to disagree without being accused of being
a self-loving Jew, I hope. I refer to a great many intellectuals who may
disagree with Chomsky and Shahak and Izzy Stone and all kinds of
people on all kinds of questions, but I think who are decent people, who
are not racists about Arabs, Muslims, or Palestinians.

With my friend Hitchens I will not try to compete in wit, nor in dis-
honesty. Hitchens and I are close friends, we can say anything we want
about each other.

The Joan Peters book was a shabby performance by an ignorant
woman. The Joan Peters book should have been refuted in my magazine,
in other magazines; it was not. It was not because I had not read the
book before I assigned it. On the other hand, within the Jewish community and outside the Jewish community, the Joan Peters book had no impact whatsoever for several reasons. One: because most American Jews
are not terribly interested by what happens exactly inside Israel. Two:
because it was a very fat book. Three: because I believe most American
Jews are no longer hospitable to the political conclusion that the Joan Peters book begs, which is that there are no such things as Palestinians.
That was the upshot of that book, and my view—it may be optimistic,
but I speak here from some knowledge and experience—is that it is simply no longer the commonly held view in the Jewish community.

The notion that anybody who disagrees with Israeli policy is either
routinely called anti-Semitic by I don't know who—the American
media, the American Jewish media, the Jewishly controlled media—the
notion that all such critics are routinely called anti-Semitic is simply
ridiculous. There has been a very bitter debate going on inside the Jewish community ever since Israeli troops captured the West Bank in 1967,
a debate at least as bitter, if not more so, than the debate that goes on
between the Jewish community and the Palestinian community, more
bitter in a way because internecine debate, fraternal struggles, are always more bitter.

I reject the notion that all Israel's critics are anti-Semitic. Some of them are, and they should not be allowed to hide behind the inelegance of calling them that. Most of them obviously are not. My view is simply that they are wrong.

HITCHENS: I want to speak directly to two points made by Professor Lewis in his second appearance at the microphone. First, his dismissal of the idea that there is any pattern in the misrepresentation that Edward Said and myself have mapped and sketched as much as we dare. And second, as he put it, that there's nothing congenital [about terrorism]. He says he knows of no one who says that the propensity to terrorism is congenital, no scholar, that is. Let me give the quotation, "The root cause of terrorism lies, not in grievances, but in a disposition towards unbridled violence." Would that meet your criteria of congenitality?

Well, that's in the introduction to *Terrorism: How the West Can Win* by Benjamin Netanyahu, who you may say is no scholar, and I would be compelled to agree with you. What he is—apart from being Israeli ambassador to the United Nations and a leading member of the hard right—all he is at the moment is a convener of scholars. His institute, the Jonathan Institute, is a recognized resource for a vast network of academic and journalistic outlets. It's routinely quoted as a source of expertise on terrorism on the news. And I think I'm being videoed by the Fletcher School of Law and Diplomacy, which produced a book, *Hydra of Carnage,* a depiction of terrorism that's entirely based on the findings of the Jonathan Institute. I don't mind debating with Benjamin Netanyahu, that is to say. What I do mind is that when I come to a seminar, I find that he's the moderator of it. I would say *mutatis mutandis* that the words terrorist, rejectionist, extremist, and fundamentalist have come to mean over a vast sway of discourse what Israeli conservatives understand them to mean. I say that that is a pattern; it is not a mere coincidence and not something that can be laughed off. It is a signal triumph of unassimilated, undigested propaganda. And it finds its triumph in the acceptance of Benjamin Netanyahu and in the emergence of terrorism as a discipline, a subject in its own right, with chairs and course codes. Now I think we may find certain root cause theories of terrorism to be simplistic and unpersuasive and propagandistic also. But I think that Ambassador Netanyahu's finding on page 204 of his book that, "the root cause of terrorism is terrorists" is open to objection on both journalistic and scholarly grounds as well as on aesthetic and grammatical ones.

The job of independent journals and the academy is not to reflect bigotry in public opinion, or to cater through special institutes and seminars to the pressures of raison d'état. Least of all is it to collude with the propagandistic and self-serving views of the world. Thank you.

Discussion with Bernard Lewis, Leon Wieseltier,
and Christopher Hitchens, chaired by William H. McNeill,
The Journal of Palestine Studies, Washington, D.C., 1987

SIXTEEN

AN EXILE'S EXILE

Can there be peace in the Middle East without a solution to the Palestinian question?

I don't think so. A lot of Palestinians don't think so. And a lot of people around the world don't think so.

What would a solution look like to you?

A solution would have to take into account the facts of Palestinian history and present-day reality. The Palestinian Arab people are the original inhabitants of what used to be called Palestine but is now the territory called Israel, plus the West Bank and the Gaza Strip, which were occupied by Israel in 1967.

The Palestinians feel themselves as a community or a nation to have been dispossessed by that act. Since then, they have become people who are either second-class citizens inside Israel, or people who were driven out and are refugees and exiles throughout the Arab world, or people on the West Bank and Gaza Strip who are an occupied population.

We're the people without a state and without a place, and in nearly every country where Palestinians are to be found, their situation is distinguished from the nationals. Even in Arab countries, they are set apart. So there's no question. There's a very strong feeling that the idea of a state is the only relief of this acute national problem of homelessness and exile.

We need a Palestinian homeland or state where our connection with the land would be reestablished.

Geographically, where should that be?

Well, I think the logical place is the occupied territories, which have the largest concentration of Palestinians today.

Would that include parts of the East Bank as well?

You mean Jordan? Jordan is a sovereign state. And, although a large population of Palestinians lives there—people who came in 1948 and were granted Jordanian citizenship—the notion that Jordan could be a substitute homeland has never satisfied either Jordanians or Palestinians. But in the last three or four years, the notion of a confederation between Jordan and a Palestinian state on the West Bank and Gaza has been discussed.

Who in your mind should represent the Palestinians at a peace conference or in negotiations?

The only representative with any credibility is the Palestine Liberation Organization. The polls show this; the various informal and international means at the disposal of the community have asserted over and over again that despite divisions and disagreements, the one thing the PLO retains without any shred of doubt in anybody's mind is the sense that they represent the Palestinians.

What are the different perceptions of the PLO in the West and among the Palestinians?

I would make a distinction even within the West. First there are distinctions between the perception of the PLO in the Palestinian world, the Arab world, the nonaligned world, the Islamic world, the Third World generally, on the one hand, and the perception in the West, or rather the United States—which is quite different from, say, that of France and England.

In the United States, the official position is that the PLO is a terrorist organization. Now recent polls show that isn't the real perception, depending on how you put the question. There is a strong popular sentiment that, whether we like them or not, the PLO is in fact a national organization of some sort. We may not like the PLO. It doesn't have a good image. Its press is obviously not good. But be that as it may, it is a representative organization.

What do you think is the sentiment within the PLO for peace and for a permanent solution? What do people want—is it a homeland on the West Bank or Jordan? Or is it still the idea of all of Palestine as a secular state?

The international consensus, the Arab consensus, and I would say even the Palestinian consensus, is the idea of a partitioned state—that is to say partly Israeli, partly Palestinian. There are still many Palestinians inside Israel today—650,000 of them—who are Israeli citizens, and many Palestinians who are originally from parts of Israel, who feel ties to that part of the country.

But the idea of a state would make that distinction, between ties—the way an American who is from Ireland feels ties to Ireland but yet has the idea that he or she is an American. The same thing would apply to Palestinians. In time, the relationship will be closer than that enjoyed between two states that are totally different. There are connections between the people.

If there were a Palestinian state on the West Bank, do you think terror as a modern phenomenon, as related to Palestinians, would diminish?

I'm not sure that terror is related. That's a popular conception.

If there were a state, would there be peace in the region?

I think there would be a greater degree of peace and a greater degree of stability. What is killing the region right now is a sense of intolerable frustration. And that is why, I think, we have this extraordinary phenomenon of religious resurgence. And it's not entirely Islamic. It's Islamic, it's Christian, it's Jewish, it's all through the region. There's a sense of impotence, a sense of standing still. And above all, among the Palestinians, the most articulate of all the Arab communities in the Middle East, there's a sense of tremendous injustice, a sense that they are endlessly being put off by the great powers, principally the United States and its ally Israel.

When you say, will a Palestinian state bring peace, will it by a magic stroke of the pen just change everything, I think so. But I am not trying to peddle a Pollyanna idea that all problems will be solved. There are other problems—poverty and inequities, economic injustices and social deformations, that will remain. I think, though, that it is difficult for any Palestinian to overestimate the importance of gaining a sense of resolution, of a just resolution to our problems.

How do Palestinians relate to Lebanon and to Jordan? Is it feasible for a Palestinian state to fit within Jordan or Lebanon?

No. You are talking about countries in such close proximity to each other, where there are all kinds of ways in which you can actually see into your own past. As people have said, if the Jews have waited 2,000 years to go back to Zion from exile, it isn't hard to imagine that the Palestinians would find forty years a very short time and wouldn't forget in forty years. Besides, about 45 percent of all the Palestinians in the world live in Palestine, so there are natural connections.

The other thing is that the countries of this region, in the period since World War II, have developed powerful national self-consciousness. The Jordanian is different from the Lebanese. The Lebanese is different from the Syrian. The Syrian is different from the Egyptian. And all of them are different from the Palestinian, who has his own sense of national identity.

And the third factor, which is very important, is that the Palestinians are seen as an anomaly in some way. I won't say outsiders or pariahs or exiles or outcasts or misfits, although they are seen that way. They are the people always on the fringes. The Palestinian is distinguished by virtue of greater education and greater political sophistication. Exile produces that. For all of these states, the Palestinians are the source of unrest.

Israel is divided on the question of the West Bank, whether it ought to be annexed, whether it ought to be returned to Jordan, whether a Palestinian state ought to be created there. It does seem to be unified on the question of Jerusalem, that it will never be returned or made an international city. If that's the case, can there ever be a solution?

I am, perhaps, an incurable optimist. I think every situation which seems frozen, irreversible, unchanging, adamantly resistant to everything, can be changed. I think there is a will; there are formulas to use for various sorts of bargaining. The nascent thing is the discovery, if possible, of the will to change.

Unfortunately, right now the preponderance of power, of military and economic strength, is so much on the side of the Israelis, who are supported by the United States almost without qualification. And there isn't enough of an Arab deterrent of any sort to make the Israelis think they're in a losing position. What you have is a debate in Israel that is more or less academic. Should we or should we not? There's a small number of people, courageous people, who are doing a lot of tremendously important work—political organizing, testimonials, helping to reduce the strains of the occupation. But overall, the Israeli position is basically that of inertia and power.

Over the years, I've met with many Israelis, and it's very striking. For the Israelis, there is a psychological and even a moral factor associated with the Palestinian that doesn't apply to other Arabs. Their problem with Syria is a problem between states, their problem with Egypt is a problem between states. But the problem between Israel and the Palestinians is much more intimate. And I think most Israelis now realize that they have no real military option against the Palestinians. The Palestinians are not all going to be murdered or sent away. They are there.

Does the presence of Israeli settlements on the West Bank make the occupation almost irreversible?

No. I don't think so. Look at France. It was in Algeria for 130 years; Algeria was a department of France. They worked it out. The French left.

Obviously the Jews in Israel today are different from the French in Algeria. They won't leave. But they will have to accommodate themselves to the reality of the situation. A lot of Jews now say this quite openly: We can't live permanently as an overlord population when the population we are on top of is growing in numbers and is certainly growing in participation and political self-consciousness. The time will have to come when we will have to deal with it. But of course it's human to put it off.

How does the United States perceive the Palestinians and why?

In the United States, particularly in the media, and for all kinds of reasons, the overall perception is extremely slanderous. The Palestinian is either a faceless refugee or a terrorist. I'm frequently struck by the extent to which this picture results not only from ignorance but also from avoidance of the Palestinian as a human being. The Palestinians and their lives and their styles, their ambitions and their achievements, go on despite the handful of incidents that causes the West to see them as a terrorist community. So ignorance is an important factor.

Another factor which is terribly important is that the Israeli foreign-policy establishment, during the middle 1970s, reached a kind of consensus that one way to deal with the Palestinians—this endless problem that won't go away—would be gradually to reduce them to the status of terrorists. This has been documented by some Israeli journalists recently. It is much easier to dehumanize the population than actually to deal with its ambitions.

If that's the case, why wouldn't Palestinian strategy, or tactics, shift away from terror? Why does the West after ten, twelve years, after Munich in 1972, still see incidents like those in Karachi and Paris?

This is likely a matter of perspective. If you look at the *ratio* of terror—and, of course, one must dot the i's and cross the t's—but infinitely greater amounts of terror have been directed against Palestinians than against Jews or against anybody else in support of Palestinians.

What are some examples?

The invasion of Lebanon in 1982, when at least 19,000 or 20,000 Palestinian and Lebanese people were killed, and a total of 600 Israeli soldiers were killed in that war.

I could reel out statistics, but there is no comparison. Palestinians are under Israeli occupation. People are killed. Yesterday a man was killed in Gaza. There are daily events. Israel figures tell you that roughly 250,000 people on the West Bank have been in Israeli jails since the occupation, which is now in its twentieth year. The destruction of houses and property, the collective punishments, village curfews, deportations: There's no comparison.

Instead, what we get is a focusing on the desperate acts of Palestinians. In my opinion, they are unforgivable acts. I've never condoned them at all; I've always been against that kind of tactic. But focusing on them and making them the issue where in fact they are by-products, is wrong. They pale in comparison to the violence visited against Palestinians throughout the Arab world.

Are Israelis able to separate what happened to them in the Holocaust from what is going on now in Palestine?

That's a very tough question to ask an Israeli, but I have often asked it. I've frequently said to them, "Look what happened to you: You as Jews are the victims of all time, really. The history of anti-Semitism is a millennial fact. And we are your victims now. How can you, having suffered victimization, in what seems to be with heedless consciences, inflict similar punishments on another people? People who, in the great scale of things, have done you very little harm—except that they were there?"

That is an unanswerable question for me. It is what puzzles me, and it is why I can't answer your question.

But I certainly know that the Israelis owe the Palestinians atonement of some sort. We haven't been the sinners in this thing. We don't live, of course, in a world of total guilt and total innocence, but in this particular conflict we have been more sinned against than sinning.

This is terribly important to peace. We need some formula that goes beyond the matter of returning land, one that involves moral restitution. The Israelis still claim, and Americans in particular listen to them, that we don't exist as a people. We are just nomads. They say the land was empty when they took it. They try to deny our humanity.

This is a true part of being a Palestinian. Not only are you denied your political sovereignty and rights, but also your history is denied and your reality as a suffering human being is pooh-poohed or ignored completely.

The essence, obviously, is mutual recognition. They have to recognize us. And we, who think what they have done to us is outrageous and illegitimate and illegal, have to recognize them. It's very difficult, but it's got to be done. Otherwise, there will be killing and endless instability for years to come.

Within the Palestinian world, there is a tradition of learning and literature. Does it translate into democratic institutions, into parliaments, into levels of representation?

As much as it possibly can, it has. Most people feel, as I do, that the Arab world in general is a pretty despotic and desolate place right now politically. Palestinian institutions are on the whole extraordinarily democratic. I mean there's an endless series of opposition parties within the Palestinian community, and every Palestinian has his own party, practically.

But the one fact that you mustn't forget about the reality of Palestinian existence in the Arab world is that there is no Palestine. We are guests in host states that, for the most part, are even more tyrannical with their own subjects. The lot of the Palestinian is, first, that he is not part of a sovereign state of his own. Second is the fact of dispersion. We are scattered everywhere, we have no central place. Lebanon, for example, is in a state of acute anarchy, but there is still Beirut, a physical capital. The Palestinians have no such thing. And that fact gives our lives its peculiar agony, isolation, and, above all, desperation.

Here in the United States, there is bias not only against Palestinians but also against Arabs in general. How would things have to change here to then change over there?

It doesn't quite work that way; it's not a direct relationship.

But you have said that Americans have to change the way we think.

Oh, absolutely. There's an ugly phenomenon in this country that needs to be underlined and said and resaid. That is this: The last permissible racism here—and by permissible, I mean it's okay publicly in the media and elsewhere—is to be racist against Arabs. You can say the most outrageous things in the most respectable magazines and newspapers and even on the air about Arabs, things you would never dare to say about any other ethnic or racial group.

Anti-Arab racism is the last acceptable or respectable racism. Now that cannot continue. In the last couple of years, a series of attacks against Arabs resulting in the deaths of some have occurred. My office was vandalized and raided a year ago. I was visited by the FBI, and the raid was publicly noted. And the leader of one of these Jewish defense groups said in an interview, "As far as we're concerned, Said, anything goes." They have threatened me and others who speak up for Palestinian and Arab rights with death. That cannot be allowed to go on. That is not only racism but murder.

Unfortunately, a lot of respectable people cooperate and collaborate in this. You read in the pages of *The New Republic,* in *Commentary,* and in the more outrageous magazines to the right of them, the most horrible things about the natural depravity of the Arab, the crazed ways of Arab culture, the inability of Islam to tell the truth from falsehood. These are clichés of popular and public discourse. And that is a uniquely American phenomenon at this moment, and a terribly frightening one.

Are there any politicians now that you feel have a sense of both sides of the question?

I think Jesse Jackson does. The most likely place where you find a sense of compassion for Jewish suffering *and* our suffering and for groups in this country who have suffered is with the blacks, various Hispanic Latin groups, and women's groups. Some politicians in Congress—members of the Black Caucus, Paul McCloskey when he was there, Paul Findley when he was there—have made courageous and unusual statements about the Palestinians. But they are gone. The Congress now, almost to a man and woman, at the drop of a hat will vote any amount of aid to Israel without any questions asked. And they will take positions about Israel and the Middle East that are totally out of keeping with reality. And that includes the liberals, who are forthright in their condemnation of apartheid.

What is American policy in the Middle East?

You can describe it in two simple phrases: Combating terrorism and fighting communism—which add up to no policy at all. Is that a policy for the complexities and the tragedies and the density of conflict, history, and tradition of the Middle East? Obviously it isn't. It's simply no policy at all, and it's tragic.

Is there a connection between the Palestinians, Libya, and Moammar Quaddafi? Does he have any standing in the Palestinian world?

No. That is one of the greatest canards of all time. In 1982, he told Palestinians in Beirut they could commit suicide. He is one of the most extraordinarily unpopular figures in the Arab world. He's an indefensible man. But that isn't to say that he hasn't been very useful to this administration, in creating a kind of foreign devil, a scapegoat.

Has Yasir Arafat been a good envoy from Palestinians to the rest of the world?

There's no question that his image in the West is very bad. And he is highly controversial even among Palestinians, who tend to debate whether doing *this* as opposed to *that* was the right thing, and so on. In my opinion, he's a very complex and even tragic figure, because he has had to do a number of things that couldn't win—for example, the business of signing an agreement with Jordan. I feel he had to do it, although I also felt it was ill-conceived, that nothing would come of it, so it's a paradox.

But he has a major achievement: He has crystallized the notion of a Palestinian community despite dispersion. Don't forget that until he appeared as a crystallizing figure in the late 1960s and early 1970s, the Palestinians were a forgotten people. I mean they were *buried* in the refugee camps or in the poorer places like Tyre and Damascus. For every one of us, our identities and our histories were lost. And then this resurgence after 1967, the shaping of the notion of a Palestinian as somebody with an identity and a possible future really is his doing—along with the PLO and, of course, the people. He is a man of the people in that respect.

What leadership exists behind Arafat, in what might be the next generation?

That's the great question; I can't answer that. I'm so out of touch, because we're all scattered. Arafat is obviously the most visible, but there are people who have been around him historically, part of his group, the founding group of the PLO.

Nevertheless, institutions exist, and that impresses me. There are financial institutions, there are charitable institutions, and medical and educational ones, that still function. Palestinians are the great self-help community of the Third World. We are responsible for the education of our children despite dispossession and dispersion. The PLO until today supports the families of people who are killed—orphans and widows and family members. There's a huge welfare network, private and official, which keeps the community alive.

I am fifty-two. The people of my generation were children in 1948, but we had some experience of Palestine. Now there is a whole generation of people who grew up under occupation or exile, entirely without any direct contact with Palestine. There are 400,000 of them in Lebanon.

That's true also in Israel and in Palestine. In Israel now the next generation is all post-1967, as in Palestine. Does that mean greater chances for war rather than peace?

I don't really know. Over the last few years, really since 1982, I have detected a greater level of intransigence among young Palestinians. Take the schoolchildren of the West Bank today: They know nothing but the occupation. To them, they are alone and they've got to fight it. They are the ones who lead the fights against the Israeli troops, with rocks and burning tires and that sort of thing. Now, what kind of horizons such people have is a frightening question to contemplate.

That they are resilient, I have no doubt. That they will not sit up and just die, just say we are going to efface ourselves, we know also for a fact. But what political modalities this is going to lead to, I really don't know. It's a tormenting question.

Interview with Matthew Stevenson,
The Progressive, Madison, Wisconsin, 1987

SEVENTEEN

AMERICAN INTELLECTUALS
AND MIDDLE EAST POLITICS

With reports of Israeli repression and Palestinian resistance in the newspapers every day, the publication of Blaming the Victims: Spurious Scholarship and the Palestinian Question *seems especially timely. Would you say that there have been changes in the nature of resistance in the occupied territories?*

The scale of resistance is what is particularly impressive and new. There have been up to 3,500 to 4,000 recorded incidents a year in the last five years, that is since 1982. And certainly the level of Israeli reprisals and punishments and repressions has been fairly high all through. For example in October five or six people were killed in Gaza. That's not considered part of this particular round, which is supposed to have begun on the 9th of December. But the scale is impressive, as is the unity between the West Bank and Gaza on the ground. That is to say, there is some coordination. And obviously, between those two areas of the occupied territories and the Palestinians in pre-1967 Israel. The thing is also that hitherto there hasn't been any report whatever of armed resistance. It's been essentially unarmed resistance—rock-throwing, burning tires, barricades.

A couple of weeks ago the New York Times *permitted itself a certain sarcasm about the Israeli policy of dragging people out of their houses and breaking their bones. Do you find any cause for encouragement in the current climate of opinion in this country, any special opportunities for reversing the special apathy of the American Left where the Middle East is concerned? Do you think there are any indications that there's likely to be a break in the systematic campaign of silence and disinformation that you describe in the book?*

I think the best thing about the present moment is that a lot of people are taking note of the heroism of the Palestinians and their refusal to capitulate. And obviously their concerted and organized resistance, which is emerging in an unprecedented way. And I think a part of this is that a lot of the media—that is, the print media, the electronic media, and of course the radio—have been reporting the events, which in and of themselves are impressive on their own. Now the one thing that hasn't changed very much is the editorial opinion, which remains suspended between the right-wing Israeli position and the hypocritical and essentially right-wing American position. This is a long and complicated issue and it's probably worth going into it a little bit. A perfect example is to be found in *The New York Times,* where you have what I think is very good reporting by John Kifner, who's essentially a police reporter, and who's reporting the events on the ground, and tries to report them from the point of view of the demonstrators, which is something new. Parallel to him you have Thomas Friedman, who has been their correspondent in Jerusalem (I'm told he's leaving now). But he's been reporting all along. He gives the sophisticated Orientalist interpretation of the events, which uniformly comes out to be scandalously tendentious. He will argue for example that the problem with the Palestinians is that they haven't supplied Israel with a view of the future and therefore, by implication, deserve to be beaten up. That's a coarse paraphrase of his argument. Or that Palestinian women really want to be raped by Israeli soldiers. He's actually said such things, although he hides behind quotations from Israeli sources. So the analysis is always in a framework that is deeply hostile to the Palestinian national movement.

In addition to that there's been a tremendous amount of attention in this country paid to the "agony" of the Israeli soul or of Israeli supporters, that is to say the problem of the Palestinians is a problem for American Jews, which turns out to be apparently an image problem. Here are pictures that are profoundly unflattering to Israel of people wilfully beating up old women and children with clubs and rifle butts. So the image and soul problem has been very much bruited about. Then you have the so-called political line, which is that the Palestinians have in a certain sense, it is true, broken new ground in resistance and political opposition to Israel in the occupied territories, but all of this is a way of moving away from the PLO, which is after all discredited, it's in Tunis, it has nothing to say, and so on. There's an article like this by another *New York Times* reporter today, Youssef Ibrahim, who tries to argue that the PLO is marginal to the revolution. (A simple seven weeks later he reversed himself completely.) Ignoring the fact that every statement from the occupied territories has repeated the phrase that the PLO is representative of the Palestinian people and that they describe themselves on the West Bank and Gaza as the children of Arafat. Most American reporters can't deal with this fact. I was on a television program last week with Morton Kondracke of *The New Republic* and Daniel Pipes of *Orbis* magazine in which the whole thing for them was the problem of the PLO not accepting UN 242 and the recognition of Israel. I've met with many Israelis who've come to speak to me behind the scenes and say, "This is a very important time and we should try for a rapprochement with the PLO and yet what we need from the PLO is some statement about recognizing Israel." The irony of it is of course that we are the people who are the victims and we are the ones who are required to produce all kinds of statements to reassure the Israelis who are beating us up.

Then finally we come to the attitude of the American Left. Let me give you an indication that seems to me perfectly symbolic of its current state so far as the Middle East is concerned. For the last two and a half months, there has been a massive insurrection on the West Bank and in Gaza of a kind that hasn't been seen since the days of the Algerian experience. In fact many of the things that have taken place on the West Bank and in Gaza remind one of scenes from *The Battle of Algiers*. There have now been two issues of the new Left magazine called *Zeta*. There isn't a word about the uprising. Now I take this as symptomatic of the general attitude of the American Left. A combination of ignorance, piety toward the cant about Israel and its being a bastion of democracy and being a place for the remnant of the Holocaust has limited the reaction of the American Left both politically and intellectually to an astonishing degree. And when they do appear to say something, for example the letter signed by Irving Howe and Michael Walzer and Rabbi Hertzberg in *The New York Times* a couple of weeks ago, or the various comments made by other prominent people who appear to be troubled by the events on the West Bank and Gaza, it's always thought to be necessary formulaically to attack the Arabs politically. As Michael Lerner of *Tikkun* magazine said on a program where I appeared with him, this is the result of forty years of Arab intransigence, the terrorism of the PLO, and so on. The scandal of it, the hypocrisy, the violence implied in these comments, is nothing short of outrageous.

I've talked with many people on the American Left. Somehow they cannot bring themselves to focus on this. All the various discussions on the American Left—the meta-theoretical issues that come up, like the role of the intellectual, the role of the Left in American policy, and so on—couldn't be better illustrated than by the fact that the United States is after all what's making all this possible by virtue of the money we spend on Israel, by virtue of the political and military subsidies that we provide to the Israelis. And yet very little concerted action happens. This is the one place, it seems to me—along with the Nicaraguan case—where American intellectuals have a very direct role to play. And yet there's nothing there. I find it astonishing. The argument used to be that if those of us who were involved in anti-war, anti-imperialist, anti-interventionary policies linked these to Israel we would lose the support of many American Jews. But I don't think that's true. If on the one hand you say that we're against providing support to repressive regimes in Latin America and southern Africa and various parts of eastern Asia, what is the problem with saying that same thing from an internationalist perspective about Israel? Moreover, what I find even more peculiar is the way I'm told by members of the American Left, well, Israel is very bad, it's true, in what it's doing to the Palestinians, but look what the Syrians did to Hamah, they leveled the city, or look at what the Jordanians did to the Palestinians in 1970–71—as if in some way that excuses Israel for what it's doing. The argument seems to be that since Palestinians have been massacred by others, why shouldn't the Israelis have the right to do that too? So I find it very difficult to understand, principally because the question of Palestine is so implicated in many of the issues the Left has been so vociferous about.

Thinking of what you said about the media organizing this story—in terms of the "agony" of the local Jewish lobby—as a way of bringing this home to an American public which can only register these things if they are "brought home," it strikes me that there's some connection be-

tween that and a way in which you bring this material home to people, especially on the American Left but also to Americans generally. Events like these seem to come to us often from very far away. Part of the force of this book for American intellectuals, and one of the reasons why your work has generated so much excitement among American intellectuals, is in its contention that something like "scholarship"—I'm thinking of your subtitle—actually matters in things like this, that there is a battle also and significantly fought out on the terrain of information, vocabulary, imagery, and so on, that is on our home turf.

To my mind it's a unique case: the support for Israel in the West and especially in the U.S. among the Left in particular. Don't forget that in the early days, in the post-1948 period, the cause of Israel was in the case of Britain, essentially a Labor cause, and in the U.S. of the Democratic Party, and large segments of the independent American Left. The International League for Human Rights, Roger Baldwin, Reinhold Niebuhr, Norman Thomas, later Martin Luther King, all these people were very powerful advocates of a Jewish state. In time, the way discourse works, through the accumulation of information and sheer density of material, it was possible for the case to be built in such a way as to completely obscure the existence of a Palestinian presence. Dispossessed in the case of the refugees, oppressed and kept under in the case of the Palestinians who remained. Of course with 1967 the splits began to appear. Israel could no longer claim that it was a beleaguered state. And you get the famous rifts within the New University Politics, amongst Left intellectuals, and the blacks who are trying to draw analogies between what was happening in Africa and what was happening in the Middle East. And this has persisted in one way or another.

But the most interesting thing is that the beginnings of a kind of revisionist scholarship in Israel, after 1982 I think, have really received very little attention in this country: the work of people like Benny Morris, Tom Segev, and Simha Flapan, and so on. These are works by Israelis, works that it's possible to publish in this country. Take the case of Simha Flapan's book, *The Birth of Israel,* or Bennie Beit-Hallahmi's book on the Israeli arms connections with various dictatorships in the Third World. These books have scarcely been reviewed or paid much attention to. Whereas it seems to me that they provide extraordinarily interesting ways of extending what we already know about the Third World and the network of arms. Take also the case of Iran-contragate where the Israeli role was completely suppressed with the connivance of Senator Inouye and Michael Ledeen and others. Now I find it particularly fraught because any piece of information that comes out inevitably adds force to the picture of an Israel that has been in deliberate and one might even say programmatic violation of virtually everything that has been said either by or about Israel in the years after 1948. For example, Israel was thought always to have been in need of and wanting and waiting for an Arab interlocutor. We now have evidence provided by Israeli scholars that the Israelis received assurances from the major states, after 1948—Egypt, Jordan, Syria—that they wanted to conclude a peace with it, but the peace was turned down by Ben-Gurion programmatically. That the Palestinians were forced to leave, that they were not asked to stay, that the various efforts to restore some kind of modus vivendi in Israel for the Palestinians and Israel in the region—all these have been positions taken routinely by the Israelis, but suppressed in the U.S. And of course there's also been a systematic cover-up of the horrific things that have been done to Palestinians in the intervening years. What I'm trying to say is that it's not just the information, which is plentifully available now, both from the Israeli press, from the alternative scholars in this country, like Chomsky and Jane Hunter and others. The interesting thing is how little of this gets into circulation. As you read reports in the press, you keep trying to tell the reporter, journalist, or commentator, why not connect this with this other material that's there? That connection has never been made.

There's an extraordinary irony that comes out in the book about the difference between Israel and the United States. Take the famous case of "the broadcasts" [Arab radio broadcasts supposedly urging Palestinians to flee their homes in 1948], according to the Kidron article: that is a myth that has been abandoned in Israel and is still going strong in the U.S.! Or the Joan Peters case, exactly the same thing. One thing I wanted to ask you about is the irony that these things should be abandoned in Israel and still going strong in the U.S.; the other is what does it say about the standards of responsible scholarship in the U.S., that in these cases people have not even looked at the evidence—that one elementary act of what one thinks of as scholarship?

One thing that comes to mind is that people have often been stopped not by the first step but by what they believe to be the second step. That is to say, let us say that we discover that these broadcasts never took place, or that Israel has systematically refused to make peace in the region, principally because it wanted to expand its boundaries—it never really had an interest in defining its international boundaries and therefore turned away any peace offers; there's plentiful evidence for that. The problem has always been, if we find that out, what follows from it politically? It's somehow thought to be unacceptable because it would mean less support for Israel, that is to say amongst the American Left who feel that they are committed to it, as Jews if they happen to be Jewish or as people who feel something about the need for reparations to the Jews after World War II. And then the next question is, supposing it's true, what are we supposed to do about it? Can we deal with the cumulative history of injustice and hypocrisy that has in fact been there? It becomes very, very difficult, because there's so much that needs to be not only re-excavated but has to be forsworn. You have to say I was wrong, I lied, I connived, I was complicit. And that's a step that's very hard to take because, as we show in this book, so massive is the scale of lying and disinformation, or at least deliberately partial information, that people are often stopped. Whereas it would seem to me, speaking for myself, that there are a number of quite concrete gestures that could be made at this point that are much simpler than renouncing the whole past, and those include recognizing the need immediately for a restoration to the Palestinians of a fairly massive sort.

One conclusion you might draw is that, as Hayden White remarked a few years ago, the Palestinians need better narratives. I don't know whether this has been a consideration of yours, or whether it's a consideration that informs Blaming the Victims, *but when you see absolute neglect of empirical evidence in the way that you've just mentioned, because it can't be fit into a larger narrative, it makes you think that if critique is a negative model for intellectual activity, there might be a need for this alternative positive model, providing narratives that people could fit the information into.*

The narratives have been there. They're of a different sort. I don't think there's a kind of "grand narrative"; it's essentially not a Western narrative. The model of wandering and exile is available; I. F. Stone always says the Palestinians have become "the Jews of the Middle East."

But that's a borrowed narrative. There's the problem that it's after all an alien culture; it doesn't speak English, it doesn't resonate with Western myths. I've become aware of this as I've gotten older. There's a kind of stubborn and somehow uninformed refusal on the part of the Palestinians to accommodate easily. It's certainly been true in the Arab world; that's become symptomatic of the Palestinians. It's difficult to describe; it's almost epitomized in the appearance of Arafat; he doesn't correspond to any known notion of what a national leader should look like.

Isn't that creative rather than a refusal . . . ?

You could say that it's creative. That's one way of looking at it. But that's at least a way of explaining the absence of an easily manageable narrative. After all, this is a narrative that always has to compete with a very powerful, already existent narrative of resurgent nationalism of the retributive kind, of the sort that one associates with Zionism. So on a lot of fronts there are formal problems. Then there's the tactical problem of where's this narrative to be formed? Because the Palestinians are locked into the "Arab" (so-called) narrative, and that's usually tied into oil, and the Arabian Nights, and a whole set of other myths, on the one hand. And on the other, in the West it's virtually impossible for the narrative to be located hospitably in any set of allied or counter-narratives. Because it keeps coming up against these problems we've mentioned. The only place where it's now appeared of course is in television news—the rock-thrower, without a history, without a name, without a face. . . . Just like the man who came over in the hang glider, you remember, who killed six Israeli soldiers. He was never even named. Most of these kids are never given names. Although we Palestinians publish them and they're perfectly available. The list of the dead in Gaza, killed by the Israelis, the hands broken, are never published in the West because they don't have a place here.

A third alternative for a narrative emerges here and there in the strangest places, like Peter Wollen's film *Friendship's Death*. Or in a remarkable new Palestinian film, *Wedding in Galilee* by Michel Khleifi. They're so programmatically eccentric and alternative that you can't think of them as partaking in the general economy of the grand narratives that we live by. And fourth and probably most important, the notion of Palestinian liberation is still unclear in the minds of many, even the Palestinians themselves, who want to be recognized, but recognized for what? This is self-criticism. The question of how we accommodate with the Jews of Israel is still uncertain. There's no formula for this. It can obviously only be done with the Jews, who have so far shown, with few exceptions, little interest in it. It's the teleology that's both missing here, and is difficult to imagine. Hence the attenuation of the narrative.

One of the book's most striking examples of the battle on the home turf of intellectuals, a battle over vocabulary, is its polemic in pieces both by you and by Noam Chomsky, against the abusive concept of terrorism. The lack of any critical reaction in the United States to, say, the Israeli bombing of Tunis or the U.S. bombing of Libya, to take two examples among many, suggests that this is an uphill fight. How do you win acceptance for a counter-term like "state terrorism"? What are your ideas on this?

That's where I disagree with Chomsky. I find the use of the word terrorism in almost any context, whether you use it as the media and the apologists have used it—as a way of creating and then attacking foreign devils—or as a label to apply to the state violence of the United States, Israel, etc., to be a largely self-defeating tactic.

It's an "ism" we should just get rid of?

I think so, but not without carefully deconstructing it beforehand. I think Hitchens has been right about this. The use of the word terrorism is usually unfocused, it usually has all kinds of implicit validations of one's own brand of violence, it's highly selective. If you accept it as a norm, then it becomes so universally applicable that it loses any force whatever. I think it's simply better to drop it. I prefer the use of the word violence, which allows for notions of different types of violence. What I've tried to do in a piece I've done since this book appeared is to look at terrorism, as well as the discourse and rhetoric and tropes of terrorism, as part of what I call the "politics of identity." These emanate out of the various identitarian forces in the nationalist world where patriotism, to be seen for example in the reinforcement of the curriculum in America of all this about "Western values," "Judaeo-Christian values," are part of the economy that creates the limitlessly expanding discourse of terrorism, by which things "we" do not like are identified with terrorism. Therefore I think it's better not to talk about terrorism and show that we're really not the terrorists or "they" really are the terrorists; rather it is better to show terrorism as having a historical semantics which connects it with other processes in society with which we can interact oppositionally, so as to prevent violence against unarmed civilians and to eliminate the causes of desperate and irrational terror. Terrorism today is so nebulous a concept, has become so infected—almost as a business concept: there are, after all, terrorism experts, handbooks on terrorism, many many books, courses on terrorism, programs. It's a situation I don't think one ought to encourage by entering the fray. Rather, give alternatives to the notion and locate it in something else, for example, in the violence produced by the politics of identity, of nationalism, of exaggerated patriotism, etc.

While we're on the subject of terrorism: as an intellectual who's also active in a cause branded by many as terrorist by definition, I wonder whether you've ever felt that there's some affinity between the two terms in the American consciousness, that is between the intellectual and the terrorist, two alien figures which, at least in the terms of American anti-intellectualism, seem to blend into one another.

Partly because of the affinity you mention between the two terms, which is obviously a hidden affinity though an affinity nonetheless, I've noticed that among the Left the use of the word intellectual has fallen into disrepute and disuse. And what instead has appeared are words like professional and scholar and academic. And the use of the word intellectual has been relegated to some pre-modern realm, partly because the intellectual as a concept suggests something rather more general than something concrete. If you want to keep Foucault's use of the word—he distinguishes between a general and a specific intellectual—than it might come back into currency. But it hasn't. And people have been much happier I think with the notion of a technical expert or the academic or the professional or the critic—a word with much more positive valences than the intellectual. I think it's partly because of the general refusal of American Left intellectuals to accept their political role, their general unhappiness with the real world of history and politics.

It's been of course deliberate state policy in Israel both to expel local leaders from the occupied territories and to deny the representativeness of the PLO. Lately in this country you've had something very similar with the effort to close the PLO mission at the United Nations. . . .

. . . and the information office in Washington.

One could take this as an attack on the idea of the representative in-

tellectual, in fact a kind of undermining of the notion of the intellectual by deliberate state policy. One wonders, when you also have within the academy, or that part of the academy that's influenced by so-called literary theory, an erosion of the concept of the representative intellectual, one wonders whether these two movements are not in some way related to one another, and whether we might have to draw some kind of conclusion: to put it schematically, whether this concept needs to be defended a lot more than it needs to be undermined right now.

It probably ought to be looked at within the context of the general suspicion of representation, the whole problematic of representation. It is assumed that there's a kind of, not so much inauthenticity, but ideological deformation taking place whenever representation is at issue. Thus the notion of the representative intellectual strikes a chord of antipathy because there's assumed to be something constitutively false and deconstructable in it, so that nobody wants to venture into that place. If you refuse to occupy the position of representative intellectual, that makes it possible to occupy the kind of Archimedean position of the critic, who's always outside the group, who doesn't represent anything, but is a force for skepticism. I wouldn't want necessarily to leave aside from our discussion the profound effect on all of this of people like Derrida and de Man, who have contributed very much to the disrespect and distrust for the discourse of politics as something by which people live, constitute themselves, fight, die, etc. This kind of suspicion, this hovering on the margins, this infatuation with the undecidable and the ironic, it's all part of this. One can only look at it as a formation of late capitalism in the American academy.

Before we get too far away from terrorism I just want to ask you one more question. I know that when the Reverend Benjamin Weir was a hostage in Lebanon he read some of your works, in Arabic I think . . .

No, it was in English.

And he appreciated them very much, as he has said. I wonder, if you can put your modesty aside for a minute, if you think there's any message in this experience—exactly the sort of thing one doesn't hear about hostages in the American media—for those who are interested in deconstructing the discourse of terrorism.

Well, it's not only Weir and his story, which you repeated, but also Jeremy Levin of CNN, who was a hostage and escaped. He has become an active partisan of the Palestinians, but also of the general adversarial attitude to U.S. policy in the region. Of course it could be put down as just an example of the "Stockholm syndrome," the man who's fallen in love with his captors. But these are people who underwent not a "conversion" but a really quite dramatic change in their perception and have become rather active in trying to understand the ramifications and unforeseen results of U.S. policy as a policy which is not benign and altruistic but which has far-reaching effects on the lives of ordinary people. There are others, too. Take Pauline Cutting, this remarkable British physician who went to Beirut and worked in the camps of Sabra and Shatila as a physician. During the war of the camps (1985–88), she would be broadcasting from Sabra and Shatila when they were besieged by the Amal militia, and she said, "They are now eating cats and dogs. They are on the verge of cannibalism." So horrific were conditions during the siege. This is a British physician who volunteered to go in; she knew nothing about Palestine. It was through a Malaysian friend, I think, that she went. She came back and she wrote this book called *Children of the Siege* which is the number two bestseller in Britain. She cannot find an American publisher for the book. So there are cases like that. The question is how little effect their voices have had on the general discourse of terrorism, which continues to characterize Palestinians and others as terrorists.

A question about Foucault and Gramsci as providing paradigms of the intellectual. You've written about both, and I know both of them have been quite important to you. I wonder whether you find both oppositions—that is, between the specific and the universal intellectual in Foucault and between the organic and the traditional intellectual in Gramsci—equally useful, and whether in your own thinking you find they contradict or complement each other.

Insofar as a lot of people have taken those to be absolute distinctions between two kinds of intellectuals in both cases, intellectuals who are more or less reified in their position, I think they're not very useful. If they're conceded to be only analytic distinctions, then I think they're interesting in a kind of momentary way, especially the general/specific distinction made by Foucault. The organic/traditional duality proposed by Gramsci I think is interesting only in one way. I think it's perfectly possible—and I think Gramsci intended it this way, as a close reading of the notebooks suggests—that the traditional intellectual had once been an organic intellectual. The cycle is what is interesting about it. All classes have intellectuals who organize their interests. Once the class has achieved a certain stability, whether by acquiring power or adjacence to power, then the conversion of the organic intellectual into the traditional intellectual is almost a foregone conclusion. But Gramsci leaves open the possibility that the traditional intellectual can also become an organic intellectual once again. He gives an instance in his essay on the Southern Question of the writer and editor Gobetti, you may remember, who was a traditional intellectual who had turned himself into an organic intellectual. So I think that's a very central and important set of distinctions and dynamic relationships.

To go back to Foucault: the specific/general distinction he makes is interesting except in the light of his later work when one begins to see that perhaps what he had intended as a legitimization of the specific intellectual turns into a kind of antecedent for his (to my mind) exclusive interest in the constitution of the self and subjectivity. If you look carefully at his analysis of specific intellectuals, it isn't that the specific intellectual only masters a particular field and has a discrete competence, but also that the specific intellectual has a particular subjectivity which is constructed as part of his or her selfhood and therefore legitimates the notion of selfhood in a particular context or setting. That is to say, Foucault already seems to be moving toward the politics of subjectivity, which becomes of course the subject of his later work, in which I find a falling off of interest. Insofar as the specific intellectual is a retreat from the world of the general, of the historical, of the social, it's an antipolitical position for Foucault to be supporting, and an invidious distinction. Most often it isn't perceived that way, of course; Foucault has achieved the status of a classic and remains an extraordinary figure.

One of your own very influential coinages has been the term "affiliation," which proposes a possible model for the intellectual's relation to a constituency or collectivity. Another term which has had an equal effect is "worldliness." I wonder whether these two terms say the same thing in different ways, or whether there are significant differences in emphasis.

Worldliness orginally meant to me, at any rate, some location of oneself or one's work, or the work itself, the literary work, the text, and so on, in the world, as opposed to some extra-worldly, private, ethereal context. Worldliness was meant to be a rather crude and bludgeon-like term to enforce the location of cultural practices back in the mundane, the quotidian, and the secular. Affiliation is a rather more subtle term that has to do with mapping and drawing connections in the world between practices, individuals, classes, formations—that whole range of structures that Raymond Williams has studied so well in books like *The Long Revolution* and *The Country and the City*. Above all affiliation is a dynamic concept; it's not meant to circumscribe but rather to make explicit all kinds of connections that we tend to forget and that have to be made explicit and even dramatic in order for political change to take place.

Since you mention Raymond Williams, he makes an interesting distinction, as I'm sure you know, between alignment and commitment, the latter being more intentional. Alignment is what you're stuck with. I wonder whether you could locate "affiliation" in relation to that distinction.

The point is of course about intention. If you want to put it in a Freudian context, it's the move from unaware alignment to active commitment that he's interested in, the bringing of social relationships to consciousness.

I didn't ask my question well. I guess I always wondered how much intention there was in affiliation, how close it was to alignment and how close it was to commitment.

Oh, I see. That's a tough one. Well, I suppose it's closer to the notion of alignment than it is to commitment. It has also to do with larger degrees of involuntary association and unconscious (or sometimes hypocritically concealed) association, complicity, and so forth than it does with active commitment. The problem of commitment is a very difficult one. It's not difficult in England, where there's a settled political tradition. Here, the notion of commitment is necessarily tactical. There is really no discourse of the Left here. There is no Left formation of any sort, unless you think the Democratic Party is the Left. So the notion of commitment becomes a very difficult one to use. That's why it struck me as not possible to employ it in the American context, except within a very limited compass.

In your critique of Michael Walzer in Blaming the Victims, *you demonstrate the political cost of his notion of belonging, and you also suggest that "critical distance and intimacy with one's people" need not be "mutually exclusive." It seems to me that this suggestion answers those critics who've accused you of erecting marginality and exile into an exclusive principle of intellectual activity. In the U.S., some leftists may be more willing to tolerate Walzer's emphasis than they should be because there's a sort of perceived relative deprivation of community. We feel that we need this more than countries like England. I wonder whether you yourself see the struggle to change American policy toward Palestine as requiring the building of new solidarities, as well as the critique of old ones.*

There are two very important issues here. I'll start with the second. The changing of our policy toward Palestine doesn't necessarily involve, in my opinion, building new forms of solidarity. All I'm asking for at this point is honesty—to apply a rigorously honest and international standard to discourse about the Middle East, the same standard that one would like to apply to writing about Central America. That's where the big gap has been. People who find it very easy to support the Sandinista revolution or to support the ANC in South Africa have said absolutely nothing about the parallel case of the Palestinians in the Middle East. So that's one very important point. The second point is that I think, unless I'm forgetting here, that I attack Walzer on this point about intimacy and belonging because of where he got it from. He got it from the Algerian connection. It was an attempt to revalorize, as he said, Camus's choice of his mother over "terrorism." What I found wrong with this— as most of the time when justifications for morally fallible and hypocritical choices are advanced—is that there's a factual inaccuracy at the base of it (you will note that I have no trouble talking about the factual). He was making it seem as if all of his life, Camus considered himself an Algerian and supported the demands of Algerian independence, and it was only when he was asked to choose between the terrorism of the FLN and his mother's life, that he in the end chose the community of the *pieds noirs*. That's a factual lie. I've studied it—the whole case of Algeria is a very interesting one—and it's true that in his early writings on Algeria Camus condemned French colonialism. But he condemned colonialism the same way Conrad condemned colonialism in Africa. Conrad condemned the abuses of the Belgians, and he condemned a little bit the excesses and the pretensions of the English, but he saw no alternative to colonialism. He said that this is the fate of this continent and this people, to be colonized by—I'm putting it crudely—their betters. And in fact when it came to writing about the existence of an Algerian nation, a separate Algerian nation that should not be colonized by France, of an Algerian-Muslim people, Camus always denied its existence, in exactly the way in fact Walzer and his cohorts have denied the existence of a Palestinian nation. Camus is explicit on this point. If you look at his *Chroniques Algériennes,* he says, "*Il n'y a pas de nation algérienne. Ça n'existe pas.*" Which is to say that this entire nation, which has been "underdeveloped," to say the least, milked, abused, exploited by France for 130 years, didn't constitute a nation in the eyes of this Frenchman of Algiers. And therefore he chose his mother. All of this background Walzer removes from the account. So to say it's a matter of belonging is simply to overlook what kind of belonging it is. There's belonging, and then there's belonging. One can certainly belong to communities in ways that don't always involve rapacity, exploitation, and the denial of equal rights to other communities.

That's the second point. The third point I want to make is that I never said anything about rootlessness and exilic marginality as excluding the possibility of, shall we say, sympathetic—I'm using a very simple word —sympathetic identitification with a people suffering oppression. Especially when the oppression is caused by one's own community or one's own polity. The example I always give is the example of a comparatist. You and I have comparatist backgrounds. The credo of Auerbach, this exiled German Jew in Istanbul during World War II, citing Hugo of St. Victor, strikes me as a very different thing from saying, on the other hand, one must celebrate wandering exilic marginality. There's a kind of exilic existence which involves the crossing of barriers, the traversing of borders, the accommodation with various cultures, not so much in order to belong to them but at least so as to be able to feel the accents and inflections of their experience. As the antithesis of Camus in Algiers, there is Genet. Genet was the man who was able in fact to rise above this French identity, to identify in *Les Paravents* with the Algerians and in his last and, some say, his greatest work, *Le Captif Amoureux,* with the Palestinians. This was a remarkable act of self-exile and repatriation in another's homeland. That's the point. Walzer seems to have missed all of that.

To some extent the discourse of exile seems to stand in the way of articulating the Palestinian problem as a problem specifically for Americans, even though of course as you were saying a few minutes ago Israel depends so absolutely on American support. I'm thinking of what I call the "Little Drummer Girl" syndrome. In the film that was made of the le Carré novel both sides of the Middle East conflict, Israeli and Palestinian, can be respected as "authentic," while the European or American, the Diane Keaton figure, in the film, who affiliates herself with a foreign cause, someone else's cause, is judged to be transgressing and is systematically broken and humiliated by the movie. In your experience trying to win a place on the leftist agenda for the Palestinian people, have you found any such "jargon of authenticity" to function as an obstacle? Is the fact that action presents itself to the American Left as a sort of shopping list of foreign causes (South Africa, El Salvador, Nicaragua, and so on) an issue that can or should be tackled explicitly?

What I think you're saying is that, whereas it's okay for the Palestinians and the Israelis on the one hand to feel strongly about what they stand for, the problem with Diane Keaton, with the little drummer girl, is that she feels she can identify with one or the other and thereby transgresses her own identity.

That's the way the film represents anyone who would, not being Palestinian or Israeli, affiliate him or herself with such a cause: that person is inauthentic. In other words, there's no room for the articulation, which is so necessary to this particular case.

I see your point. There are two things to be said—both of them about the le Carré novel, which I read at the time it appeared (I didn't see the film). One is that the novel conceals what is in fact an ideology of the outside observer who can negotiate the claims of the two people. It is the prerogative of the Western white overlord who could stand outside and see and adjudicate the conflicts between these two warring rabbits, the two small parties. Of course Charlie's mistake is to go from one camp to the other in whole solidarity with one at the expense of the other. The critique of that is that one should stand above those camps: that is proper role of the Western referee/umpire. I felt at the time that this book was in fact a vindication of Western imperialism. Whereas of course by many Israelis it was taken—given of course le Carré's writing about the war in 1982, when he wrote for *The Observer*, in sympathy with the Palestinians—it was taken to be a sympathetic account of the Palestinians. But in fact, in the structure of the book and its epistemology, there really is a legitimization of the outside disinterested observer who could only be male, white, Western, and WASP, and who is entitled to this perspective.

Number two: the other side of it is that there is assumed to be a kind of symmetry here, which "we" on the outside can perceive. Whereas from my point of view, I see the artificiality of the perspective of symmetry and balance which you find in le Carré, in the *MacNeil/Lehrer Report,* in the use of words like "objective" and "balanced" and all the rest of it, that people adopt in the discourse of American political science and governmental expertise. It's fundamentally flawed because in any conflict, it seems to me—and this is another problem that I have with Walzer—there's a question of justice, of right and wrong, comparatively speaking of course. The major task—I say this actually without any qualification whatever—the major task of the American or the Palestinian or the Israeli intellectual of the Left is to reveal the disparity between the so-called two sides, which appear rhetorically and ideologically to be in perfect balance but are not in fact. To reveal that there is an oppressed and an oppressor, a victim and a victimizer, and unless we recognize that, we're nowhere. We'll endlessly be going around looking for formulas the way the United Nations and American diplomats are always looking for the right formula.

One idea that has been much repeated in conversations about intellectuals and their relation to collectivity, especially among feminists, is the necessity to accept "the risk of essence," a phrase associated with Gayatri Spivak and Stephen Heath. Does that formulation have any resonance for you? Does it seem at all generalizable or useful in the case of the Palestinians?

As I understand "the risk of essence," it means the insistence on the nativist essence in a national or gender struggle. There's a very good point here. The history of modern and indeed pre-modern nationalism suggests that the telos of nationalism is the fundamental reinforcement of a kind of native identity which becomes tyrannical in the end and of course dissolves or occludes important questions as well as issues of class, race, gender, and property. In my opinion, on the other hand, there is no way around the fact that struggles such as those of the Palestinians and other oppressed people, struggles that have to do with the attempt on the part of their oppressors to exterminate them—I don't mean physically only, but in an ethnic sense, to destroy the essence of the Palestinian, to make the Palestinian an "Arab" again or to drive them out, or any of these things associated not merely with Kahane but with elements of the Labor Left, who say the Palestinians can go somewhere else—in this context, there's no substitute therefore for the struggle for identity. But I think that the struggle for nativist identity must always be linked to a further perspective leading to liberation, the perspective offered by people like C. L. R. James and other anti-nativist critics like him for whom I have great respect. On the one hand you want the right to represent yourself, to have your own ethos and ethnos, but unless they are linked, on the other hand, to a wider practice which I would call liberation, beyond national independence—liberation that would include attacking the question of the relationships between classes, between other "tribes" if you like—then I'm totally against it. It seems to me a violently dangerous and awful trap. Nowhere is this more evident than in the Israeli case. And to a lesser degree, in the case of the Lebanese Christians.

One last question. After the Last Sky *was a much less overtly political book, though it also offers, in a somewhat different literary mode, a sort of "profile" of the Palestinian people. What response have you had to it, and do you expect or hope for a different kind of response to* Blaming the Victims?

The response I've had to *After the Last Sky* has been on the whole very good. People have read it; it's sold respectably—obviously not well—and it was well reviewed and frequently analyzed with precision, tact, and interest. It was meant to be a personal book and it was meant to be a collaborative effort with Jean Mohr, a man I admire—specifically an outsider, a non-Palestinian photographer, whose pictures had struck a rather profound chord for me. And it was meant to be a book written out of exile. Because I realized in the end that I could only use the pictures to connect myself with Palestine, because I couldn't go there and actually see the places or the people that he had photographed. On the other hand *Blaming the Victims* is meant to be a book that should hopefully stir debate and challenge political perceptions and processes in a fairly massive way. I feel without having much evidence at the moment that, in the mainstream culture, it will not be as discussed or re-viewed as *After the Last Sky* because it advances theses that are terribly difficult to deal with. [Note added May 1988: The first printing sold out in two months in both the U.S. and U.K.] I'm sure, for example, that *The New York Times* will not review it. Neither will *The New York Review of Books,* etc. But I'm hoping that it will become a kind of tool kit for further discussion on some of these issues. There was nothing foreseen about its time of publication, its moment, which is quite uniquely con-junctural. But I hope that it will be useful in that way. And to judge by the response I've had from a lot of people—I'm not talking about jour-nalists or the media—which on the whole has been pretty good about it, it seems to me not an entirely unhopeful sign.

Interview with Bruce Robbins,
Social Text, Duke University Press,
Durham, North Carolina, 1998

EIGHTEEN

THE NEED FOR SELF-APPRAISAL

This interview appeared simultaneously in English and in Arabic. It was the first time I took so critical and public a stand against the PLO, and it presaged my later break with them. Others, of course, had criticized Arafat from a party point of view. Mine was done from the standpoint of an independent intellectual. E.W.S.

Before we begin this interview, I would like first to make the following remark about the need for self-appraisal. My opinions must be viewed as part of the effort to back the Palestinian stand and the PLO as the sole, legitimate representative of the Palestinian people. Therefore, I am not speaking as an outsider. I am part of the PLO, I took part in the long struggle which led us to the Algiers declaration. But I am worried because we are beginning to lose the things for which we have sacrificed a great deal. It is this concern which has driven me to say what I want to say. The aim or criticism from within rather than from without.

The U.S. Government justifies its acts by saying that it is under the pressure of Israeli supporters to halt the dialogue and curtail the PLO's activities in the United States. Hence, it takes such measures. Where do the limits of the Israeli pressure end—and specifically the role of AIPAC (the American-Israel Public Affairs Committee)? Where do U.S. excuses begin?

It is common knowledge that AIPAC is the Israeli lobby in this country. It is an extremely influential lobbying force and is capable of imposing its will on the U.S. government. Nevertheless, it is possible to confront it and resist it. . . . Their objective is to defend Israel's interests. These interests are firstly, to supply financial aid and provide unlimited political support for Israel; and secondly, to prevent the Palestinians from having their right to self-determination. . . .

What impact does this [AIPAC's] measure [to halt the dialogue and deny Arafat entry visas] have on the U.S.–PLO dialogue?

My reply is that ignorance is not an excuse. The PLO has been participating in UN activities constantly since 1974. It has had the chance to study the state of affairs in the United States. . . . The question I would like to pose is the following. When will the PLO try to use the resources that are available to it to deal with the United States in a serious and confrontational manner? I would like to repeat the following: The United States is not the great white father. It is not an arbitrator. It is a party to the conflict and supports Israel. Without U.S. support, Israel cannot pursue its barbaric practices, its massacres, and the human rights violations which we now witness in the West Bank and the Gaza Strip.

In my opinion, it is a tragic mistake to place ourselves at the mercy of the United States and some pro-Israeli elements in this country who claim they are interested in a dialogue between Israel and the PLO. There are many persons, organizations, and institutions in the United States that support Palestinian rights. These forces should be mobilized. Instead of doing this, the PLO unfortunately, depends on persons who claim to be friends, who, in reality, represent other interests and objectives. These are the brokers and intermediaries between the Palestinian struggle and the American people. I believe this is a gross mistake.

U.S. officials say that the Palestinian–U.S. dialogue has produced no tangible results. How do you assess this dialogue and where do you think it is going?

. . . These meetings have not served our interests. When we ask questions about U.S. policy, we do not get replies. Most of the time, the meetings have taken place at the U.S.'s request, not ours. We must learn to deal with the United States the same way the Vietnamese dealt with Henry Kissinger in Paris and the same way the Algerians dealt with the French. This is not a match between a child and an adult. It is a struggle between two parties, between two adversaries, who are involved in a real conflict; one party, the Palestinian people, is struggling for its rights while the other parties, the United States and Israel, are working to suppress Palestinian rights. That's why one must view this issue very carefully and seriously.

The dialogue is not based on a complete, serious, and detailed knowledge of American society and its relationship with American policy, a correct understanding of the available resources in this country, and knowing how to mobilize them. For example, as far as I know, we have not embarked on a planned campaign to reveal to the world what the United States is trying to achieve through the dialogue sessions. We should reveal how the U.S. side is expressing, without shame, Israeli concerns without dealing with any of our concerns. We must reveal this to the press. All that we see in the United States are reports issued by the Americans and Israelis saying that they are not satisfied because the United States is holding a dialogue with the PLO or because the PLO is not responding positively to U.S. requests. There are no attempts to explain the Palestinian stand to the outside world. I am speaking about this country. They believe that we are a stubborn and silent people who have nothing to say. I believe that this is a horrible distortion of the Palestinian mind.

Is this a call to stop the dialogue?

No. I have always believed that dialogue is a good thing and I support it. I supported the Algiers resolutions. I have always believed in the solution based on two states. I have called for this for years. And this is a firm stand. I believe that in the end we will reach a formula through which the two states and peoples can live side by side on the same land. I completely agree on this. However, I worry because we misunderstand this complicated and difficult situation. And our dealings with this situation are based on weakness. We are incapable of using our stands and achievements represented by the *intifada* effectively. This is our mistake.

The Israeli and U.S. governments are our enemies. Logically, what we do must be on the same level of what they do as enemies. We cannot say: Please speak to us. There is a big difference. Anyhow, we are weaker; we do not have a strategic ally or enough armed forces. We have a brave and creative people who have an unlimited commitment to the struggle against the occupation in the West Bank and Gaza. This is our basic resource. In order to use this resource we must have representatives and a representation that reflects this fairly so as to convey this reality to the American arena. And this has not been achieved so far.

The two basic arenas of the Palestinian struggle today are the Occupied Territory and the United States. Nothing has been achieved in the United States. You have been in New York for one week; have you heard any Palestinian voice? Have you seen Palestinian representatives on television? Have you seen any announcements or writings? Have you seen demonstrations? The silence is deafening. . . .

The time has come to ask a question about Palestinian activity in the United States. Why has the United States become an arena where the small Palestinian shops fight among each other over the spoils? This is not beneficial and no use for us in places like Washington, Boston, San Francisco, and one or two places in New York. Why is this allowed to become an alternative for the tremendous political and national duty—that is, the issue of cleverly and logically presenting the Palestinian cause in the United States—because in the final analysis we will succeed if we do that the right way.

. . . There are many institutions in this country, universities, cities, professional unions, and numerous community sectors which support us completely. However, they have never been mobilized, exploited, or asked to do anything. Everything is arranged between Tunis and Washington behind closed doors. They come here, leave, and that is the end of it. Our need for a Palestinian presence in the United States should be coordinated and studied accurately—an intelligent and resistive presence, coordinated and planned for strategically. This presence should be at the forefront of our priorities of activity; otherwise, we will not reap the rewards of our West Bank and Gaza Strip people's brave struggle. Their deaths will be useless. Here is what the PLO should do: it should organize the U.S. arena and deal with it seriously; otherwise, it will be left to coincidences and individual efforts.

. . . As I said, the dialogue must not stop, and it should be broadened. We must employ pressure—the pressure of the dialogue—in the service of our objectives. For example, as of now the PLO is officially considered a terrorist organization. In light of the existence of this dialogue, we must refuse to hold talks with the United States until our status in this country changes from a terrorist organization to that of a political organization or a national authority. Thus, all factors of give-and-take, pressure and bargaining must be employed in this case. We simply cannot sit there in Tunis and listen to the U.S. ambassador repeating the Israeli position for us.

The United States is not merely a curious onlooker. It is a party to the conflict and it gives Israel over U.S.$4 billion a year. The money Israel requests to settle the Soviet Jews will come from taxes paid by the U.S. citizen. The PLO has not issued any statement on this subject although it has been known for the past five years that the problem of Soviet

Jewry's immigration will be resolved through settlement in the West Bank and Gaza. Until now, we have not taken a stand in this regard.

How can we read the U.S. stand toward the Israeli elections plan and the role of the so-called Egyptian points?

I think the objective is to end the *intifada*. There is a difference in political viewpoints between President George Bush's administration and the Likud on how to achieve this. Shamir simply wants to halt U.S. progress on the right to self-determination, but the Americans are eager to have this achieved with the least possible damage. However, they admit the existence of a reality which the Likud denies.

Therefore, the Egyptian-sponsored negotiations among Yasir Arafat, Hosni Mubarak, and Shimon Peres are particularly important because they deepen the differences inside the Israeli government and the United States. On that basis, they are good but not good enough. More is required. What is required is to further publicize the Israeli occupation in the media, through politics, and through U.S. society in general.

Therefore, our main task must be to emphasize the illegitimacy of the Israeli occupation of the West Bank and Gaza. This must be our first priority. The occupation of the West Bank and Gaza is only possible because of U.S. aid. This is the simple issue. And, if this is not understood by a larger number of people in the United States, we will never be able to win the tactical and political battles which are now being fought. . . .

Clearly, you do not believe in a military option against the occupation. But can the Palestinians get rid of the occupation through political and diplomatic activity?

Yes, they can do that, but only if they use all the means provided them. Here, I am talking about the United States. I cannot discuss what is happening in the West Bank because I do not live there. However, if we do not view our task as one of struggle in which all the resources at our disposal are used—the mental, political, moral, and representational—we will have no hope in succeeding because we are locked in conflict with very strong enemies. However, even strong enemies can be defeated, as the *intifada* has defeated the Israeli occupation.

. . . We face a difficult task and perhaps it is the most difficult task we have faced so far. Contrary to the situation with the French and Americans, we do not face an ordinary enemy. We confront Israel's Jews representing the survivors of the Holocaust. There, they have a special moral situation. We should understand this situation, appreciate it, and deal with it seriously. In addition, they enjoy the support of the most important military and economic power in the world today. This power is determined to support them. . . .

How do you view Soviet positions toward the Palestine question in light of "glasnost" and do you see any worrying signs?

Soviet policy based on "glasnost" is about easing the tension of the Cold War. As you know, I am not an expert on these matters, but my impression is that the Soviet retreat in general from extending support to its allies in Third World countries covers all fronts. The Soviets have withdrawn from Cuba, Namibia, Nicaragua, and Afghanistan to some extent. All this is part of the new Soviet–U.S. relationship. My impression is that our situation has been weakened by this Soviet policy. I have no doubt that the interests of the two superpowers differ from those of the small nations which struggle to realize their right to self-determination. Consider, for example, how successful the Israeli pressure on the United States is. Israel pressures the United States to pressure the Soviet Union into allowing more Jews to emigrate to Israel rather than any other place. This campaign has succeeded and will cost us much because these Jews want to settle in the West Bank and Gaza Strip. Therefore, we have to deal with these issues.

How do you view the controversy raised by the question of issuing a visa to Yasir Arafat and the U.S. position on that issue?

The argument about whether he will obtain a visa or not is humiliating us as a nation. If I were Arafat, I would put an end to this by saying that I would visit the United States only if I were officially invited. But to continue this public comedy about the issue of a visa will harm our people. . . .

Interview with Hisham Melhem,
The Dawn/Al-Fajr, Karachi, Pakistan, 1990

NINETEEN

A FORMULA FOR
MORE HUSSEINS

This discussion took place at the time of the Gulf War. E.W.S.

There have been a number of press accounts of Palestinians and other Arab peoples rallying in support of Saddam Hussein.

Palestinians are not fools, and Saddam Hussein is not seen as their savior. What is ballyhooed as Palestinian enthusiasm for Hussein is an expression of frustration and hopelessness at the situation decreed on us by Israel and the United States. Every Palestinian knows that a tyrant and a reckless adventurer and a man whose record in the Arab world is frightening cannot represent any hope for Palestinians. Moreover, every Palestinian with sense knows that if his threats to retaliate against Israel with chemical weapons are carried out, they will kill at least as many Palestinians as Israelis. So we are not particularly grateful.

However, the defiance of Saddam, which is both stupid and deplorable, nevertheless allows people the chance to speak up for an Arab world which is characteristically disregarded, save for its oil.

But there isn't an Arab who isn't tremendously alarmed, dismayed, and petrified by what is likely to take place. People I've spoken with by phone in Saudi Arabia are horrified by what has been visited on them by Iraq and the U.S. The dislocation and relocation of homes and families is considerable. All through the Arab world, people are fleeing.

How do you gauge the reaction to the American intervention?

You don't bring in a midsize American city, as Bush put it, without causing some tremors. Even the people most against Saddam are not filled with great joy at the prospect of the U.S. destroying Iraq. The U.S. moved too quickly and too challengingly. An Arab solution ensuring a full withdrawal might have taken place.

Accordingly, each of the rulers who sent troops (which is the result of rigorous American pressure), with the possible exception of Hassan of Morocco, is going to be challenged in his own country. The Saudis are in a tough position. It is in their interest to pry open some breathing space, to see if some other modality besides a massive military confrontation will work. The PLO is undertaking this, as are the Jordanians and the Egyptians, in their tarnished way. Arabs aren't sitting back with hands folded watching war come. They are desperately trying to rescue the situation.

In what way?

One might be an announcement from the Saudis that they are willing to let an Arab force stand between the Americans and the Iraqis. A second would be a discussion to resolve the disputes between Iraq and Kuwait, leading to a withdrawal from Kuwait. No one in the Arab world expects the annexation of Kuwait to be permanent.

What has been the effect of the crisis on the Palestinians?

Immediately, it's been little short of disastrous. Palestinians in the West Bank and Gaza depend on remittances from Palestinians who live in the Gulf—especially Kuwait, which has the largest concentration of Palestinians outside of the immediate homeland area. As well, the relationships between the various Gulf sheikdoms and the PLO are threatened financially. My feeling was that it was a mistake for the PLO to be involved in the Arab League discussions at all. The PLO is not a country. Its position [on the condemnation of Iraq] was one of abstention, but it has been misrepresented in the press. It has been perceived as voting against Kuwait, which it wasn't. Finally, the crisis has furthered the apparent ascendancy of the Israeli right wing, which now can say it has been somewhat confirmed in its views of the Arab world.

Still, the Palestinian question is bound to recur, because there is a Palestinian population that raises issues that are central to Middle Eastern politics. And given the international response to the aggression and annexation in the case of Iraq, this response will be raised by other Arab parties in the Palestinian context. Some attention to the twenty-three-year-old occupation of Arab lands has to be paid.

What kinds of Western policies would promote the development of more secular, democratic, progressive regimes in the Arab world?

To begin, some limitations on Israel, whose ability to get away with anything has greatly increased the resentment against the U.S. in the region and has stimulated the growth of this atavistic Muslim reaction. Second, a serious attempt to deal with the region by means other than arms, and with priorities other than U.S. vital interests. Third, there is a kind of cultural iron curtain between the Arab world and the West, the U.S. in particular. For instance, over the past five years, there's been a huge number of major works of Arab literature translated into English, not a single one of which has been reviewed here. There's a sense that the Arab world is a seething den of mad Muslims or terrorists. A lot of this *should* be blamed on the Arab world, but much of the writing here has made it difficult for any other image to be established. There's a huge amount of "learned" material, by Bernard Lewis and others, on "the rage of Islam" or "the madness of Arabs." It's not scholarship or history. It's demagoguery. It makes it impossible to take stock of the past and move on to the future.

Lastly, there's the whole question of the modality by which resources such as oil in the Arab world come under the sovereignty and authority of Arabs. What matters to the U.S. is compliant rulers who can assure easy access and supply. That's a formula for more Saddam Husseins.

But the absence of any motion, of any change in U.S. policy, gives rise to things for which we pay a heavy price. It leads to national-security states like Syria and Iraq, that say, "We must repress in the interest of defending the Arab nation." It gives rise to religious desperation, to people saying the West will only listen to hostages and terror. It gives rise to a disenfranchised bourgeoisie, that is interested only in making money. Look at the Gulf, at the pact between the rulers and the foreigners who came there and their own middle class. The understanding is: make all the money you want, but don't engage in politics. There's no civil society. Even the university is considered part of the apparatus of the security of the state.

Saddam Hussein, for all his brutality, cannot be isolated from the environment that produced him—and it's an environment shaped by U.S. policy.

Interview in *L.A. Weekly,*
Los Angeles, 1991

TWENTY

PALESTINIAN VOICES
IN THE U.S.

Lately you have been critical of Palestinian efforts in the United States. What was the reaction of the PLO leadership to such criticism?

I was just recently in Tunis and I tell you quite frankly most Palestinians I have seen in the United States, in Europe, and in the Arab world are very supportive of my position because it is a fact that our dealings with the United States are done largely out of ignorance and without enough attention paid to what is, after the occupied territories, the most important place of struggle.

I am somewhat pessimistic and discouraged by the fact that the level of awareness of the Palestinian leadership of what in fact America is, of what American politics are all about, of how the various pressure groups work, of how the Congress works, of how the media work, of how the various sectors of the culture work; all of these are totally unknown to our people in Tunis. And they are making, in my opinion, not enough effort to understand it better. They are dealing with the United States from a position of a tremendous relative weakness and ignorance. It is very sad and I don't think they are doing enough to remedy that because they are not taking it seriously in my opinion.

You were harsh in your criticism of the Palestinian offices in the United States for their lack of effectiveness and organization. What was the effect of such criticism on the leadership in Tunis?

As a result of criticism that various people, including myself, have made there seems to be a move now to clean our act up. And I hope within the next few weeks there will be some important changes. It is necessary and obligatory to make these changes because the peace process is grinding to a halt and we are slowly being forced into more and more concessions with fewer and fewer results. The Palestinian message is not coming through to the American people. The real obstacle here is the U.S. government which is incredibly cautious and obviously for domestic reasons very pro-Israeli, and is exacting from us five concessions to one Israeli concession. That is unacceptable and we have to put more pressure on them. We have to launch, in my opinion, a public campaign to deal with the incredible unfairness and double standards of the U.S. government against us.

Let me ask you the following question and I hope you will answer it honestly. What do you think of the latest interview with Chairman Arafat on NBC's "Meet the Press"?

I didn't think it was a good performance. I think he can't be expected to know in detail what the American media are like, maybe. That is our role to explain to him. But I certainly don't think he should speak in English. Gorbachev has shaken the world in the last five years, more than anyone has, I think, and he has never spoken one word of English. He only speaks in Russian. And my feeling is that Chairman Arafat should speak exclusively in Arabic instead of sort of going back and forth with the questioners. He should make his statements in Arabic, not in order necessarily to answer the question but to deliver a message to the American people. The Palestinian message of peace and moderation and political vision of the future.

Have you had the chance to talk to him about this?

No, I haven't. But when I went to Tunis I took with me a cassette of the NBC interview and gave it to one of his aides, as something that could be profitably studied!

Does Chairman Arafat have media experts to help him deal with the Western media?

He doesn't. He has nothing!

Some people blame intellectual Palestinian Americans, yourself included, who have access to Arafat and who could provide him with expert advice on such matters.

He has a lot of gifted young people who help him as best as they can. But what he needs is a full-time media adviser who is in touch with and understands perfectly the role of the media in political life. The media, television in particular, is not just appearing on the screen, it is a major instrument of politics in the late twentieth century. And that, I think, we don't understand. What Arafat needs is a person whose full-time job is to exploit the possibilities of the media in this country in particular, television again, and that can only come from a professional who understands the Palestinian and the American worlds perfectly, and who understands the uses of television. This is a highly specialized job of the utmost importance which is totally neglected. Arafat cannot possibly do this because of his way of life, the condition of exile imposed on him, the lack of a political base or center in the Arab world. This work should be done for him, he can't possibly do it himself, and it can't be done by somebody sitting in Tunis.

Lately there have been reports in the Arab press that the PLO wanted to have a Palestinian American like yourself or Abu-Lughod to be in charge of information in the U.S. Have you been approached about this?

We talked about it, and I must tell you that there was a very very positive reception to our ideas in Tunis. I went with Professor Abu-Lughod and we spent four days and saw the Executive Committee and Chairman Arafat and we told them what I am telling you now. The response was very positive and there seems to be a great receptivity. Of course the important thing is to act on these ideas, and I am hoping it will work out.

The PLO has recently announced some changes in its diplomatic personnel around the world, including the transfer of Mr. Hassan Abdul Rahman from the Washington office. Do you think this came as a result of your criticism?

That seems to be an indication of how seriously they are taking it, which is good! All diplomatic services change their ambassadors, it is time we changed ours, and it is important in America, for example, to put Palestinian representation in at the very highest level with the most competent and the best people. The one thing I would complain about is the total absence of coordination of Palestinian activities in the United States. There are major Palestinian figures from the PLO leadership who have been here, for example, for two or three weeks in this country, and have talked to nobody. They just do their own stuff and they go home. It would seem to me that the better part of wisdom is to at least be in touch with Palestinians in this country who follow events and can help and give evaluation.

What, in your opinion, is the solution to the lack of an effective Palestinian information policy in the United States?

For me, speaking as an intellectual and an independent, we have to keep saying it publicly to our people, to keep insisting on what we need and do it. We have to organize an effective Palestinian presence and voice in this country, and we are doing it now. We are going to set up a kind of *majlis* which will be called "The American Council for Palestinian Affairs," which is going to try to collect Palestinian efforts in order to give it an intelligent and coordinated presence in this country; to be the Palestinian voice that expresses the views of our people and the *intifada.*

What is your evaluation of the peace process, and what do you expect will come out of the upcoming meeting in Washington between the U.S., Egypt, and Israel?

I think from our point of view it is an impossibly slow and even comic process which is very heavily favored toward Shamir and the right wing of the Likud party. The administration is extremely cautious, unimaginative, and very hostile to Palestinian aspirations. One should note the hypocrisy. This is an administration that welcomes the drive for democracy in every other part of the world, but somehow they exclude the Palestinian revolt against Israeli oppression and tyranny. My feeling is that they are the same thing and indeed the movement in Eastern Europe has learned from the Palestinian *intifada.*

Given all the negative things, one must also say that there is no doubt, as one reads the Israeli press, that the Israelis are also, from their own point of view, being forced for the first time to confront reality and I think it is a tiny opening, and one should not exaggerate it and say it's the thing we have been waiting for. But it is an opening. Therefore, we require at this point, particularly when they meet, we require the maximum of political coordination, intelligence, strategic thinking, correct evaluation and assessment, in moving forward. We cannot move forward and improvise in a careless sort of spontaneous way. I think this is perhaps the most difficult period because it is very easy to get discouraged. The important thing is to engage in a detailed way with this very complex moment and to maximize it to our number one priority, which is going to be very hard because we don't have any important strategic ally.

Interview with Munir Nasser,
Arab American News, Dearborn, Michigan, 1990

TWENTY-ONE

THE INTELLECTUALS
AND THE WAR

How would you characterize the portrayal of the Gulf crisis and war in the U.S. and in Europe?

Representation of the conflict in the West, by the first week of the crisis in August, had succeeded, first, in demonizing Saddam; second, in personalizing the crisis and eliminating Iraq as a nation, a people, a culture, a history; and third, in completely occluding the role of the United States and its allies in the formation of the crisis.

But there were divergent opinions on the crisis, particularly among intellectuals.

I'm talking about policymakers and mainstream media. The media mobilized for the war in perfect synchrony with the administration. Even among the alternative media and intellectuals there's been a reluctance to deal with the Middle East. One reason is its setting and the people involved. Then there's so-called postmodernism. The United States, as the last empire, has, in the case of its intellectuals, internalized imperial rule. That generally sets intellectuals above such issues, perhaps because of a widespread sense of helplessness, impotence, and fragmentation due to specialization.

The American intellectual community in the main doesn't consider itself sufficiently bound by responsibilities toward the commonweal, doesn't feel responsible for the behavior of the United States internationally. In the Middle East, the United States has routinely obstructed struggles for human rights. The U.S. has sided with every entrenched and rooted power against struggles for women's rights, for minority rights, for rights to free assembly and free speech. All as matters of policy.

With regard to this history, which has very little to do with the Palestinians, the large body of American intellectuals are basically provincial, drawn only by virtue of expertise. If they're Latin American specialists, they don't talk about anything other than Latin America.

There is no sense of affiliation with the public sphere, with a cause. I remember once a friend of mine, a literary Marxist in this country, said, "Well, you're lucky, Edward, you were born Palestinian, but this other person, who's an American, doesn't have a cause to which he was born." As if there's some tremendous privilege to being subjected to the travails of the Palestinians. If you are an American, you're above all causes. Unless you're born to the thing or you've been given a degree in the subject, it doesn't matter.

The senior Middle East experts were dying to be called to Washington. They were not saying things that would disturb the policy train. The rest of us were fragmented, didn't have access to the media, and had to rely on *samizdat* publications.

Contrast this situation with the remarkable interview in January with the French scholar Jacques Berque, in which he was able to distinguish between Saddam and Iraq and the Arabs and imperialism, between the state of human rights in the Arab world and in Europe historically, and point out that butchery and violence are by no means the monopoly of Iraq. And get it published prominently, in *L'Autre Journal* [February 1991]. Nothing like that happened in this country, where mainstream scholars of his stature, almost to a man or woman, affiliated themselves with the administration.

Yet French intellectual circles, just as in the U.S. and the U.K., generally failed to respond coherently and with principle. Has this crisis challenged the intellectual class to begin to examine its own history?

Not really. They were perhaps glad it was as short as it was. The problem is a history of disengagement from international questions, above all from the Middle East and the Arabs generally. The small number of us who tried to engage intellectuals in general questions of responsibility were too few. In the meantime, this country has produced an entire literature of instant expertise and knowledge, all of which puts forward a view of the Middle East and of this conflict in particular that largely supports the administration's position.

How has this cult of expertise developed? Who are the main practitioners of intellectual policing today with regard to the Middle East?

During the Vietnam War there emerged a powerful and vocal group in the universities that challenged the administration. And this had a noticeable effect upon the media. The difference with this war is that Vietnam evolved over a longer period of time. And the presence of Israel is a complicating factor.

With very few exceptions, the leading Middle East scholars gravitated either toward Washington or to the media and were made use of there. Their sights were not focused on the region; they were focused on ways to the region as provided by CBS, NBC, *The New York Times* and whatnot, or by the policymaking institutions in Washington. You didn't see the emergence of a strong, well-profiled opposition sympathetic to the Arabs as a people and a culture, to Iraq as a nation, one that opposed the Iraqi invasion and annexation of Kuwait but also opposed the U.S. military presence.

Instead, the media hooked on to the war policy, in its wake bringing up a lot of retired military men—men, always men—and what I call the scholar-combatants—Fouad Ajami, Daniel Pipes, Bernard Lewis, and so on—and with them a handful of journalists like Tom Friedman who were virtually indistinguishable from policymakers.

These scholar-combatants also have engaged in a kind of curriculum-building.

There was a reading list publicized by National Public Radio which didn't have a single work on it either by or about an Arab. *The New York Times* published a list that covered an entire page in which there wasn't a single book about Iraq after about the seventh century B.C.! Iraq was left pretty much at Sumer! There were five Israeli novels, three or four histories of the Jews, Conor Cruise O'Brien, but nothing on the modern history or culture of Iraq.

What you have is a canon, which now includes Samir al-Khalil's *Republic of Fear,* Fouad Ajami's *Arab Predicament,* the instant books by journalists, and of course Thomas Friedman's *From Beirut to Jerusalem,* David Fromkin's *Peace to End all Peace* and, occasionally, Albert Hourani's book. Now if you exclude Hourani's *History of the Arab People* (which, although it's now on the bestseller list, is not a book to be digested easily), these books are generally unsympathetic to the Arabs and advance the thesis that the feuds and the violence in the Middle East are due to, relatively speaking, prehistoric causes, inscribed in the very genes of these people. Such things as a rational argument presented by the Arab people of the twentieth century about their own sense of history, their identity, their achievements—all of these are dismissed as fraudulent and essentially self-deluding. In the words of Ajami, the problems of the Arab world are the result of "self-inflicted wounds." This literature pretty much exonerates the United States and its policymakers, and of course Israel, from any role in this appalling mess we're living through today.

In his book *Teachers, Writers and Celebrities,* Régis Debray advances an interesting argument that relates to the situation we are discussing. These authors are all without significant scholarly attainment or expertise. Fromkin's book has no real connection with the Middle East in terms of scholarship or anything that he wrote prior. Friedman is a journalist. Ajami is a mediocre scholar who has written one twenty-year-old collection of essays and a dismissable history of Musa Sadr. These people belong to the genre of media celebrities discussed by Debray rather than to that of university teachers or to that of artist-writers. They have no particular anchor in the process of intellectual work or in institutions of intellectual production. They are therefore, paradoxically, much more difficult to dislodge, precisely because they belong to no particular institution, except the corporate media. They are creatures of the moment.

What effect has the Gulf crisis had on Arab political culture?

My impressions are roughly as follows. Almost all of what is now published in the daily newspapers in the Arab world—one can always find exceptions—is politically motivated, in the narrow and most vulgar sense. To write, you have to be affiliated with a particular line or regime or ruler. If you're independent, unorthodox, creative in some way, it's either extremely difficult or impossible to make a break.

Has the Gulf crisis destabilized those structures to allow for a reconfiguration of intellectual projects?

The credibility of the Right has been undermined. Since almost everything that is written today directly reflects a political influence in the most literal sense, nothing anyone writes is going to be above question. Opportunities will open up, new alignments will take place. But the first question people will ask is not whether what the writer is saying is true or not, but who is this person really speaking *for.* As they say in Arabic, *min warrah?,* "who's behind him?"

There is now, because of the war, a general collapse of cultural institutions in the Arab world. Patterns of funding and staffing have been changed in ways we're only now beginning to assess. There's a seismic shift in the intellectual and cultural topography of the Arab world, which is very hard to assess but which can't be good.

An Arab world divided between victor and vanquished. The Palestinians are losers. The Egyptians are desperately trying to cast themselves as winners. This has an effect on the micro level, at institutes, at cultural and political endeavors.

Suspicion across borders has increased. The Saudi deportation of 800,000 Yemeni workers was not about a fifth column or destabilization: it was an act of petty vengeance against an entire people.

There's also something quite new in the Arab world: the idea that inside these borders people are homogenized in some way, that Syrians are homogeneous Syrians, and so on. This is something quite foreign to our culture and history, because the essence of the region is precisely that it comprises a tremendous diversity. There's no purity at all; it's a consecrated hybridity almost unique to Islam. And that's why people objected to the various comical nationalisms that appeared in one or another of these countries. But now it's become a situation in which, for example, the king of Jordan claims, "I am a sharif." There's now a contest to ground one's identity in some distant, pure and primitive first state, whether that is Islam or a tribe or a border. That's not the world I grew up in.

What has been the effect of all this on the Palestinian movement?

A part of it is quite different from the other nationalisms: it is in a certain sense transnational, it's about principles. But we don't live in a vacuum. In 1985, I went to Kuwait as a guest of Kuwait University. Because I was an outsider, both the Kuwaitis and Palestinians who worked there sought my ear to accuse the other of malfeasance, usually on national grounds. You can sympathize with the Palestinian who is a minority in a country like Kuwait, but it breeds that whole atmosphere of people being identified ethnically and through the prism of a very narrow and narrowing nationalism; it breeds even in the victim a general lack of generosity. Of course, I'm privileged, I live in New York, but I was very disappointed when Palestinians on the West Bank and Gaza identified with Iraq bashing the Kuwaitis. Even if the Kuwaitis are arrogant, why would a victim identify with the oppressor? That's one of the roles intellectuals and leaders could play: to say that this is a matter of principle. Invasion is invasion.

Do you see, within the Palestinian intifada *right now, any possibilities for rehabilitation?*

I'm relatively optimistic about that. The difficulties are tremendous and the sufferings horrific, but there has been a cataclysmic shake-up. If it doesn't kill one, that can induce a clarification of priorities. The alliance of the Palestinian national movement with Gulf money has not been such a wonderful thing. Building hospitals, libraries, and kindergartens with help from the Palestinian community in the Gulf and from the Gulf States themselves was important, but the political price has been high. It's taught an entire generation of Palestinians to depend on shortcuts created by easy money. Now Palestinians are thrust back on the resources and the energies of the people themselves, and not outside interests.

One could say that this crisis demonstrated the failure of the Palestinian movement to provide leadership for the democratic forces within the Arab world, leaving a vacuum into which Saddam Hussein was able to move.

Palestinians will tell you that Arafat's positions during the war followed from the fact that Palestinians in the West Bank and Gaza took those positions. I disagree. One of the things that leaders do is lead. Many of us failed in this role. It would be unfair to ascribe it entirely to the Palestinian leadership: it's a general failure over the last two years, the abandonment by the Arab states and regimes of the *intifada.*

I've often felt the PLO has been remiss in not releasing publicly the minutes of the U.S.–PLO meetings in Tunis, so that people could see what little we got as a result of our historical compromise. Palestinians need to make political gains out of the lessons of the *intifada,* which are a blueprint for democracy and solidarity between people. We are the only national movement still in existence today in the Arab world that functions according to democratic, largely non-coercive and inventive modes of association and coordination, which remain for the most part secular.

It would be foolish not to recognize that the odds against us are horrifically great. But one of the lessons we've learned in the last twenty years as Palestinians, and I think many Israelis have also learned, is that we have no military option against each other. They could slaughter us, but they're not going to get rid of every Palestinian, and they won't snuff out the flame of Palestinian nationalism. Conversely, we have no military option against the Israelis. What we do have is a vision, a way of including them in the Middle East based on the respect of nationalities for each other, the right to live within secure and safe borders, and to coexist in a profitable way with other peoples.

That is our main weapon, but most of us have not realized it. We still believe in the outdated and useless slogans of an Arab nationalist movement based on military might, on the one-party state, and above all on the cult of the great leader. Those are not necessary to the Palestinian struggle and have never been central to it. To the extent that we are still a part of the Arab world, that we speak Arabic, that we read the same literature, that we employ the same discourses, it's very important for our discourse to emerge as distinctive from that of the others, and lead the others, rather than to drown—as we did.

In the Arab countries democratic movements are more or less moribund at the moment. How can those movements be reactivated?

There are generally two time frames we have to work on. One is the immediate: that agenda is dominated now by the regimes. As the events in Iraq demonstrate, even the worst of them are not easily dislodged, or if they are it is simply by alternative versions of themselves. And the game of the regimes is now dominated by the United States and its allies. There are some fairly opportunistic things to be done, given the presence of the Palestinian issue high on the agenda. You have to play that game, not always very hopefully.

Then there's the other agenda, a "slow politics" that takes place over a long period of time, which can allow for coalition-building. The really popular position in the Arab world, if you were to study it carefully, is a rejection of what Saddam stands for, and the disastrous results which he brought to his own country and people, and a rejection of the American military solution.

The necessary coalition would be between people in different parts of the Arab world who are actively involved in local struggles for democracy, economic justice, women's rights, human rights groups, university groups—for example, the Jordanian student university movement of the mid-1980s. There are gatherings of intellectuals in some transnational Arab institutes, like the Institute of Arab Unity and the Arab Human Rights Organization, various lawyers' groups, university and intellectual groups that collaborate on small projects, journals like *Muwaqqif* or *Fusul* or *Alif*. There are serious discussions between secular and Islamic forces for the first time.

What we really need is a critical language and a full-scale critical culture, not name-calling or the rhetorical equivalent of political murder. One purpose is to assess and critique power in the Arab world. Not according to grandiose schemas imported from Hegel and Stalin and so on: many of the miseries of the Arab Left are ascribable to the importation of methodological instruments or Orientalist models from abroad having no relation to our life. We must indigenously and imaginatively develop composite or hybrid models of the sort, for example, of Abdallah Laroui in North Africa, or Anwar Abdel Malek, or Muhammad Jabri. Like-minded individuals have to give such a critique of power greater currency in their discussions.

We also need a language of appreciation based not on dogmatic orthodoxy or reverence for Quranic and authoritative ideas, but rather one that develops out of this critique of power. We need to be able to say what we are *for* in our world and in our lives, as opposed to using the fundamentalist model of saying that we're for the way it was done in the past. We need a developed sense of what it is that we care about.

Out of this combined critique of power and discourse of care and attention can come accountability. This can lead to participation, which is something in Arab intellectual life that has struck me as very problematic. There is in the Arab world a tremendous sense of provincialism and isolation. We're not—whether in our literature or intellectual work—part of the ongoing debate in the world. Our inability to take part is largely due to ourselves. We are the focus of a lot of world attention, but we're always outside it, we're not participants, intellectually, in the determination of our own future, although God knows our complaints and grievances (rather boring ones) are well known enough!

This brings us back to the role of the intellectual—Arab and non-Arab—here in the U.S.

Yesterday I heard a panel discussion on the lessons of the Gulf War. One participant was Samir al-Khalil. What struck me as extraordinarily sad, not to say desolate, was his appeal to the United States, which had just devastated his country militarily, to enter further into Iraq and unseat Saddam Hussein. For him the only issue is the one that he as an Iraqi, genuinely in pain, feels. That seems to me to be part of the misery of this whole story. He is intelligent, fluent, but unable to attach himself to anything but an issue of the moment, with no realism in his perspective. He's suddenly discovered he's got to do something, and what does he do? He appeals to the United States, which has just destroyed his country, to come and rescue him! It's astonishing.

One of the roles Arab intellectuals play in the West is that of a sort of guinea pig witness. Since you're from Iraq, you tell us about Iraq. When we're not interested in Iraq, we don't want to hear from you. The native informant. That's simply an unacceptable role. We have to be everywhere. We have to deal not only with general problems in the Arab world, but we have to be able to say things about *this* country, where we live and work.

You can't just burst in and do this kind of Tolstoyan grandiloquence which is going to rescue your people. Al-Khalil appeals to the very same people who are responsible for a large part of the present tragedy of his country. They collaborated with Saddam and now they're propping him up after destroying the infrastructure. After such knowledge, what can possibly emerge?

In 1967, in the context of the U.S. war in Vietnam, Noam Chomsky wrote his essay "The Responsibility of the Intellectuals." What would be the main components of such an essay today?

One would have to pretty much scuttle all the jaw-shattering jargonistic postmodernisms that now dot the landscape. They are worse than useless. They are neither capable of understanding and analyzing the power structure of this country, nor are they capable of understanding the particular aesthetic merit of an individual work of art. Whether you call it deconstruction or postmodernism or post-structuralism or post-anything, they all represent a sort of spectacle of giving back tickets at the entrance and saying, we're really out of it. We want to check into our private resort and be left alone.

Re-engagement with intellectual process means a return to an old-fashioned historical, literary and, above all, intellectual scholarship based upon the premise that human beings, men and women, make their own history. And just as things are made, they can be unmade and remade. That sense of intellectual and political and citizenly empowerment is what the intellectual class needs.

There's only one way to anchor oneself, and that is by affiliation with a cause, with a political movement. There has to be identification not with the secretary of state or the leading philosopher of the time but with matters involving justice, principle, truth, conviction. Those don't occur in a laboratory or a library. For the American intellectual, that means, at bottom, that the relationship between the United States and the rest of the world, now based upon profit and power, has to be altered to one of coexistence among human communities that can make and remake their own histories and environments together. This is the number one priority—there's nothing else of that magnitude.

Universities cannot afford to become just a platform for a narcissistic Molière-like specialization. What you need is a regard for the products of the human mind. That's why I've been very dispirited by some aspects of the "great Western canon" debate, which suggests that the oppressed of the world, in wishing to be heard, in wishing their work to be recognized, really wish to do dirt on everything else. That's not the spirit of resistance. We come back to Aimé Césaire's line, "There is room for all at the rendezvous of victory."

Within certain university contexts there have been lately two major issues: the Gulf War and multiculturalism. I have not seen any linkage between the two.

Even inside the university, the prevalence of norms based upon domination and coercion is so strong because the idea of authority is so strong, whether it's derived from the nation-state, from religion, from the ethnos, from tradition. It is so powerful that it's gone relatively unchallenged even in the very disciplines and studies that we are engaged in. Part of intellectual work is understanding how authority is formed.

Authority is not God-given. It's secular. And if you can understand that, then your work is conducted in such a way as to be able to provide alternatives to the authoritative and coercive norms that dominate so much of our intellectual life, our national and political life, and our international life above all.

Interview with Barbara Harlow,
Middle East Report, Washington, D.C., 1991

TWENTY-TWO

WHAT PEOPLE IN THE U.S.
KNOW ABOUT ISLAM
IS A STUPID CLICHÉ

Edward Said is known for his abiding interest in the Urdu poet Faiz Ahmed Faiz. Holding him to be a great example of the post-colonialist intellectual at work, Said often mentions Faiz's name along with that of the great Kenyan writer and intellectual, N'gugi wa Thiong'o, to illustrate for the uninitiated the nature of the Third World literary and political landscape. In fact, in Said's hands, Faiz almost becomes an epigram, a fact evident in an oft-quoted article which the Palestinian writer contributed to New York–based Harper's *magazine in 1984:*

"To see a poet in exile—as opposed to reading the poetry of exile—is to see exile's antinomies embodied and endured. Several years ago, I spent some time with Faiz Ahmed Faiz, the greatest of contemporary Urdu poets. He had been exiled from his native Pakistan by Zia ul-Haq's military regime and had found a welcome of sorts in the ruins of Beirut. His closest friends were Palestinian, but I sensed that although there was an affinity between them, nothing quite matched—language, poetic convention, life history. Only once, when Eqbal Ahmed, a Pakistani and fellow exile, came to Beirut, did Faiz seem to overcome the estrangement written all over his face. The three of us sat in a dingy restaurant one night and Faiz recited poems to us. After a while, he and Eqbal stopped translating his verses for my benefit, but it did not matter. For what I watched required no translation, no enactment of homecoming steeped in defiance and loss, as if to say exultantly to Zia: 'We are here.' Of course, Zia was the one who was at home."

The Herald *thought it would be proper to begin the interview with some more thoughts on the significance of Faiz before asking Professor Said about the importance of being Edward.*

You say, "Of course Zia was the one who was at home." But if he was, and indeed we know he was, what was in it for Faiz? And if in countries like Pakistan, we are to espouse this Faizian model of the post-colonial intellectual, what in the end is gained and lost? Tell us why the world maybe needs another Faiz. Why we must continue to turn to the Zias of the world and continue the chant, "We are here."

First, a couple of things. The article came out in 1984 but my meeting with Faiz was in '79 or '80. Also, even though I had no way of knowing this at the time, I understand Faiz went back to Pakistan. In fact, he died there.

Now, I don't know the precise reasons because of which he left Pakistan in 1979 (or thereabouts), but I assume it was because his freedom was threatened. He may have been put in jail, or silenced in other ways. As I remember it, he was the editor of *Lotus,* which was an Afro-Asian writers' magazine and, to the best of my knowledge, he was the responsibility of the Palestinians. There was a man there by the name of Mu'in Besseisso, a Palestinian poet who has since died also, who worked at the magazine and understood Faiz's stature, and so on. Since this was a particularly lawless period in Beirut's history, I think he (Besseisso) secured the protection of the Palestinians so that Faiz's safety and comfort were assured.

What I say in that article, and the point I am leading up to here, is that in spite of all this, exile is not such a bad thing. I think that in order to continue working, in the case of a writer or an intellectual (like Faiz) it might be necessary sometimes to leave and to find another place to continue. At the time of the meeting, I didn't know Faiz would return, and what I was doing was contrasting his condition with my own. I left Palestine in 1947 and never went back to the part of Palestine I am from, which later became Israel. I was on the West Bank in 1966, one year before the Israeli invasion, but I haven't been back there either. In fact, I did return later, in June 1992.

And what about this exultant and defiant retort to Zia, "We are here," as a larger sort of condition, as opposed to whatever it may be construed as meaning in a narrower Pakistani sense. As a general condition, what does that statement say?

Look, as a general condition, India and Pakistan on the one hand, and the Arabs on the other, share a common background of colonial tribulation followed by independence and sovereignty. And at least in our case, speaking of the Arabs, what has happened is that although there are now twenty plus independent Arab states, the Arab world itself, with its rulers and regimes and kings and presidents, is a catastrophe. You have regimes, all of whom, with the exception of a few, are deeply unpopular. You have the resurgence of Muslim religious political feeling. You have a significant brain-drain; a lot of people are leaving. And above all, from my point of view, you have a cultural class, let's say, who are either silent or in hiding or abroad.

So, very frequently in a situation like this—when the situation is hopeless—it is important to turn to a symbolic figure, like a poet or a writer or an intellectual, to a Faiz Ahmed Faiz, who is not co-opted, who is not corrupted, who is not silenced, and to say what he or she is doing is enough for us. Of course, in reality it's not enough. What we are talking about are situations where political change has often been set back. There has been no political change.

You are also a writer exiled from his country. Tell us, is your situation essentially different from a Faiz or, say, N'gugi wa Thiong'o, the Kenyan, who you also sometimes mention? Does being in America make the situation distinctly different? And I ask you this because in one of the essays in The World, the Text, and the Critic *you talk about Erich Auerbach, the Jewish, Western-trained and -educated intellectual who wrote* Mimesis. *You note that he was exiled by the Nazis and wrote the book in Istanbul, an odd place for such an important Western work to be written in, since that city at the time still represented what Europe regarded as the Ottoman menace. Then you go on to discuss Auerbach's condition in more detail. But it sounds almost as if you are talking about yourself. After all, you are also in the belly of the beast, a Palestinian at work in the United States. Is that so?*

Well, obviously, there are many parallels, but I wouldn't want to suggest that my life is a very difficult one. Due to a series of fortunate circumstances, I am in a field which allows me to teach literature and to maintain a position as a professor, with great luxury and ease. I mean, it's a wonderful job. It's the best job in the world. So in that sense, I can't really complain. But I must say that there is no question that I live in an alien environment. And all said and done, it is very difficult because my relationship with the culture and the surroundings is adversarial. People are always waiting for me to say something in order for them to utter a rebuttal.

Nothing I say is easily accepted; it must be fought over. Not to mention the fact that I come from a part of the world that most people here are completely ignorant of: the Arab world, and the Islamic world. Nothing is known about it at all. What is known, as I tried to show in *Orientalism,* is extremely attenuated and a series of stupid clichés: violent this, despotic that. And then, if you say, well, can you name a writer, an Arabic writer, these people come up with no names. There is nothing. They draw a blank. So it's a tough situation.

You described an occasion once, before Naguib Mahfouz won the Nobel Prize, when an American publisher called you and asked for a list of writers. Could you tell that story for the benefit of our readers?

I will tell you exactly. The publisher called me sometime in 1980 or '81 and asked for a list of Third World writers, because he wanted to start a series, and I put Mahfouz at the top of the list. A few months later I saw this publisher and I said, Well, what have you picked? So he told me that Mahfouz was not one of the writers that he had chosen. I asked him why. After all, Mahfouz was the greatest Arabic writer and a world figure. Why would he drop him? He said: "Well, you see, Arabic is a controversial language." The language is controversial! I mean, what are we talking about here?

I'll give you another example. There is a great deal done in American universities, in their literature departments, with medieval studies: medieval English, medieval French, and so on. And the phrase medieval is understood to cover the entire Middle Ages. Yet, not a single instance can I think of in which medieval courses and programs ever include Andalusian, Muslim civilization, which was exactly contemporary with that of, say, Dante, Chaucer, Aquinas, et cetera, et cetera. And on a much higher level, whether it be science or literature or theology or medicine, it's just left out! So, if you live in this culture and you come from that part of the world (the Arab and the Islamic world), you have to pay the price of this, lapse, let's call it.

Now, on the other hand, your own works are very widely distributed in the West and equally sought after in the Third World. With Orientalism, you had a profound galvanizing influence on an entire generation. It has been translated into seventeen or eighteen languages, and to many among us, it represents a manifesto, so to speak, a state of mind. Tell us, have you had the time, so many years since 1978 when that book came out, to sit down and scrutinize the changes in perception it has brought about?

Well yes, I think it has changed perceptions. In the West, for instance, in certain fields, such as anthropology, history, cultural studies, feminist studies, it has influenced people to think about problems of power relationships between cultures and peoples, where dominance includes the power to represent and create, to control and to manipulate. In other words, it makes the argument for the connection between the production of knowledge and power. And specifically, because it was a historical work, it really looks at all of this in the age of empire.

Now, one of the things I was slightly disturbed by, in terms of the book's influence in the Muslim world, was that it was considered by some to be a book in defense of Islam, which it was not at all. I have nothing to say about Islam; what I talk about are representations of Islam, rather than Islam itself. I suppose somebody could write a book about portrayals of the West in the Islamic world and come up with roughly the same distortions. But what I am really interested in, to make my point, is not just distortion, because distortion always occurs, but rather in trying to facilitate an understanding of how it occurs and what might be done to ameliorate it. So, that is one point.

Another reflection is that since *Orientalism* came out in 1978, I have myself started thinking of the problem of Orientalism in a wider context. Beginning in 1984–85, I started working on a book, nearly finished now and scheduled to come out later this year, which is a kind of sequel to *Orientalism*, but looks at the problem in a global context. In other words, I try to look at Africa, I look at the Middle East, I look at India and Pakistan, and I try to discover what the role of culture was in forming imperialism in the West. In the middle of the book, I look at the role of culture in the process of decolonization and resistance to imperialism—in other words, what role culture played in resisting empire in places like India and what is now Pakistan, in Africa, the Caribbean, and so on. And then, in the last chapter, I look at the role of the United States after the classical empires were dismantled in World War II, to see, since the extraordinary role that the United States played as the last remaining imperial power, and the influence of that role upon knowledge and the production of knowledge. And all of this really comes out of my work on Orientalism. I have tried to extend it and take it further, looking not only at the aggressive aspects of empire but also at the resistances to empire that people like you and I were able to mount. After all, empires didn't last. India gained its independence in 1947. So, something happened, and that is what I look at in this book.

Getting back to Orientalism *itself. Tell us, was there a sequence of events in your life which led to the writing of* Orientalism?

Well, there are several germs. One was when I was growing up after we left Palestine and were in Egypt. Although my family was well off and I went to colonial schools in Palestine and Egypt, I realized that no matter what I was by virtue of family or education or language, to a ruling Englishman—and this is colonial Egypt in 1948–49—I would always remain a wog. It was brought home to me in an episode I will never forget. I was about ten at the time, and I was walking home across the fields of the Gazira Sporting Club in Cairo, a great colonial sporting club of which my family was a member. It was a club really for the English but they admitted a few locals. So, I was walking home (we lived near the club) and the man whom I saw coming toward me on a bicycle was the secretary of the club, an Englishman named Mr. Pilly. He stopped me and said: "Boy, what are you doing here?" and I replied, "I'm walking home." And he said: "Don't you know you're not allowed to be here?" and I said, "Yes, I am allowed to be here, because my family is a member." And he said "Boy, you are not allowed here. You are an Arab boy. Get out." Now the irony of this is (and by the way, I did get out: I was scared) that Mr. Pilly's son was a classmate of mine at school. Now these are the sort of formative experiences where you come to understand that race, in the colonial context—no matter what else goes on—is determining.

Another germ was 1967, when I was a professor at Columbia. I was not at all involved in politics. I was a student of European literature and a professor of it. But then the war broke out and I realized the enormous cultural hatred and bias toward Arabs and the Arab world, and that politicized me. That is to say, being an Arab, I identified with the Arab losses and I realized how much of the loss was due to the fact that we were considered to be an inferior people. I began to try to understand where that image that they had of us came from.

The last point that I want to make about *Orientalism* is that I don't think I would have written that book had I not been politically associated with a struggle. The struggle of Arab and Palestinian nationalism is very important to that book. *Orientalism* is not meant to be an abstract account of some historical formation but rather a part of the liberation from such stereotypes and such domination of my own people, whether they are Arabs, or Muslims or Palestinians.

It's good you brought it up, Professor Said, since we were about to turn to Palestine anyway. You concluded The Question of Palestine *by saying: "We must not forget that Palestine is saturated with blood and violence, and we must look forward realistically to much turbulence, much ugly human waste, in the short term. Unhappily, the question of Palestine will renew itself in all too well-known forms. But so too will the people of Palestine—Arabs and Jews—whose past and future binds them inexorably together. Their encounter has yet to occur on any important scale. But it will occur, I know, and it will be to their mutual benefit." Now, with the advent of direct negotiations (and the third round of negotiations in Washington will already have taken place by the time this is printed) do you think that the encounter, so to speak, has occurred?*

Yes, I think it really began to occur with the beginning of the *intifada* in December of 1987, and it has continued to occur. The Israelis have had to confront the reality of the Palestinian nation. I am not talking about rioting individuals or of throwing stones. I am talking about a nation. For the first time in their history, Israelis are dealing with an entire population which constitutes a nation because, of course, that entire population in the occupied territories is tied with people like myself, who live in exile. More than half of the Palestinian population lives outside Palestine. Forty-five percent live on the land of historical Palestine, that is to say the occupied territories and present-day Israel, and 55 percent live abroad. This has made Israel confront, first through the *intifada* and then through the declaration of Palestinian statehood in Algiers in 1988, then the recognition of Israel by the Palestinians, and now through these talks, the reality of the Palestinian nation. It's coming. It is very, very slow. But I have no doubt that at the end of the process there will be an independent Palestinian state.

I also have no doubt, however, that Israel as a nation—and I am not talking about individuals but rather an establishment—has made very little progress toward us and toward what we have done as a people. They still will not recognize the PLO. They still will not recognize Palestinian nationalism. I don't know if you notice this, and most people in the West are not aware of this, but when Shamir and Netanyahu (Israel's deputy foreign minister) speak they never speak about the Palestinians, they always call them the "the Palestinian Arabs." They connect them back to the Arab world. Why? Because if you call them Palestinians, you give them a separate identity. So, they say "We are ready to talk with the Palestinian Arabs." That's still a part of their political makeup; that we (the Palestinians) are not a people.

So you don't exist?

Well, we do exist, but they refer to us as "aliens" who live on the land of Eretz Israel. The more honest Likud settler in Israel refers to the Palestinians on the West Bank and Gaza as "aliens" on the land of Israel. So, they have made no progress yet in coming to terms with our reality as a nation. The same is true of most American Jews. I can't speak of Jews in the West, but American Jews, with a few exceptions, still cannot reconcile themselves to the existence of our nationhood. And one of the reasons is that the whole enterprise that brought Israel into being was premised upon our nonexistence. Now, suddenly, after forty-five years, they discover that not only are we here now, but that we have been here all along, and it's something that's just very difficult for them to accept.

Do you think that an encounter on a major scale, at this point in time (and we are talking about, say, the next two years), is at all possible without the PLO and Yasir Arafat coming overtly into the picture?

No, it's not. And, in fact, it is taking place with the PLO. In other words, there is this tremendous illusion, mainly because of this ludicrous, puerile attitude of the Americans and the Israelis, that if you exclude the physical presence of the PLO, the PLO will go away. The delegation sent to Madrid and to Washington was chosen by the PLO.

Everything they say or do is referred to and approved by the PLO. The delegates receive directives from the PLO. Many of them are supporters of parties within the PLO. And all of them recognize the supreme authority of the PLO as the national organization representing Palestinian identity as a nation. So, I think this "we are not talking with the PLO" business is a reflection on the juvenile qualities of the Americans and the Israelis. They say "Well, you know, we're not dealing with them." But on the other hand, they are dealing with them in this roundabout way. They are prisoners of their own silly ideology that the PLO is nothing but a terrorist organization. If you believe that kind of lie then you can't really deal with reality. That's why I am really proud of the fact that Palestinians are mature and are able to deal with the Israelis as they are. We don't need ideological fiction. We can say: "We are dealing with Israel." We are not dealing with "the Zionist entity." And it's true, we are the ones who want to deal with the Israeli government; they are the ones who have difficulty sitting with us. In the last round of talks in Washington, they refused to sit in the same room with the Palestinians. They said we don't recognize you. We must sit only with the Jordanians. And that is what they are stalling. But I think in their hearts they know that the inevitable is upon them. They are going to have to deal with us. The real question now, of course, is how much and how long America is going to indulge them in this fantasy of not dealing with us.

There has been some criticism of this specific administration, the Bush administration, over its decision to join this month's United Nations resolution condemning Israel for its latest deportations of Palestinians. How do you feel about that?

I don't take very seriously the changes that have occured in the policies of this country under the Bush-Baker administration. I think it is very important to remember that this is the first American administration to attempt and partially succeed in destroying a major Arab country. This is an administration that uses the United Nations to continue to violate the sovereignty of Iraq, which is one of the two major Arab countries. It is an administration that has granted nothing to Palestinian nationalism at all except cosmetic improvement in its image after the end of the Gulf War. It needs a "Peace Victory" to make up for what it was not able to do in Iraq to bring down the regime of Saddam. He is a tyrant, I will say it, and what he did in Kuwait was absolutely wrong, but the Americans have not solved the problems of the region. They have caused rifts between Arab states. They have caused a huge amount of human suffering and waste and death and violence. What they are doing now with this so-called peace process is, I will repeat, a cosmetic attempt to restore the luster of George Bush's image as a peacemaker and, at the same time, to express a sort of petulance at Israel's behavior.

But petulance is not enough. Israel continues to settle and appropriate the land. Israel continues to deport. Israel continues to kill. Israel continues to imprison. Israel continues to clamp down the curfews, twenty-four hours a day. And the United States has not withheld one cent of the five billion dollars annually sent to Israel in U.S. aid. That is against the law of this country. The law says that gross violations of human rights have to result in curtailment of U.S. aid to the recipient country. That has never happened.

So, I am not one of those people who think it's a historical breakthrough that the United States has changed its policy. They are still exacting from the Palestinians concessions they are too scared to ask from the Israelis. I will give you a simple example. The two Palestinians who negotiated with Baker for six months, from March until the beginning of August, were Hanan Ashrawi and Feisal Husseini, and Baker praised them publicly in Madrid for their negotiations. Now, neither one of them was allowed to be a member of the delegation. Neither one of them was allowed to come to the Peace Palace in Madrid because Israel said we cannot have these people since they are affiliated with the PLO and they are real leaders. The official reason they gave was that they were from East Jerusalem. And America accepted these conditions, so what are we talking about? We are talking about an administration that is too afraid, too tied to the past, too subservient to whether it's Saudi Arabia on the one hand or the Israeli lobby on the other, to make any courageous advances in the progress toward peace.

Is it true that Shamir had once objected to George Shultz meeting you?

Not only that, he wouldn't allow me into the country. In the spring of 1988, I wanted to go with my family and he wouldn't allow it. I am an American citizen but he expressly forbade me from entering the country. We are dealing with a really lousy situation here. And, to get back to the point, I don't see that a vote in the United Nations where the United

States condemns a flagrant violation of the Geneva Convention is all that significant. First of all, who is going to enforce the resolution? What astonishes me is the Arabs accepting that as a reason for coming back to the talks. We got nothing from it. Just a condemnation. So what. There are already sixty-four UN Security Council resolutions condemning Israel for one or another abuse of Palestinian rights. Not one of them has been implemented, and the reason they haven't been implemented is the United States.

Talking of resolutions, you gave an interview once to Salman Rushdie in which you described Zionism as the touchstone of contemporary political judgment in America. You said a lot of people who are happy to attack apartheid or to talk about U.S. intervention in Central America are not prepared to "talk about Zionism and what it has done to the Palestinians." You said that here, in the United States, if you say anything about Zionism you are seen as "joining classical European or Western anti-Semitism." Therefore, you said, it has become "absolutely necessary to concentrate on the particular history and context of Zionism in discussing what it represents for the Palestinian."

The important part of that phrase is "for the Palestinian." Zionism for the Jew was a wonderful thing. They say it was their liberation movement. They say it was that which gave them sovereignty. They finally had a homeland. They established institutions which they never had before, et cetera, et cetera. The list is very long. So, I am not talking about that. That's good. It's fine. But so far as the Palestinians are concerned, we are the victims of Zionism.

But this undertaking itself, of making this position known, how will it be affected by the reversal of the United Nations resolution equating Zionism with racism?

Well, look, I was never happy with the resolution. To say that Zionism is a form of racism is to be insufficiently clear about, and insufficiently sensitive to, what Zionism did for the Jews; for the Jews on the one hand and to the Palestinians on the other. In *The Question of Palestine*, I talk about it. To me, Zionism is Zionism. I don't have to equate it with anything else.

But for the Palestinians today, Zionism means: number one, the shattering of their society; number two, the dispossession of their population; and number three, and most importantly, the continuing oppression of the Palestinians as a people. To give you an example, Israel is the only state in the world which is not a state of its own citizens, it is a state of the Jewish people. If you happen to be a non-Jew in that Jewish state (and there are some 800,000 Palestinians who are Israeli citizens) you are referred to as a non-Jew and you are discriminated against simply because you are not Jewish. Jews are allowed to return to Israel by the law of return. I was born there but I can't. Jews can buy and lease and rent land in Israel. Palestinians cannot. And on the West Bank and Gaza, in the occupied territories, Palestinians are discriminated against in ways that Jews are not discriminated against. Settlers on the West Bank and Gaza can take away land from Palestinians and just live on it.

However, in spite of all these things, I must say that the resolution on Zionism and racism was a tremendously unfortunate episode. It was partly the euphoria of the early seventies, with the Afro-Asian movement in full bloom, and the Soviet Union still a player, and the Islamic movement heating up, which caused it to come about. It was badly thought through, insufficiently sensitive as I said, and as a result of it we, the Palestinians, have paid a very high political price. It became a stumbling block. But that is in the past now.

You were just saying that you are not allowed to buy land. One of the most important pieces of land at issue, of course, is Jerusalem itself. The peace process which has just been started is torturously slow. Do you believe, by the time this process comes to fruition, there will be any chance left at all for non-Jews to lay claim to Jerusalem?

I don't see any way of resolving the problem if Israel continues to hold on to the whole of Jerusalem. I am not saying that I am for the repartitioning of Jerusalem. I am not. I think it should remain a united city. But there should be an imaginative way for Palestinians to see in Jerusalem, of at least Arab or East Jerusalem, their capital. It has to be. It means a lot to Palestinians. And, of course, it also means a tremendous amount to the Islamic world. Jerusalem is not just a Palestinian city. It is also a city with great significance for a billion Muslims. So, some arrangement has to be made whereby Israel cannot go on dispossessing Palestinians within Jerusalem. But I must repeat I am not for the repartitioning of the city. I think something should be done in an imaginative way so the city, which is a universal city, can express the hopes and traditions of the three faiths: Judaism, Christianity, and Islam.

Something on the lines of the Vatican, would you say?

Something like that, without necessarily internationalizing it. But something of that sort, rather than cutting it up again or keeping it unified under Israeli control.

Now let's talk about intimidation. And we know it's a sensitive issue. As a highly visible spokesperson for the Palestinian cause, you have been targeted by various groups who turn out and protest when you deliver papers, who attack you in print, hand out leaflets quoting you out of context, and so on. They call you an Ambassador of Terrorism. All these unpleasant incidents have taken place.

Well, there have even been death threats. What can you do?

Tell us what bothers you the most about all this.

Well, what bothers me most, I think, is the lying and injustice that's involved, mounting a vicious campaign not only to continue to hurt my people but also to heap all kinds of lies and opprobrium upon me, calling me a terrorist.

Number two, in America, I have no real way of responding. Many of the people who have attacked me and written about me in slanderous and libelous ways have entire magazines at their disposal. *Commentary,* for instance, the magazine of the American Jewish Committee, gives them space to write whatever they want. So, it's very hard, if you know what I am trying to say. In other words, there is no organized equivalent to the platform that the enemies of the Palestinians have in this country.

The third, most galling thing of all, is that the Arabs and the Muslims, in this country and elsewhere, have never organized themselves together and tried to put forward a credible, alternative view to that put forward about us—not about me necessarily but about us—by the Zionist lobby in this country. We are the inheritors of a great tradition and a great civilization. We have many talented people and yet we cannot, just cannot, work together. The Palestinians work not only in five different directions but frequently in opposing ones. The Syrians work by themselves. There is no attempt to take ourselves seriously as members of a nation. And it really goes back to what I said earlier about the condition of the Arab world: It's a sink. It's a sink of corruption and mediocrity and the most appalling and murderous tyrannies. There are no democratic freedoms. It's just a dreadful place. And yet, it's a place to which I feel attached; it's where I am from, and my family is from, and my wife is from. I mean, I am not about to give up. And I won't do what the Samir al-Khalils and the Fouad Ajamis of this world want to do, which is to set up in this country, the United States, and to become apologists for the enemies of the Arabs. I won't play that game.

You once described Fouad Ajami (the Middle East expert of The New Republic, *a Washington based anti-Palestinian magazine) as* The New Republic's *"resident anti-Arab Arab."*

That's right. He's a disgrace. Not just because of his viciousness and his hatred of his own people but because what he says is so trivial and so ignorant. He, much more than me, is a professor of Middle Eastern studies. That's what he does for a living. Yet he doesn't know anything about the Arab world. He doesn't care about it. What he writes is simply used by the Zionist lobby and the establishment in this country against the Arabs.

Samir al-Khalil is the author of the book entitled State of Fear, *which is about Iraq and gained wide currency during and after the Gulf War. Would you put him in the same category?*

Roughly. He perhaps doesn't have the venom. He hasn't been at it long enough. In some ways, he is a much more confused man. Ajami, at least, has the virtue of clear-sightedness. He knows what he wants. He wants to attack the Arabs. This man, I don't know what he wants. He is a confused, emotionally distraught figure who has leapt to a kind of sudden prominence on the basis of this basically negligible book. So, it attacks Saddam—fine. But it's not a historical contribution, it's not a scholarly contribution to understanding Iraq and it was useful as part of the mobilization of this country against Saddam Hussein. Khalil has played that role and he has played it well and I really don't see him doing anything else. When this postwar euphoria in this country is over, he will pass from the scene.

So you think he will indeed disappear?

I think so, yes. He hasn't really written anything of lasting consequence, in my opinion. He's not a scholar.

There is some talk of a new Palestinian leadership, and many Ameri-

cans mention Hanan Ashrawi, for instance, as a new kind of leader. Give us your thoughts on that.

Well, you know she was a student of mine. She was at the University of Virginia, not here at Columbia, but they asked me if I would like to supervise the writing of her dissertation and it interested me, so I said yes. After that, for about two or three years, she would send me the chapters of it, and so on. She is a very intelligent and interesting woman. Lately, she has received a lot of attention too.

In my point of view, however, it is unfortunate that this has been used invidiously against Arafat. I am referring to the speculation and the attention that you asked about. In a certain sense, if you look at it honestly, she is unthinkable without Arafat, if you see what I mean. But it's all a part of the racism of the West. They think they like her because she speaks English well, the same reason they used to like me, because I spoke English well. As if that's it, if you don't speak English well, you're really not in the same world with their exalted highnesses.

Which brings us to a final question, one I know you are keen to address, about yet another person who speaks English well: Salman Rushdie. If you could just outline for us your position on Salman Rushdie. And we ask this because there are a lot of people who would be very interested to know precisely what Edward Said thinks about the whole Rushdie affair.

Well, my feeling is the following. And there are two or three points to be made.

Number one, I am an absolute believer in absolute freedom of expression. As a Palestinian, I have fought Israeli attempts to censor my people in what they can write or read. A lot of our battle for liberation has to do with freedoms of thought and opinion and expression. I firmly believe in them. So, let me say, regardless of the reason, I believe there should be no censorship at all. That's number one.

Number two, Salman Rushdie is an old friend of mine whom I have known for about ten years. I first met him in 1980–81 in London. I'm a great admirer of his writing, especially *Midnight's Children*, which I think is one of the great novels of the twentieth century. I also liked very much the book of short stories he wrote for his son, *Haroun and the Sea of Stories,* which I reviewed here in the United States. *Shame* I like less than *Midnight's Children*. I read it only once, and maybe if I read it again I will be able to get more into it.

The Satanic Verses, I think, is an interesting novel. It's a large, confused, in many ways brilliant book that is designed to be provocative. I mean, I am not going to sit here this evening and give you my precise literary critical analysis of his work, but he is a very gifted and extraordinary man and I deeply regret all the things that have happened to him. I also urge you not to censor what I am saying and to print it as I say it, knowing that you will be under pressure to decide how much you want to print about him.

So, as I was saying, I really regret that reactions to him have been as violent as they have been. Personally, I don't myself believe that it is in the nature of Islam or a part of the best traditions of Islamic civilization to suppress the writings of an offending dissenter, let us say. So, the hullabaloo about him has been deeply regrettable and, in many ways, unacceptable to me. Now, I can understand that a lot of Muslims are offended by *Satanic Verses*, even though, I must say, I am not sure if very many of them have even read the book. That's one of the great comic events of all time. All these people screaming about this book being an offense to Islam when most of them, at least in the Arab world, can't read the English language. After all, it is in English. But they just take the word of some ulema who claims this or that is what he says. That's garbage. It's terrible.

So, I am very disturbed about the whole thing and I just wish that Salman Rushdie could lead a normal life. I have seen him since he went underground and the toll this has taken on him has been terrible. It's a huge price to pay for an individual. He has lost the ability to be free. He can't move around as he wishes. He can't see his son. His second marriage failed while he was in hiding. And the sense of persecution and insecurity is tremendous. I feel it shouldn't happen to anyone. Our world is big enough to have people like Salman Rushdie writing as they do and to debate what they say. But to condemn him to death and to burn his book and to ban it—those are horrible, horrible things.

This coming Sunday, by the way, in *The New York Times*, they asked a number of people, including me to give their opinions about whether Wagner should be played in Israel or not. What I have done is written a few paragraphs comparing the attitudes of Israelis to Wagner with that of Muslims in the case of Salman Rushdie. And I oppose both views. Art and ideas one doesn't like have to be discussed, they can't just be thrown out of the window the way it was done during the inquisition. It's a great crime and I think it would do our world a great disservice if we let that view prevail.

Interview with Hasan M. Jafri,
The Herald, Karachi, Pakistan, 1992

TWENTY-THREE

EUROPE AND ITS OTHERS:

AN ARAB PERSPECTIVE

This interview was done in connection with a television program in Ireland.   E.W.S.

As an outsider looking in, do you think there is such a thing as a distinctively European tradition?

I think there is no question but one can talk about a European tradition in the sense of an identifiable set of experiences, of states, of nations, of legacies, which have the stamp of Europe upon them. But, at the same time, this must not be divorced from the world beyond Europe. In the Algerian context there is a good phrase for this—"complementary enemies." There is also a complementarity between Europe and its Others. And that's the interesting challenge for Europe, not to purge it of all its outer affiliations and connections in order to try to turn it into some pure new thing.

What is becoming of the "European intellectual" today?

The idea that the intellectual is a professional who is rewarded for his or her services has meant in the United States and in Europe that you have this extraordinary gravitation toward centers of power, that the intellectual thinks that the reward or the goal for what he or she does is a policy-playing, a policy-forming role, to be an opinion maker, a policy-maker. Whereas my view is that the intellectual role is essentially that of, let's say, heightening consciousness, becoming aware of tensions, complexities, and taking on oneself responsibility for one's community. This is a non-specialist role, it has to do with issues that cut way across professional disciplines. Because we know about professional discourse. I mean, it becomes a jargon, speaking only to the informed, keeping them essentially in a state of acquiescence, and promoting one's own position in the end. That's something I find deeply abhorrent, because it seems to me that society is made up of two kinds of people. There are the maintainers, the ones who keep things going as they are, and there are the ones who are the intellectuals, who provoke difference and change.

And you would introduce here an ethical scruple of responsibility for one's fellow citizens.

Yes, I think that's the essential thing.

And if that means a contamination or confusion of realms, then so be it?

So be it, exactly. For me, what has been terribly important is that I have a sense, maybe it's an accident of birth, that I'm affiliated with a national community—Palestine. Partly because of the universality of the cause, Palestine is not just a simple nationalist struggle, it involves the cultural problem of anti-Semitism. We have become the inheritors of European anti-Semitism: we are the victims of the victims, if you like. It's a complicated role. Nevertheless, having some connection with a national community—or community, never mind national—keeps one honest.

But is this where you would see a social and moral role for the intellectual, where in inventing or reinventing our traditions, we can actually take apart and analyze the myths and the symbols? There's a lot of talk at the moment about the creation of a new Europe. Do you think there might be a danger that we could witness the emergence of a new form of cultural imperialism?

I think the likelihood of a kind of imperialism that one associates with nineteenth-century European imperialism is not very great. And I think the overshadowing power and influence of the United States is also a kind of impediment to it. One would like to think that Europe— at least that's the way I think from the point of view of the Arab world—is a kind of counter to the United States; that it provides, partly because of the Mediterranean links between some of the southern European countries and North Africa, a kind of exchange of cultures that is not imperial, and that there is more give-and-take than before.

But has Europe succeeded in acknowledging the Other in its midst: the traditional Other, in this instance, being the Arab or Islamic world?

No, I don't think so. I think there's a problem. Take Italy. Italy now sees itself as saddled with about a million Muslims, all of them from North Africa, largely from Libya and Tunis, some from Egypt. This is unacknowledged, as opposed to France, which has also two or three million Moslems, which is a political issue. But I think discussion and debate, even the kind of rancorous debate that you get between Le Pen and some of his more liberal opponents, is better than the silence you find in Italy. Nevertheless, there is a presence there which is going to provoke more discussion and more awareness. And, interestingly enough, there is now in the Arab world a set of writers, thinkers, and intellectuals who are very serious about a Euro-Arab dialogue, exchange between the two that will break down some of the hostility, the kind of blanket, "Arabs versus the West" kind of thing. It's very different from the United States where there's none of that. The United States still regards itself as at war with the Arab world, or Islam, or fundamentalism, or something of that sort. So the cultural issue is never really even tapped.

But when it comes to concrete political decisions, it would seem that Mediterranean Europe, which has been open, both in terms of migrations and culturally, to the Arab world, was not able to stop a war taking place in that part of the world.

Not only that, but in the case of Britain, participated rather more avidly than one would have liked. On the other hand, in the postwar period, the Italians and the French did try to broker a political, as opposed to a military, settlement. The Italians have been very active since the war on a negotiated political settlement, obviously not of the Gulf situation, but of the crux, which is the Palestinian issue. Now, they haven't been able to stand up obviously to the Americans for a number of reasons. Partly because their efforts are individual. They're not done in the name of Europe. I mean, the Council of Europe has taken very good positions, but they haven't acted together as a Community, and probably won't until after '92, if then. Individually, they are caught. On the one hand, they're pressured by the U.S. On the other hand, they need oil from what are essentially conservative, reactionary Arab regimes who are very opposed to a change in the status quo. So their position is difficult. I'm really talking on a cultural level, where I think there is greater movement.

You've spoken a lot about the phenomenon of "Orientalism," a cultural phenomenon which basically represents a stereotypical attitude in Europe, and in the West generally, toward the Arab world.

Absolutely. It's really very powerful. You don't have to look in the jingoistic press. One thinks of the commentaries that one reads in *The Times* by, to mention names, Conor Cruise O'Brien, who still talks about the Muslim family as a depraved family full of incest, and the Muslims and the Arabs as violent and depraved people, or books like *The Closed Circle* by David Pryce Jones, which could not be written about any other ethnic cultural group in the world today.

This is a sort of racism?

It's racism, it's xenophobia, it's a kind of paranoid, delusional fantasy.

And why has Europe needed this?

I'll tell you why. With regard to the Arabs Europe has always had Islam at its doorstep, so to speak. Islam, don't forget, is the only non-European culture that has never been completely vanquished. It is adjacent to and shares the monotheistic heritage with Judaism and Christianity. So, there is this constant friction. And unlike, say, the British in India, the problem has not been settled. The idea of the West, I would argue, comes largely from opposition to the Islamic and Arab world. I think it probably goes back in its root to theological issues. The prophet Mohammed, who saw himself as a continuer of the line of prophecy that begins with Abraham, Moses, Jesus, and concludes prophecy, is seen initially in the first polemics against Islam in the seventh and eighth century as an upstart, a terrifying emanation from exactly the world that produced Christianity and Judaism. So I think it's a unique case, and the sense of cultural contest is further enhanced by military, and you might say economic and political, contests where a tremendous amount of ignorance pervades, and people are not entitled, are not able therefore, to look at the concrete experience between Muslims and Europeans which is in reality much more complicated than sheer animosity. I mean, there is a tremendous dependence, for instance, in Europe on Islamic science, on the transmission of science and philosophy from the Greeks to the Muslims and back to the West.

I am struck as a philosopher by the crucial role played by Arab thinkers like Avicenna and Averroes, the Córdoba school, the Andalusian school, and so on.

Absolutely. And the idea of the university flourishes in the Arab world. The idea of a college, you know, *the collegium,* is, in fact, an Islamic idea.

We've had some rather dramatic examples, haven't we, of the confrontation between the European and Arab worlds in recent times? I'm not just thinking of the Gulf War, but also of controversies within Europe itself. We've had the Salman Rushdie affair, which raised all kinds of issues around universal rights versus the right to differ; and, in France, the famous controversy over the wearing of the veil by Muslim girls in secular schools. It's been a common argument that if Arab immigrants come to Europe, and have every right to do so having been colonized by Europeans for so many hundreds of years, they should leave behind them their cultural, religious differences and conform to this secular, universal space which is modern Europe.

I think there are universal principles of free speech to which Muslims as well as everyone else conform; and I think it's important that there is in the Arab world—I can't speak with the same certainty about *all* the Islamic world, Pakistan, Bangladesh, and so on—a very important struggle taking place today between the forces, broadly speaking, of what one would want to call *secularism,* to which I attach myself, and the forces that could be broadly described as *religious.* Now, fundamentalism is a frequent topic on the television, but I think it would be wrong to associate fundamentalism with everything that takes place in the Arab and Islamic world. I mean, there are different brands of that. There is a debate going on, and I think we are now at a point in the Arab world where the religious alternative has been shown to be a failure. You can be Muslim, but what does it mean to have Muslim economics, Muslim chemistry? In other words, there's a universal norm when it comes to running a modern state. But the question is, what of those people who represent another side of Islam, which is Islamic resistance to the West? On the West Bank in Gaza people consider themselves Islamic militants fighting Israeli occupation, because that's the last area of their lives that the Israelis have not been able to penetrate, as was the case in Algeria during the French occupation. So there are different kinds of Islam, there are different kinds of secularism. To come back to the Rushdie question, there were many Arab writers and intellectuals, including myself, who publicly supported Salman Rushdie's right to write whatever he chose, and that has to be underlined. But what we also drew attention to is the fact that there are many Muslim writers in the Arab world, in the occupied territories for example, who were put in jail by the Israelis as journalists and novelists for reasons of political expediency. For instance, speaking of banning books, on the West Bank today, because of Israeli law, you cannot buy and read Plato's *Republic*. Nor can you read Shakespeare's *Hamlet*! There is a proscribed list of many hundreds of books, prohibited by the Israelis for reasons nobody can understand. Now, where were the Western writers who stood up for Salman Rushdie—I'm glad they did, and I stood with them—when it came to the advocation of Palestinian freedom of expression on the West Bank and Gaza today? I don't know whether you know this, but the use of the word Palestine is a punishable offense. If you use the word Palestine you can be put in jail for six months. So what about a single standard for all these things? Why hypocritically use this? We're in the same fight with you. We want also to fight against that kind of thing, but let us fight on *all* fronts.

There's been much talk in recent times about creating a new European order, a federal Europe of regions or nations, and there's been talk about creating a new world information order—I'm thinking especially of the UNESCO Report sponsored by the late Sean MacBride. Are you suggesting we should interpret this as a struggle to create a secular universal order?

I'm not sure I know. I'm not in favor of an abstract universalism, because it's usually the universalism of whoever happens to be most powerful. If you look around today, the language of universalism is proclaimed by the United States, which is the superpower—one would like to think it's the last superpower. Without wishing to preach to the converted, it does seem to me that Ireland could play an important role in all of this, because Ireland has a colonial past. Although European, it is different from Europe, noticeably from continental Europe, and it would seem to me that instead of the submergence of various European countries like Ireland into the general European personality, highlighting the differences would be very important for dealing precisely with other parts of the colonial world. For instance, it seems to me that Ireland has a very special role to play, not only in Palestine, by virtue of the divisions in this country, but also in South Africa. Highlighting differences and allowing that to engage Europe's others in a kind of exchange could be very important in breaking down the idea of the world in great cultural camps, which in the end become armed camps. No, I have nothing but suspicion for the kind of universalism that is sometimes talked about.

But would you have some hope that we can in the Western world, and in Europe in particular, overcome the traditional antagonism between "them" and "us"? Do you see the possibility of some kind of solidarity being created between those in Europe struggling for basic liberties and rights, and those within the Arab world who are doing exactly the same thing?

Yes, I think that is the hope, precisely that. It *is* a common struggle. But even more important than that, what struck me the most about the war and about the behavior of the Iraqis and even the response of Palestinians, was that this was a war of decrepit or diseased nationalism. I think the great problem is the whole issue of national identity, or what I would call the *politics of identity*—the feeling that everything you do has to be either legitimated by, or has to pass through the filter of, your national identity, which in most instances is a complete fiction, as we all know. I mean, an identity that says all Arabs are homogeneously the same and against all Westerners who are all the same. There are many Westerners, there are many Arabs. I think the principal role of the intellectual at this point is to break up these large, national, cultural, transcultural identities.

Whether it is pan-Arab nationalism or Euro-nationalism?

Yes. I mean, there is an Arab people, there is an Arab nation. It doesn't need defense, we know that. But what we need is to reclaim it from the rhetoric of nationalism which has been hijacked by regimes in the Arab world. You tell me what the Saudi Arabian regime, government, or the Syrian government, or the Egyptian government has to do with Arab nationalism. I tell you, zero, nothing. They are in the business of *using* Arab nationalism. Or take their defense of Palestine. They have betrayed the *intifada,* they do nothing for it. And they use the notion, not only of a national identity but of a beleaguered national identity, which produces the national security state, the repressive apparatus, the secret police, the army, as an instrument of repression. The same in Israel. The same idea, it's everywhere. The same in the United States. Can anyone persuade me that what the United States was fighting in the Gulf was an aggression that threatened the United States? Does security enter into it? That's total, absolute, complete nonsense. But the resurgent American identity needed and used the security issue. What about the real struggle for freedoms? Human freedoms which are central—freedom of expression, freedom of assembly, of opinion, and so on. And then, the political freedoms. Where today, for example, we know it's a scandal in South Africa that a vast majority of the inhabitants are not allowed the right to vote. But also the states of Europe and the United States who underwrite, subsidize, the denial of democratic freedoms for an entire nation, the Palestinians. I mean, that's a scandal also. But you have to get beyond the politics of identity to be able to talk about these things.

Are you then advocating a movement beyond the rival nationalisms of the Arab world on the one hand, and of Europe on the other hand? And do you see a danger of a relapse into nationalisms in Europe that would again be a mirror image for a similar occurrence in the Arab world?

I think that's obviously the great trap. What I would prefer to see is a Europe that is more aware, for example, of its colonial history. In other words, not to simply say, well, we've superseded that, we're something else now. Your history as Europeans is also a colonial history; and North Africa, for example, has to be dealt with as a fact that informs your present behavior and informs your relationship with these former colonized cultures.

Do you mean acknowledging also the immigrants who are a part of us?

There has to be an understanding, finally, that there is no political or national grouping that is homogeneous. Everything we are talking about is mixed, we deal in a world of interdependent, mongrelized societies. They are hybrids, they are impure.

Which is a strength and a virtue.

To me it's a virtue. What you're beginning to see now is a rhetoric of purification. I'm talking about the Far Right, let's say, in France, Le Pen. The idea that Europe is for the Europeans, you're beginning to hear it now. On one level, of course, it's fighting off the United States, and also Japan. Look at the rhetoric of Japan-bashing. The fundamental question is education. Most systems of education today, I believe, are still nationalist, that is to say, they promote the authority of the national identity in an idealized way and suggest that it is incapable of any criticism, it is incapable of any fault, it is virtue incarnate. There is nothing that lays the seed of conflict in the future more than what we educate our children and students in the universities to believe about ourselves.

Would you advocate multiculturalism, that we should read the texts of other traditions as well as the great Western texts?

I think so. Take America, for example. There has been a tremendous debate recently about the figure of Columbus. I mean, we're in 1992, which is the five hundredth anniversary of the discovery of the United States by Columbus. The figure of Columbus itself is a highly controversial one, but he has been domesticated, sanitized into this wonderful hero who discovered America, whereas, in fact, he was a slave trader, he was a colonial conqueror, he was very much in the tradition of the *conquistador*. Now, which is better, to prettify and sanitize or to admit the truth? And there is this ridiculous idea that if you don't do this inventing of tradition, which will produce a hero figure, who's basically a conqueror—you threaten the fabric of society. I say just the opposite—the fabric of society, particularly American society, but it's also true of Europe, contains many different elements, and one has to recognize them. I think children are perfectly capable of understanding that. It's the adults who don't want to understand that for base reasons.

Interview with Richard Kearney,
Visions of Europe, Dublin, Ireland, 1992

TWENTY-FOUR

SYMBOLS VERSUS SUBSTANCE:

A YEAR AFTER THE DECLARATION OF PRINCIPLES

It has now been a year since the Israeli-Palestinian Declaration of Principles on Interim Self-Government Arrangements (DOP) was signed in Washington. To what extent have your initial expectations about this agreement and its consequences been fulfilled?

Well, I wasn't very sanguine about the results, although I did think that there would be a more general Palestinian effort to rally around and make this terribly bad accord better, to improve the conditions, to change the context perhaps. But I've been very disillusioned, because not even that has happened. I think the Israelis correctly banked on Arafat's incompetence and the continued hold he seems to have on the Palestinian mind, which enables him to remain in Gaza and Jericho as a kind of local enforcer with extremely limited and dwindling power.

I've also been disappointed that the opposition to the DOP hasn't become more coherent. The DOP consolidated Israeli occupation with Palestinian acquiescence; it gave the Israelis sovereignty, control over water, security, external relations, and the veto power in everything of consequence occurring in the autonomous areas. Jerusalem, the settlements, and the roads remain in their hands, with no restrictions at all. People haven't tried to formulate an alternative. So what you have is four groups: quite a large group of silent and disappointed Palestinians, a second group of loyalists, a third group waiting around to see if things will get better for them, and, lastly, a group opposing the process and Arafat who can't seem to get it together. There haven't been any generalized meetings, and not more than a few general petitions have been signed. The result is a feeling of drift along with confusion and all-around pessimism.

I think what is most disappointing to most people is the fact that the money hasn't shown up. I had expected that. There were many promises made, but in the first long article I wrote, "The Morning After," I said that the whole notion of the place being flooded with dollars, projects, businessmen, and jobs for everyone was a fantasy. Because such arrangements in the past, in other parts of the world, have all proved illusory.

It seems that opposition to the DOP could basically take two directions: it could engage in a wide-ranging and broad national dialogue with the Palestinian leadership in an attempt to get it to change its program and implement reforms, or it could institutionalize itself as an opposition, probably with the more ambitious goal of removing the current leadership. Yet neither of these seem to be happening. As a member of this opposition, how would you like to see things proceed?

Well, I think these two have happened, at least the first one has. Beginning in October 1993, I was involved with others in the diaspora—loyal nationalists, genuine Palestinian patriots—who were convinced that the DOP was a bad bargain but believed that it was all we could get and we now had to help Arafat proceed. I went along with that, and signed a couple of early petitions asking to reform the mechanisms of the PLO [Palestine Liberation Organization], to bring in more competent people, to create institutions, and so on and so forth. And, alas, that stream of petitions—all of them useless—has continued.

Since then, I have taken the position, based upon the evidence I have gathered, that the leadership is obdurate and unreformable. They neither listen to each other—Arafat and Abu Mazen [Mahmoud Abbas] and Abu Alaa [Ahmed Qurai], to mention just three, are now no longer on speaking terms with each other—nor are they interested in listening to anyone else. They are simply interested in perpetuating their own positions and their own risible power.

I therefore think that the number one priority for the opposition ought to be a coherent program asking the PLO leaders to leave. They must be made to resign. I think noncooperation with them is the essential first step, just as the *intifada* was a form of noncooperation with the

Israeli occupation authority. Remember that the West Bank town of Bayt Sahur refused to pay taxes to the Israeli authorities. That's what we need now. Because not only are we still fighting the Israeli occupation, but in fact we are fighting an enforcer of the occupation—namely the PLO—which has the distinction of being the first national liberation movement in history to sign an agreement to keep an occupying power in place. So I think the preeminent responsibility of every Palestinian is not to cooperate with an authority that is a surrogate to the Israeli occupation and an incompetent one at that.

The PLO's main concern is security. Arafat has not been able to clean the streets of Gaza, but he has been able to establish five intelligence services all spying on each other. I think it's an outrage. He closes newspapers, people are bullied into silence, and so on. And the net result is that the very disturbing circumstances of the occupation remain the same if not worse.

A couple of weeks ago, the day after the early empowerment agreement was signed, General Danny Rothschild made a statement in which he said, "We're still the real power in the West Bank and Gaza Strip." And when journalists then asked what Israel had given the Palestinians, he replied: "We've given them the right to deliver services to the residents." That's the real meaning of early empowerment, and the PLO cannot exercise even these extremely limited responsibilities effectively.

It's interesting that you consider the opposition's priority as involving the Palestinian leadership rather than negating the DOP. Does this mean that you accept the DOP as an irreversible fact?

Not necessarily. I just think that the Palestine National Authority (PNA), the agents on the Palestinian side in charge of keeping the agreement in place, has occupied the place formerly reserved for the Israeli occupation authorities. People should refuse to cooperate with them, though selectively—it is possible, for example, to accept the notion that Palestinian education is in the hands of Palestinians. But insofar as the PNA is the security force that in a certain sense works for the Israelis, arresting Palestinians because the Israelis say they should be arrested, as has happened several times in the last few weeks, these are things I don't think people should cooperate with. And by that I mean not just saying, "I won't cooperate," but trying to set up different kinds of councils, for example, where local needs are taken care of by the communities, which is exactly what happened during the *intifada*. That's what I think the first priority should be.

The second thing is for the DOP to be modified. For this you need the diaspora, the vast majority of Palestinians who don't live in the West Bank and Gaza Strip and whose rights have been denied. I think it's very important that they should be inserted in the process in some meaningful way, to urge questions like Jerusalem, the settlements, and the rights of return and repatriation and compensation. Let's not forget that the Palestinian struggle began in the diaspora. The people in Israel and the occupied territories have always been prisoners, and this hasn't changed. The solution therefore has to be partly initiated from outside.

And number three—very important—concerns reparations. One of the most shocking aspects of the accords is the fact that no provision is made for any kind of Israeli reparations. The Israelis not only completely destroyed Palestinian society in 1948, they also destroyed the economies of the West Bank and Gaza Strip during the last twenty-seven years of occupation. Yet no reparations have been demanded of them. The Iraqis occupied Kuwait for a matter of weeks and they will be paying for what they did, financially, for a long time to come. The Israelis should be made to pay too. It's true that we're very weak, but since 1982 this leadership has not attempted to mobilize its people or the resources available to it. I mean, Nelson Mandela was in jail for twenty-seven years and still he was able to remain steadfast in his devotion to certain principles. And through the African National Congress (ANC), which was completely exiled or underground, he was able to mount an international campaign, which is what turned the tide. We've never done that. And I think that's what we should do.

In light of what has transpired during the past year and your views on these events, how do you reconcile the apparent contradiction that for many years you were seen as a leading advocate for American recognition of the PLO, and of Yasir Arafat in particular, and that you are now among the most prominent critics of the PLO and Arafat?

I felt that Arafat was genuinely a representative of Palestinian nationalism, far transcending his actual role as a human being. And so publicly, in the West, I was always supporting him as a way of supporting the Palestinian national idea. The PLO was our institution; I was defending it as something that represented us. I publicly defended Arafat insofar as he was attacked—which in the West was consistently the case—as the personification of the Palestinian national idea, but did not consider it my business to defend his person or methods when these were at issue.

As for my own relationship with Arafat and the Palestinian leadership, I never was a close adviser. I lived too far away from them, in more senses than one. I would see them when I would go to Beirut and then to Tunis, and before that to Amman, and these relations were always quite critical. I never tried to get anything from Arafat. What I was most interested in was trying to make him understand the nature of the West, and America in particular—about which he had absolutely no idea—and to try to convince him of some of the things I mentioned earlier, such as the need for a campaign, the need to organize it.

I also tried to get them not to focus so strongly on the administration. I lost in that, because in the end what they wanted was to get in bed with James Baker and George Bush. They thought that was their greatest achievement, that the secretary of state spoke to them. But before he spoke to them, he spoke to me. I saw Secretary of State Vance in 1979. I had access to him. I had access to them all, living in America and knowing everybody as I do. I saw Secretary of State Shultz in 1988 with Ibrahim Abu-Lughod. We weren't instructed to see him by the PLO. What we told Shultz and then told Arafat—or rather what Abu-Lughod then told Arafat—made no impression on them at all.

My idea has always been that the Palestine question in the United States and in the West in general is an issue of the opposition, not of the establishment, and that we should work with our constituency. The leadership was never interested in that. As of the fall of 1989, when I did a long interview with the Kuwaiti newspaper *al-Qabas,* I have been publicly critical of their behavior.

And during the summer of 1991, when I was involved in the run-up to the Madrid Conference, trying to define a Palestinian strategy for dealing with the conference and exactly what we wanted from the Americans, I finally realized that all they wanted was acceptance. They weren't interested in fighting, in being equal, they just wanted the white man to say they were okay. That's all. I was astonished. That's when I broke with them, and now I have no relationship with them at all. I refuse to talk to them. It's hopeless. This leadership is what Frantz Fanon used to call "Black Skin, White Masks." They're desperate to be white. That's not what our struggle is about. But even before this break, my relations with them were always critical. Cordial, but critical.

I wonder if you could expand upon another theme you've addressed in your writings since the signing of the DOP, namely, what you term the "discipline of detail" and your view that the Palestinian leadership lacks this discipline.

What I mean by the "discipline of detail" is best illustrated by a small story. In the negotiations that went from Oslo to Cairo, all—literally all—of the facts, documents, figures, and even the maps that were used were produced by the Israelis. The PLO has been unable to produce one item of information that is not derived from an Israeli source. And this is about our land! This is what I mean by the discipline of detail. If you're going to negotiate with your enemy—and Israel is our enemy—you need maps that you yourself make. We need a strategy on the ground, above all for Jerusalem, which the Israelis have been taking bit by bit. Their historical motto was "Another Acre, Another Goat." Historically, the Palestinians have never produced a counter-strategy.

In Jerusalem there's a Dutch geographer, Jan de Jong, who has documented what they've been doing and what their plan is. It's there for everybody to see. Yet the Palestinian leadership has never responded to it at all. The settlements are growing and, along with their road network, have largely been built with Palestinian labor. We've never formulated a strategy for preventing Palestinian labor participation in the expropriation of our own land.

And above all, in the years that I've known this leadership, they've never had the vision, or the seriousness, to develop a systematic strategy in which each detail is an organic part of the whole. The way you develop a real strategy is by gathering around you people who are willing—not for money but out of dedication—to devote themselves to the idea of liberation. But this leadership is not interested in liberation, which requires effort and the discipline of detail, where even a square inch actually liberated is much more important than getting general principles like the DOP signed in Washington. We will need an entire generation to be trained in what is effectively a modern struggle.

I refuse that my fate as a Palestinian should be that of nineteenth-century Africans or American Indians where the white man gives the chief a few trinkets and says, "Okay, now you're the leader, but we're the real power here." We have to feel that we are equal, that we can fight them on technical and scientific grounds, that we know what we are talking about—that we have discovered the information that we have for ourselves. Last summer there was talk of two hundred technical committees in the West Bank and Gaza studying issues like refugees and water and land, and so on, but no results have appeared. We have only one decision maker, namely Mr. Arafat, and he's a man of no education, he cannot read a foreign language, he's distracted, and he is governing an entire nation of six million people who have the leading doctors and lawyers and engineers and intellectuals in the Middle East and the highest rate of university graduates in the region. It's a disgrace.

Arafat says that we have confidence in Rabin. But the fact of the matter is that the situation has gotten worse since the DOP was signed. The Israelis are out not only to take everything from us—they already did that—but to humiliate us in the full sense of the word. What's so outrageous about the period since the signing of the DOP is that Rabin and his gang, who have remained essentially unchanged military men, are being billed as men of peace and vision and courage and all the rest of it even while they continue to apply the policies they always had based on notions of the Palestinians as an inferior people. The implementation of this accord in a sense embodies this idea insofar as it makes us dependent on them—we are to have no authority, they retain all real power, they know better. Even the people with whom they signed the agreement, like Arafat, are humiliated—he is being searched in Gaza. The Palestinian negotiators are unable to get from the Israelis even the right to pass from Gaza to Jericho, a distance of ninety miles. And this leadership has gone along with it, because it's sort of Abu-'Arab, you know, "It doesn't matter." But all of these things matter very much.

It's as if they are snowed by this agreement, where the only thing the Israelis conceded is that the PLO is the representative of the Palestinian people. And Arafat was received in the White House. But today in

America, the PLO is still considered a terrorist organization. We still haven't gotten a cent from the United States. Just for moving a few troops around in Gaza so that Arafat could come in on 1 July, the Americans added $180 million to the aid budget for Israel. We got nothing. There's this idea that we have to accept what's given us, which I don't understand at all.

In your initial reaction to the DOP you did say that Israeli recognition of the PLO was not something to be underestimated. But current views seem to be that the PLO is more about symbols than substance.

Totally. Do you know what they were negotiating the last night before the signing of the 4 May Agreement, according to the British press and according to a friend who was there? Whether Arafat could put his likeness on the postage stamps! That's what's of interest to him. And a friend of mine who was on the PLO Executive Committee at the time told me that during the negotiations in Oslo between chief Palestinian negotiator Abu Alaa and the Israelis, Arafat only took interest in those sections that had to do with him. So it's all about symbols over substance. It's a disgrace that we should accept such nonsense. He arrived in Jericho with an Israeli helicopter guarding him. Imagine how Palestinian prisoners must have felt seeing the "Maximum Leader" escorted by their jailers. That's the situation we're in. And that's why I think that Arafat, if he had any decency, if he had any backbone—and the same goes for all those leaders and negotiators that surround him who had a hand in this appalling process—would say, "This is all we can do." In my opinion, we need a referendum.

The whole issue of democracy has been pushed to the forefront during the last year. It does seem that a key element of any program of reforms, particularly now that the PLO is for all intents and purposes centered in the occupied Palestinian territories (OPT), is to hold elections and referenda there. At the same time, don't you feel that elections in the OPT, even if they were free, fair, and fully democratic, would further marginalize Palestinian communities in exile?

That's perfectly right. I think there's been a vast exaggeration of the importance of "free and open" elections. First of all, I don't think there can be, under the present circumstances, constitutively, free and open elections at all, because there is an Israeli occupation army, and a Palestine National Authority whose power and authority derives from the Israeli occupation, and also because the only permitted alternatives are Arafat and the PLO on the one hand or the Israeli occupation authorities on the other.

So I'm not one of these American-style liberal Palestinians proliferating now in America and elsewhere who heap all the responsibility and blame on Arafat for denying democracy. I mean, Arafat is not part of any democratic setup. He is mandated by the Israelis to enforce what they call their security, and therefore you can't have democratic elections in any meaningful sense of the term.

And second, as you said, unless the exercise is accompanied by the enfranchisement of the diaspora Palestinians, then it further marginalizes them. I completely agree. So that's why I keep talking about the need for a census, for assemblies constituted by Palestinians no matter where they are, in the West Bank and Gaza Strip, inside Israel, in Lebanon, and elsewhere. And I'm surprised this hasn't happened. And until there's some sense in which the Palestinians constitute themselves as a political body, you can never have democracy. You can't have democracy legislated from above by decree. That's kind of a parody of the whole thing. So, I've never spoken about elections as the panacea or the answer to the problem. There are elections in Syria, Iraq, Egypt. They are described as democratic and open, in which anybody can vote, and so on and so forth. But what do they mean? What is needed is a culture of democracy, not just a few democratic pretenses suddenly appearing that are supposed to solve all our problems.

Concerning the Palestinian exile communities, there seems to be an increasing hostility to the Palestinian presence in several host countries on the part of either the government, sections of the population, or both. How do you view this challenge?

One of the achievements of the PLO in the decades prior to the DOP was a unity of the Palestinian people, by which I mean that we think of ourselves as one people, whether we live in Nazareth, or Nablus, or Beirut, or New York. Now this sense is dissipated, and Palestinian communities that are relatively unprotected, like in Lebanon, are now open to the hostility of the host governments, which in a sense can't be blamed. Lebanon is a precarious republic, as it has been called, and to try to enfranchise and give citizenship to 400,000 Palestinians is unimaginable for them. In Jordan, there's the problem of dual citizenship, of Palestinians carrying Jordanian passports.

With the Oslo agreement, the PLO suddenly stopped this process of mobilizing and attracting Palestinians to a new concept, which has to be based on the gradual repatriation of Palestinians, and, second of all, pressing for modifications in the Israeli "Law of Return." These things can be done, not easily, but at least they're talking points, part of the negotiation. The Israelis are masters at making past oppressors pay for what they did to them. They got over $40 billion in reparations from the Germans. They're in absolutely no position, moral or otherwise, to tell us to forget about the past and apologize for what we did to them, and that we are the ones who should pay the price.

There has to be a collective effort. And what I don't understand, and what I find deeply disturbing, is why we have been unable in the year since the signing of the DOP even to set up a forum in the diaspora. So the problem of the diaspora is a problem of leadership, or the absence of leadership; the notion that, to most people, the problem appears to be solved, coupled with a sense of desperation and confusion, with the poorest and the underprivileged—the large majority—in the worst possible position.

Now, I think that what is happening in the PLO itself, from what I've been able to gather, is that there is now a dispute between Arafat, who is confined by the terms of this agreement mainly to the Gaza Strip, and the PLO in Tunis. Faruq Qaddumi, the head of the PLO political department and the senior PLO official in Tunis, seems to be advancing the thesis that Arafat can occupy himself with the PNA in the West Bank and Gaza Strip according to the terms laid down by the Israelis—he has no choice—but that this does not commit the rest of the PLO, with its offices and embassies and few remaining institutions and, above all, its capital. His argument is that we should be able to use what's left of the PLO to remobilize and to advance the process that had begun already in the late 1960s. There may be some hope there.

Some of your critics have faulted your position on the DOP for failing to offer alternatives. I know you have addressed this point in your writings, but could you expand on it here, both with regard to alternatives prior to the signing of the agreement and alternatives today, a year later?

There were alternatives all along, including the Egyptian–Israeli Agreement at Camp David. I was one of the many, certainly including the PLO leadership, who said, "We won't have any part in it." The question that I need to have asked of Arafat and company after the DOP is, "Why have you turned down all these other alternatives, about which we all know, only to take this one?" That's where the principle of accountability comes in. These people have never been made accountable for their actions, which have led to one disaster after another. Actually, this question about alternatives should not be asked of *me*, but of *them*. That's point one.

The second point is, I'm not a politician. I don't know how to suddenly create a new leadership, and so on and so forth. These are issues that concern a community, not just individuals sitting on a chair somewhere saying, "Well, this is what should happen." I've never believed that. But what I'm really concerned about is the need to raise the level of participation to enable people to feel they are doing something to advance the cause of our people. And I would say that maybe 80 percent of Palestinians today, whether in the West Bank and Gaza Strip, inside Israel, or abroad, don't feel a sense of participation, but feel excluded. But the only way not to be excluded is to speak out and take part in what's going on.

One way of participating is in projects in the occupied territories, including self-help projects financed from abroad that will build institutions. But most of the projects that I've heard about are not infrastructural. For example, take the Builders for Peace chaired by Vice President Al Gore, which includes a lot of Arab and Palestinian businessmen as well as Jewish businessmen. What are they going to build? They are going to build a hotel. They are going to build a water-bottling plant. They are going to build more tourist facilities. There is talk of an airport in Gaza. Is that really what is needed, or should we not be more concerned about rebuilding houses, rebuilding parts of Jerusalem or being involved in the building of parts of Jerusalem that are still available for public projects? We have not been able to finance one public project in Jerusalem by private Palestinian money committed to a national cause. There's a health problem in the West Bank and the Gaza Strip, there's an education problem, there are sanitation problems. Those are the issues that need to be addressed. But I don't think it's going to be done by some "Maximum Leader" who comes up and says, "Let's do this and let's do that." As I understand it, it has to be something generated by the people themselves.

Your generation was very much present at the inception of the contemporary Palestinian national movement and, even more so, during its rise to international prominence in the period after 1967. I'm wondering how, more than a quarter of a century later, you see the ambitions, aspirations, and ideals that initially motivated you. Did you ever think you would be in the position you are in today?

No. I tell you, my major insight into the period of the last twenty-five or thirty years has been that we have still not been able to—well, let me put it this way. The successes are obvious: the institutions, the PLO, the sense of national consciousness, and so on and so forth. The failures we've just been talking about.

But one of the things that haunts me is that, like most of the Arabs— and this may be a cultural thing—we've only been able to think in terms of survival, steadfastness, *sumud*. We haven't turned the corner to think in terms of actually winning, which is quite a different thing. To stay in one place, in order not to lose what one has—that's very important and to a certain degree we've done that. We've remained a Palestinian people despite all the deprivations and the pressures and the Declaration of Principles, and so on. There is a Palestinian national consciousness which is there. But we haven't been able to find a mechanism or a method or a politics for converting dispossession into repossession, for converting defeat and loss, which is really the history of the last forty-five years, into something resembling an actual victory.

That is what haunts me—why we've been unable to do that. Why we can't think collectively in the same terms that a very successful Palestinian businessman can; he creates a company and reaps the profits and creates something that lasts. Or like a Palestinian intellectual when he or she does research and produces an important book. That's something reclaimed, something substantiated. But nationally, all our institutions, almost without exception, have a half-life of about ten years, and then they die and we start all over again. We reinvent the wheel and start from scratch. So the question is why we're satisfied with persistence and steadfastness, and not concerned enough with actually defining something, the sort of thinking that produced the slogan "Another Acre, Another Goat." There's very little of that.

The discipline of detail?

The discipline of detail. I don't know why it's missing. It's not missing in the personal lives of many of us, but collectively it's not there. Our leaders embody the kind of defeatism and passivity that led one of them to tell me after Oslo that we had to accept the fact that all we will get from Israel is what Israel gives, that otherwise we can have nothing. Why? What happened to our will? What happened to our purpose? They are never factored into the equation.

An example that haunts me, again, is when I went to South Africa in 1991 shortly after Mandela was released—I think I was the first Palestinian to go there—and I saw Nelson Mandela and Walter Sisulu. And I said to them, "How did this happen? You were terrorists, exiles, and prisoners." And they said: "Number one, we never let go of our principles. We never changed what we were fighting for. Number two, we focused on the international dimension, because our international success in delegitimizing apartheid gave hope to the people inside to continue the struggle." In contrast, we are nothing now but an international laughingstock. How do most Palestinians feel when they see Arafat strutting around pretending that he's the leader of something when he works under the thumb of the Israeli military authorities? You need a qualitative change of consciousness where you move from simply trying to be there to trying to liberate and move and win. That's what I think has been the failure of my generation.

If you compare the Palestinian experience with that of South Africa, the ANC began with a program committed to the establishment of a unitary, nonracial, democratic state, and in the course of its struggle was prepared to make any compromise or concession provided it did not undermine that ultimate goal. . . .

In other words, they were strategically very firm and tactically very flexible. We're exactly the opposite.

And on that basis critics could say that you were one of the most prominent advocates of a negotiated compromise with Israel on the basis of a two-state solution, whereby 77 percent of Palestine would be permanently conceded to Israel and the possibility of a unitary, secular state precluded. Couldn't they see a contradiction in your present opposition to a solution they would contend is the logical consequence of what you supported in the past?

I've just collected my political writings in a volume, and I think the record is quite clear. I've always been very consistent. First of all, I never said anything about simply accepting X percentage of land; I talked about fighting for it.

Second, I've always believed that neither side had a military option. So essentially, for all kinds of structural, international, ideological, and cultural reasons, it's a kind of stalemate, and the only way you can go forward is to negotiate a political agreement between the two sides. But I've always specified that it has to be an agreement between two sides with equal claims as far as rights are concerned, so that if we lost land in 1948, that doesn't mean we lost the claims to repatriation for those Palestinians who would want to go back. We still don't even know how many Palestinians from 1948 want to go back. We've never bothered to find this out, among other things. And certainly compensation. I've never believed in giving that up. If we lost it, then it has to be paid for by the Israelis.

And, third, I certainly had no conception other than of two states with equal rights for the citizens of both states where, let's say, there were free-flowing borders. I was for a Palestinian sovereignty and an Israeli sovereignty that were necessarily in interaction with each other, and in the end would perhaps create a situation like the cantons of Switzerland. And this is in a certain sense part of the notion of equality and, let's say, shared sovereignty. So I really haven't changed my views. I still believe in the concept of a unitary state, but you can't impose that on your opponent, which is what the early PLO formulation involved— telling them that this is what they have to have. I believe in democratic choice, which means that if the Israelis want their own form of what is in my opinion a deformed nationalism, imbued with the kind of religion that is going to be very problematic for them in the years to come— there's a kind of standing civil war now in Israel between religious and secular forces—but if that is what they want, then let them have it. But we should also be entitled to make a choice for ourselves.

The question of land is a question of realism, and negotiations, and of claims that can be settled retrospectively. If I lost my family's property in Talbiyya I should be allowed to claim it back as my own and at the very least to claim compensation for my loss. The curious thing is that the house I was born in, my family's house, is now the International Christian Embassy, given to them by the Israeli state. What right does the Israeli state have to dispose of Palestinian property in that way? This leadership that we have never even raised the issue. So I don't think I've changed. I think they've changed. But I'll never change.

Interview with Mouin Rabbani,
The Journal of Palestine Studies, Washington, D.C., 1995

TWENTY-FIVE

THE ROAD LESS TRAVELED

Professor Said, your contributions to the intellectual and academic ter-rain of not only this country, but to the world at large have been re-markable and singular in that they have had an enormous impact in shaping some of the cultural debates of our times. And yet, one gets the feeling that it is your involvement and commitment to the Palestinian cause that is most important. In many ways you could be called an ac-tivist. How would you respond to that?

Yes, of course. I like to think of myself like that. I just came back last week from Palestine and it is a terrible situation over there . . .

One does not get much inside information on this. I read about the work of Sara Roy on the Gaza Strip for instance, and there are some articles in magazines and papers, but not nearly enough is really known . . .

There has been almost a total press blackout, because once something appears on the White House lawn, two people shaking hands in the name of a peace process, nobody pays any attention to the details. All of which is terrible for the Palestinians. The Israelis have got a fantastic deal.

Have you distanced yourself from the leadership, from Arafat?

Oh, totally. I am an outspoken, some would say too outspoken an opponent. I didn't find anybody who defended him when I was there. I even had a long meeting with one of his ministers, a very close adviser of his whom I have known since the days of Beirut and he was just excoriating. He said the man is corrupt and even if you leave that aside, there is his capriciousness, his desire to control everything, and he is a despot.

And the way it all started out, in the beginning . . .

Well, exactly. It is very hard for somebody like myself who has been involved in the struggle for Palestinian national rights for thirty years to discover that the man I have supported and defended in this country has betrayed everyone. Incidentally, I used to be known in America as Arafat's man because I was quite close to him and I did it out of commitment, because he was the leader of a popular movement, and so forth. And now he is the enforcer, the Israeli kind of right-hand man on the West Bank. It is not only shocking but starkly dramatic. The first day I was there. . . . My son is living there. I was driving to the Palestinian military headquarters of Ramalla and there was a demonstration and so we stopped and we got out and there were students demonstrating against the Palestinian authorities, against them for picking up that day 50 students and arresting them. Exactly what they used to do with the Israelis, except that now the Palestinians are doing it instead of the Israelis.

What is the way out now?

I am uncompromising in my belief that two things have to happen. One is that we have to rid ourselves of the present leadership. Arafat is unreformable. He is a brilliant tactician but he cannot build a nation and he is without vision, really obsessed with the tiny details of power and above all, he is saddled by the burdens of the Oslo agreement. We have no territorial sovereignity, no territorial continuity. To get from one town to another we have to pass through Israeli barriers. For him to leave Gaza to come to the West Bank which is a distance of about 65 km he has to get Israeli permission. Second, we need a new peace movement that will proceed to negotiate with the Israelis on the basis of equity. It is a long struggle because we are very weak. We don't have support like the Israelis do from the United States, and they are a first world country. If you drive now from Jerusalem which is now part of Israel on the road to Ramallah which is the West Bank capital, it is like going through southern California, passing through a military barrier and you are immediately in Bangladesh. The road gets to half its size, is full of potholes and there isn't a single repair crew around. The houses are ramshackle, people are poor and there is 70 percent unemployment. The Israelis control the economy, they control the security, they control the borders, they control everything. So how can a nation get its independence? This has to go.

What about social development?

Every conceivable social development is being inhibited. Arafat is a terrible role model. And now one of the things I noticed, it's just an impression, that all the NGOs that are now starting up . . . some of them are quite laudable, vocational training, information services, educational inputs, curriculum development, and so on . . . Most of them are one-man shows. Somebody who has never been elected has been there for twenty years. *You* understand what I am saying? It is the same in many parts of the Third World. India has definitely gone beyond this but, unfortunately, we haven't. And unless we set a new model for collaborative or cooperative life and learning, how to work together, you know, not to attack people behind their backs, and all the minuscule details that make up a civil life. And until we do that, we will just remain where we are. We are a Fourth World country, incredibly underdeveloped.

Is it worse than, say, Bangladesh or Nepal?

No question about that. Because don't forget, those countries are poor for natural reasons and whatever; some political reasons. But in our case, take Gaza. As Sara Roy pointed out, [it] was deliberately de-developed by the Israelis. They destroyed the economy and the same is true of the West Bank. Israel has been in military occupation for twenty-nine years . . . it's the second longest military occupation in the twentieth century, and that meant that they deported people, they broke up organizations, they closed schools, they closed universities. We have a whole generation that is uneducated. So all this is a very heavy burden to bear. Now there is the bourgeoisie, a middle class, and they are prosperous and know how to take care of themselves, but I am talking about the large mass of the people . . .

So how important a part of your work is all this?

It is very important. I mean it is not the main thing, but it is one of the main things I do. Because I think we are at a very critical juncture in our history. I think in the past I used to think of myself as a soldier, you know, we were trying to mobilize people and I did what I could, which is to speak and write. Of course, I live in exile and am part of the expatriate community. Over 50 percent of the Palestinian people live outside Palestine and most since 1948. Then after the Oslo agreement I felt it was my duty to produce a book about this. It is my duty now to speak out and tell the truth. It is important to provide a record of what is happening, so I published a series of essays originally written for the Arab press that chronicle the whole betrayal and the crimes against our people.

Peace and Its Discontents?

Yes, that's it, but now I feel I have to be more involved. I have been ill for some time. Periodically I have to have chemotherapy, but I am okay, you know. I can manage although it is a fairly serious disease . . .

I find this extraordinary, courageous . . .

No, it's absolutely necessary. The alternative is to become an invalid and just sit around and mope and feel sorry for oneself. I really need to fight this. I was also tremendously encouraged by the fact that my son has gone out there, and I mean this is a New York City kid and he taught himself Arabic, which is not his native language, and although my wife and I speak it, he grew up as an American. And now he translates from Arabic to English and English to Arabic and he is living there as a volunteer on his own money on less than $100 a month because he thinks it's important to do this. Now I didn't force him, it is out of his own commitment and that is what encourages me now, this new generation . . .

Was there something in your own childhood, the fact of exile maybe, that pushed you into political activity?

No. Because my family is completely apolitical. I have no history of this in my immediate family, but I have relatives scattered around, and some of the extended family were involved in politics, but not my parents. I think it was the experience of living in America, where you can become radicalized very quickly, because one is so aware . . . I came here in the early fifties.

The kind of commitment you have shown in spite of your academic work and pressures and your recent illness is extremely unusual. How many intellectuals do this sort of thing and do you think that intellectuals should play this kind of role?

I think they should, exactly. To be perfectly honest, I am rather sad about it. And unfortunately, in the case of Palestine, very few do it and that is the thing I haven't been able to understand and figure out. In order to make the situation possible today, we did have an intellectual capitulation before it happened and this particular "peace process" to me represents capitulation and surrender. Of course in every battle there is a winner and a loser, and they are powerful and have money, etc. But there is a difference between giving up and throwing yourself at the mercy of your conqueror on the one hand and acknowledging this one defeat and saying, well, that was one battle, but we have to go on to the next step. I was just talking to this very intelligent, very resourceful Palestinian American who runs a think tank, and he keeps saying there's no alternative. We certainly are more credible now than we were before, and he keeps saying there is no alternative. Now that's part of the defeat, people saying this, but of course there is an alternative.

What about the role of intellectuals and academics in the Western world, in the U.S. for instance?

Did you see my book on the intellectuals which were the Reith Lectures I gave to the BBC in 1993 called *Representations of the Intellectual*? Well, basically, what has happened is that they have become caught up in professionalism and expertise, that is, the narrow focus. You know, in fact there has been quite a dramatic willingness on the part of so-called policy intellectuals who are concerned with the economy, with social issues, women's issues, to work with the powers that be. The idea of the intellectual as somebody who represents the powerless, the dispossessed, doesn't exist.

Why not?

It is hard to know why. There are historical reasons of course, and the distance of the academic from the world, and the notion that academics should not be involved, the notion of respectability. I've paid a very heavy price in terms of the abuse at different times. I have a button in my house that was installed there about ten years ago, and if I press it rings at the police station and they come immediately. My office has been burned, ransacked, and in print I've been called all sorts of things. There was an article in a very respectable magazine that called me "the professor of terror." So you have to really put up with a lot, and people don't want to. And then there are prizes and awards, and honorary degrees and they want them.

Do you see this trend everywhere?

In some parts of the Third World, it is disgraceful. Take Palestine or any of the other Arab countries. Intellectuals have just lost touch with their own people, they've become Americanized, they serve the regimes. One has to also say that they live in a very difficult situation, because we're talking about uniform despotism and tyrannies in the Arab world. It is so difficult to stand up when one could be silenced, imprisoned, or killed. But some people still do that. There is a Jordanian intellectual, a good friend of mine who in a lecture criticized King Hussein going to Rabin's funeral and said that there has been a Hashemite-Zionist alliance, and they have put him in jail for that. He has been in jail for five months now and without charge. Just because of speaking. In fact he was tried on an action of what the ancien régime in Europe would call *lèse majesté*. In Arabic there is a phrase, "his tongue got too long and stretched out to the king" and that is a penal offense. For giving a lecture he's been jailed for three years. But he did it and even though it may be difficult, some people still stand up.

The fact that people distance themselves from issues of this nature, issues that infringe on basic fundamental rights, seems more shocking in countries like India and the U.S., which are democracies, where people can protest—in that sense, do you see intellectuals, and even literature, culture, and the arts as somehow being estranged from some of the very basic concerns of society?

Totally. I mean they become ornamental. The idea that art is not political is the reigning dogma of the late twentieth century. You know, the idea that art and culture are above politics. That there is something ennobling and redemptive about them and they can't be sullied by involvement which is totally untrue. Historically you cannot find an instance of great art in the Western tradition which hasn't been involved in politics.

In Culture and Imperialism, *you have talked about the need to read the great novels of the nineteenth century in that way, but does this take away from an enjoyment of them as just novels, just art?*

No, not at all. Novels are about the world. For example, the novels of Jane Austen that I talk about in that book are about the world of men and women, and about the world of history, the world of eating and drinking and growing up, and dying and marrying. And necessarily, they are involved in questions of power, of justice, questions of wealth and poverty, and so on.

Is it also the duty of the intellectual, the academic to decipher or decode art and literature to the wider public?

Well, I suppose everyone cannot be engaged in doing this, but certainly as a teacher that is what I would do, and what I am mostly interested in is in developing this critical attitude among my students, to be able to read self-consciously and be skeptical as well as inquisitive.

What about the kind of literature that is being produced right now? There seems to be a huge gap between popular literature on the one hand, and the more literary kind of writing, the serious novels that are also being produced. Which of them reflect national culture more?

America's mass culture is interesting, and some of these novels do reflect the consumers' tastes, but they also reflect a basic lack of attention on the part of the public, you know, what is now called the airport novel—John Grisham, Tom Clancy, etc. They represent the apprehensions, the obsessions, the interests of the mass public, whether it is sex or political violence, or the time of the Cold War. Other than that, there is what we would call quality literature, novels by people like Updike and Philip Roth, who are popular but literary, and they are on the whole reflective of the national moment. They are sort of in touch with the first group but are obviously of a better quality and they are more self-conscious and more attention is given to the writing. Then there is the third kind which you might say is literature that aspires to the status of a classic, and what is interesting about this third group is that it has an international quality about it, and it includes not only American writers like Thomas Pynchon but European and Third World writers like Rushdie and García Márquez.

Does this kind of writing build bridges between people and cultures?

Yes, because it has an international audience.

In that sense do they have a message, a kind of common language of understanding, and will they work as agents of change in society?

Oh, very much so. Much more than the other two categories, these novels can work as agents of social, intellectual, and cultural change, because they introduce whole new worlds. To give an example, for an English-speaking reader to read Rushdie is to really read something completely new. I mean it has connections with the world of Kipling and Forster, but it is transformed, it is post-colonial and has its own magic, its own brilliance. And it also introduces a particular kind of hybrid experience into English.

Does the mass media have a role to play in the dissemination of this kind of literature to the larger public?

They do have a role but they don't play it. I just know about America really, the quality is so low and in my view it just purveys lies and stereotypes and propaganda. For me it is virtually impossible to look at TV and to even read papers like *The New York Times* without the need to correct them because they are so deceitful, so full, in my opinion, of wrong perspectives, and the contexts are often wrong.

But you don't keep away from them?

Not entirely, but the opportunities afforded one are very limited. They don't want to hear from me, they want to hear from people who more or less reinforce the national policy and say the things that they expect. But I feel it is my duty up to a point to make an intervention whenever I can.

In Culture and Imperialism *you talk about the resistance to empire that gradually built up; now in the present-day situation of neo-colonialism and the economic dominations of America, do you perceive any kind of resistance to this?*

Of course. Unfortunately, it is not to my taste, it is not secular resistance. Look at some of the Islamic movements, Hamas on the West Bank, the Islamic Jihad, etc. They are violent and primitive forms of resistance. You know, what Hobsbawm calls pre-capital, trying to get back to communal forms, to regulate personal conduct with simpler and simpler reductive ideas. Now I am not at all for them, and violence for its own sake is to be condemned absolutely, but they are essentially protest movements. In most instances they arise out of two principal factors. One is the corruption, the incompetence and the inability to serve the needs of the domestic populations by local regimes, and the other is, as in the case of Iran, the resistance to the hegemony and dominance of the United States, which is the only world power that has made no secret of its eagerness to impose itself for reasons of its own economic gains, strategic advantages, and a sheer hegemonic drive. It is very difficult to watch this happen, especially the way the U.S. uses regional powers like Egypt, Israel, or Saudi Arabia and very often these regimes are aligned against their own people. Warren Christopher talks about terrorism every day, but the main issue is not terrorism but people want to eat.

There is one more question I would like to ask. You have often discussed the idea of the resurgence of national identities in a postcolonial world. In some cases, it has become the resurgence of narrower identities, such as communal identities, religious identities, as in the resurgence of Hindutva in India for instance. How would you view this?

I am uniformly opposed to this. I was in Greece just now, and the same question was raised there with the conflicts between Greece and Turkey, Macedonia, the former Yugoslavia, the Serbs and the Croats, and so on. Those are all in my opinion a legacy of imperialism. The idea of narrow and separate identities is not really historically based but that we belong to much larger identities, ones that are more healing, and more generously defined. This idea of Hindu versus Muslim, etc., goes back to the days of Partition and British policy in India. I am not saying there was a rosy period when everyone was happy but I am talking about the exacerbation that has occurred, and people are afraid of changes, and it is natural to hold on to what you think is nearest and dearest. Also, people only with very great difficulty accept the idea that identity is not just one thing but several things, so they prefer to hold out for one thing in order to fight against another. In all these instances it goes back to the Greeks and the Barbarians. You know, you're a Greek because you are not a Barbarian and being a Barbarian means somebody who doesn't speak Greek. In other words, it is an antagonistic national identity and it plays a very negative role. It is very constricting, and third, I think the most important factor that is often overlooked in the case of raised identities is the role of education. Most traditions of education are narrowly nationalistic, that you come from a great tradition, the founding fathers and all that; but to also indicate that other traditions are inferior, now that goes on and it is terrible and we need to urgently change that, to emphasize a larger and more comprehensive and generous vision of humanity.

Interview with Nirmala Lakshman,
The Hindu Magazine, Chennai, India, 1996

TWENTY-SIX

RETURNING TO OURSELVES

JACQUELINE ROSE: *I'm hoping that we can use this discussion as an opportunity for you to reply to some of the criticisms, not to say misrepresentations, that on occasion you rather dramatically seem to provoke. I have a personal interest in this. I'm here as a Jewish woman and a feminist with a long-standing commitment to psychoanalytic thinking and, let's face it, none of these epithets could be said to apply to you. I'm therefore also hoping that we will have a chance to demonstrate the possibility of undreamt-of forms of dialogue across what have often seemed to be insurmountable barriers of historical difference . . .*

You've talked about writing throughout your work and, at one point, you say: "for a man who no longer has a homeland writing becomes a place to live." You also say: "the main hope of the intellectual"—this is a bit surprising—"is not that he will have an effect on the world, but that someday, somewhere, someone will recall what he wrote exactly as he wrote it."

Your quote about the hope of the intellectual, that somebody would read their words, I borrowed from Adorno at a time when I felt that things were going very wrong for the Palestinians, and that being left out of the progress of history is a fate which I didn't want to settle for. I was writing at the time of the Oslo accords when there was universal celebration and people on television were talking about this earth-shaking event, and I was feeling exactly the opposite. I thought it was a very bad moment. From then on, I felt it was important somehow not to let things escape. I've been suspicious, for as long as it's been around, of deconstruction: people who say, well, it all depends on how you look. I believe in facts and very often the facts get abused, or left out, or embroidered or hidden or forgotten . . .

One of my strongest images of you was indeed after Oslo, when you were speaking at the School of Oriental and African Studies at the University of London, and you stood in the room and just drew in the air the roads that were being built through the so-called, about-to-be-liberated, newly independent territories. In a stroke, you demonstrated to me—and it has stayed with me ever since—the economic non-viability of what was happening for the Palestinians. That would be consistent with the life of a spokesperson whose task is, as you have put it, "the fusing of the moral will with the grasping of evidence" or "speaking truth to power." On the other hand, in much of your writing, especially on literature and music, your passion is for modernism which, by your own account, is skeptical of certain concepts of truth, certainty, and so on. Can you say something about how you square or how you see the connection between the Enlightenment and modernist components of what you do?

In many ways, they're really quite as different as you suggest. If you're writing about modernism with all of its skepticism and, above all, irony, then you're really talking about something quite different from what a particular political actor has done, what a political settlement or a political process might be all about. But what I think connects them is a certain sense of exploration and provisionality . . .

I've always been very suspicious of a number of things which I see as ultimately related. Officials. I think officials always lie. I. F. Stone, the great American journalist who died a few years ago and who I knew reasonably well toward the end of his life, used to publish a little magazine out of his home that became very influential in Washington, beginning I think in the Eisenhower years, but also during the Kennedy and Johnson years, and especially around Vietnam. He was a remarkable reporter, extremely irreverent, and he said that the working rule for the journalist is to assume that every government report is lying. It's certainly true of most journalists—it's the laziness of the twentieth-century journalist—that they repeat the government report. You should always assume that officials representing a position, administrators, people who have authority and power over others, et cetera, are all involved in keeping their places and their authority intact. It is therefore the role of the intellectual, at least as I see it, to keep challenging them, to name names and cite facts.

Writing about modernism is a totally different thing because first of all it's much more private. It's a mode of reflection and meditation and perhaps much more uncertain. Also, even in writing about modernism or music, I think of myself as a historian, where what you're trying to do is to put the work of art in a larger perspective and connect it to things that normally are not connected to it. In the case, let's say, of opera, it's very interesting to see a kind of politics of the moment, because operas were written for particular occasions in the past, whereas most people think of them as classical works—you go to the opera and you wear your tuxedo and all that kind of thing. But, in fact, they were combative in many ways, with specific objectives as well as other aims. And the same is sometimes true of works of literature, which may mean connecting them, not just to a cultural and political situation, but also to the privacy of the writer's life.

Let me pick up the point about privacy. You're writing your autobiography at the moment. I think everybody here would love to have you talk about that a little bit, if you can.

I've resisted the use of the word "autobiography." I call it a memoir, because I don't try to account for a public trajectory. I felt that I had something to understand about a peculiar past. My family was of course Palestinian, but we seemed to live in two or three different worlds. We lived in Egypt. My mother is partly Lebanese, so we lived in Lebanon. This was all during the colonial period. We had an extremely strange— because my father sort of invented it—a very strange, constructed life. I went exclusively to colonial schools, so I know, or knew at the time, a great deal about the Enclosure Act. I was thinking about it when I came down on the plane. I see these pastures, and I remember a question in school that I got a very high grade for: "The Enclosure Act of (I forget what year it was) was a necessary evil. Discuss." I was living in Egypt at the time, but if somebody had asked me about the irrigation system of Egypt, I couldn't have said a word about it. And because my father had lived in the United States for a while and had served in the First World War, we, my sisters and I, all inherited American citizenship. So, here I was, Palestinian, living in Egypt with a very peculiar first name in the circles I moved in (Edward is not your basic Arabic name). I think probably the main thread of the memoir is to trace the effects of this sort of imprisoning or limiting life that I had as a child, perhaps because my family felt that they had to protect me . . .

What does it feel like to be living in New York as what has become the chief spokesperson in the West for the Palestinian people? How does that work for you, in terms of where you put yourself and where you belong?

It goes all the way from death threats to the more common thing, which is abuse. About ten years ago, my office was burned at Columbia University. The police and the FBI—I was assigned an agent—told me that part of the Jewish Defense League, who were found in the basement of the building where I live, had done it and were threatening to do more. In New York especially you also get a tremendous amount of hate and anger. I remember, for example, one night, it must have been twenty or twenty-five years ago, when I had already been made a professor, and there was a party for a departing colleague. Everybody got fairly drunk. And the wife of a colleague of mine who is herself Jewish came up to me and said—I'll never forget this—that of course she wouldn't have normally said it, because I had run into her on the street, but that under the influence of alcohol she felt slightly released: "Young man!"—she was barely ten years older than I was—"Young man, I want to talk to you about some of your ideas . . . why do you want to kill Jews?" There was an article written about me called "The Professor of Terror." I think now they've gotten tired of doing that, because somehow I've survived it all.

The most peculiar thing has been the number of people, mostly Jews actually, who have wanted either to come to my house or to see me over a meal, to see how I "live." This literally happened to me, maybe half a dozen times. A very well known Jewish woman psychologist who lives in Boston—we had participated in several seminars in the 1980s about conflict resolution—came to New York and rang me from New York University, which is downtown, and said: "Can I come and visit you?" I was taken a bit by surprise and said: "Yes, of course." She came up, entered the apartment, came into the living room where I have a grand piano: "Oh, you play the piano," looked around a bit more, asked to see my study and then, when I said, "Why don't you sit down? I mean, it's a long subway ride from downtown," said: "No, no, I have to go . . . I only came up to see how you lived." Another person at a distinguished publishing house refused for weeks, perhaps even months, to sign a contract until I came to Boston and had dinner with him so he could observe me and my table manners.

Can I respond to this with an anecdote of my own?

Of course.

About three years ago I gave a lecture at Yale University and the next day one of the distinguished literary critics asked me over lunch if I had any "Jewish blood" in me and when I replied, thinking that it was a strange question but I'd answer it, that as far as I knew I had only "Jewish blood" in me, but why had she asked, she replied: "Because we thought you were Jewish, and then we realized you couldn't be, because in your lecture you cited Edward Said."

One more story. This is actually quite poignant. About ten years ago, I went to Emory University in Atlanta to give a series of lectures and seminars. At the last seminar, as I was entering the room, I was stopped by a young man who introduced himself to me as a graduate student of English who was going to attend the seminar and who very much, he said, wanted to drive me to the airport afterwards. And I said: "Well, that's very kind of you, but it won't be necessary because Professor X is going to do that." He said: "No, listen, it really means a lot to me to drive you to the airport; it really is a matter of some sort of personal privilege." When I asked why, he explained that he had been a student at Columbia in English but had never taken any of my courses: "I went to a Jewish school in New York where the rabbi said that you were the devil, and we were not to have anything to do with you, so I didn't. But I feel that it was such a stupid and wretched thing to have done that if I could drive you to the airport it would sort of make up for it."

I'm now going to slightly play devil's advocate, with a question about Jewishness and Judaism, because it obviously does shadow your work. There are a number of ironies here: the fact that your present criticisms of the Palestinian authorities have earned you the epithet of "Friend of the Zionist enemy"; the fact that Martin Buber moved into your house when your family had to evacuate it in 1948. At the end of Orientalism, *you say: "By an almost inescapable logic, I found myself having written a history of a strange and secret sharer of Western anti-Semitism." I would very much like you to talk about the way Jewishness and Judaism or anti-Semitism figure in your writing. There are some moments that*

*make me uncomfortable . . . Would you just talk about what "Semi-
tism" means for you and how you do or don't distinguish that from individual Jewish thinkers, scholars, friends, and so on?*

Those generic classifications, which one encounters really from the
end of the sixteenth century in European literature—like the idea of "the
Semites," which of course mainly means Jews, but by the nineteenth
century means everybody in the Semitic East—have always struck me as
constructions that were foreign to me because I'd grown up in a mixed
environment. The schools I went to in Palestine and Egypt were all full
of Arabs, of course, Christians and Muslims, Greeks, Italians, Armenians, Jews, both Oriental (as they used to be called) Jews and occasionally here and there, not too many, European Jews. I saw this kind of
construction worked out in the literature of anti-Semitism and found an
interesting parallel between that and the notion of the "Oriental," because in both instances Europeans were trying to talk about exotic peoples. In a wonderful phrase, Disraeli asks, "Arabs, what are they?" and
answers: "They're just Jews on horseback." So, underlying this separation is also an amalgamation of some kind.

Throughout my life when I've met Jewish people, individual Jews in
class, in society, and so on, I've always felt a certain kind of affinity. Because in a sense we've been—like now—thrown together, sometimes not
too pleasantly and sometimes very pleasantly. It's a very complicated
thing, because I'm one of the few people who says that our history as
Palestinians today is so inextricably bound up with that of Jews that the
whole idea of separation, which is what the peace process is all about—
to have a separate Palestinian thing and a separate Jewish thing—is
doomed. It can't possibly work.

I remember in 1988 I was participating in a forum, organized under
the auspices of the Jewish magazine *Tikkun,* in which the Jewish philosopher Michael Walzer, who is famous in the United States and a great
antagonist of mine, was also participating. He's a man of the Left supposedly, but a quite extraordinarily dogged Zionist. It was organized because the Palestinian National Council, of which I was then a member,
had just recognized Israel and had spoken about the need for two states
for the first time explicitly, and this was seen to be a new opening. I kept
insisting that it was not simple. At one point Walzer said to me: "Alright,
listen. You've recognized Israel. You obviously have or can have your

own state. But don't keep speaking about the past. Let's talk about the future." This is very often said to me by my critics; that I always talk about the past, that I dwell too much on the injustices done to the Palestinians, and so on and so forth. The audience was, I would say, about 99 percent Jewish. When he said it, my mouth hung open, but I didn't say anything, because a woman in the audience—I'll never forget this as long as I live—got up and started vociferously attacking Walzer. She said: "How dare you say that to a Palestinian? How dare you say that to anybody? Because of all the people in the world, we ask the world to remember our past. And you're telling a Palestinian to forget the past? How dare you?" It was an extraordinary thing. And he didn't utter a word after that.

Lastly, of course, there is a deep—and I say this with great sorrow as perhaps the hardest thing to accept—irreconcilability between Arab and Jew which in my generation will not be overcome.

Arab and Jew or Arab and Israeli?

Well, both. I think it's quite plain. I live in the United States. It's very hard to find anybody there who's Jewish who doesn't identify with Israel. And I understand . . .

I know lots, Edward, I know lots of Jews in the United States who don't identify with Israel. We speak to different people. Clearly we do.

Let me just finish this, if I may. You may be right. But the idea of separation is an idea that I'm just sort of terminally opposed to, just as I'm opposed to most forms of nationalism, just as I'm opposed to secession, to isolation, to separatism of one sort or another. The idea that people who are living together—this happened, for example, in Lebanon—should suddenly split apart and say Christians should live here and Muslims there and Jews there and that sort of thing is, I think, just barbaric, unacceptable. And yet there's a very deep rift caused by real history, and it takes a lot of working through to get over it. There's too much that's gone on between us in this way, between let's say Arab and Israeli. But I feel it very strongly in the United States. People will tell you it's an emotional thing. When the pogroms start we need a place to go to, and my answer is, of course, go to Palestine, go to Israel, but don't displace another people when you're doing it. That's the problem. We have been dispossessed. Our society has been destroyed. It's very difficult to forget that. And, lastly, I think the flaw in the peace process, the basic psychological or cultural flaw in the peace process, is that Israelis and their supporters have been insulated from the very facts which made their society in Israel possible. With very few exceptions—one of them being Israel Shahak who, quite remarkable in that respect, is willing to talk about it.

And Leibowitz.

Yes, I mean you can count them, Leah Zemel, Felicia Langer, et cetera. And later in his life, Matti Peled, who was a general in the Israeli army during the 1967 war.

It depends too, of course, on how you draw the lines. As you know, Ella Shohat has written extensively about the different political configuration you would get in Israel if the Palestinians and Sephardic Jews, who are another repressed minority within the Israeli community, should seek some kind of political affiliation, how the whole map would change.

It seems to me that one of the things you've been talking about is what I would want to call, not the irrational, but the non-rational dimension of political identities. In his extraordinary book, The Third Way, *Raja Shehadeh, the Palestinian lawyer working in the West Bank, says of the Israeli: "I dream the dreams that he should have." So there's a quite terrifying and chilling sense of unconscious histories repeating themselves across the red line in Israel and Palestine and through the unconsciouses of the participants. If we go back to your project of speaking truth to power, of making explicit demands, of one injustice being remedied but not at the cost of forgetting the injustice that was done to the Jews: if we assume this could be done rationally, what nonetheless do we do about this non-rational, unconscious, almost pathological dimension of political processes?*

That's obviously a very difficult dimension. For example, I've spent a long time criticizing Israel and Israelis, but one must say that Palestinians have a lot to answer for. There's very little real knowledge of Israel or of the need to address a constituency of conscience in Israel, or to try and create one amongst Palestinians. There's either the slavish "white man's nigger" attitude typified by Arafat and his crew—because the Israelis are more powerful and have the United States behind them, we have to be their slaves. That's no good. Or there's the view that they are all aliens and intruders. If they go away, like the Crusaders went away, that would be the best thing. If they don't, we want nothing to do with them. Neither attitude is okay.

What we haven't done, I think, is to intrude ourselves upon the Israeli conscience: conscience, not consciousness. I mean, they're aware of us—who builds the settlements today, the Israeli settlements? Palestinians build them and the top contractor for the settlements is a Palestinian who is a minister in the Palestine Authority. That's unacceptable, because there politics and interests are being used to camouflage a really deep complicity which is not the solution. We're in a position of such subordination and such weakness vis-à-vis Israel that our number one priority is to seize and understand ourselves and our history. To this day, there is no decent Palestinian history written by Palestinians. Our own history is unrecorded. There are interesting books, monographs written about the history of Nablus, a short history of Haifa, a little bit here and there, synoptic kind of histories of Palestine, but if you want to look for an authoritative history of the Palestinian national movement, you have to read an Israeli book or an American, English, or German book. But that moment of real self-consciousness is not the consciousness-building of the 1970s and the 1980s, when we thought of ourselves as carrying on the struggle of Fanon and which dissipated very quickly. You need institutions, you need to build education.

I'll give you another example. Just two months ago [i.e., March 1997], 19,000 public-sector teachers in secondary and primary schools went on strike. Why? Because they were getting salaries of between $200 and $300, which is half the salary of the driver of a director general in the ministry, of which there are now 750 in only twenty-six ministries. They have, of course, no real jobs. They're simply being paid from the public purse to keep them loyal to Arafat. So what happens? The authority refuses to even talk to them. They pick up twenty-five of the "leaders" of the strike. They jail them. They torture them. None of them—I'm very proud of this as a teacher myself—none of them capitulates. Arafat then says: "Bring them to me." So the twenty-five leaders are brought to his office. Arafat curses them for one hour, trying to break them, insulting them in the most obscene and filthy language. (The correspondent of the *Guardian/Observer*, who is himself not Arab but knows Arabic, rang me from Jerusalem and said: "Did you hear what he did to those twenty-five people? Where did he learn that kind of street language?") They didn't break. They then accepted a 2 or 3 percent increase in their salaries, but 85 percent of them said that they would go on strike again as soon as the school year was over (exams were coming up). That argues a very poor attitude toward education. Those things have to be addressed. It's a very long and difficult process.

In After the Last Sky, *you say: "All of us speak of return, but do we mean that literally or do we mean we must restore ourselves to ourselves? The latter is the real point, I think." As you've said many times, Jews all over the world are allowed to return to Israel, but you cannot return. But there you seem to be suggesting more a psychic state of being than a concrete, literal return. Could you say some more about what you meant by that?*

I don't how many people know this, but I'd say at least 55 percent of all Palestinians today don't live in Palestine, or in historical Palestine, whether inside Israel as Israeli citizens or on the West Bank and Gaza. So there's a very large community which is made up of refugees of various categories. Some in Lebanon, for example, 300,000–400,000—destitute, unable to work, unable to travel, unable to move. They're the wretched of the earth and the peace process has nothing to say about them. In Syria roughly the same number, sometimes prosperous, mostly not prosperous refugees; 1.2 million in Jordan; 130,000–140,000 in Egypt, and so on throughout the Arab world. In Western Europe, the United States, and Latin America, there are a fair number of Palestinians, perhaps half a million or more. For most of them, I think the idea of return—it's very difficult to say this—is unlikely in their own lifetime. And many of the younger generation never lived in Palestine; so either they don't know it or they know it only from their parents. What's impressive is that they still keep the accents, they still keep the sense of where they're from. They may not ever have been there, but they say we're from Nazareth or from Ramallah, and so on. So that sense of a tie of some kind is on the one hand metaphorical, but also comes through family who remained and other friends and connections. As against that, Israel has a law of return which entitles every Jew anywhere to become an Israeli citizen. There's nothing comparable to that for Palestinians. And if suddenly by some miracle there was a repatriation allowed for all Palestinians, I don't know—and I don't know anybody who does know—how many Palestinians would actually go back. So, for me, therefore, the question of an actual return is deferred. I certainly won't be able to go back and I'm not sure that I would want to. And maybe I'm not an untypical case; maybe many Palestinians are like that.

But what return does mean to me is return to oneself, that is to say, a return to history, so that we understand what exactly happened, why it happened and who we are. That we are a people from that land, maybe not living there, but with important historical claims and roots. Many of our people will continue to reside there. But we have a common self-consciousness of not the most, but one of the most interesting twentieth-century experiences of dispossession, exile, migration. And not only because it's in and of itself connected to the Holy Land, which is saturated with all kinds of significance, but also because it's part of that twentieth-century experience. That's where I feel I have tried to place my emphasis. To speak our case, when we suffer and go through all the terrors of exile and dispossession and the absence of rights. People write to me and say, look, I don't have a passport. If you live on the West Bank, it says on the passport "Identity unconfirmed or indeterminate." If you have a refugee's piece of paper in Lebanon, it says, "Nationality: Stateless." The name is never mentioned. When you look and see Palestinians, as I do all the time, it's very difficult to say that this is just metaphorical, because it's terrible, it's lived. I think one must never forget that, and that we should try to erect on the ruins of our national history some sense of common purpose, which we still haven't got. We don't know what we are doing.

How compatible would that process be with any kind of statehood? You cite Eqbal Ahmed and his use of the expression "the pathology of power." Can you envisage a benign, non-coercive form of executive authority? You personally have said: "I have never found it interesting to be close to power." Is the idea of a non-pathological authority a contradiction in terms?

I think it is. I can't imagine it. Speaking in a utopian vein—since you mentioned the Oriental Jews in Israel—I think our best hope is a common struggle with Israeli Jews in historical Palestine to devise a method of coexistence with a minimum of coercion—there's no such thing as no coercion—whether it's through cantons, the way the Swiss have tried to do it, or other ways. But I think the idea of separation or partition, in our time, simply can't work. It simply can't be done, physically. For the Israelis, there's always this tendency to think of us as aliens and therefore the fewer of us around the better, and the best are those you don't see at all. Hence those roads on the West Bank, the so-called by-passing roads. What's so extraordinary is that what the Israelis are now doing on the West Bank and Gaza is really repeating the experience of apartheid and what the United States did to the Native Americans. Put them in reservations or just exterminate them, which the Israelis haven't done, but put them as far away as possible, then the problem will go away. The hope is somehow to break out of those enclosures and to try to work out some method of coexistence with Israelis who are interested in this. I think more can be done in time . . .

One final question. The occasion of your being in England is to inaugurate the Empson Lectures at Cambridge University. You've chosen to talk about "Transgression and Authority in Opera." I was fortunate enough to hear the first of these lectures when you gave it at the Collège de France. You talk about Mozart's vision of the "protean, unstable, undifferentiated" nature of human identity, his view that the "stabilities of marriage and the social norms habitually governing human life are inapplicable, because life itself is elusive and inconstant." It seemed to me that you were saying that what Mozart understood about death casts its shadow back across the pretensions, the false and killing certainties of social norms and conventional human arrangements. It seemed a new departure for your work, incredibly moving and quite inspiring. How can that kind of insight be linked into the kind of political vision and hopes you have for the future?

I don't think it can. But it's there. I know it's there in the sense that I feel—and I don't mind talking publicly about it—and have for the last few years felt the impress or weight of mortality. So whatever sense of urgency I feel, whatever sense of hastening toward the end, I think Mozart was right about. It is basically almost Schopenhauerian, there's a kind of indistinguishable, seething, endlessly transforming mass into which we are going. It really is very much part of what I'm writing about. One of the reasons for this is that I've become very, very impatient with the idea and the whole project of identity: the idea, which produced great interest in the United States in the 1960s and which is also present in the return to Islam in the Arab world and elsewhere, that people should really focus on themselves and where they come from, their roots, and find out about their ancestors—as in the book and television program *Roots*. That strikes me as colossally boring and totally off the mark. I think that's the last thing that we should be thinking about. What's much more interesting is to try to reach out beyond identity to something else, whatever that is. It may be death. It may be an altered state of consciousness that puts you in touch with others more than one normally is. It may be just a state of forgetfulness which, at some point, I think is what we all need—to forget.

Interview with Jacqueline Rose,
The Jewish Quarterly, London, 1997–98

TWENTY-SEVEN

A STATE, YES, BUT NOT
JUST FOR PALESTINIANS

Your Minneapolis talk is titled "The Consequences of 1948: The Palestinian Catastrophe." Can you give a brief overview of the consequences of 1948?

Well, my point of departure is the fact that the peace process sponsored by the United States, which began in 1993, has been a total fiasco. Certainly, for Palestinians, their situation has only gotten worse. They are unable to move freely; more of their land has been taken; they have not gotten anything like self-determination; the Israeli occupation continues. Palestinian forces control only about three or four percent of the land area of the West Bank. And in those areas, the Palestinian Authority acts as an enforcer for Israel. Arafat has accepted the sort of Bantustanization of the West Bank. [This refers to a South African policy during apartheid under which native tribes were given small homelands, called Bantustans, in a phony appearance of self-rule.]

Not only does this situation and this peace process not fulfill Palestinian aspirations, it doesn't begin to address the fundamental problem which began in 1948, when as a people we were driven off the land, lost the entire land of Palestine and have remained refugees or second-class citizens ever since.

But I also argue that despite gaining control of Palestinian land and lives, Israel's security has not been assured. Fifty years after its establishment, Israel is a less secure place.

You used to be much more supportive of Arafat. If his position is as meritless as you now believe, what do you think motivates him to pursue it?

Well, I think that in 1993, he found himself at an impasse. He had sided with Iraq during the Gulf War. He had been effectively isolated by the Palestinians on the West Bank and Gaza during the *intifada* [1987–91 uprising], which was their movement. He either had to accept his irrelevance or he could accept a deal that guaranteed his survival but, alas, did not advance the best interests of his people. He took the latter. And that's why I separated from him.

I think he persists now because he has no other choice. He has become a prisoner of the peace process. He has a little authority, because he has 50,000 men under arms, but effectively, he does Israel's bidding. He is a prisoner of the Israelis. I mean literally. He can't go in and out of Gaza without their permission. But he is a strutting dictator in his own territory. I think he's betrayed his people's interest and their dreams of self-determination.

If he has delivered so little for those who elected him, how does he retain their support?

I don't think he does, except for those he directly employs. He has an enormous and unproductive bureaucracy. According to the World Bank, he employs in the bureaucracy about 80,000 people, which we don't need at all. I mean, it's totally unproductive. But if you add up the security forces and the bureaucracy and multiply them by seven or eight, which is the number of dependents of each person he employs, you'll find that he, in effect, employs about 700,000 or 800,000 people. And that's where his support comes from. People who are indebted to him. . . .

I have every conviction that if somebody were to challenge him now—if there was a real organized opposition, which, alas, there isn't—he would lose. Of course there are individual opponents. His own ministers talk very critically about him to me. I think his support now is basically the power of the purse and the fact that he has an army that compels and cows the citizens. There is an atmosphere of fear, and there is censorship. My books were banned by him in 1996.

The other fact that keeps him in power—and I'm ashamed to say this as an American citizen—is that the United States supports him and all these unlawful and undemocratic practices.

In your piece in the Times, *you argued that not only the current peace process, but any attempt to solve the problem by creating a separate Palestinian state out of the occupied territories, is doomed to fail.*

Well, because the Israelis have now sunk their tentacles on the land of Palestinians in the West Bank and Gaza. Now, 40 percent of Gaza has Israelis on it, namely in the form of settlements. I would say that if you add Jerusalem to the West Bank, where there are settlers, and the fact that they have expanded the city limits of Jerusalem something like ten times what it was when they annexed it in 1967, you're talking basically about 90 percent of the West Bank. I was just there last month. There are these bypassing roads that go all through the West Bank, connecting the settlement to Israel and going all around Palestinian towns and villages.

By their own aggressive zeal, the settler movement and the Israeli government and army have in fact involved themselves so deeply in Palestinian life that in my opinion there is no separation between them, or only the separation of apartheid. But demographically there are two populations living together. In about ten years there will be demographic parity.

Therefore, the only conclusion to be drawn from this is to devise a means where the two peoples can live together in one nation as equals—not as master and slave, which is the current situation.

Are you saying a two-state solution can't work because the intermingling of the two populations is too great to undo, or is it that no two-state solution can address the tragedy of the Palestinians since '48?

Both, and for more reasons. Within Israel—now, I'm not talking about the West Bank and Gaza—there are at least a million Palestinians, 20 percent of the Israeli population. They are Israeli citizens, and they are discriminated against because Israel is advertised as the state of the Jewish people, not as the state of its citizens. There are laws which discriminate very clearly within Israel itself between Jews and non-Jews. So, wherever you look, Jews and Palestinians live together, but live together as unequal populations, although theoretically equal in human rights.

So, even if you could solve in some way the problem of the bypass roads and reduce the number of Israeli settlements in the West Bank and Gaza, there is still no way to create a Palestinian state out of those territories?

That's my profound belief. What would be left would be in effect a kind of tiny rump, which is an affront, not to say an insult to Palestinians, offered to them as their separate state. It's not worth it.

And, as I say, the problem of 1948 has never been addressed. How an entire people can simply be thrown off the land as we now know—thanks to the work, not just by the Palestinians who have said this all along, but by Israeli historians, the so-called revisionist historians, who proved that there was a plan during the 1948 war to get rid of Palestinians, to evict as many of them as possible; close to a million were kicked out deliberately in 1948.

So, the whole project has been to diminish Palestinian feeling about land and about their past. Well, this hasn't happened. Palestinians still cling to the past; they still cling to the land. And they simply are not going to go away. So, my sense of realism is such that the only way this problem is going to be settled, as in South Africa, is to face the reality squarely on the basis of coexistence and equality, with a hope of truth and reconciliation in the South African style. You have to say that these are equal peoples and they have to live together as communities, each with its own sense of itself. . . .

I think that is the way to go. This other way is not working. Separate states, separate populations on a tiny land, drenched in the history of two peoples who have been living with and fighting each other for the last hundred years, is simply unrealistic. I don't think it can work.

I'm sure you know that no group with any political support in Israel has been willing to consider anything like this for many decades, if ever. Do you have some reason to believe that idea could become a thinkable thought in the Israeli political spectrum?

Absolutely. Over the past year, I've spoken to numerous Israeli, both Palestinian and Jewish, audiences. I think there is a new generation to be found in the universities, amongst intellectuals, independent writers and thinkers. I'm not talking about a large mass of people, but I know a lot of people who are thinking along these lines. . . .

I know it seems like a longshot and an improbable thing now, but I think that within the working out of the history and the unfolding of time, it becomes a more and more attractive idea.

If you could identify one or two aspects of the conventional wisdom about the Israeli/Palestinian situation, at least as received by consumers of American media, that you would most like to challenge, what would those be?

One is that the Palestinians are a kind of motley crowd of aggressive terrorists who are disturbing Israel's presence. I think that is why '48 is so important. I think it has to be understood that we were the people dislodged from the land. We were the indigenous inhabitants who were thrown out to make way for a Jewish state. We are, in fact, victims of the victims.

I mean these are the people who went through the horrors of anti-Semitism and the Holocaust. But in establishing a state for themselves for perfectly understandable reasons, they destroyed the society of another people.

Second, I think the existence of a Palestinian desire to live in peace and tranquillity is much more long-standing than that of Israel. The press has talked about Palestinian terrorism, has talked about Palestinian fanaticism, and so on and so forth without paying any attention to the vastly, vastly greater amount of violence wreaked upon us by Israel, which has, after all, nuclear power, has been supplied hundreds of billions of dollars by the United States and has flouted every international convention, whether it's the Geneva conventions or the conventions on the laws of war, or all of these things. This is not widely known. We are thought of as kind of nasty people who are doing damage to the Israelis, whereas the fact is the opposite is true.

Those two are the principal things I would like to correct.

Last question. I apologize if it's too personal. You made a reference to your leukemia and I had read a quote in which you said you feel you're entering the final phase of your life. I wonder if you feel that this sense that you're nearing the end of your life has affected your view of the question of Palestine?

Well, only insofar as I think it deserves more time and attention than I may be able to give it. I'm fighting very hard, and I'm going now through a good period where my disease is in remission. I feel encouraged by that and that gives me the privilege of fighting for what I believe is just and right.

Interview with Eric Black,
The Star Tribune, Minneapolis, 1999

TWENTY-EIGHT

ORIENTALISM, ARAB INTELLECTUALS, MARXISM, AND MYTH IN PALESTINIAN HISTORY

The front cover of one of your books shows a photo of a Hamas slogan on a Palestinian wall saying that Hamas is the resistance or something similar. Did you choose the picture?

No, the publisher chose the physical form the book took.

Did you have a different vision for it?

No, the issue does not concern me much, and I have nothing against it, because it is only the form. What holds importance for me is the content of the book.

Is there any particular significance for choosing this picture?

Yes, there was a reason for this choice, as the book's topics include anger and protests; writing on walls is one of the means to express anger as well as one of the forms of protest.

Does it concern you that among your best Arab readers are intellectuals who belong to the neo-Islamic groups, and some of these increasingly cite your ideas and writings in their studies' footnotes?

Certainly, and I have frequently expressed my concern on this subject. I find my opinions misinterpreted, especially where they include substantial criticism of Islamist movements. First, I am secular; second, I do not trust religious movements; and third, I disagree with these movements' methods, means, analyses, values, and visions. It is very possible to read a given author according to a certain interpretation, and this happens often, resulting in misunderstanding. In my introduction to the new edition of *Orientalism*, I insisted on this issue, pointing out the vast difference between me and the Islamic reading that some accuse me of. In *Orientalism* I do not talk about Islam, but rather the portrayal of

Islam in the West, offering a critique of the foundations and the goals upon which the coverage is based.

Does your study of intellectual activities in the Arab world, mainly through the elements of conflict and debate within Arab culture, reveal to you signs pointing toward a post-colonial discourse?

Do you mean the existence of a post-colonial school?

Or signs?

I doubt that.

Do you think reading trends in Arabic show that Orientalism, *which had a great impact in India, Latin America, Japan, and Africa, is being read in Arabic with as much importance as in other languages?*

Let me return to examples I have used before: the influence the book had in India, Japan, or South Africa seems to me at a deeper level of analysis than in the Arab world. The Sub-Altern Studies in the field of history in India, for example, in my opinion, is the most important school in the Third World that produces post-colonial discourse in writing and analyzing history, etc. This school, which was greatly influenced by *Orientalism*, is significant to the extent that no history department in U.S. universities is without one of its representatives. In fact, no equivalent to this school exists in the field of Arab and Islamic studies. The Sub-Altern Studies school has influenced the trends of analyzing and writing American history itself, as well as influencing other world universities. *Orientalism*, I think, was read more profoundly in other places than in the Arab world.

What is the reason?

The reason is that *Orientalism* was basically used by Arab readers as a means for conflict and not for developing an analytical thought based on ideas. This factor made the term "Orientalism" an insult. If you want to insult someone, you call him "Orientalist." This is one of the negative consequences of the caricatural reading of my book, because I do not say or imply anything like this.

But you often presented deplorable examples of this term in your book.

Maybe, but it was in a much larger context than to reduce *Orientalism* and its circumstances to the level of insults. I admit that as the author I am biased, but the most important thing about the book is the method of analysis, the theoretical framework according to which results are organized—and not the negative consequences themselves, which should not be simplified to the point of saying this Orientalist was our enemy, that one was against us and that one likes or hates us, etc. It appears that as an Arab society we remain prisoners of these modes, for we have not been able to develop something that allows us to be emancipated from the dark past.

To be fair with those who are just readers, those who did not respond to your theories with the written word, I think many of them have received the ideas of the book within the contexts you propose, through the broad vision that you want as the framework for analysis and revision. The difference here is that the reading did not become writing.

This is condemned to be mere reading, for it neither became a written response nor added to the debate. But let me add something: *Orientalism* was published in 1978, and during the past twenty years I wrote about ten books, including *Culture and Imperialism*, published in 1992. These books cover topics like literary criticism, philosophy, and other themes.

Does this mean you want to free yourself from the confining stereotypes, or from the dominant popularity and prominence of Orientalism *over your other writings among Arab readers?*

Do you mean, to renounce my book?

I mean, do you want to free yourself from the dominance of the book?

I think an author should continuously attempt something new, centering on all that he has, to prevent a reduction of his works. Knowledge of all an author's different writings leads to understanding the developments in his/her thinking and research from one area to another. It is important to me that people read my books, but my major interest centers on writing rather than revising what I have written. I mean, I want to continue my journey a little bit further.

In this context, and viewed from the revision perspective, how would you describe the "addition" to Orientalism?

It is a very small and limited addition that could have been more developed, but as I said before, I don't have a lot of time for revision.

Do you think current trends of events in the Arab world are not re-

flected fast enough in intellectuals' ideas, analysis, and research, and thus these intellectuals appear shocked by facts, often producing reactions rather than effective thinking?

This is correct to some extent in the Arab world, although not quite new. My personal problem is that I live isolated from the region, and my daily, weekly, monthly, and yearly job is naturally connected to the Western society in which I live. Excluding two American universities in the region (Cairo and Beirut), I regret not having a relationship with any other Arab universities that would enable me to know the daily situation of the researcher, professor, or Arab intellectual, except what I gather on hurried visits. Thus, I feel I lack accurate details of the situation, but through the available information I have, I can conclude that your observation that events unfold with a great speed is correct. There is no intellectual position that reflects these events to the degree to which they influence consciousness and the course of events.

During the past few years, Hamas, Hizballah and the Islamic Jihad has focused on a purely romantic image of the fighter and the strong rejectionist, while on the other hand, the image of the leftist rejectionist (the Marxist and the nationalist) has faded. Furthermore, the leftist rejectionist became for a large segment of people the symbol of one colluding with the corrupt regimes that wage bloody wars against part of society. The avant-gardist intellectual appears paralyzed before this new equation. What is your commentary on that?

I agree with your characterization of the situation. There appears to be great confusion. It is certainly easy to say that, although I am geographically distant from the facts and events, not to mention that I do not have any political ambition, but it seems to me there is a similarity between the practice and the function of the intellectual on the one hand, and politics on the other. What I find at this time is an urgent need for total separation between the two. The most dangerous and worst scenario for intellectuals is to be involved in both the intellectual and political realms, that is to combine functions in their political life and political ambitions (seeking positions and offices) and their functions as intellectuals. This image of the politically invested intellectual has been reinforced nowadays to the point that it pollutes the cultural discourse and this has led, as you say, to accusing the intellectual of connivance, a warranted accusation indeed. Arab intellectuals have quickly given up to the change in their position from opposition to participant in government without any real attempt to preserve their independent status and protect their position as free intellectuals.

Could you still see the possibility of reviving Marxism as an opposition discourse, for as I understood from remarks you made earlier on the subject, you seemed to be questioning whether or not this is possible, and the question appeared quite serious and open. But did I feel even the traces of hope about reviving Marxism in the current world crisis?

I do not like to discuss the question of Marxism because I do not want get involved in the problematics of terms—the questions of what is Marxism and whether or not I am a Marxist. I am not concerned with schools of thought if the issue is membership. What I see is completely different. As a free and independent intellectual, I give little importance to slogans, whether they are Marxist or non-Marxist. Undoubtedly, the Marxist analysis, or let us say the materialist analysis, includes lessons and elements very useful to understanding the situation we live in now, especially concerning economic relations. Here I refer to the Marxist analysis through the contributions of Gramsci and Lukács. It is possible to benefit from these contributions in analyzing what Marx did not think of; it is something we can use in the current situation. We need neither the reproduction of traditional Marxism nor reviving the slogans, but instead we must eclectically choose specific elements and reformulate them in a new approach through our new discourses.

What do you think about the "permanent" exile of Jacques Derrida, and is it the same for the Palestinian?

Maybe.

What then is the difference between the two situations?

The difference is that the Jewish people claim that their relationship to Palestine goes back 3,000 years, and that they were exiled from it and displaced 2,500 years ago. But the expulsion of the Palestinians from Palestine began just yesterday. Still, we should not forget that the Zionist official history was founded on the diaspora and the idea of permanent exile—this history uses many myths. I think we as Palestinians should avoid myths, and it appears to me that we as intellectuals must focus on the historical and concrete facts and refuse to utilize mythological dimensions. I cannot accept the notion that the Palestinian refugee will remain a refugee forever. I am among those who think that there will not be a realistic solution unless it deals with the current situation of Palestinians as refugees. Thus the question is: is it possible to relive our past and restore history to pre-1948? I doubt that. We suffered a loss; it can be said that our people lost the battle temporarily. The question is to what extent? I do not think that anyone at the present has a final answer to this question. What we have to do now is to limit this loss.

The Jews used the term diaspora to describe a collective nostalgia toward a mythical place. Some Palestinians have adapted this term and used it to describe their expatriation from Palestinian geography. Do you think that Palestinians' use of this term may imply other meanings, especially when the Palestinian exile is from a geographically existent, very real place—real to the extent that they were expelled from homes to which they still keep the door keys? Is there an alternative term to diaspora which you propose the Palestinian use?

In Arabic I use the word *shatat* (dispersion) despite my continuing caution and criticism of many terms based on myths of imagination. I naturally reject the term "diaspora." But nothing can prevent the term being used. The Jews used it to fulfill their own imagination, but we are talking about a different situation for the Palestinian. The Palestinian situation and the society Palestinians desire is peculiar to that nation.

Interview with Nouri Jarah,
Al Jadid, Los Angeles, 1999

TWENTY-NINE

MY RIGHT OF RETURN

This was not the first interview I had with Israel's leading daily, but it was certainly the largest and the best prepared. Ari Shavit spent three days talking with me in early August 2000 in New York. What is striking about such an interview is that it could (and of course did) appear in an Israeli daily, but certainly not in a U.S. equivalent. E.W.S.

Shortly before leaving for New York, I went to look at the house. I didn't have far to go—it is about 300 meters from where I live, and overlooks the public garden where my daughter likes to play. It is not an impressive structure: two stories, angular, projecting a kind of dry, Protestant-like functionality. It is not one of those splendid, well-hewn houses in which the Christian Arabs of Talbieh invested their all; it is businesslike, rectangular, with a fine palm tree in the front yard, a small staircase and a touching entryway. This is the entryway that Edward Said constantly refers to. This is the palm tree he remembers. And how there were no other buildings around the house then. Until one day he heard a conversation that threw him into a panic: someone was talking about the danger embodied by the Jews. And someone else said there was nothing to be afraid of. That when the time came the young men with the clubs would gather and eject the Jews. Get rid of them.

No, Said does not remember the exact moment when his family left the house. He has no memory of the last day, the last time. All that happened was that at the beginning of the winter they returned to their house in Cairo, as they did almost every year. It was only some time later that he heard that something terrible had happened in Palestine. And slowly, very slowly, he understood that they would not be able to go back. That Jerusalem was lost to them. That some of his relatives and some family friends had lost everything. Were now refugees.

In early August, at the height of the summer vacation, the half-

abandoned campus of Columbia University in New York is a melancholy place, and gloom stalks the corridors of the building that houses the philosophy department. But the fifth-floor office of Professor Edward W. Said is spacious and well-lit. A not unpleasant disorder reigns in it, of documents and piles of books and journals in several languages. And among all this, in a corner, hangs an old, familiar poster of the Yesh Gvul (there is a border/limit) movement: "Don't say 'I didn't know.' " And above it, on one of the shelves, a map of Palestine. The Whole Land of Palestine. Gilded.

His hair has turned gray over the past year. The cancerous growth in his stomach bothers him too. Nevertheless, Edward Said is still a very handsome man, punctilious about his appearance and his dress. A silk handkerchief protrudes from his jacket pocket and the gold watch on his wrist glitters when he stretches out his hand to take a sip from the bottle of Pellegrino on his desk.

He exudes charm. The most widely known Palestinian intellectual in the West, he is warm, learned, and cunning. Highly political, emotional, with a sense of humor. He skips lightly and gracefully from poetic quotations from Dante to Zionist-damning quotations from Sternhell—and back again. He takes obvious delight in moving between the various languages and between the cultural levels on which he lives. Between the different identities that skitter within him. As though celebrating his ability to be British and American and Arab all at the same time. Both a refugee and an aristocrat, both a subversive and a conservative, both a literateur and a propagandist, both European and Mediterranean.

Before I turn on the tape recorder, Said inquires at length into my background. How long I have been in Israel, where my family came from. And gradually we come to talk about our common neighborhood. He lived there, for some of the time, more than fifty years ago. I live there now. And we talk about the various buildings that we are both familiar with. About the various family names we are both familiar with. Trying to circle carefully around what is most sensitive: for he is my Other. I am his Other. And this strange intimacy, this tragic intimacy, between us. Between him and me and Talbieh.

Professor Said, many Israelis—and not only Israelis—were astonished to learn that you, a distinguished scholar, threw stones at an Israeli army post on the Lebanese border earlier this summer. What led you to take such extraordinary action, after Israel pulled out of southern Lebanon?

I was in Lebanon for a summer visit. I gave two lectures and stayed with family and friends. Then I had a meeting with [Hizballah spiritual leader] Sheikh [Hassan] Nasrallah, whom I found to be a remarkably impressive man. A very simple man, quite young, absolutely no bullshit. A man who adopted a strategy toward Israel quite similar to that of the Vietnamese against the Americans: We cannot fight them because they have an army, a navy, and a nuclear option, so the only way we can do it is to make them feel it in body bags. And that's exactly what he did. In the one conversation that we had, I was impressed by the fact that among all the political leaders I met in the Middle East, he alone was precisely on time, and there were no people around him waving Kalashnikovs. We agreed that as far as reclaiming Palestinian rights, the Oslo accord was a total mess. And then he told me that I must go down south, and so I did, a few days later.

There were nine of us. My son and his fiancée, my daughter and her friend, myself and a few others, and a guide from the Lebanese resistance. First we went to Khiam prison, which made a very strong impression on us. I've seen a lot of unpleasant sights in my life, but this was probably the worst. The solitary confinement cells, the torture chambers. The instruments of torture were still there, the electrical probes they used. And the place just reeked of human excrement and abuse. Words cannot express the horror, so much so that my daughter started crying, sobbing.

From there we went straight to the border, to a place called Bowabit Fatma, Fatma's Gate, where hundreds of tourists faced an enormous amount of barbed wire. About 200 meters further down stands a watchtower, also surrounded by barbed wire and concrete. Presumably, inside the tower were Israeli soldiers, but I didn't see them. It was quite far.

What I regret in all this is that the comic quality of the situation did not come out. The assumption was that I was throwing stones at someone. But there was nobody there. And in fact what happened was that my son and some of the other young men were trying to see who could throw stones furthest. And since my son is a rather big fellow—he is an American who plays baseball—he threw furthest. My daughter said to me, "Daddy can you throw a stone as far as Wadie?" and that of course stirred the usual kind of Oedipal competition. So I picked up a stone and threw it.

Throwing stones at Fatma Gate when Israel had just ended its occupation of southern Lebanon seems to be not only a celebration of liberation, but a very basic rejection of something. Of what?

A rejection of Israelis. The feeling is that after twenty-two years of occupying our land, they left. And there is also a sense of dismissal. Not only are you leaving, but good riddance to you. We don't want you to come back. So the atmosphere is rather "carnivalesque," a sense of healthy anarchy, a triumphant feeling. For the first time in my life, and in the lives of the people gathering at Fatma Gate, we won. We won one.

Professor Said, this summer Israelis and Palestinians are trying to put an end to the hundred-year conflict between you and us. Can it be done? Can the conflict be resolved?

Yes, I think it can. But I don't think Yasir Arafat can sign off on the termination of the conflict. Nor does he have the right to do so on an occasion provided by Bill Clinton at Camp David. Until the time comes when Israel assumes moral responsibility for what it has done to the Palestinian people, there can be no end to the conflict.

What is needed is a "bill of particulars" of all our claims against Israel for the original dispossession and for the occupation that began in 1967. What is needed, at the very least, is an acknowledgment of the destruction of Palestinian society, of the dispossession of the Palestinian people and the confiscation of their land. And also of the deprivation and the suffering over the last fifty-two years, including such actions as the killing at Sabra and Chatila refugee camps.

I believe that the conflict can only end when Israel assumes the burden of all that. I think an attempt should be made to say "this is what happened." This is the narrative.

What is the narrative? What is the conflict all about?

It is an almost sublime conflict. I was telling [Daniel] Barenboim the other night, think of this chain of events: anti-Semitism, the need to find a Jewish homeland, Herzl's original idea, which was definitely colonialist, and then the transformation of that to the socialist ideas of the moshav and the kibbutz, then the urgency during Hitler's reign, and people like Yitzhak Shamir who were really interested in cooperating with Hitler, then the genocide of the Jews in Europe and the actions against the Palestinians in Palestine of 1948.

When you think about it, when you think about Jew and Palestinian not separately, but as part of a symphony, there is something magnificently imposing about it. A very rich, also very tragic, also in many ways desperate history of extremes—opposites in the Hegelian sense—that is yet to receive its due. So what you are faced with is a kind of sublime grandeur of a series of tragedies, of losses, of sacrifices, of pain that would take the brain of a Bach to figure out. It would require the imagination of someone like Edmund Burke to fathom. But the people dealing with this gigantic painting are "quick-fix" Clinton, Arafat and Barak, who are like a group of single-minded janitors who can only sweep around it, who can only say let's move it a bit—let's put it in the corner. That's how I see the peace process.

Is this a symmetrical conflict between two peoples who have equal rights over the land they share?

There is no symmetry in this conflict. One would have to say that. I deeply believe that. There is a guilty side and there are victims. The Palestinians are the victims. I don't want to say that everything that happened to the Palestinians is the direct result of Israel. But the original distortion in the lives of the Palestinians was introduced by Zionist intervention, which to us—in our narrative—begins with the Balfour Declaration and events thereafter that led to the replacement of one people by another. And it is continuing to this day. This is why Israel is not a state like any other. It is not like France, because there is continuing injustice. The laws of the State of Israel perpetuate injustice.

This is a dialectical conflict. But there is no possible synthesis. In this case, I don't think it's possible to ride out the dialectical contradictions. There is no way I know to reconcile the messianic-driven and Holocaust-driven impulse of the Zionists with the Palestinian impulse to stay on the land. These are fundamentally different impulses. This is why I think the essence of the conflict is its irreconcilability.

Are you saying we should not have come?

Your question is too much in the realm of "what if." The actualities are too strong. To say that you shouldn't have come, is to say you should leave. And I'm against that. I've said it many times. I'm totally against you leaving. The furthest I would go is to say that, given the logic of the Zionist idea, when you came, you should have understood you were coming to an inhabited land.

I would also say that there were those who thought that it was wrong to come. Ahad Ha'am, for one. And had I been there in 1920, I would have cautioned against it. Because the Arabs were there, and because I myself am not terribly enamored of movements of mass immigration and conquest. So I wouldn't have encouraged it.

Are you willing to acknowledge that we had a need to come? That most of those who came in the 1920s and '30s would have perished in Europe had they not come?

I am one of the few Arabs who have written about the Holocaust. I've been to Buchenwald and Dachau and other death camps, and I see the connection. The chain of events. I am willing to accept that much of the evidence suggests that there was a felt need to come. But am I deeply sympathetic with those who came? Only modestly. I find it difficult to accept Zionism as Zionism. I think European Jews could have been accommodated in other countries, such as the U.S., Canada, and England. I still blame the British for allowing Jews to come to Palestine, rather than accommodating them elsewhere.

How about later: Would you have accepted the 1947 Partition Plan?

My instinct is to say no. It was an unfair plan based on the minority getting equal rights to those of the majority. Perhaps we shouldn't have left it there. Perhaps we should have come up with a plan of our own. But I can understand that the Partition Plan was unacceptable to the Palestinians of the time.

And in 1948, does the moral responsibility for the Palestinian tragedy of that year lie only with the Jews? Don't the Arabs share the blame?

The war of 1948 was a war of dispossession. What happened that year was the destruction of Palestinian society, the replacement of that society by another, and the eviction of those who were considered undesirable. Those who were in the way. It is difficult for me to say that all responsibility lies with one side. But the lion's share of responsibility for depopulating towns and destroying them definitely lies with the Jewish-Zionists. Yitzhak Rabin evicted the 50,000 inhabitants of Ramle and Lydda, so it is difficult for me to see anyone else as responsible for that. The Palestinians were only responsible for being there.

When you look at this sequence of events, the narrative as you see it, what is your emotional reaction?

Anger. I feel tremendous anger. I think it was so mindless, so utterly, utterly gratuitous to say to us in so many ways, "We're not responsible for you, just go away, leave us alone, we can do what we want."

I think this is the folly of Zionism. Putting up these enormous walls of denial that are part of the very fabric of Israeli life to this day. I suppose that as an Israeli, you have never waited in line at a checkpoint or at the Erez crossing. It's pretty bad. Pretty humiliating. Even for someone as privileged as I am. There is no excuse for that. The inhuman behavior toward the other is unforgivable. So my reaction is anger. Lots of anger.

Do you hate us?

No. Funny, hate is not one of the emotions I feel. Anger is much more productive.

But in your version of the Palestinian narrative, hate seems almost inevitable.

What do you feel about the Germans?

Is it the same?

I'm not saying it's the same. I'm just wondering. If you have been massively wronged, what do you feel?

I suppose I do hate the German Nazis, but hate alone cannot encompass it.

It's a strong emotion, especially because we are still being wronged. It hasn't stopped. It's not as if Oslo brought an end to it. No, it still continues. Go and see Khiam. Go and see Erez. It's appalling.

So you feel you're facing evil? That even an Israel that retreats to its pre-1967 borders would still represent ongoing evil?

It's a set of evil practices, whose overall effect is a deeply felt, humiliating injustice. And it is ongoing. Every day. In every conceivable way.

That's what strikes me about it. That it is willfully maintained. Now

I'm not talking about every Israeli. There are all kinds of Israelis. But the ensemble of practices, the Israeli practices vis-à-vis Palestinians, are profoundly wrong. And it's profoundly stupid. What can Palestinians harbor in their hearts and minds? Not only a feeling of "I want it to stop," but a feeling of "I want my turn," of "One day you're going to get it."

Do you see it happening? Do you feel that the balance of power is beginning to shift toward the Palestinians?

I never use terms like balance of power. But I think that even the person doing the kicking has to ask himself how long he can go on kicking. At some point your leg is going to get tired. One day you'll wake up and ask, "What the fuck am I doing?"

In my opinion, not enough people in Israel have woken up to that understanding. In my reading of the last hundred years, there has been an assumption on the Israeli-Zionist side that if we fight hard enough, and beat them down long enough and if we erect enough walls and if we make it hard for them in every way possible, they will give up.

But that didn't happen. It didn't work. Today, among Palestinians, there is an even greater desire not to give up. On the evidence of my subjective experience, I can say that Palestinians of all generations feel a very strong sense of injustice. They feel that justice denied compels them to go on struggling. That's why they feel that arrangements like those discussed at Camp David in July would not be satisfactory, would not bring real reconciliation.

Are you saying that for Palestinians, without justice there can be no peace?

Yes. No one gets absolute justice, but there are steps that must be taken, like the ones taken at the end of apartheid. Israel and South Africa are different, but there are commonalities. They are not entirely incomparable. One of these commonalities is that a large part of the population feels itself denied access to resources, rights, ownership of land, and free movement. What I learned from the case of South Africa is that the only way to deal with a complex history of antagonism based on ethnicity is to look at it, understand it, and then move on. What I have in mind is something like the Truth and Reconciliation committee. And I think we, the Palestinians, are the ones who have to do it. Just as

Desmond Tutu and the blacks did it. Of course, they had first won. They got rid of apartheid.

To what extent would a post-occupation Israel still resemble the old South Africa?

There is certainly an ideology of difference. The sense that Israelis created a system in which one people has more than others. Is it total apartheid like it was in South Africa? Probably not. But there are similarities. The Afrikaners had a proto-Zionist ideology. They felt they were chosen by God.

But what is more important in my mind is the question of responsibility. I think it should be in the consciousness and conscience of every Israeli that his state obliterated the Arab life of pre-1948. That Jaffa was formerly an Arab city from which the Arabs were expelled. And I think Israelis should be aware that their presence in many places in the country entails the loss of a Palestinian family, the demolition of a house, the destruction of a village. In my mind, it is your duty to find out about it. And act in consequence, in the Kantian sense.

Many Israelis resist this because they think the consequence would be to leave. Not at all. As I told you, I'm against that. The last thing I want to do is to perpetuate this process by which one distortion leads to another. I have a horror of that. I saw it happen too many times. I don't want to see more people leave.

What you are saying is that Israelis should know that, like white South Africans, they have a right to stay as long as they give up their ideology.

Yes, an ideology that denies the rights of others.

So what is needed is a process of de-Zionization?

I don't like to use words like that. Because that's obviously a signal that I'm asking the Zionists to commit hara-kiri. They can be Zionists, and they can assert their Jewish identity and their connection to the land, so long as it doesn't keep the others out so manifestly.

Following this logic, it would then be necessary to replace the present Israel with a New Israel, just as the New South Africa replaced the old. Unjust state mechanisms would have to be dismantled.

Yes. Correct. Let's say reformed. I am ill at ease with talk of dismantling. It is apocalyptic language. And I would like to use words that are as little as possible taken from the context of apocalypse and miraculous rebirth. This is why I don't say de-Zionize. It's like waving a red flag in front of an angry bull. I don't see what purpose it serves. So I prefer to talk about transformation. The gradual transformation of Israel. As well as the gradual opening of all Middle East countries.

Two years ago you wrote an article in The New York Times *endorsing a one-state solution. It seems you've come full circle—from espousing a one secular-democratic-state solution in the '70s, to accepting the two-state solution in the '80s, back to the secular-democratic idea.*

I would not necessarily call it secular-democratic. I would call it a binational state. I want to preserve for the Palestinians and the Israeli Jews a mechanism or structure that would allow them to express their national identity. I understand that in the case of Palestine-Israel, a binational solution would have to address the differences between the two collectives.

But I don't think that partition or separation would work. The two-state solution can no longer be implemented. And given the realities of geography, demography, history, and politics, I think there is a tremendous amount to be gained from a bi-national state.

Do you think the idea of a Jewish state is flawed?

I don't find the idea of a Jewish state terribly interesting. The Jews I know—the more interesting Jews I know—are not defined by their Jewishness. I think to confine Jews to their Jewishness is problematic. Look at this problem of "Who is a Jew." Once the initial enthusiasm for statehood and *aliyah* subsides, people will find that to be Jews is not a lifelong project. It's not enough.

But that's an internal Jewish question. The question for you is whether the Jews are a people who have a right to a state of their own?

If enough people think of themselves as a people and need to constitute that, I respect that. But not if it entails the destruction of another people. I cannot accept an attitude of "You shall die in order for us to rise."

Are you saying to Israelis that they should give up the idea of Jewish sovereignty?

I am not asking people to give up anything. But Jewish sovereignty as an end in itself seems to me not worth the pain and the waste and the suffering it produced. If, on the other hand, one can think of Jewish sovereignty as a step toward a more generous idea of coexistence, of being-in-the-world, then yes, it's worth giving up. Not in the sense of being forced to give it up. Not in the sense of we will conquer you, as many Arabs think when they call Arafat Salah-e-Din—which means that he is going to kick you out. No, not in that sense. I don't want that dynamic. And you don't want that dynamic. The better option would be to say that sovereignty should gradually give way to something that is more open and more livable.

In a bi-national state, the Jews will quickly become a minority, like the Lebanese Christians.

Yes, but you're going to be a minority anyway. In about ten years there will be demographic parity between Jews and Palestinians, and the process will go on. But the Jews are a minority everywhere. They are a minority in America. They can certainly be a minority in Israel.

Knowing the region and given the history of the conflict, do you think such a Jewish minority would be treated fairly?

I worry about that. The history of minorities in the Middle East has not been as bad as in Europe, but I wonder what would happen. It worries me a great deal. The question of what is going to be the fate of the Jews is very difficult for me. I really don't know. It worries me.

Do you personally have a right to return, a right to return to Talbieh in Jerusalem?

For me, Talbieh is a house. The family house, located on Brenner Street, by what is today a small park. When I went there for the first time in 1992, I had with me a deed to my family's house, given to me by my cousin. He wanted me to see what could be done. Four years later, he came himself and registered with some organization in order to get the house back. He wanted the house back.

So this is a very specific thing. If you ask me in the abstract, I would say that I have a right to return just as my Jewish colleague has a right under the Israeli Law of Return. But if you ask me specifically, I would affiliate with my cousin, whose father's name is on the deed, and would like to get some recognition that it was taken from him. That the house is his.

Do you really expect to go back to that house? Would you really want to return to Talbieh?

I wonder. I feel the pressure of mortality. For me to disconnect myself from my life in New York would be difficult. But, would I want to return to those places of my youth, not as a tourist—I'd say yes. And in the case of my son, he wants to be able to go back there. To the house. He would like that. Yes, why not?

So the demand to return is not abstract. It's not only a metaphor. Do you really mean it?

Yes. It's a real problem, and a real attachment for real people. That's what it has been all along. A lot of Israelis say, well, in that case, that's the destruction of the State of Israel. But I don't see it like that at all.

The refugee problem is the most difficult to solve, because it involves moral questions of expulsion. But I think Israel must acknowledge the plight of the refugees. And I think the refugees must have a right to return. I'm not sure how many will want to return, but I think they should be entitled to return.

Studies have been written that address feasibility and what I can only call decency regarding this issue. How you can accomplish it with the least harm. Without literally throwing people off land they cultivated. According to these studies, you could quite easily settle a million people in present-day Israel with a minimal disruption. I think this could be a beginning. A good point to discuss and converse about. Of course, it must be a regulated return. Not just anyone getting on a boat and coming back.

Let's go back to Talbieh. How would this work in the neighborhood where you lived fifty-five years ago, and where I live today?

My relatives whose names are on the deed believe the house is theirs, so they should have a right to it. In the case of that house, there is no problem because it is not owned by an Israeli family. It is owned by a fundamentalist Christian organization. From South Africa, by the way. So my family should have the house back. Will any one of them go back to live there? I think, yes. But in this particular case, they should definitely be given the option. Regarding other houses, which people live in and have been living in for years, my instinct is not to drive them out. I think some humane and moderate solution should be found where the claims of the present and the claims of the past are addressed. I don't have easy solutions, but I told you, I'm averse to the notion of people leaving their houses, forced to leave. Even if it's on behalf of an international tribunal, or a people that says this is our right. It is their right. But to actually put it into practice in that particular way—I can't do it.

Aren't you worried that among Palestinians there are those who feel differently? That given the right to return, there would be an impulse of eviction?

I suppose, but I would oppose that. I'm totally against eviction. My entire philosophy is designed to prevent that. I'm not sure I'll be around when it happens, but if I am, I shall fight it very strongly.

I look at this in terms of the Zimbabwe situation. There is no doubt in my mind that the people there—the whites who farm the land—have a very powerful attachment to the land, the property, the cultivation they made possible. I believe they should stay. As long as they admit the others were dispossessed and robbed of their rights. The same applies here. But it's a very troubling ethical question. It far exceeds the capacity of any one person to answer.

So what you envision is a totally new situation in which a Jewish minority would live peacefully within an Arab context?

Yes. I believe it is viable. A Jewish minority can survive the way other minorities in the Arab world survived. I hate to say it, but in a funny sort of way, it worked rather well under the Ottoman Empire, with its millet system. What they had then seems a lot more humane than what we have now.

So as you see it, the Jews would eventually have a cultural autonomy within a pan-Arab structure?

Pan-Arab or Mediterranean. Why should it not include Cyprus? What I would like is a kind of integration of Jews into the fabric of the larger society, which has an extraordinary staying power despite mutilation by the nation-state. I think it can be done. There is every reason to go for the larger unit. The social organization that would be required is something I haven't really pondered, but it would be easier to organize than the separation that Mr. Barak and his advisers dream of. The genius of Arab culture was catholicity. My definition of pan-Arabism would comprise the other communities within an Arab-Islamic framework. Including the Jews.

So in a generation or two, what we will have is an Arab-Jewish minority community in an Arab world?

Yes. Yes. I would have thought.

Many Jews would find that frightening.

As a Jew, you obviously have good reasons to be afraid. But in the long run, one should move toward less rather than more anxiety. Maybe I'm wrong, but the way I read it, the present existence of Israel is based largely upon fending off what's around and preventing it, as it were, from crashing in. That's an unattractive way to live, I think. The nationalistic option created an anxiety-ridden society. It produced paranoia, militarization, and a rigid mindset. All for what? The other way, the option I'm talking about, would give you, the Jews, a much more mobile and open life. It would give the project of the Jews coming to Palestine, to Israel, a much saner basis.

Are you a refugee?

No, the term refugee has a very specific meaning for me. That is to say, poor health, social misery, loss and dislocation. That does not apply to me. In that sense, I'm not a refugee. But I feel I have no place. I'm cut off from my origins. I live in exile. I am exiled.

The title of your recently published memoir is Out of Place. *What does that mean?*

Not being able to go back. It's really a strong feeling I have. I would describe my life as a series of departures and returns. But the departure is always anxious. The return always uncertain. Precarious. So even when I go on a short trip, I overpack, on the chance that I won't be able to return.

You always have the feeling you don't belong. You really don't belong. Because you don't really come from here. And the place you do come from, someone else is saying it's not yours, it's his. So even the idea of where you came from is always challenged.

Given that, did you have to invent yourself?

In a very particular meaning of the word. In Latin, *inventio* is to find again. It was used in classical rhetoric to describe a process by which you find past experiences and rearrange them to give them eloquence and novelty. It's not creating from nothing, it's reordering. In that sense, I invented myself.

First, under the influence of [the Italian historian] Vico, I saw that people make their own history. That history is not like nature. It's a human product. And I saw that we can make our own beginnings. That they are not given, they are acts of will.

But in recent years, when I was facing terminal illness—with a tremendous amount of uncertainty—I discovered that I wasn't afraid of death. Not even of the suffering associated with the terminal phases of the disease. But I was afraid of not being able to recapture and to restate and to reinterpret those aspects of my life that I thought had some value.

It was then, while looking back, that I realized that the world I grew up in, the world of my parents, of Cairo and Beirut and pre-1948 Talbieh, was a made-up world. It wasn't a real world. It didn't have the kind of objective solidity that I wanted it to have. For many years, I mourned the loss of this world. I truly mourned it. But now I discovered the possibility of reinterpreting it. And I realized that it's true not only for me, but for most of us: We move through life shedding the past—the forgotten, the lost. I understood that my role was to tell and retell a story of loss where the notion of repatriation, of a return to a home, is basically impossible.

So for you personally there is no return?

While I was writing my memoir, my dear friend Abu Lughod, who is a refugee from Jaffa, went back to Palestine and settled in Ramallah. That was an option for me, too. I could have gotten a job at Bir Zeit. But I realized this is something I cannot do. My fate is to remain in New York. On a constantly shifting ground, where relationships are not inherited, but created. Where there is no solidity of home.

Are you addicted to homelessness?

I don't know if I'm addicted. But I don't own any real estate. The flat I live in is rented. I see myself as a wanderer. My position is that of a traveler, who is not interested in holding territory, who has no realm to protect.

[Theodor] Adorno says that in the twentieth century the idea of home has been superseded. I suppose part of my critique of Zionism is that it attaches too much importance to home. Saying, we need a home. And we'll do anything to get a home, even if it means making others homeless.

Why do you think I'm so interested in the bi-national state? Because I want a rich fabric of some sort, which no one can fully comprehend, and no one can fully own. I never understood the idea of this is my place, and you are out. I do not appreciate going back to the origin, to the pure. I believe the major political and intellectual disasters were caused by reductive movements that tried to simplify and purify. That said, we have to plant tents or kibbutz or army and start from scratch.

I don't believe in all that. I wouldn't want it for myself. Even if I were a Jew, I'd fight against it. And it won't last. Take it from me, Ari. Take my word for it. I'm older than you. It won't even be remembered.

You sound very Jewish.

Of course. I'm the last Jewish intellectual. You don't know anyone else. All your other Jewish intellectuals are now suburban squires. From Amos Oz to all these people here in America. So I'm the last one. The only true follower of Adorno. Let me put it this way: I'm a Jewish-Palestinian.

Interview with Ari Shavit,
Ha'aretz Magazine, Tel Aviv, 2000

CREDIT ACKNOWLEDGMENTS

The interviews and discussions in this book originally appeared under the following titles in the following publications:

PART ONE:
PERFORMANCE AND CRITICISM

"Beginnings," Interview in *Diacritics* 6.3, Fall 1976, Department of Romance Studies, Cornell University, Ithaca, New York. Responses copyright © 1976 by Edward W. Said. Reprinted with permission of Cornell University.

"In the Shadow of the West," Interview with Jonathan Crary and Phil Mariani in *Wedge* no. 7/8, Winter/Spring 1985, New York. Responses copyright © 1985 by Edward W. Said.

"Overlapping Territories: The World, the Text, and the Critic," Interview with Gary Hentzi and Anne McClintock in *Critical Text,* Spring 1986, New York. Responses copyright © 1986 by Edward W. Said.

"Literary Theory at the Crossroads of Public Life," Interview with Imre Salusinszky, Responses copyright © 1987 by Edward W. Said, in *Criticism in Society* by Imre Salusinszky, Routledge, London, 1987. Reprinted with permission of Routledge.

"Criticism, Culture, and Performance," previously titled "Criticism, Culture, and Performance: An Interview with Edward Said," Discussion with Bonnie Marranca, Marc Robinson, and Una Chaudhuri, Responses copyright © 1991 by Edward W. Said, in *Performing Arts Journal* 37, January 1991. Published in *Interculturalism and Performance: Writings from PAJ,* edited by Bonnie Marranca and Gautam Dasgupta. PAJ Publications, New York, 1991. Copyright © 1991 by PAJ Publications. Reprinted with permission of PAJ Publications.

"Criticism and the Art of Politics," Interview with Jennifer Wicke and Michael Sprinker in *Edward Said: A Critical Reader,* edited by Michael

Sprinker. Blackwell Publishers, Oxford, England, 1992. Copyright © 1992 by Edward W. Said. Reprinted with permission of Blackwell Publishers.

"Wild Orchids and Trotsky," Interview with Mark Edmundson, Responses copyright © 1993 by Edward W. Said, in *Wild Orchids and Trotsky: Messages from American Universities,* edited by Mark Edmundson. Penguin Books, New York, 1993. Copyright © 1993 by Mark Edmundson. Reprinted with permission of Viking Penguin, a division of Penguin Putnam, Inc.

"Culture and Imperialism," previously titled "An Interview with Edward W. Said," Interview with Joseph A. Buttigieg and Paul A. Bové in *boundary 2: An International Journal of Literature and Culture* 20, no. 1, Spring 1993. Duke University Press, Durham, North Carolina. Copyright © 1993 by Edward W. Said. All rights reserved. Reprinted with permission of Duke University Press.

"*Orientalism* and After," Interview with Anne Beezer and Peter Osborne in *Radical Philosophy* 63, Spring 1993, London. Responses copyright © 1993 by Edward W. Said. Reprinted with permission of *Radical Philosophy.*

"Edward Said: Between Two Cultures," Interview with Eleanor Wachtel, Responses copyright © 1996 by Edward W. Said, in *More Writers & Company* by Eleanor Wachtel. Alfred A. Knopf Canada, Toronto, Canada, 1996. Reprinted with permission of Alfred A. Knopf Canada, a division of Random House of Canada Limited.

"Peoples' Rights and Literature," Interview with Jonathan Rée in *Alif: Journal of Comparative Poetics* 13, The American University in Cairo, Cairo, Egypt, 1993. Responses copyright © 1993 by Edward W. Said. Copyright © 1993 by the Department of English and Comparative Literature, The American University in Cairo. Reprinted with permission of the American University in Cairo.

"Language, History, and the Production of Knowledge," Interview with Gauri Viswanathan, Colgate University, Hamilton, New York, 1996. Responses copyright © 1996 by Edward W. Said.

"I've Always Learnt During the Class," Interview with Damayanti Datta, *The Telegraph,* December 22, 1997, Calcutta, India. Responses copyright © 1997 by Edward W. Said.

PART TWO:

SCHOLARSHIP AND ACTIVISM

"Can an Arab and a Jewish State Coexist?," previously titled "Q & A," Interview with Timothy Appleby in *The Globe and Mail,* November 8, 1986,

Toronto, Canada. Responses copyright © 1986 by Edward W. Said. Reprinted with permission of *The Globe and Mail*.

"Scholars, Media, and the Middle East," previously titled "The MESA Debate: The Scholars, the Media, and the Middle East," Discussion with Bernard Lewis, Leon Wieseltier, and Christopher Hitchens, chaired by William H. McNeill, *The Journal of Palestine Studies*, 1987, Washington, D.C. Responses copyright © 1987 by Edward W. Said. Copyright © 1987 by Institute for Palestine Studies. Reprinted with permission of the University of California Press for the Institute of Palestine Studies.

"An Exile's Exile," Interview with Matthew Stevenson in *The Progressive*, February 1987, Madison, Wisconsin. Responses copyright © 1987 by Edward W. Said. Reprinted with permission of *The Progressive*.

"American Intellectuals and Middle East Politics," previously titled "American Intellectuals and Middle East Politics: An Interview with Edward W. Said," Interview with Bruce Robbins in *Social Text* 56, Fall 1998, Duke University Press, Durham, North Carolina. Copyright © 1998 by Edward W. Said. All rights reserved. Reprinted with permission of Duke University Press.

"The Need for Self-Appraisal," Interview with Hisham Melhem in *The Dawn/Al-Fajr*, February 5, 1990, Karachi, Pakistan. Responses copyright © 1990 by Edward W. Said.

"A Formula for More Husseins," Interview in *L.A. Weekly*, August 30–September 6, 1991, Los Angeles, California. Responses copyright © 1991 by Edward W. Said.

"Palestinian Voices in the U.S.," previously titled "Efforts Redoubled to Build Effective Channels for a Palestinian Voice in the U.S." Interview with Munir Nasser in the *Arab American News*, 1990, Dearborn, Michigan.

"The Intellectuals and the War," Interview with Barbara Harlow in *Middle East Report*, July/August 1991, Washington, D.C. Responses copyright © 1991 by Edward W. Said. Reprinted with permission of the Middle East Research and Information Project, Inc.

"What People in the U.S. Know About Islam Is a Stupid Cliché," previously titled "What People in the U.S. Know About Islam and the Arab World Is a Series of Stupid Clichés," Interview with Hasan M. Jafri in *The Herald*, February 1992, Karachi, Pakistan. Responses copyright © 1992 by Edward W. Said.

"Europe and Its Others: An Arab Perspective," Interview with Richard Kearney, Responses copyright © 1992 by Edward W. Said, in *Visions of Europe* by Richard Kearney. Wolfhound Press, Dublin, Ireland, 1992. Reprinted with permission of Wolfhound Press.

INDEX

ABOUT THE AUTHOR

Edward W. Said is University Professor of English and Comparative Literature at Columbia University. He is the author of twenty books, including *Orientalism,* which was nominated for the National Book Critics Circle Award, *Culture and Imperialism, Representations of the Intellectual, The End of the Peace Process,* and *Out of Place: A Memoir.*

ABOUT THE EDITOR

Gauri Viswanathan is Class of 1933 Professor in the Humanities at Columbia University. She is the author of *Masks of Conquest: Literary Study and British Rule in India* and *Outside the Fold: Conversion, Modernity, and Belief,* which won the James Russell Lowell Prize, among other distinguished awards. She has also published numerous essays on education, religion, and culture.